KU-015-613

IRELAND
HISTORY
of a NATION

Yet the nation, as imagined or even forged community, is far older than the nation-state. It existed before the political mobilisation made possible by the print revolution. It will, in fresh mutations, exist when the nation-state has passed into history.

Neal Ascherson, Black Sea

> Once, in the Giant's Ring, I closed my eyes
> and thought of Ireland,
> the air-wide, skin-tight, multiple meaning of here.
>
> When I opened them I was little the wiser,
> in that, perhaps, one
> with the first settlers in the Lagan Valley
> and the Vietnamese boat people of Portadown.

Frank Ormsby, Home

IRELAND
HISTORY
of a NATION

NEW EDITION

David Ross

WAVERLEY
BOOKS

Select Bibiliography

Bardon, Jonathan, *The History of Ulster.* Belfast, 1992
Beckett, J.C., *The Making of Modern Ireland, 1603–1923.* London, 1966
Bence-Jones, Mark, *Twilight of the Ascendancy.* London, 1987
Brady, Ciaran, O'Dowd, Mary, and Walker, Brian, *An Illustrated History of Ulster.* London, 1989
Connolly, S. J. (ed.), *The Oxford Companion to Irish History.* Oxford, 1998
Curtis, Edmund, *A History of Ireland.* London, 1936
Dillon, Myles and Chadwick, Nora, *The Celtic Realms.* London, 1967
Harbison, Peter, *Pre-Christian Ireland.* London, 1988
Harkness, David, *Ireland in the Twentieth Century.* Basingstoke, 1996
Henry, Françoise, *Irish Art* (3 vols). London, revised ed. 1965–70
Johnson, James H., *The Human Geography of Ireland.* New York, 1994
Lee, J.J. (ed.), *Ireland, 1945-70.* Dublin and New York, 1979
Loughrey, Patrick (ed.), *The People of Ireland.* Belfast, 1988
Lydon, James, *The Making of Ireland.* London, 1998
McDowell, R.B., *Public Opinion and Government Policy in Ireland, 1801–1846.* London, 1952
MacKillop, James, *Dictionary of Celtic Mythology.* Oxford, 1998
Martin, F.X. (ed.), *Leaders and Men of the Easter Rising.* London, 1967
Ó Gráda, Cormac, *Ireland, A New Economic History, 1780–1939.* Oxford, 1994
O'Kelly, Michael, *Early Ireland.* Cambridge, 1989

Picture Credits

Courtesy of **Ingram Publishing**:
Page 247, Oscar Wilde
Courtesy of **Maurice Mechan**:
Page 23, W. B. Yeats by Maurice Mechan
Page 23, George Bernard Shaw by Maurice Mechan
All other illustrations by Henry Doyle, from
The Illustrated History of Ireland, 1868
Courtesy of **Shutterstock**:
Page 20, Jim Larkin Monument, copyright © Patryk Kosmider
Page 33, David Lloyd George, copyright © Neveshkin Nikolay
Page 37, Michael Collins' grave, copyright © Rodrigo Garrido
Page 54, de Lorean car, copyright © Albo
Page 243, Memorial to Charles Stewart Parnell, copyright © Tupungato

This edition published 2014 by Waverley Books, an imprint of
The Gresham Publishing Company Ltd,
Academy Park, Building 4000, Gower Street, Glasgow, G51 1PR, Scotland
www.waverley-books.co.uk

First published 2002
Reprinted 2006, 2008, 2010, 2014

© David Ross 2014

All rights reserved. No part of this publication
may be reproduced, stored in a retrieval system or transmitted
in any form or by any means, electronic, mechanical, photocopying,
recording or otherwise without the prior permission of the copyright owner

ISBN 978 1 84934 178 3
(Previously 978 1 84205 164 1)

Printed and bound in spain by Novoprint, S.A.

CONTENTS

FACT WINDOWS

Introduction: Twenty-first Century Ireland

FREE FROM THE 'TROIKA'

In the early months of 2014, the people of the Irish Republic were given a piece of good news and a piece of bad news by their government. The good news was that after three years Ireland was able to dispense with the controlling power of the 'Troika' – having completed the economic programme imposed and overseen by the agents of the International Monetary Fund (IMF), the European Commission and the European Central Bank. The bad news was that the policy of austerity was to be maintained into the future – Ireland might no longer be a stretcher case in economic terms but it was still on the danger list.

How very different it all was from 2005, when official European Union statistics showed Ireland as the second richest member of the (then) 25-member EU. Only tiny Luxembourg had a higher per capita gross domestic product. Previous centuries had formed an enduring image of relative poverty in Ireland compared to the industrialised countries. The Irish had had only a few years to get used to riches, which were in any case unevenly distributed, but attitudes had changed. Until 2001 Ireland had been a country that said 'Yes'. Since the mid-1960s it had been a valued supplier of troops for United Nations operations, its neutrality an asset in policing sensitive regions of the world. It had said 'Yes' to joining the EU, to the Maastricht Treaty, and to adopting the euro in place of the Irish punt. Ireland gained more from European funds than it contributed. The notorious referendum of 2001, when a majority of voters (little more than a third of the whole electorate) rejected enlargement of the EU, suggested a rather bergrudging attitude to other countries which wanted to follow the same road to prosperity. That verdict was overturned, to official relief, in the following year, but in 2008 yet another referendum rejected the Treaty of Lisbon, with its revised, more centralist, proposed constitution. Again, a second try in 2009, after some minor concessions in the treaty, resulted in a substantial 'Yes' vote.

In the years after 2005, the Republic's economy had roared ahead to such a degree that its partners within the 'eurozone' and the European Central Bank, were concerned enough to speak out publicly. The rate of inflation was running above the European average, and rising. The Fianna Fáil government's response was nonchalant. The Budget announced for 2008 showered increases in social benefits, pensions, health-care and education even as the financial skies were darkening. For another two years the government seemed to be in half-denial that there was a huge problem. Other authorities, too, failed to see what was becoming very obvious. In April 2008 the Organisation for Economic Co-operation and Development said of Ireland, 'the economic fundamentals remain strong . . . Irish banks are well capitalised and profitable.' But Ireland's prosperity was unreal, a bubble of soaring property prices and expansion of the construction industry, puffed up by ever increasing lending from the banks. The banks in turn relied on borrowing huge sums in the international money market. This could not go on indefinitely, and events outside Ireland brought the collapse. Not only Irish banks had been allowed to run wild, and an international banking crisis, originating in the USA but swiftly spreading, blocked the Irish banks' chances of further borrowing. Confidence in the property boom slumped, and borrowers who relied on further loans, or rising property prices, to pay off earlier debts and mortgages, instead found loans refused and property prices tumbling. Late in 2008 the government made the fatal pledge to guarantee the debts of the Irish banks, without knowing what these were. Soon it emerged that some €90 billion of toxic debt had to be covered. All that the banks had were worthless securities against which they had lent vast sums, mostly for construction projects which had come to a sudden halt with the collapse of the property market.

Taxpayers had to bear the brunt, as a succession of emergency Budgets followed, with almost every aspect of public expenditure heavily cut back. Brian Cowen's government was increasingly enmired, as rumours, then revelations, began to emerge of the extent of the complicity between bankers, property developers, regulatory bodies and senior government figures in driving the property boom. Regulation had been minimal at best, and the chief financial regulator took early retirement in January 2009. The Anglo-Irish Bank (AIB) was taken into state ownership. A National Assets Management Agency was established to take over the property-related loans made by six banks, on which they had lost an estimated €100 billion. In November 2010, after prolonged hesitation and faced with national insolvency, the Irish government reluctantly requested assistance from the IMF, the European Commission and the European Central Bank (the 'Troika'). A bail-out loan totalling €75 billion was granted, under rigorous conditions.

Cowen's attempts to bolster his much criticised leadership by means of a large cabinet reshuffle collapsed early in 2011, and the Green Party withdrew from the coalition, forcing a general election in February. A humiliating defeat for Fianna Fáil saw its representation slump by 75 per cent. For the first time, Fine Gael was the largest party in the Dáil, with 76 out of 168 seats, and its Labour ally was second largest with 37, giving their coalition, led by Fien Gael's Enda Kenny, a comfortable majority. Fianna Fáil, for so long the dominant party, lost 57 members and retained only 20 seats. The Greens lost all of their 6 seats.

Change of government did not lead to a change in the austerity policy, and the new ruling parties rapidly found their popularity falling. In fact, under the terms of the bail-out, a change of policy would have been impossible. During 2011, however, the interest rates on large parts of the monster loan were reduced from 6 per cent to levels of 3.5 per cent and 2.5 per cent, a large relief to the Irish economy. In the course of 2013 signs of economic recovery, helped by continuing exports, were becoming apparent, and by the end of 2013 the government had successfully extracted itself from the close control of officials of the 'Troika', which, as in other bailed-out countries, had become ever more resented for its authoritarian nature and inflexibility.

Kenny hailed the policy of 'internal devaluation' (i.e. wage and benefit cuts) which had made the country pull itself up by its bootstraps, and ministers were quick to salute the Irish people as the 'heroes' who had borne the struggle through pay and benefit cuts, higher taxes, and, for many, negative equity, having paid far more for their homes than the post-recession value. But most economic pointers remained gloomy: economic growth hovered around the the 0.2 per cent mark through 2012–13, and the target of a maximum budget deficit of 3 per cent of gross national income had not been attained. By 2014 it was still 7.6 per cent. Significantly, against increasing international criticism, the government stuck to one of its main economic weapons, the low 12.5 per cent rate of corporation tax for international companies, while denying that Ireland was operating as a 'tax haven' for multinationals. Critics claimed that the real level of corporation tax was often well below the official figure.

A 'DOUBLE WHAMMY'

For the Irish people, such a reversal in their national and personal fortunes inevitably led to introspection. How could this have happened? Who was to blame? Was there something intrinsically amiss in national governance? 'Dysfunctional' became a byword, reached for to describe any shortcomings in public administration. As if economic collapse were not enough, there was further unpleasantness to come, in a sort of 'double whammy'. The sense of national malaise was deepened by increasing evidence of cronyism and collusion between government and business. Publication in June 2013 of taped

11

telephone conversations between top AIB officials revealed a startling degree of irresponsibility, cynicism and mendacity in their dealings with the state.In early 2014 three AIB executives went on trial for making illegal loans and falsifying details. But it was not clear how the endemic culture of cronyism, embracing government, official agencies and business from the national to the parish level, could be tackled. It was not even clear whether the government had the constitutional authority to launch a sufficiently effective investigation. The lack of accountability, the sense that many of the wreckers would never face inquiry or trial, deepened public anger and cynicism.

At the same time, other spectres from the past were making an appearance. For years stories had circulated about the sytematic abuse of children in institutions run by the Roman Catholic Church, notably the 30 or so 'industrial schools'. For many people, they were too shocking for belief, perhaps part of a campaign to defame the Catholic Church. In 1999, with evidence mounting, the Commission of Inquiry into Child Abuse was finally set up, and its findings published as the Ryan Report in 2009. Only then did the scale and duration of the physical, mental, and sexual abuse of children in these places, from 1936 onwards, come fully into the open, along with the efforts of top churchmen to cover up what was happening and to protect, not the innocent, but the guilty. Government-imposed restrictions, and a legal case brought by the Congregation of Christian Brothers in 2004, meant that no names were included in the report and no prosecutions resulted directly from it. Nevertheless its impact was very great. The *Irish Times* described it as 'the map of an Irish Hell'. Respect for the Catholic Church as an institution fell sharply, and it was dealt a further blow by another report, into the workings of the 'Magdalene laundries' between 1922 and 1996. Operated by four orders of nuns, these 'asylums' were workhouses to which over 14,000 girls and women were consigned, around a quarter of them placed there by state agencies. Many were single mothers or otherwise considered to be 'fallen women'. Often their own families colluded in this incarceration. While the level of physical violence was vastly less than that inflicted on boys and girls in industrial schools, the inmates were virtual prisoners subjected to a repressive and intentionally demoralising regime. As Taoiseach, Enda Kenny made an official apology to the 'Magdalenes', though it was noted that he stopped short of admitting the Irish state's role (it is somewhat ironic that the laundries did the government's washing, from the president down). The Catholic Church's role in social care has been hugely reduced following negotiations with successive governments over the transfer of property in return for non-prosecution. Survivors of abuse still have access to civil courts and in 2014 one man was awarded €370,000 damages against the Brothers for sustained instances of rape and sexual molestation whilst in their care. Fines and out-of-court payments have eroded the finances of numerous once-wealthy satellite organisations of the church. In another national institution, the bones of a further skeleton began to rattle when the Garda Commissioner abruptly resigned in the wake of exposure of the fact that the police force had been routinely but illegally recording non-emergency calls to and from stations from the 1980s to November 2013. Originally linked to allegations of corrupt wiping of traffic offence points ('celebrity favours'), the revelation threatened to affect both ongoing and past cases where improperly obtained evidence might have been used. Suggestions of corruption, and of attempts to deter the actions of 'whistleblowers', within the police force were the last thing people wanted to hear at this time.

WHITHER IRELAND?

Against this sombre background, a minor industry emerged in 'Whither Ireland?' conferences and seminars, all concerned to seek not just a way out of economic depression, but some means of grappling with the social forces which contributed to it and whose roots run back into the scandals of the not-so-distant past. A great need to retain and reinforce national self-respect was felt, perhaps as a preliminary to remaking the country's international reputation – looking for what is best and what can be built on. In one such gathering, in January 2013, one of Ireland's leading historians, Professor Roy Foster, remarked that under 'inadequate and venal' governments, Ireland had rebranded itself from the 'Celtic Tiger' into 'How to blow it all away'. But he also noted that Irish history is not a smooth continuity but has always been a series of radical shifts, with discontinuity and unpredictability as the constant motif. One future for the country dissolved in 2008. With the centenary of the Easter Rising due in 2016, what kind of Ireland would be celebrating it?

In his noting of the country's capacity to take new directions, Professor Foster perhaps permitted himself a glint of optimism. Even during the fat years, many people had deplored the materialism that had grown up, with its culture of greed and its hunger for easy money. The traditional Irish virtues of frugality, community, and a sense of the deeper aspects of life, were the victims. But now there was an opportunity for a new start and another shift, hopefully for the better. Social and economic issues, interlinked, are integral to Ireland's future, though their resolution does not lie wholly within Ireland's boundaries. These issues are also bound into the two great and continuing themes of contemporary Irish history. The first is chiefly political: the two-stranded theme of achieving (and maintaining) an independent state, alongside the surviving sense of separate identities – differences 'in hearts and minds' – between the two population groups in the six counties forming Northern Ireland. The second theme is mainly social: the emergence of a democratic society and its transition from cultural isolation and relative poverty behind a 'green curtain' to a secular state forced to modernise its institutions and be a player not only in Europe but in a wider sphere which contains the world-wide web as well as the IMF.

Northern Ireland, with the political machinery in place since 1999 for devolved and democratic government based on power-sharing between former antagonists, has found that mutual suspicion and the urge to confrontation, take a very long time to subside. The Assembly was suspended for several months in 2000 and for five years between 14 October 2002 and 7 May 2007. Unionism seemed to have dug itself into a very deep trench when Ian Paisley's new Democratic Unionist Party (DUP) overtook David Trimble's old Ulster Unionists in the 2005 general election. The St Andrews Agreement of 2006, worked out between the British and Irish governments and the Northern Irish parties, at last found a way forward, with Sinn Féin accepting the role of the Police Service of Northern Ireland. Paisley surprised his supporters and many others by accepting the principle of power-sharing, becoming first minister in May 2007 with the once-militant republican Martin McGuinness as his deputy. Once again, in the not-quite ended history of British imperialism, a man formerly branded a terrorist was now a government minister – but here former extremists of both sides were cooperating. There is a high-mindedness in this which earned respect from all but the most obdurate, despite the occasional spats and the evidence, as in the scandal over Mrs Iris Robinson's undisclosed loans in 2010, that Northern Irish politics suffers from the same kinds of localised rot as in the Republic. Paisley stepped down in May 2008 and Peter Robinson replaced him as leader of the DUP and first minister. The violence that erupted late in 2012 over Belfast City Council's decision to fly the British flag on only 18 days a year, leaving 163 policemen injured and 560 people charged with various offences, was a powerful warning that community passions remained strong, and that change should be both considered and measured.

A LONG HISTORY

So much had changed in a few years and 'change' remained the position of the barometer needle across all of Ireland. But, although this book begins with contemporary events and modern times, these are the always-advancing front of a very long history. As a national history, Ireland's has unusual aspects. Normally the historian can count on being able to record the positive statements and actions of a people – or at least of those who governed and spoke for the people – over a lengthy period of time. In the case of Ireland, this is not possible, because from the twelfth to the twentieth century, Ireland did not function as an independent nation-state. Elsewhere, across the seas, monarchies and republics rose and fell, frontiers were marked and erased again; for the greater part of a millennium, Europe seethed, churned and changed, while Ireland remained with no government of its own, claimed as a dominion by the King of England, though sometimes only technically, and rarely found in a peaceful condition. And yet it cannot be said that colonial Ireland played no part in the long and varied catalogue of events which, stitched together, form modern Europe – quite apart from its pre-colonial contribution in exporting both Christianity and culture. For hundreds of years, the Irish question figured strongly in the international policies of France and Spain. Irish soldiers played conspicuous parts in battles in many countries, from the Thirty Years War in Germany to the American Civil War – usually on both sides. On the soil of Ireland itself, much more was at stake in 1690 than whether James or William should rule, or whether the country should be Protestant or Catholic.

But Irish history remains elusive. Historians of medieval and later Ireland, in which so much of the action was initiated, or dictated, by the English and their government (from 1707 the British government) have found it hard to avoid shaping their narrative into the history of England-in-Ireland. An effort has been made, in this book, to always bear in mind that the enduring, underlying element in Irish history – indeed, what gives Ireland a history – is the Irish people. Ireland did not, after all, become West Britain, despite the best efforts of its near neighbour. And, for all its massive impact on life in Ireland, and Irish self-awareness, England is only one of the influencing factors. Scotland and Ireland have experienced a complex relationship for much longer, and each country has given the other highly significant sets of immigrants at different times, with profound and permanent consequences in every case. Norwegians, Danes, Welsh, Normans and Flemings have also participated in forming the present-day people of Ireland. As the descendants of successive incomers came to assume an Irish identity, the overall notion of Irishness was each time subtly altered. But much the largest element in the population stems from the people who came to call themselves the Gaels. Recent genetic research, carried out under the auspices of the Royal College of Surgeons in Ireland, indicates that the major contribution to the Irish gene pool was made during the initial, or a very early, human colonisation of the island. Inhabitants of the land from an immemorial period, speakers of now unknown languages before Gaelic and then English, inheritors and passers-on of an increasingly rich cultural tradition, sometimes silenced for generations

15

at a time by the noisiness of lately come proprietors, the Irish people have succeeded in maintaining a clear identity for a very long time.

One of the fascinating aspects of their history is the way in which that identity has developed and changed while remaining effortlessly distinctive and always renewing its links with a far distant but still relevant past.

CHAPTER ONE

Twentieth-century Ireland

IRELAND IN 1900

WHEN exploring origins, one finds that beginnings in Irish history are as elusive as mountain summits: just as the topmost ridge seems to be reached, a further horizon rises up beyond it. The year 1900 was in no sense a definitive one in Irish history, but it marks the beginning of a decisive century.

At that time, the entire island of Ireland, with a population of 4,459,000, had been incorporated within the United Kingdom of Great Britain and Ireland for a hundred years. Its monarch was Queen Victoria. Its political centre was the Palace of Westminster, in London, where a hundred Irish members represented their constituents in the House of Commons, and twenty Irish peers represented the aristocratic interest in the House of Lords. A Lord Lieutenant, based in Dublin, represented the monarch in Ireland.

In 1900, the 81-year-old Queen made a state visit to her Irish capital. Her government hoped that the royal presence would both damp down the force of Irish nationalism, and help in recruiting soldiers for the colonial war being fought against the Boers in South Africa. The results were mixed. There was loyal acclamation, but also protest. Maud Gonne, daughter of an English colonel but a stormy petrel of the Nationalist cause, made a famous speech whose burden was 'Go home, Queen!' An Irish Brigade was formed by her future husband, John MacBride, to fight on the side of the Boers against the British Empire: not for the first or last time, Irishmen would fight on opposing sides in someone else's war.

Ireland was not an oppressed society. Within the country, there had been democratic control of district affairs for two years, since the formation, in 1898, of councils for the counties and urban and rural districts. All adults were eligible to vote for these councils, including (for the first time) women. The Royal Irish Constabulary (RIC), though armed and housed in small district barracks, was a civilian police force. Relatively few troops were stationed in the country, most of them at the Curragh Camp in Kildare. The press was free, indeed writers had more freedom than in England, since the Lord Chamberlain's censorship of plays did not extend to Ireland. There was freedom of worship. There was abundant evidence of commercial enterprise

17

and expansion. Belfast was a major industrial city, a centre of shipbuilding and of linen manufacture, and all their ancillary trades. Dublin, apart from its huge brewing businesses, had a vast range of industrial activity from locomotive works to chinaware. These cities and every other town also acted as markets, processing points and supply centres for the products and needs of a varied land-based economy. It was still an essentially rural country, with agriculture as the basis of society and economic life. The Wyndham Land Act of 1903, named after the Chief Secretary for Ireland, who introduced it, would be the next major stage in a process of reform which was transferring ownership of much of the land from rent-collecting landlords to owner-occupier farmers. Steam railways linked every town of importance in a national transport system. Early motor cars were beginning to oust horses from the stables of country houses. These houses themselves, distributed throughout the landscape, especially in the more green and pleasant parts, harboured a 'gentry' population which, although diminished in power by the establishment of elected local councils, remained influential in many ways. Telegraphic links enabled rapid communication across the land and sea. The country was administered from Dublin Castle, where a team of British or Anglo-Irish civil servants worked for the Chief Secretary for Ireland, a member of the government. In 1900, some

---

THE FERGUSON TRACTOR

HARRY George Ferguson (1884–1960) was born at Growell, Co. Down, and showed a mechanical bent from his boyhood. In 1902 he joined a motor-cycle repair business, set up by his brother, in Belfast. In 1909 he made the first powered flight in Ireland, at Hillsborough, Co. Down, in a plane built by himself. By 1911 he was in business on his own account, an enthusiastic advocate of the motor tractor as a replacement for the plough horse. Ferguson's great achievement was the hydraulically controlled plough which could be raised or lowered to different depths. His success attracted the attention of the American motor magnate, Henry Ford, but he preferred to set up his own US operation in 1926. A commercial agreement with Ford followed in 1938. The Ferguson tractor became a worldwide symbol of agricultural modernisation, though the lack of capital among Irish farmers and the small size of many farms made its take-up relatively slow in Ireland, apart from large farms where its labour-saving potential made it immediately profitable. Ferguson himself retired from his business after a merger with Massey-Harris in 1953.

---

men destined for later fame were still young. Patrick Pearse and Eamon de Valera were university students. Michael Collins was a boy of ten, in Clonakilty. Sean Lemass was a one-year-old infant.

HOME RULE AND UNIONISM

An established political and social structure, and the daily pattern of work in field, factory or storehouse, did not mean that society was either contented or united. One proof of this was that in the Imperial parliament, following the general election of 1900, eighty-one of the Irish MPs were committed to the policy of 'Home Rule for Ireland'. John Redmond was elected their leader, though they were not a very united group. Nationalism embraced a number of visions of the possible future. Home Rule, to most adherents, implied the running of Ireland's affairs from within Ireland, without the English having any say. Ireland would remain a kingdom, sharing a monarch with Great Britain. For some, this was all they wanted; for others, it was as much as they thought they could get. After all, in the 1880s, such devolution had seemed to be just around the corner. A minority, unrepresented in parliament, wanted complete separation from Great Britain, in an independent Irish republic, and accepted that this could only be achieved by violent means. A smaller minority were organised to put their beliefs into practice, in secret groups like the Irish Republican Brotherhood (IRB). This spectrum of nationalist opinion was accommodated in various public organisations, mostly of recent origin. The newest were Cumann na nGaedheal, 'Association of the Gaels', founded in 1900 by Arthur Griffith, a 29-year-old journalist recently returned from South Africa, which linked a number of Nationalist clubs, and Inghinidhe na hÉireann, 'Daughters of Ireland', founded in the same year by Maud Gonne. The latter was intended to be a means of educating women in Nationalist ideas and of putting these ideas into practice, in such ways as not buying British-made goods, and discouraging young men from joining the British armed forces. Intended to be non-political and non-sectarian, the Gaelic Athletic Association, sixteen years old, and the Gaelic League, established in 1893, were specifically intended to reawaken the people's interest in the nation's past, its traditions, and not least, its language. Neither of these aims could be accomplished without opposing the growth of 'foreign' – that is, English – games like soccer, and the ever-increasing dominance of the English language, and despite resistance from the Gaelic League leaders, the two movements were steadily becoming more closely associated with political Nationalism. There was also a more volatile and sporadically active element in the Nationalist camp, the popular mob which, especially in Dublin, could quickly assemble to protest or to celebrate. It had its counterpart in Belfast, though that city had two mobs, reflecting the visceral Unionist as well as the Nationalist point of view, and also an entrenched division between Catholics and Protestants that transcended any sense of working-class solidarity.

A substantial section of Irish society was content with the established system. They supported the Union and did not think that Home Rule was either necessary or desirable. Full independence was naturally even more unattractive to them. Unionists, though most strongly established in the industrial districts and broad farmlands of north-east Ulster, were to be found throughout the country. They too formed a spectrum of opinion: particularly outside Ulster, not all Unionists were Protestant and by no means all Protestants were Unionists. Belief in the Union and in Home Rule were not incompatible. Many staunch Unionists were in favour of Home Rule for all internal matters. Supporters of the Union ranged from those who felt that on the whole it brought economic or social value to Ireland, to those who did not believe that the country could survive without it. Unionists were rarely a majority in any non-Ulster parliamentary constituency: the main exception was the Dublin university seat held by Sir Edward Carson.

RADICAL POLITICS

The Nationalist–Unionist divide, and the different forms of nationalism and unionism, overshadowed but did not wholly stifle other forms of political thought, shared by Ireland with other countries. Capitalism was the economic system of the United Kingdom, and in Ireland, as in Britain, the rise of trade unions and of a Labour Party reflected the working class's sense of self-awareness and communal support that had developed in the later nineteenth century. As it happened, there was more support for the workers from those who believed in abolition of the Union. Those who supported the Union were more likely to have vested interests to defend. But the Irish industrial 'proletariat' was small, certainly not a majority of the working population, and socialism

The Jim Larkin monument in Dublin

20

AN ARMAGH TEA PARTY

' LORD and Lady Aberdeen were a thoughtful pair, but they never really understood the Irish. When they visited the Protestant and Catholic Archbishops of Armagh, they somehow felt it would be tactless to let either prelate know of their visit to the other one. So having lunched at the Palace with the aged Protestant Archbishop Alexander and his unmarried daughter Nell, who did hostess for him now that the hymn-writing Mrs Alexander was dead, the Viceroy and Vicereine suddenly took their leave without saying where they were going. They then drove round to the opposite side of Armagh city to have tea with the Catholic Archbishop, Cardinal Logue. To their great surprise, on arriving at the Cardinal's residence, they found Nell Alexander there, waiting to pour out the tea, having been asked by the Cardinal to come and do hostess for him.'

Mark Bence-Jones, *The Twilight of the Ascendancy.* [The Earl of Aberdeen was Lord Lieutenant in 1886 and from 1905–15.]

---

and labour activism were confined to certain districts of the largest towns. Labour's most prominent figure was James Larkin, a Liverpool-born man, who organised and led the Belfast dockers before moving to Dublin in 1909, where he formed the Irish Transport and General Workers' Union. The radical tradition in Ireland was much older than the rise of industry and owed far more to Tom Paine and his advocacy of the 'rights of man', than to the economic and social theories of Karl Marx. Industrialists and other large employers in Ireland viewed organised labour with the same suspicion as their counterparts elsewhere, and the notorious 'Dublin Lockout' of 1913, led for the employers by the tramways magnate, William Martin Murphy, a prominent home-rule Nationalist, was a temporarily successful attempt to break trade unionism among the workers.

LITERARY CONTROVERSY

Driven by similar ideals, and with the same energy as the Gaelic movements, the literary scene had great vibrancy at this time. It too was a channel for Nationalist sentiment, though its most public and provocative form, the Literary Theatre founded by W.B. Yeats with the help of the Anglo-Irish Lady Gregory and the wholly English Annie Horniman, proudly stood for the Republic of Letters, and its productions were as likely to outrage Nationalist as

Unionist sentiment. Though both sought inspiration in Irish tradition, there was a wide gulf of attitude between Yeats, who never learned Gaelic, with his London house and English friends, and someone like Douglas Hyde, who believed that a return to Gaelic was not only desirable but essential for the future of Ireland. A corresponding gulf existed between those who held a relatively relaxed view not only of literature but also of social behaviour, and those who held a decidedly strait-laced one.

Since the formal restoration of the Catholic hierarchy in 1850, a puritanical strain in Irish society had emerged. There is something of the ethos of a counter-reformation in this. Catholic Ireland did not need a counter-reformation, having kept its adherence to the essentials of the faith, but the clergy felt the need to underline their authority, and no doubt there were many opportunities to correct laxness of all kinds in daily life. As with all such trends, it focused strongly on matters relating to sex. The modesty of Irish girlhood, in particular, was set up as an ideal. The combination of this repressive attitude to any hint of sexual reference or display, plus the veneration of Irish tradition, caused a riot when J.M. Synge's *The Playboy of the Western World* was put on at Yeats's Abbey Theatre in 1907 (the Abbey had opened in 1904). The Nationalist–libertarian poet sent for the Imperialist police to quell the rage of his Nationalist–Catholic fellow-citizens.

THE HOME RULE BILL

The complex, multi-layered Irish society revealed different patterns of formation according to how its concerns and interests were cut across, but it was nevertheless largely united by the desire for Home Rule. While this was to be expected among the Catholic majority, there were many Home Rulers from the Protestant section of the community, who formed a significant minority in and around Dublin and in Leinster, and whose views were often different to those of their co-religionists in the North. But in 1900, with a convincedly unionist Conservative government in power, there was no chance whatever of Home Rule: Redmond's band of MPs was an impotent force. The situation changed with the general election of 1905, in which the Irish result was much the same, but in Britain the Liberals were swept into power. Home Rule was back on the agenda. In that year Arthur Griffith and Bulmer Hobson founded the Sinn Féin League, which became simply Sinn Féin in 1908, by which time it had absorbed a number of small groups with a mixture of republican, pacifist and feminist aims. But what was offered by the Liberals in 1907 – still remembering how the issue had almost destroyed their party in the 1880s – was an Irish Council of limited power, far short of a parliament. In the face of Irish contempt, the half-baked proposal was withdrawn. Only in 1912, with the

THE NOBEL PRIZE FOR LITERATURE

SINCE the prize was founded in 1901 it has been won four times by Irish writers: William Butler Yeats (1923), George Bernard Shaw (1925), Samuel Beckett (1969) and Seamus Heaney (1995). It is a remarkable record. The propensity for imaginative writing among the Irish is closely linked to their success in fashioning the English language into a form of distinctively Irish expression. Modern English is a commonwealth of many nations, into which Ireland regularly pays more than its due. Other roots go far back into the Gaelic tradition of story-telling, of word usage and word-play; and there is still a legacy of Gaelic's combination of verbal obliquity and mental precision in modern Irish thought and utterance. Commentators have not failed to point out that three out of the four laureates lived their adult lives wholly or to a large extent outside Ireland. Heaney was the home-based exception, and he lived in an Ireland that, for all its strains, was a more open and outward-looking society than that of his predecessors. But the writer's predicament with Ireland had been summed up by one who did not win a Nobel prize, but who can claim to be among the most influential writers in English of the twentieth century – James Joyce. Another self-sentenced exile, he wrote: 'When the soul of a man is born in this country, there are nets flung at it to hold it back from flight. You talk to me of nationality, language, religion. I shall try to fly those nets.' (*A Portrait of the Artist as a Young Man*)

William Butler Yeats   *George Bernard Shaw*

23

Irish phalanx once again controlling the balance of power at Westminster, did a Liberal government again introduce an Irish Home Rule Bill, which was passed by the House of Commons on 7 July 1913. The following week, the House of Lords rejected it. Though their veto, which had wrecked a previous Home Rule Bill in 1893, had been abolished by now, they could still enforce a two-year delay on legislation to which they objected.

OPPONENTS OF HOME RULE

The consequences of this new political momentum were swiftly appreciated in the north-eastern Ulster counties where Protestants and Unionists outnumbered Catholics and Nationalists. The Home Rule parliament likely to be set up in Dublin would have little resemblance to the Irish parliament of the eighteenth century, which had been an assembly of the Protestant landowning class. New conditions of parliamentary suffrage – if only for men at this time – and the powerful influence of the Roman Catholic hierarchy, could only mean an assembly dominated by the Catholic interest. A phrase was coined that encapsulated a simple viewpoint, 'Home rule means Rome rule' – and they were going to have none of it. In the light of later events, it is important to try to identify the reasons for this stance.

The Ulster Protestant community was spread across two large denominations, the Presbyterians and the Church of Ireland, with small numbers of Methodists, Baptists and other sects. Religious views were strongly held, and their historical significance, back to1689 and before, was not forgotten. The Presbyterians had equally not forgotten their own churches' experience as a victim of the establishment, even though they had long been prosperous and free. Their organisation was essentially local and provincial, and emphatically without any hierarchy. The Church of Ireland, with almost as many communicants in Ulster as the Presbyterians, was a hierarchy, with bishops and archbishops, and also with a structure that extended throughout all the provinces of Ireland. This prevented the Church, though not its individual members, from taking a narrowly provincial view, but with its close links to the Church of England, it had little to gain from Home Rule.

The commerce and industry that had transformed the North in the previous century was based on close trading links with England and Scotland. For many of its population, the British 'mainland' was the place their ancestors had come from, a place they did business with, a place whose Protestant forms of religion they shared. For many decades now, politics in Ulster had split on the Nationalist–Unionist divide, closely matched by the Catholic–Protestant divide, and confrontations and riots had occurred through the nineteenth century. The Unionists in the North saw the prospect of a Nationalist-dominated parliament as an economic threat: their province's factory-based industrial economy had no real parallel elsewhere, and they knew that the Nationalists had no bonds with the North's main trading partner. They also saw it as a real religious threat. This fear was heightened by a papal decree, *Ne temere*, of 1907, setting out strict rules for marriage between Catholics and Protestants, and which, interpreted in a rigorous manner, could suggest that the Protestant rite of marriage had no validity at all. There was also a threat to their political and social dominance. Within the Irish context, the Protestants of the North knew themselves to be part of a minority, though a substantial and influential one. Within the context of the United Kingdom of Great Britain and Ireland, they were part of an overwhelming majority.

There was no dialogue between the two sides. The constitutional nationalists, still led by Redmond, had no figure who could talk to the Ulster Protestants, or at first even discern what they were about. Joe Devlin, leader of the northern Nationalists, was a sturdy defender of their position but no tribune of the people. The Protestants themselves had no wish to talk to anyone other than their Conservative allies in Britain, who added their own imperialism to the other factors in the situation. Irish nationalism was seen by them as a threat to the Empire which, if not fought, would send a dangerous message to other British possessions. The utterances of British Tory politicians like Bonar Law matched the truculence of the northerners. New slogans joined the old ones, such as 'Not an inch', crystallising the view spelled out by Sir Edward Carson: 'There can be no permanent resting place between complete union and total separation.'

THE UNIONIST–NATIONALIST DIVIDE

Ulster was by far the most prosperous province, even if its wealth was unevenly weighted towards the rich arable and dairy farmlands of the east and centre, and the industrial zone of Belfast (in 1911 a more populous city than Dublin) and its hinterland, rather than in the west and south. It was of course by no means an exclusively Protestant province. More than 40 per cent of its population was Catholic. But the majority of Catholics were in the west and south, including the three counties, Donegal, Cavan and Monaghan, which would eventually be separated from the historic province. The economy of the region, and the administration of its towns, were solidly under Protestant control. What the Catholics of Ulster, 650,000 or more in number, were to make of the impassioned Protestant declarations on behalf of their province, does not seem to have been considered. The Ulster Protestants found their leader in the perhaps unlikely figure of Sir Edward Carson, the Dublin-born MP for the Dublin University constituency and a highly successful barrister, whose scalps, as a prosecuting counsel, included that of his former contemporary at Trinity College, Oscar Wilde. But Carson had already been a Conservative government minister, had excellent connections in London political circles and an oratorical skill which other leaders of the resistance, such as James Craig, could not match. His very lack of Ulster connections helped to make the cause seem less provincial. And indeed Carson's great desire was always to keep all Ireland within the Union; according to the historian J.C. Beckett, 'To kill Home Rule was the governing purpose of his life.'

With the passing of the Home Rule Bill, pressures on behalf of the Ulster Protestants increased. Old icons were unearthed. At an emotional rally in the Ulster Hall, Carson was presented with an ensign said to have been carried at the Battle of the Boyne. A nationalist paper commented: 'If that flag ever saw the Battle of the Boyne, all we can say is that the man who manufactured it deserves undying fame for the strength and durability of the material.' Demonstrations were also held in London. Bonar Law, the Conservative leader, referred darkly to 'things stronger than parliamentary majorities'. Armed rebellion in Ulster was openly discussed. The Prime Minister, Asquith, was sufficiently alarmed to tell Redmond that the Home Rule Act would require to be amended before it was put into effect.

THE BIRTH OF THE ULSTER VOLUNTEER FORCE

In September 1912, taking a leaf out of old Scottish history, 470,000 persons in Ulster signed a Solemn League and Covenant, which included the pledge to use 'all means which may be found necessary to defeat the present conspiracy to set up a Home Rule parliament in Ireland'. In 1913 the Ulster Volunteer Force (UVF) was established and recruitment was rapid, bringing it to almost 80,000 by the end of the year. Arms and ammunition were openly imported, including 24,000 rifles and three million rounds of bullets from Germany, landed at Larne in April 1914. Protestant magistrates obligingly issued licences for the UVF to carry out drilling and manoeuvres. The extent to which the Protestant Unionists enjoyed sympathy within British institutions was made clear when it was revealed that General Sir Hubert Gough, Commander of the Third Cavalry Brigade, based at the Curragh, and many of his officers, would refuse to march against a Protestant insurrection in Ulster. Not since the seventeenth century had the British army attempted to involve itself in politics, and a considerable shock wave ran through society. As a result of the 'Curragh Mutiny', over 130 officers resigned their commissions. But it was plain that the government could not rely on the army to support an Act of parliament, and the official urge to accommodate the Ulster intransigents, rather than confront civil war, was further strengthened.

RMS *TITANIC*

IN the early years of the twentieth century, the transatlantic passenger trade was growing dramatically. One of the leading shipping companies was the White Star Line, which had long-standing links with Harland and Wolff's Belfast shipyard. Marine technology was enabling the building of ever-bigger ships, and Belfast led the world in this respect. The yards also sustained a whole range of auxiliary industries, from rope works to cabinet-makers and from sawmills to fabric printers. In 1911 the 46,328-ton *Titanic* was launched, the biggest ship the world had yet seen, 'an unabashed celebration of opulence and technical wizardry' according to one marine historian. With a double steel hull and fifteen transverse bulkheads, she was also thought to be the safest. The last port to see her on her one and only voyage was Queenstown (now Cobh) on 12 April 1912. Three days later, the *Titanic* struck an iceberg and foundered, with the loss of over 1,600 people. The shock of the disaster was intensely felt in Belfast, where memories of the proud launch were still so recent.

THE INTERVENTION OF WAR

In August 1914, the focus of British attention shifted drastically with its declaration of war against Austria and Germany. John Redmond agreed immediately with Asquith that the thorny question of how Irish Home Rule was actually to be achieved should be put aside until the end of the war. Carson was brought into the government. The UVF became the basis of an army division. Redmond, no less determined than Carson to be constitutional in the crisis, offered the services of the Nationalist Irish Volunteers, a body formed in direct response to the founding of the UVF. The Secretary for War, Lord Kitchener, declined their services. Though many Irish Nationalists were to fight on the British side, it was in one of the existing Irish regiments, or in non-Irish units.

Redmond's act of British patriotism was not endorsed by all Nationalists and was repudiated by the Republican movement. If the constitutional parties on both sides of the Irish Sea thought that Ireland would cease to be an issue while the British Empire was at war, they were to be forcibly made to realise otherwise. While most of the Volunteers remained loyal to Redmond, and many joined the British army, others did not. Slightly over one per cent of the 170,000 formed their own organisation as the Sinn Féin Volunteers. From

1907 the Irish Republican Brotherhood had begun a new phase of activity, driven by a new generation of activists, mainly Ulster-born, with a programme of education and propaganda; by 1914 the membership was around 1,600. There was much overlapping of membership between different societies, particularly between the IRB and Sinn Féin.

With the advent of war, a diverse group of men saw an opportunity for their own causes. One was James Connolly, veteran Scots–Irish socialist and trade unionist, a leader of the small 'citizen army' formed in 1913 to defend strikers against the Dublin Metropolitan Police, who had killed two men in baton charges against demonstrators in the city centre. Believing, as did many socialists at the start of the war, that the conflict was a capitalist plot that the workers would repudiate, Connolly supported the idea of an armed uprising that would simultaneously deliver national independence and a workers' republic, not only in Ireland but in other nation-states too. Sir Roger Casement, knighted for his humanitarian work as a British consular official, was an active participant in gun-running and acted as a link with American–Irish Republican sympathisers. In the early part of the war he also went to Germany, both to encourage Irish prisoners-of-war to change sides, and to propose a German landing in Ireland or German aid for an Irish uprising. Thomas Clarke was an IRB veteran who had served fifteen years in prison for his part in the British bombing campaign of 1883. Eoin MacNéill, a founder of the Gaelic League and also a founder of the Volunteers, became Chief-of-Staff in the Irish Republican Brotherhood. While MacNeill, an academic, was drawn to the *engagés*, a fellow founder, Douglas Hyde, resigned from the League in 1915 because of its politicisation in the Republican cause. Other key members of the IRB were Patrick Pearse, named as Director of Military Organisation, Joseph Plunkett, Director of Military Operations, and Thomas MacDonagh, Director of Training. They were in no doubt that they were preparing for a rising.

Equally certain were the founders of Cumann na mBan (Association of Women), set up in 1914 as a supportive and auxiliary force. Outside Ireland but deeply involved in discussions and plans, was John Devoy. Long-established leader of the American association Clan na Gael and editor of *Gaelic American*, he was influential on both sides of the Atlantic. Before America's entry into the war, his links with the German embassy in Washington enabled the visits to Germany made by Casement and by Joseph Plunkett, another of the youthful members of the IRB's Military Council.

In Dublin, tension was high even before war was declared. Armed Nationalist Volunteers paraded openly. In July 1914 a troop of the King's Own Scottish Borderers turned with rifles and bayonets on a jeering crowd in Batchelor's Walk. Three civilians were killed and thirty-five wounded. But the

British administration in Dublin Castle was not greatly perturbed. Ireland was not doing badly out of the war, which had promoted industry of all kinds and improved the market for farm produce. Many thousands had joined up to fight against the Germans, while Casement's efforts to recruit a pro-German Irish Brigade were an almost total failure. And Home Rule was just a matter of time.

THE 1916 EASTER RISING

One of the most remarkable things about the 1916 Easter Rising was that, although Dublin was buzzing with rumours, no one knew just what was being planned, or when, or even by whom. Eoin MacNéill, as Chief of Staff of the Volunteers, had laid down that an armed revolt should happen only if conscription were introduced or if action were taken against the IRB and the Volunteers. Some time before, Pearse had ordered Sunday 23 April to be a day for drills and manoeuvres by Nationalist Volunteers; this was taken as a routine exercise. The seven or so men who organised the rising kept it secret not only from the government spy network but from some of their closest colleagues. On 19 April, they convinced MacNeill that the British were about to act against the Nationalist Volunteers, who were consequently put into a state of readiness to fight. MacNeill countermanded these orders on Saturday 22 April, but by then, as Pearse told him, it was too late.

Armed Nationalist columns were nothing new in Dublin. On Monday 24 April, a Bank Holiday, armed columns of Republicans converged on the city centre, but this time took possession of a number of buildings, most notably the General Post Office, from whose portico Pearse, as head of the provisional government and commandant-general, read the celebrated document proclaiming an Irish Republic. The administration, and the city's inhabitants, were taken completely by surprise, and it was not until the following day that serious fighting began, as troops and guns were hurriedly summoned. The Rising lasted until half past three on Saturday 29 April, at which time, faced with overwhelming odds, Pearse surrendered unconditionally and ordered his fellow commanders to do the same.

Nothing on a scale like this had happened in more than a hundred years. The GPO was a ruin and many other buildings were shattered. The central streets were filled with wreckage and lined by smashed and looted shops. Around 500 people were dead and 2,500 injured, among them 521 troops and police. There was evidence of indiscriminate killing, including three shootings by a junior officer, Captain Bowen-Colthurst, later court-martialled and pronounced insane. The country was placed under martial law. For the moment, the supreme and unchallengeable ruler of Ireland was the newly arrived army chief, General John Maxwell. Under military law, summary trials were held, guilty verdicts issued, and executions followed without delay.

The great majority of people reacted to news of the Rising as something futile and even stupid. A week after the surrender, the pro-Home Rule *Freeman's Journal* called it 'an armed assault against the will and decision of the Irish nation itself, constitutionally ascertained through its proper representatives'. To Unionists it was also a stab in the back, delivered in the middle of a war, and Germany's hand was seen in the proclamation's reference to 'gallant allies in Europe' even before it became public knowledge that a German arms ship, the *Aud*, had been captured off the west coast on Friday 21 April, and that Casement had been arrested on the same day after landing in Kerry from a German submarine.

A SHIFT IN OPINION

Centuries before, the Irish had known and codified the forms of martyrdom in the name of Christianity: the red, the black and the white. It was in the name of Ireland that the leaders of the Rising deliberately set themselves on the same course. None died before the surrender, though Connolly was injured. Their red martyrdoms were duly conferred by the outraged Imperial power. Fourteen men were shot by firing squad in Dublin, and one in Cork. Casement was hanged in London, as a traitor. At the same time, a wave of searches, arrests, interrogations and trials was taking place as the forces of authority reacted. Some 3,500 men and 80 women were rounded up and arrested.

During the course of these events, a decisive shift in public opinion was taking place. The general reaction to the executions was immediate and hostile. It was not a short-term response: as the import of what had been done sank in, the temper of the Nationalist-minded community changed from moderation and even apathy to separatism and firm determination. The cause of constitutional nationalism, mired in the arguments over Ulster and stalled by the war, was left behind in this new mood. Redmond's deputy, John Dillon, spoke up with courage in a hostile House of Commons: 'It is not murderers who are being executed, it is insurgents who have fought a clean fight, a brave fight, however misguided.' He proclaimed his pride in them. For the Ulster Unionist members, his words showed the Nationalists to be all of one cloth, and in the words of Ronald McNeill, it justified 'the whole basis of Ulster's unchanging attitude towards Nationalism'. A few months later, the enormous losses suffered by the 36th (Ulster) Division of the British army in the Battle of the Somme were seen by many as a grievous but freely given price paid by the province for its continuing place in Union and Empire.

THE RISE OF SINN FÉIN AS A POLITICAL FORCE

For a time it looked as if Home Rule would be rapidly implemented. But again it ran onto the same rocks. Ulster, said Carson, would not be in. Ulster, said Redmond, could not be out. Redmond, however, was fast becoming irrelevant as the pro-Sinn Féin tide swept on. Republican clubs were forming in large numbers throughout the country, and young people, especially, were attracted to them. Under the new British Prime Minister, Lloyd George, and encouraged by the United States government, separate British negotiations with National- ists and Unionists took place, dragging on for two years, during which the Republican movement grew ever stronger.

Sinn Féin rapidly shaped itself into republicanism's political wing. From October 1917 its leadership passed from Arthur Griffith to Eamon de Valera, one of the district commanders of 1916, whose American birth had gained him a reprieve from his death sentence, and who, with other prisoners, was released from internment in June 1917. Griffith was a dual-kingdom National- ist; de Valera was a firm Republican. In the spring of 1918, the British govern- ment empowered itself to extend conscription to Ireland, arousing a furore of opposition. Even the Irish bishops affirmed that the Irish had the right to resist being forced into the British army. The powers were never implemented, but an easy propaganda victory had been handed to Sinn Féin. In May the govern- ment banned the party and arrested some of its leaders, including de Valera. In the general election held in December of that year, Sinn Féin won seventy- three Irish seats, the Unionists twenty-six (twenty-three of them in Ulster), and the old Nationalists only six. Following their proclaimed policy, the Sinn Féin MPs did not take up their Westminster seats. In January 1919, twenty- five met in Dublin, named their gathering as Dáil Éireann, the 'Irish Assembly', and reaffirmed the independence declaration of April 1916. De Valera, who had escaped from an English prison, was elected as President of the Dáil in April 1919, and appointed a governing cabinet of eight members. Another thirty-four elected MPs were in British prisons.

'THE TROUBLES'

The Sinn Féin government set about establishing its own writ wherever pos- sible, and the majority of local authorities acknowledged it. The British admin- istration remained intact. It was not a tenable situation, but it took until August for the Dáil to be officially proscribed by London; meanwhile the Republicans sent delegates to canvass political support from the USA and the Versailles Peace Conference, which had been established following the end of the war. Financial support from Irish–Americans was also sought and supplied.

The Irish Volunteers were reconstituted as the Irish Republican Army (IRA), though they practised a guerrilla form of warfare, in fast-moving small units, and wore plain clothes. The aim was not to wage a conventional war but to employ harassing and disruptive tactics, especially against the police, that would make the country ungovernable. Their numbers, no more than 3,000, widely dispersed, made any other strategy impossible. A quick effect was to reduce the ranks of the Royal Irish Constabulary through resignations and lack of recruits, as well as assassinations; and to supplement the dwindled force, the British government recruited a semi-regular force, mostly of ex-soldiers, whose khaki uniform, with black police caps and belts, earned them the nickname of 'Black and Tans'.

It became a kind of semi-secret war, which the British government was anxious to hide from its own people, constantly minimising its scale and impact, whilst hoping that the Black and Tans together with another irregular force, the police Auxiliaries, would contain or beat down the IRA. There was no concealing it within Ireland. Its byname, 'the Troubles', is a feeble euphemism for the intimidation, violence, arson, destruction, assassination and terror inflicted, with little political control, by both sides. The struggle became a bitter stalemate. The IRA could not expel the British forces, which could not defeat the IRA. Trouble was not confined to the counties where Nationalists were a majority – in 1920–21 there were shootings, large-scale riots and intimidation in Belfast and the north-east. The sources were chiefly within the majority group, and a sectarian element was much more apparent in these hostilities. As a result of threats, riots and attacks, large numbers of Catholic families moved from districts where they had been long established.

PARTITION

In September 1920 the British government put forward a new Home Rule Bill, which was passed in December (without the participation of the Sinn Féin members). This specifically provided for the partition of Ireland, with six of the nine Ulster counties forming a separate unit with its own parliament, beyond the rule of Dublin. Both parliaments were to have limited powers, with both parts of Ireland still being represented also in the Imperial parliament. The partition arrangement was presented as a temporary one, and a council of Ireland, with ill-defined powers, was to be created with twenty members from each parliament.

Though anguished protests came from their fellows in the three excluded counties about being 'thrown to the wolves', the Ulster Unionists, whose prime objective had always been to preserve the position in their own stronghold, accepted this arrangement with a degree of reluctance which was partly just for show. Carson was by now out of the political struggle, having become an appeal court judge: for him partition would have been a poor sort of victory. There was distress among many Unionist-minded inhabitants of the twenty-six counties, just as there was in those Catholic and Nationalist districts which would be retained within the partitioned six. Overall, the Nationalists rejected the proposal with contempt.

When elections were held in May 1921, forty out of fifty-two Northern Ireland seats were won by the Unionists, now led by Sir James Craig, and he proceeded to form a government to work within the bounds laid down by London. Its composition was wholly Unionist. Even had the notion of power-sharing been considered, the state of relations between the Unionist and Nationalist communities would have made its success extremely dubious. The

David Lloyd George

result for the Dublin parliament showed the impossibility of any solution dictated from London. Out of 128 seats, 124 were won by unopposed Sinn Féin candidates, who of course had no intention of taking their seats. Dáil Éireann continued to be their forum. The vicious war of skirmishes, raids and reprisals continued. But in London it could hardly now be claimed that a minority were causing the 'trouble', and the pressures on Lloyd George's government to seek a negotiated solution were intense. A truce was agreed on 10 July 1921, and de Valera, an absconded 'guest' from King George V's Lincoln Jail, returned to England for official talks with the British government.

THE DILEMMA OF DIVISION

The British position was clear from the outset. Ireland — the Ireland of the twenty-six counties — was now offered full independence from Westminster rule. But it must remain a part of the British Empire, under King George – like Australia and South Africa, whose Prime Minister, Smuts, was much involved as a 'facilitator' – and Britain would retain full use of naval port facilities at Berehaven, Queenstown (Cobh), Lough Swilly, Haulbowline, near Cork, and Rathmullen: the 'treaty ports'. The six Ulster counties were to be excluded

33

from the settlement. Craig and his government refused to attend the negotiations: hardly more trustful of London than they were of Dublin, they were making haste to set up their institutions.

Once again the Irish negotiators writhed on the prongs of the Ulster fork. Pragmatically, they all knew that a million unwilling people could not be coerced into the Irish state. Equally, they all held in hearts and minds the concept of Ireland as it had always been: one, indissoluble. Siren voices – and Lloyd George was a master of suggestion – might say: 'One day, Ulster will have to join you. Only be patient.' To such hints he added the offer of a boundary commission to investigate the division between the two parts of Ireland, with the implicit prospect that this commission would slice off such a large amount of the six-county state as to make it completely unviable.

The delegates were in an extraordinarily difficult situation. On the one hand, here was the real substance of independence. To turn it down would lead to renewed warfare and the attrition of Ireland's resources, perhaps to the loss of such an opportunity for generations to come. To accept it might be to accept a divided Ireland for the foreseeable future and to consign the Catholic population of the six counties to a permanent existence as second-class citizens. There was division in the Dáil, and, at first, in the delegation. Arthur Griffith, who had from the beginning believed in independence under the monarchy, was prepared to accept the British offer. Michael Collins, who had been both the Republicans' finance minister and the IRA's director of organisation and intelligence, at first was not, but changed his mind. The six delegates at the final meetings in London were given plenipotentiary powers: that is, they were empowered to speak and decide for their colleagues. But they were also instructed not to sign a treaty until the terms had been approved in Dublin. De Valera, whom the Dáil had elected as President of the Republic of Ireland in August, was not in the delegation, and it is hard to see his role at this time as anything other than waiting to see how things balanced out between the pro-Republic hardliners, led by Cathal Brugha and Austin Stack, and those ready to accept the 'Irish Free State' as offered by Lloyd George. In the end, the delegates signed their names to the treaty that established the 26-county Irish Free State, on 6 December 1921. Part-blandished, part-hustled, by Lloyd George, who had said that failure to sign would mean war 'in three days', unable to contact de Valera who was out of Dublin, and aware – in Collins's case at least – of the lack of resources to maintain a further military campaign, they signed, knowing that the treaty would anyway have to be ratified by the Dáil.

Collins, who saw dominion status as a staging-point to full independence, defended the treaty to the IRB Supreme Council as the freedom to achieve freedom – and subsequent events proved this attitude correct. De Valera finally aligned himself with those who believed that the Republican ideal had been betrayed. The final vote in the Dáil, on 7 January 1922, showed sixty-four in favour of ratification, fifty-seven against. Whether or not this was the result de Valera expected, his reaction was to resign as president and to exit, with the Republicans, from the Dáil. The stage was set for civil war.

For a short time there were four powers in Ireland. One was the new Northern Ireland government; another was the majority group in the Dáil, with Griffith as president, and Collins and Kevin O'Higgins as its strongest members, which now formed the Provisional Government of the Irish Free State. The other two claimed all-Ireland control. The British, not yet departed, still asserted the ultimate authority of Westminster. The Republicans, with de Valera at their head, proclaimed themselves as the government of all Ireland, and the true heirs of 1916 and the long Nationalist tradition before it.

1920–22: VIOLENCE AND CIVIL TURMOIL

Events in the new Northern Ireland took their own course. Many businesses were hit by a boycott of Ulster products, led by the IRA, from mid-1920, as a retaliation against attacks on Roman Catholics. There was little communication between the two new governments. Within the six counties, the Catholic and Nationalist population, deeply hostile to the idea of partition, and still holding some belief that it would be short-lived, were disinclined to participate in Home Rule, with its built-in Unionist majority. As a result, an already abrasive situation became inflamed and the resulting violence, political and sectarian, made Ulster the most disturbed part of Ireland. Following the shooting of a senior policeman in the summer of 1920, already over 8,000 Catholic workmen had been forced out of shipyards and factories in Belfast. More than 450 civilians were killed in the North between 1920 and 1922, most of them Catholics. To Republicans, the Ulster state was a piece of Imperialist land-snatching, justifying an armed response, and frequent cross-border incursions further soured relations between the two governments. And, as J.C. Beckett noted, 'the fact that IRA activity was almost invariably based on predominantly Roman Catholic areas, strengthened the Unionist tendency to regard all Roman Catholics as "rebels"; and the rift between the two groups became even wider.'

Determined to enforce its authority, and fearful of repercussions from London or Dublin if it failed to do so, James Craig's government took strong measures. It raised an Ulster Special Constabulary (USC), with three grades of special constable, armed with the rifles intended for the UVF in 1914. An all-Protestant force with no links to the Catholic–Nationalist population, its methods were confrontational and it operated in a similar way to the Black and Tans. USC detachments frequently seemed to be waging their own war with no control from higher authority, and IRA reprisals maintained a vicious spiral that threatened to lead to civil war. In the event, civil war in the Free State diverted the attention of the Republicans. There was also a meeting between Craig and Collins, in London, in March 1922, at which it was agreed that the boycott of Ulster products would be called off, and the IRA cross-border attacks cease, in return for a promise of greater attention to the interests of the minority population in the six counties. By the end of 1922, the situation in the North was quieter, though in the Nationalist districts, it was a sullen and suspicious calm.

THE IRISH FREE STATE

On 16 January 1922, the last Viceroy of Ireland handed over the keys of Dublin Castle to Michael Collins. Saorstát Éireann, the 'Irish Free State', was a reality. So was Northern Ireland, with its more limited self-governing powers and its voluntary subordination to Westminster (it continued to send MPs there). Richard Mulcahy, IRA Chief of Staff, became Minister of Defence and his forces became the new state's army. But a substantial minority allied themselves with the pro-Republicans and prepared to continue the conflict as though nothing had changed. On 14 April, a detachment of these 'Irregulars' occupied the Four Courts in Dublin, in open challenge to the new government. A general election was held, resulting in ninety-two seats for the Free State Party and its allies including Labour, and thirty-six for the pro-Republic Party. Taking their example from 1916, when a general election would certainly not have supported the cause of Pearse and the others, and from earlier precedents, the Republicans felt that their historic aim overrode any transient popular vote. Their members abstained from the Dáil, and the warfare intensified, both in the North and in the Free State. The existence of the Northern Irish parliament meant that IRA violence also continued in Great Britain, and in June the shooting in London of Field Marshal Sir Henry Wilson, who was also an Ulster Unionist MP, brought threats of a British military reprisal.

Collins, Chairman of the provisional Free State government, did not take serious action against the Irregulars until the occupiers of the Four Courts took General O'Connell, Assistant Chief of Staff of the new army, as a prisoner. Borrowed British artillery bombarded the Four Courts and forced a surrender on 30 June. This was not the end, but the beginning of a more intense conflict.

1922–23: FULL-SCALE CIVIL WAR

Civil wars are always bitter and long-remembered. The armed struggle between June 1922 and April 1923 still underlies Irish politics. To some, what was at contention seemed very little, to others, it was very great. Under the treaty with Britain, finally passed on 5 December 1922, the Irish Free State remained part of the British Commonwealth (a term now for the first time substituted for 'Empire') and members of the Dáil had to sign an oath of allegiance to the king as head of state. The Viceroy was replaced by a Governor-General, intended to exercise the powers of a constitutional monarch, above the arena of party politics. In some respects the struggle resembled a contest of will and determination between formidable chiefs and

*Michael Collins' grave,
Glasnevin Cemetery, Dublin*

their supporters. De Valera was not a man to yield easily. Nor was Collins, and when Collins was shot dead in August 1922, William Cosgrave, the new Chairman, and Kevin O'Higgins, Minister of Justice, proved redoubtable opponents of the pro-Republicans and their irregular militia. Griffith had died, exhausted, earlier the same month. Things were done which the British would never have dared to do. More than 12,000 Republicans were imprisoned. Between November 1922 and April 1923, the Free State executed more than twice as many people as the British had in seven years between 1916 and 1921. The overall toll of deaths exceeded 8,000. O'Higgins signed the death warrant of Rory O'Connor, captor of the Four Courts, not after a trial but as a reprisal, with three others, for the shooting of a member of the Dáil. O'Connor had been his best man at his wedding. Throughout the country, friendships, families, loyalties, were shattered.

The Free State government had a powerful ally in the Roman Catholic Church, whose bishops issued a pastoral letter in October 1922 stating that 'the killing of national soldiers . . . is murder before God.' But some individual priests stood out for the Republicans, and the condemnation by the Church was not enough to stop the war. In 1916, the Catholic Church had been hostile: *The Irish Catholic* had condemned the rising as 'partially socialistic and partially alien'; and in this matter the ardent Republicans could feel it had little authority.

In early 1923, although the resolve of many of his fellow-Republicans was undiminished, it became clear to de Valera that the war could not be won.

With considerable difficulty he persuaded the army council of this. On 23 April, in his capacity as 'President of the Government of the Republic of Ireland' he issued a proclamation of cease-fire to his troops. It was not couched in the terms of a surrender:

> The Republic can no longer be successfully defended by your arms. Further sacrifice of life would be vain, and continuance of the struggle in arms unwise in the National interest. Military victory must be allowed to rest for the moment with those who have destroyed the Republic.

In this way the war ended, with a defiant claim of moral superiority from the Republicans. Sporadic violence and revenge killings continued. Many Republicans were still detained, or were now arrested, including de Valera, who was held without trial from 15 August 1923 to 16 July 1924. The Sinn Féin Party was formed to fight the general election of August 1923, still on the abstentionist platform. They won forty-four out of one hundred and fifty-three seats. A minority government was formed by Cosgrave's new Cumann na nGaedheal, the largest party, with sixty-three seats. Sinn Féin members (if not in jail) stayed away, but the slow process of rebuilding a battered and divided state could begin. An important priority was the reduction in size of the army, to about half its current strength of 50,000. The difficulty of this was heightened by an IRB faction within the army attempting to dictate to the government, but the 'mutiny' was faced down and the role of the army confirmed as an agency of the state. This was a substantial achievement, as was the conversion of the Royal Irish Constabulary into the unarmed Garda Siochana.

BORDERS AND RELIGION: CONSOLIDATION AND ENTRENCHMENT

In 1923, the Boundary Commission, promised in the treaty, made its report. For the Free State government, lured by Lloyd George into expecting great things, it was a severe and embarrassing disappointment. Only minor exchanges of land in south Armagh and eastern Donegal were recommended. In the end, not even this happened. On 2 December 1925, the governments of the Free State, Northern Ireland and Great Britain agreed to scrap the commission's report, and a number of financial concessions were made to the Free State as a form of recompense. To the Unionist government in the North, this was a great relief, removing the last threat to the future of its province. In 1922 it had abolished the proportional representation system intended to ensure balance in local elections, and had begun to redraw ward boundaries in order to build in Protestant majorities wherever possible. By 1924 only two councils of any significance in the six counties were controlled by Nationalists.

Both parliaments also took steps to entrench the role of religion in political and daily life. In the North this may be seen as religion enlisted in the service of the state, since Protestantism and Unionism were virtually synonymous. With Lord Londonderry as Education Minister (in Ulster the Ascendancy could still claim a role), primary schools were initially planned as non-denominational, but demands from the churches and the Orange Order ensured instruction in the Protestant form of worship in all schools other than those which were specifically Catholic (and which were at first denied building and maintenance grants from the state).

In the Free State, it was more like the state enrolling itself in the service of religion. The reasons for this are not so clear. There was far from being any direct identification of republicanism and Catholicism before 1916. But the leaders of the Easter Rising, all of whom died as Catholics, were very soon gathered into a popular hagiology that gave them a transcendent status to the generation that followed. To Cosgrave, it seemed virtually axiomatic that a free Ireland must not only be Catholic but must be seen to be so; he actually proposed a kind of theocratic Upper House which would review the acts of the Dáil in terms of acceptability to Catholic doctrine. Recent history, so full of bloody events condemned by the Church as 'dastardly', 'outrage', 'atrocity', may also have led to a feeling that the traditional source of ethical and moral values must be embraced. To many people, the country must have often seemed on the slide to a bloodbath of anarchy and spiritual ruin. The setting up of film and publication censorship by a religious board indicated how much the Church was being allowed to encroach upon general public life; and the banning of divorce in 1925 brought an impassioned speech by Senator W.B. Yeats on behalf of the Protestant community of Ireland, the people, as he chose to remind everyone, of Grattan, of Emmet, of Parnell.

THE BIRTH OF FIANNA FÁIL

De Valera, who combined serious faith with careful political calculation, perceived the value of the Catholic Church in sustaining an Irish government. On his release from prison and following a visit to Rome, he had come to believe that Sinn Féin ought to participate in the Dáil's parliamentary process, oath to the king notwithstanding. At a specially called Árd-fheis in March 1925, he tried to make this official policy, but there was heavy opposition, notably from the fiery Father O'Flanagan, to the 'usurping legislature set up by English law in Ireland'. Unable to persuade the radicals, de Valera resigned and proceeded to set up his own party, Fianna Fáil – the Republican Party. Many joined him but the irreconcilables remained in Sinn Féin, and the IRA remained as its military component. In the general election of June 1927, Fianna Fáil won forty-four seats and Cumann na nGaedheal forty-seven. Sinn Féin was reduced to five. Cosgrave's minority government continued. The Fianna Fáil members attempted to take their seats without taking the oath, and were locked out of the chamber. It was April 1928 before the 'mere formality' of the oath was stomached by the Fianna Fáil TDs' covering up its text while they signed their names in the register of members.

On 10 July 1927, Kevin O'Higgins was gunned down on his way to Mass. The assassination was a harsh reminder that an active section of the population did not consider the war as over; and the government assumed even further powers in the interest of maintaining what still seemed a fragile grip on law and order. A second general election in September confirmed that most people saw politics as a contest between Cosgrave and de Valera. The former had sixty-two seats, the latter was very close behind with fifty-seven, and for the first time, a real two-party system emerged in the Dáil. This was the first election in which radio played a part. Station 2RN, Ireland's first, was established in Dublin in 1926.

AFTERMATH

A modern economic historian, Cormac Ó Gráda, has written that 'One of the ironies of Irish history in the 1920s is how a group of tough but talented gunmen became . . . staid and rather conservative rulers.' The socialism of Connolly and Pearse was not carried through. The destruction inflicted by the war was more to the fabric of society itself than material or industrial. Railway lines, which had often been attacked, were soon restored to working order, and pragmatic north–south co-operation ensured the continued working of the Great Northern line between Dublin and Belfast and other cross-border lines like the Sligo & Northern Counties railway. Agricultural productivity had continued throughout the troubled years.

But everywhere great country houses stood as burned-out shells, and in many districts, especially in the west, and with the support of Sinn Féin, their farms and fields had been taken over by locals. Many landlords, anxious to sell out, were disappointed by the Free State Land Act, which fixed purchase prices at the current depressed rental level. Compensation was paid for burned houses, normally conditional on rebuilding within Ireland, which many owners did not want to do. Large numbers of the former Ascendancy left Ireland to live in England, or France. But the revolution did not have disruptive fiscal or financial aspects. The newly established Irish pound remained at par with the pound sterling. Trade and commerce continued as before, with no protection of Irish industry or tariffs on crucial imports. Though much rural and urban poverty remained, there was no destitution. The Free State abolished workhouses in 1923.

THE 1930s: REBELLION AND RETALIATION

Economic life became more difficult in the years of world-wide slump that began with the Wall Street Crash of 1929, and it was in the depths of the Depression that, in the general election of February 1932, Fianna Fáil was returned as the largest party, with seventy-two seats to the Cumann's fifty-six. De Valera formed his first fully constitutional government, and high on his agenda was the constitutional question. The oath of allegiance had to go, and despite delays in the Senate, it went, in May 1933. The role of governor-general was depreciated until it became an absurdity. Of more direct concern to many, given the militant past of the new government's ministers, was the release of Republican prisoners and the suspension of many of the special powers that the Cosgrave government had assumed. The IRA and other banned organisations were able to resume activities.

Such actions were viewed with hostility from Stormont, and with concern by London, but it was when the Free State suspended payment of land annuities to Britain, worth the substantial sum of £5 million a year, that action was taken, provoking the 'Economic War' of 1932–38. The annuities were to pay back the British Treasury for funds given as compensation to Irish landlords, and were in turn levied as a tax on Irish farmers. In 1932 many could not, others would not, pay. Britain promptly levied import duty on Irish cattle, first at 20 per cent, later at 40 per cent. Since live cattle represented over 40 per cent of all exports, and Britain was the prime market, this was a substantial blow. Other agricultural products were also taxed, to obtain the same value as the suspended annuities. The government retaliated by placing duties on British imports, and although it was a largely one-sided 'war', the economy of the Ulster state was seriously affected by the restriction of exports to the South. However, a bloodless dispute with the ancient enemy was nothing for a Fianna Fáil government to quail at, and indeed they made the most of it in propaganda terms. For ordinary people, it exacerbated the problems of the thirties and for the government it made a useful excuse. Farmers' living standards fell by 15 per cent between 1929 and 1933.

THE EFFECTS OF THE DEPRESSION

In 1929, the Northern government abolished proportional representation for parliamentary seats. The permanence of partition was underlined by the

41

ceremonial opening of the dominating parliament building at Stormont, outside Belfast, in 1932. With its more industrially based economy, the North suffered badly in the slump, with 27 per cent of the workforce unemployed in the early thirties. The big Workman-Clark shipyard went out of business in 1935. Linen manufacture was in steep decline, demand reduced not only by the depression but also by competition from artificial fibres. The province's isolation and the fact that its government had scanty funds to devote to job creation meant that few new industries were set up. In one short instance of proletarian solidarity, Catholic and Protestant workers rioted together for a higher unemployment 'dole' in 1932; otherwise sectarian disputes and violence continued, reaching a peak in the early summer of 1935. The level of communal rapport is indicated by a remark of Sir Basil Brooke, later to become the province's prime minister. He encouraged Protestant employers to avoid hiring Catholics, 'who were really out to cut their throats if opportunity arose'. Dialogue between the two Irish regimes hardly rose above a 'tit for tat' level, with the pro-government papers on each side scanning events to shock their readers with 'Mob burns Catholic homes' and 'Wanton attack on Protestants' stories. For a number of reasons, including a lower birth rate, a higher average age, emigration and mixed marriages, the Protestant proportion of the Free State's population was in steady decline, while the Catholic proportion in the North was slightly increasing.

THE EMERGENCE OF THE REPUBLIC

In the Free State, the government, led by de Valera, was taking successive steps to move from that designation in the direction of a republic. Despite the democratic structure, with two major parties, that had emerged, politics was not an easy-going activity. Bitterness and rancour were still around in plenty. The IRA did not wither on the bough in the heat of a Fianna Fáil sun, but continued to flourish. In 1931 the Army Comrades' Association was founded, composed largely of ex-soldiers, as a foil to the IRA. In 1933 it found a leader in General Eoin O'Duffy, who had led the Free State Army, and had been removed from the post of Commissioner of the Gárda by de Valera. For a time the movement, grown to around 48,000 members by 1935, looked like a serious force in political life. On the model of European organised movements of the same time, it was known by its uniform, as the Blueshirts. Although it was not affiliated to Cumann na nGaedheal, its members were united in opposition to Fianna Fáil and the IRA. It might have seemed that each party now had its own army and that civil war was again a possibility. In 1934 the Dáil banned Blueshirt parades and uniform, but the Senate, still a thorn in de Valera's flesh – it was 1936 before he was able to abolish it – delayed implementation of this. O'Duffy may have had his own dreams of becoming an Irish Mussolini, but they shrivelled from 1935. And in March 1936, the IRA was banned again, following a number of shootings, including that of a retired British admiral. Independent militias were no longer to be tolerated, even if they were notional supporters of the governing party.

Pushing on with his programme, de Valera submitted the draft of a new constitution to the Dáil and to the people. The general election of 1 July 1937 showed a majority both for his party and for his constitution, the latter by 685,105 votes to 526,946. All mention of Crown, King and Commonwealth was gone: instead a republic was inaugurated, with a president as head of state – an essentially ceremonial role (Douglas Hyde was the first president). The state was named Eire, and its first language was to be Gaelic. The constitution recognised the special position of the Roman Catholic Church, whilst also acknowledging other religious denominations. The ban on divorce, already established in law, was built into the constitution. All these things were to be expected. In Belfast and London, however, Article 2 stood out in letters of fire: 'The national territory consists of the whole island of Ireland, its islands and the territorial seas.' The claim thus made, entirely reasonable to an Irish Republican, quite the opposite to an Ulster Unionist, stiffened Unionist and British attitudes. Article 3 however accepted that the jurisdiction of the Republic was over twenty-six and not all thirty-two counties of Ireland.

Despite the controversy over Article 2, and even as a new European war was looming, Britain lifted its claim to the strategic 'treaty ports' in 1938, as part of the deal with which the 'Economic War' was ended. Some progress had been made in improving relations from 1934, and an Anglo-Irish Agreement was concluded in 1938. On the British side, the making of this was eased by an understanding that Ireland remained a member of the British Commonwealth. A lump sum of £10 million was paid by the Irish government in settlement of all financial claims (apart from a small annual payment relating to property damage in the 1919–21 period), Commonwealth preference was restored to Irish exports to Great Britain, and penal duties on British imports were dropped.

Meanwhile, the diehard element of the IRA continued to call de Valera's government illegal and issued its own proclamations on behalf of the Second Dáil Éireann. One effect of such actions and developments was to consolidate not only the one-party nature of government in Ulster, but also the increasingly gerontocratic rule of Sir James Craig, or Lord Craigavon, as he became in 1929. There was chafing and irritation with the personalities, style and methods of the government, and a Progressive Unionist faction emerged, led by W.J. Stewart, only to be worsted by the old guard in an election called in the spring of 1938, in the wake of the de Valeran constitutional controversy.

With his constitution approved, de Valera felt comfortable enough in late 1938 to open a dialogue with the North. He still regarded partition as an affront, and made a public but informal appeal, through the press, to the northerners, offering a form of Irish unity that would maintain their parliament, under the aegis of Dublin rather than of London, and provide a range of guarantees for the Catholic–Nationalist community. It was duly rebuffed in icy terms by Craig: 'We have learned in Northern Ireland to place no value whatever on Mr de Valera's promises or even guarantees . . . We are here now to say in no circumstances whatever will we listen to the rattling of the sabre, or, for that matter, the cooing of the dove where the integrity of Ulster is concerned.'

WORLD WAR II: THE EMERGENCY YEARS

In January 1939, a new phase of IRA militancy opened with a bombing campaign in Great Britain that lasted throughout the year. IRA leaders also made overtures to the government of Germany. In the same year the Irish government assumed powers to intern prisoners without trial, heralding a fierce and unremitting campaign against the IRA throughout the war, with many activists imprisoned and interned for the duration. There was to be no fifth column in operation. Well before the German invasion of Poland, it had been made clear that the Republic of Ireland would remain neutral in the forthcoming war. That stance was not shaken even in June 1940, when British diplomatic initiatives – to the horror of the ailing Craig (he died in November) – offered Irish unity in return for participation in the war effort, including British use of Irish ports and the establishment of air bases. But it could not remain unaffected. In September 1939, the government announced a 'State of Emergency' which continued until the end of the European war in 1945. An Emergency Powers Act was passed in September, giving the government very wide powers to deal with 'securing the public safety and the preservation of the state in time of war'.

Warfare in the seas and skies all around disrupted trade and communication. The country could feed itself, but every imported item, from tea and coffee to petrol, steel and coal, was in short supply, and rationing was introduced. Press and other forms of censorship were strict. Even the Charlie Chaplin movie *The Great Dictator* was banned, in case it should be interpreted as showing undue pro-Allied tendencies. Northern Ireland was drawn immediately into the British war effort, though strong representations from Dublin persuaded the British government, despite Craig's urgings, not to introduce conscription in the six counties. Many from the North joined the forces anyway, as did many from the Republic.

Many more from the Republic crossed to Britain to find work as the war economy got under way. Belfast suffered, like other British industrial cities, from German bombs, and on 15–16 April 1941, when around 700 people were killed by bombs, fire brigades were sent from Dublin, Drogheda and Dundalk, on a request from the authorities, to help put out fires in the blitzed city. 'Any help we can give them in the present time we will give them whole-heartedly,' said de Valera. But when the United States entered the war, and Winston Churchill, the British Prime Minister, sent a message to the Irish Taoiseach: 'Now is your chance. Now or never. A nation once again,' the overture was politely turned down.

Enthusiasm for the German National Socialists and their policies was scant, and though the government was careful to maintain a diplomatically correct neutrality, it was also resolved in a secret cabinet meeting of 1941 that, if the Germans should invade Ireland as a base for attacking Britain, they would be resisted as far as possible, and that, *in extremis*, British aid would be requested. But in 1942 an official protest was made against American forces being based at Londonderry, perhaps partly in pique at no prior intimations from the American or British governments; and in 1944, the government resisted Allied pressure to expel German and Japanese diplomats from Dublin. Most famously or notoriously, in May 1945 de Valera paid an official visit of condolence to the German legation in Dublin on the death of the German head of state, Adolf Hitler. Such *punctilio* was felt to be all the more necessary and important as the government knew very well that some 50,000 of its citizens were serving in the Allied forces and an even larger number were voluntary workers in British industry. The numbers of those actively involved on the German side were negligible.

The Emergency years underlined the independence, and the staying-power, of the Republic. Even in his victory address in May 1945, Winston Churchill could not conceal his bitterness about the Irish government's neutral stance. De Valera made a dignified statement in reply. Although some stray and mistaken German bombs had fallen in the Republic, most seriously on the North Strand in Dublin on 31 May 1940, when thirty-five people were killed, Ireland emerged from the Emergency with its economy and infrastructure far less drastically affected than those of the warring nations. Rationing came to an end in 1947.

But it was still a 'backward' European nation. More ground was now under crops, as the shift from stock towards arable farming continued, but the donkey was still the most common form of traction on the Irish farm, often pulling a sledge rather than a cart. Many of the country's wage-earners were earning that wage in England or Scotland; and remittances from emigrants in the USA, Canada and Australia were still important to the livelihood of thousands of families. Emigration was running at a level that recalled the torrent of the late 1800s. The wartime neutrality also meant a degree of later diplomatic isolation – Russia's veto kept Ireland out of the United Nations until 1956. But neutrality remained the government's policy, and Ireland stayed out of the negotiations to form the North Atlantic Treaty Organisation (NATO) in 1948–49. Sean MacBride made the position clear in a speech to the Dáil in July 1948: 'The continuance of partition precludes us from taking our rightful place in the affairs of Europe.'

FULL INDEPENDENCE AND CONFIRMATION OF PARTITION

The post-war period showed the apogee of 'de Valeran' Ireland. But it was a Fine Gael–Labour coalition government formed in February 1948 under John A. Costello – including the transient Clann na Poblachta Party led by Sean MacBride – that formally proclaimed the separation of the Republic of Ireland from the British Commonwealth, in December of that year. Costello made the initial announcement at a Commonwealth gathering in Ottawa, Canada, in September. The move prompted criticism on the grounds that it confirmed the partitioned state of Ireland. It was greeted with hostility in Belfast for another reason: the fact that Britain and the other Commonwealth countries maintained the Republic's privileged status in trading and citizenship. In 1949 Britain passed the Ireland Act, accepting the independence of the former Free State, and giving its citizens a special status in the UK. It also set out to reassure the Unionists of the status of Northern Ireland as an integral part of the United Kingdom: 'It is hereby declared that Northern Ireland remains part of His Majesty's dominions and of the United Kingdom and it is hereby affirmed that in no event will Northern Ireland or any part thereof cease to be a part of His Majesty's dominions and of the United Kingdom without the consent of the parliament of Northern Ireland.'

This clause, reaffirming partition, was heavily criticised in Dublin, where the government had not been advised of its inclusion in the Act. But the British government recognised that the Irish government had put the priority of complete separation above that of ending partition. The clause satisfied the government of Northern Ireland, though it was notable that it appeared to transfer the responsibility for maintaining the province's status as part of the United Kingdom from Westminster to Stormont.

1951–59: AN IRISH IDENTITY

In 1951 Fianna Fáil was returned to power, the start of a 22-year run of office. Eight years later, Eamon de Valera was elected President and Sean Lemass replaced him as Taoiseach.

The ethos of both parts of Ireland at this time was in many ways an embattled one. The Republic was still young, threatened from within and still constitutionally incomplete. The tenor of life was strongly Catholic. Deferred to by government, the hierarchy of the Catholic Church asserted control over most aspects of daily life, especially in moral behaviour. Books and films remained subject to censorship. The import and sale of contraceptives was banned. There was a genuine desire to repel the increasingly godless and socially permissive culture of the West.

But when Church leaders adopted the notion of 'vocational' social groups, in which, suitably guided, those with a common interest – be it teachers or industrial workers – could combine with management to run their activities, the government ignored it. Church and state combined in an alliance of undefined terms, which worked so long as each kept to its own preserve. The Church's hostility to the Mother and Child Scheme, intended to provide free health care for mothers, and children up to the age of sixteen, caused a political crisis in 1950 until the Minister, Noel Browne, withdrew the plan. In the eyes of the bishops it was a 'socialistic' state intrusion into family life: a field in which the state had no business to trespass.

But many people resented the officious and often arbitrary behaviour of those who tried to manage Irish life. De Valera had stated in 1938 that he put the policy of 'a really Irish Ireland' above even the consideration of ending partition. The opponents of all this spoke of a 'Green Curtain' to rival the 'Iron Curtain' that shut off the Soviet empire, and behind which Ireland's leaders sought to foster an illusive national spirit of faith, chastity, continence and obedience. They complained of a culture of 'backwardness'. Many children were not educated past the primary school stage; secondary schooling had to be paid for by parents, and as late as 1962, the Council of Education could define education as the religious, moral and cultural development of the child. Even science teaching at secondary level was officially described as 'cultural rather than practical'.

Trust in authority, especially religious authority, meant that considerable power in the care of children, the elderly and the ill was placed in the hands of priests and nuns, with minimal supervision. The idealistic view of a Catholic Ireland outstripped the reality of human nature and a minority of those in power abused the powerless ones in their care. The subsequent uncovering of such scandals did much to discredit the social and pastoral role of the Church later in the century.

In other ways the vision had its negative effects. Emigration was running at around 50,000 a year through the 1950s – and the dangerous drain of young people was compounded by a falling marriage rate and a tendency for marriage to happen later in life. The population was ageing, and dwindling.

THE TURF BURNER

IN the late 1940s there was a continuing shortage of coal and fuel oil. In an effort to make use of Ireland's major natural resource, the national transport board, Coras Iompair Éireann, authorised the construction of a turf-burning steam locomotive in 1949. The prototype ran trials on goods trains between Dublin and Cork, but there were acute problems associated with raising steam, and the project was abandoned. Bord na Móna (The Peat Board), established in 1946, was more successful both in developing mechanical methods of turf extraction, and in selling turf for power generation.

ECONOMIC AND CULTURAL EXPANSION

Under de Valera as Taoiseach, economic management had been prudent and conservative. Stability was more important than growth. When Sean Lemass took over as Taoiseach in 1959, he had been in charge of the Irish economy for many years (he was first appointed Minister for Industry and Commerce in 1932). But, working with T.K. Whitaker, who was appointed Secretary of the Department of Finance, he now presided over an opening up of the economy that prompted, or coincided with, a similar opening up in social life. What the *Economist* magazine described as 'autarchic social conservatism' was replaced by a drive to install systems of innovation, planning and development in business and industry. The First Programme for Economic Expansion, launched in 1958, had stimulated growth; the Second, of 1964, consolidated the trend towards a 'corporate state' in which the civil service worked to encourage and prod industry and commerce in the direction of a market-oriented, growth-minded, profit-motivated approach to management, in which education and training played vital roles. Lemass's achievement was remarkable. In the words of J.J. Lee, 'he threw a time-bomb into Irish history . . . He was confronted by that pervasive mediocrity which gave the Irish, after nearly forty years of independence, the lowest living standards, the highest emigration rates, the worst unemployment rates, and the most intellectually stultifying society in northern Europe.' Living standards in the Republic rose by a remarkable 50 per cent in the decade of the 1960s, and the decline in population was at last reversed.

On 1 January 1962, a state television service, funded by advertising, began, and Telefís Éireann played an important part in bringing political, ecclesiastical and other authority figures under greater public scrutiny and questioning than ever before. As John Whyte notes in *Ireland, 1945–70*: 'Most of the major controversies of the decade seemed to start off with a television programme.'

Among Lemass's most important innovations was a new insistence on the value of education both to the individual and to the community. Secondary and tertiary level education were greatly expanded and modernised; at last secondary schooling became universal and free. Some traditional aspects of policy remained. In all their acceptance of a Republican state, the Irish people had never paid more than lip-service to one of the passionate causes of de Valera, Douglas Hyde, and others – the reinstatement of Gaelic as the primary national language. Their own form of English remained supreme, and the Gaeltacht grew ever smaller. Children learned compulsory Gaelic at school, and forgot it. Applicants for official posts mugged up on their obligatory Gaelic, and once appointed, never used it. To be part of the English-language speech area was a boon to Irish writers, to exporting businesses, and a great help to the hundreds of thousands of emigrants. But it also made Ireland open to the new 'permissive' culture of Western society and all that accompanied it, from a challenging attitude to authority to an openness about sexual behaviour and an increasing tolerance of obscenity. The lofty television aerials of eastern homes, set high to capture the British transmissions, even with a home-produced channel available, told their own story of willing absorption of external influences.

NORTHERN IRELAND IN THE POST-WAR DECADES

In the six counties of Northern Ireland, a different, but equally embattled, ethos prevailed. As part of the United Kingdom, it shared in the establishment

---

ST ENDA'S SCHOOL

PATRICK Pearse's nationalism was deeply rooted in Irish culture. He had edited the Gaelic League's journal and lectured in Irish at University College, Dublin. In 1909 he founded *Scoil Éanna* (St Enda's School), a bilingual Irish–English secondary school intended to foster a Gaelic spirit. It was also based on principles of education far different from the conventional schools of the day. These relied heavily on formal group teaching, severe discipline, and a rigid system of tests and examinations. Pearse, like other educational innovators of the time, aimed to develop the talent of the individual child and to develop a love of learning in a context that was encouraging rather than repressive. Another of the signatories of the 1916 proclamation, Thomas MacDonagh, also worked with Pearse at St Enda's.

---

of the 'Welfare State', though its Unionist government viewed the post-1945 Labour administration with deep suspicion. A free Health Service was established from 1948. Education was reformed, made free for all children of school age, and made more accessible to Catholics at secondary and university level. A post-war slump was less marked than it had been in the 1920s, but there was a steady decline in the province's major industries of shipbuilding and linen-manufacture. Although unemployment ran at a higher level than in other parts of the United Kingdom, the social security system had been much improved. Living standards drew ahead of those in the Irish Republic, by as much as 20 per cent. The basic tenet of the province's government was however to maintain its own Unionist stance and ensure that the Protestant–Unionist section of the population exercised political and social control. Until 1971, the electoral register for local elections was heavily biased towards property owners, who might have up to six votes.

The Catholic proportion of the population was rising slowly, and by 1961 was 34.9 per cent, but its virtual exclusion from political life led to a huge vote and two Westminster seats for Sinn Féin in 1955, and a renewal of IRA violence in 1956–62.

By 1962, a softening of relations between Belfast and Dublin, and the growth of a moderate National Democratic Party, pledged to work for Irish unity by consent, seemed to offer hope to non-Republican Nationalists. Sir Basil Brooke, now Lord Brookeborough, retired in 1963, and his successor, Terence O'Neill, took a more conciliatory approach to the minority population. In 1965, for the first time, the Prime Ministers of the Republic and of Northern Ireland exchanged official visits. But O'Neill and his successors hoped to neutralise nationalism in the North, rather than bring it into a democratic context. A vigorous civil rights movement, the CRA, arose, with a new generation of Nationalist politicians taking peaceful action on the streets to demonstrate their lack of representation. Meanwhile a Protestant Unionist Party was formed by those who objected to O'Neill's softer line.

Through the 1960s a vigorous programme of new factory building and other developments had been under way, driven to a large extent by the Minister for Commerce, Brian Faulkner. But the bulk of this was in the east of the province, and unemployment remained proportionately much higher in the districts where Catholics were a larger element in the population. There was particular anger in the Catholic–Nationalist community that the new town of Craigavon, and the new University of Ulster, were placed in the Lagan valley and at Coleraine respectively, rather than in the less-developed west and in the province's second city.

A NEW ERA OF VIOLENCE

In 1969 sectarian violence flared in a way not seen since the 1920s. The RUC was unable to cope and British troops were sent into Belfast and Londonderry. Seen at first as protectors of the minority, they were later cast as defenders of imperialism, and from 1969, the newly formed Provisional IRA began a campaign of shootings and bombings. Under pressure from Westminster, many of the civil rights demands were met, but the combination of Protestant resentment against these 'concessions', and an upsurge of Republican nationalism, meant that violence from extreme elements on both sides continued to grow. A number of moderate Nationalist and left-of-centre parties combined as the Social Democratic and Labour Party (SDLP), led first by Gerry Fitt and from 1979 by John Hume. Another new party, the Alliance, tried to unite moderate opinion on both sides of the sectarian divide, but it was to remain peripheral. In 1969 the Irish government formally appealed to the United Nations Security Council to send in a peace-keeping force, on the grounds that the British government was not in control and the RUC was not accepted as an impartial police force. The UN decided to take no action. Two government ministers in Dublin, Charles Haughey and Neil Blaney, were dismissed from office in 1970 over accusations of supplying weapons to the North for terrorists' use. Charges against Blaney were dropped; Haughey was put on trial and acquitted of the charge.

In 1971 there were changes in alignment among the Unionists. The paramilitary Ulster Defence Association was set up, and the Democratic Unionist Party was established by Desmond Boal and the Rev Ian Paisley as a successor to the Protestant Unionists: its strategy was to outflank the traditional Unionists both in rhetoric and in street demonstrations. As civil tension and terrorist activity continued to mount, Brian Faulkner, now Premier, introduced a policy of internment without trial for suspected terrorists. Since this was directed only at the extreme Nationalists, it was, as one Ulster historian put it, 'viewed as an act of war by almost the entire Catholic population'. Civil disobedience followed, and the Nationalists withdrew from the Stormont parliament. Between 1969 and 1972, over 400 people were killed. The events of 'Bloody Sunday', on 30 January 1972, when British paratroops shot dead thirteen people during an anti-internment march in Derry, cemented the hostility felt towards theBritish army. Three days later, the British embassy in Dublin was attacked and burned by a rioting mob. On 30 March 1972, Stormont was suspended and direct rule imposed from Westminster. In that year, there were 467 politically related killings in Northern Ireland.

THE TWO COMMUNITIES IN EUROPE

In 1969, the Irish government, under Jack Lynch as Taoiseach, had warned the British government that it could not stand by while violence raged in Northern Ireland. In February 1972, the government, still led by Jack Lynch, was considering military intervention in the North. For a short time, a return to open warfare seemed possible. The intervention of London, with the appointment of a Secretary of State for Northern Ireland, and a flurry of diplomatic activity between the capitals, took some of the heat out of the situation. By this time, the economy of the Republic was dramatically changed, and Ireland was on the verge of joining the European Economic Community. The past and the future both beckoned. The future won. Two referendums that year defined a new social and economic era; the first accepted membership of the EEC, the second agreed the removal of the special status of the Roman Catholic Church in the constitution.

With Britain also joining the EEC on 1 January 1973, the two sovereign Irish governments formed parts of the same supra-national union. But sectarian violence seemed to have settled on the North, with atrocities committed by both sides, and bombings and assassinations happening also in the Republic. A 'power-sharing' Assembly was set up from 1 January 1974, with a split within the Ulster Unionist Party. In May the Assembly was abandoned after a two-week general strike called by the Protestant Ulster Workers Council. Direct rule from London resumed. The short-lived prominence of organisations like the Peace People, whose founders won the Nobel Peace Prize in 1976, testified to the yearning for an end to bombings, shootings and terror, but violence continued with a momentum that seemed to be unstoppable.

In 1979, under a new Fianna Fáil Taoiseach, Charles Haughey, the Republic joined the European Monetary System, ending almost sixty years of parity between the Irish punt and the pound sterling. The Irish currency was now linked to a rate of exchange fixed by the European Central Bank, anticipating the eventual introduction of the euro in January 2002. Though Britain was still the major trading partner, its overwhelming importance was falling: its share of Irish export trade fell from 75 per cent to 43 per cent between 1960 and 1980, at a time when exports were rising rapidly. Irish trade with Europe and further afield was being steadily developed, helped by the state-funded Industrial Development Authority. Cross-border trading was stimulated as consumers went north or south in search of cheaper goods. The population was expanding steadily now, with emigration much reduced, and economic activity regularly reaching new heights.

By this time, Northern Ireland's lead in living standards was much less apparent. The notion of 'convergence' between the two economies was being much discussed. Whereas fifty years before, heavy industry had typified the North, now its decline, and the rise of light industry, often little more than assembly plants, both there and in the Republic, meant that the general mix of agriculture and industry was increasingly similar. Increasing prosperity in the Republic also had the effect of reducing whatever unquantifiable 'cushion' of economic benefit might have tempered the urge of northern Nationalists for Irish unity. By the same token, the 'economic' argument of moderate Unionists for preserving the British link was being gradually undermined.

THE ANGLO-IRISH AGREEMENT

The deaths of ten IRA hunger strikers at the Maze Prison during 1981 served to underline the sense of commitment that republicanism could still inspire. The strikers' leader, Bobby Sands, was elected to Westminster as a Sinn Féin MP before his death. As the governments, with Fine Gael in power under Garret Fitzgerald from June 1981, continued to probe for ways forward in what was coming to be called 'the peace process', there was extensive debate and discussion between interested parties, notably in the New Ireland Forum convened by Fitzgerald in May 1983. The Unionists remained aloof from this, though they were the only parties to participate in the new Northern Ireland Assembly. Following secret discussions, an Anglo-Irish Agreement was signed at Hillsborough on 15 November 1985, by the Taoiseach, Garret Fitzgerald, and the British Prime Minister, Margaret Thatcher. This provided for a wide range of inter-governmental co-operation between Britain and the Republic, including consultation on policy in Northern Ireland, and was received by the Unionist parties with what Professor David Harkness described as 'outrage, panic and hysteria'. Their effort to mobilise support through a general election, though it generated 418,239 votes, fell short of their half-million target. The second attempt at a provincial Assembly was dissolved in June 1986 and direct rule from London was resumed again.

A NEW GENERATION OF LEADERS

It was only in the later years of the century that politics and national life ceased to be dominated by men who had come to maturity during the struggle for independence and the fraught decades that followed. John Hume of the SDLP, James Molyneaux of the Official Unionists, Charles Haughey, and his Fine Gael opposite number Garrett Fitzgerald, were all children of the post-1916 generation. In a way, Molyneaux, Hume and their Northern Irish colleagues, crossing to London to sit in the Westminster parliament, preserved a nineteenth-century Irish tradition already forgotten in Dublin. But all politicians nurtured their roots. In 1970 it was possible to shake hands with a man who had shaken hands with a man whose parents had lived through the Great Famine. A sign of the times was splits in political parties, with the emergence of the Provisional Sinn Féin, and the Official Sinn Féin becoming the Workers' Party in 1977, and later the Democratic Left. The Progressive Democrats broke away from Fianna Fáil in 1985. Unionist splinter movements formed and re-formed, with the essential divide always being between the 'official' party, willing to discuss new constitutional arrangements, and the more entrenched elements, typified by the Rev Ian Paisley's Democratic Unionist Party, which believed that a whole way of life was at stake, and preferred the 'Not an inch' approach of old. Like Sinn Féin, the more extreme Unionist groups preserved links with outlawed paramilitary organisations. The Irish electorate held back from awarding decisive majorities, and Fine Gael–Labour or Fianna Fáil–Progressive Democrat coalitions came and went.

EUROPEAN COMMUNITY INFLUENCE

As one of the poorer member states of the European Community (from 1993 the European Union), Ireland benefited substantially from grants and subsidies, and, while it lasted, from the Common Agricultural Policy. These helped to drive forward an already expanding economy, with commerce and industry overtaking agriculture as the main generator of national income. As a poorer province of the United Kingdom, Northern Ireland also was well supplied by EC regional funding and able to offer inducements to incoming industry. The eagerness to welcome new industry led to occasional embarrassing disasters, as with the demise of the de Lorean car factory in Belfast, amidst accusations of fraud and incompetence and with the loss of many millions of pounds of taxpayers' money. The managers of both Irish economies accepted that the

A de Lorean sports car

KNOCK AIRPORT

THE Marian shrine in the village of Knock, Co. Mayo, has been a place of pilgrimage since March 1880, with as many as one and a half million visitors a year. In 1979, during a visit to Ireland, Pope John Paul II visited the village. After a long and tireless campaign, the parish priest, Mgr Horan, succeeded in having an airport built to allow pilgrims from around the world to come directly to the shrine at Knock. The airport was completed in 1986, despite criticism from transport experts who pointed out that even if Ireland needed another international airport, Knock was not the obvious place to site it. The long neglect of Mayo, and a sense of guilt relating to the Gaeltacht area generally – so important culturally, so backward economically – helped to make the discussion a somewhat confused one, in which sentiment played its part. Although its few scheduled flights are internal or to the UK, Horan International Airport (renamed Ireland West Airport Knock) remains in business.

enticement of international companies, with all its uncertainties of external ownership, was the only way to develop the manufacturing side, and both found that a skilled and educated workforce was a powerful inducement to industry.

LIBERALISATION IN THE REPUBLIC

The trend towards an Irish Republic more integrated in its *mores* with the rest of western Europe was not a steady one. Often the older 'de Valeran' attitudes showed through. A referendum in 1983 agreed the insertion of an anti-abortion clause in the constitution, and successive votes failed to obtain a majority to legalise divorce (it was finally passed by a wafer-thin majority in 1995). These were flagpole issues, with powerful groupings for and against. Many other issues of women's and children's rights were quietly conceded. In 1990 a woman, from the minority Labour Party, and with some strongly 'progressive' opinions, was elected as president of the Republic. Mary Robinson's role in what was an essentially honorary position helped to mark out Ireland as a country facing the future rather than the past, and her inaugural speech held out a vision of an 'open, tolerant and inclusive' Ireland. With the pace of change speeding up, that other country of the 'past' could be well within the average lifetime. The 1950s began to appear remote, slightly primitive, but also innocent, unspoiled, still rooted in the traditional values so often appealed to by Eamon de Valera. By the 1990s, the encouragement of entrepreneurial attitudes fostered by the Lemass government in the 1960s was criticised as having led to a culture of get-rich-quick financial manipulation and an obsession with material possessions. Observers sensed the original keen air of planning, business discipline and careful investment turning into a murky atmosphere of political favouritism, shady accountancy and commercial bribery.

THE PEACE PROCESS AND THE ASSEMBLY

In 1994, after three years of negotiation and 'talks about talks', the long, slow, often frustrating and always uncertain 'peace process' in Northern Ireland was visibly seen to be moving forward. It became known that there had been secret contacts between the IRA and the British government. The IRA announced a cease-fire on 30 August; the Loyalists followed suit on 13 October. Sinn Féin, formerly a prohibited organisation, was allowed access to the public media, and preparations began for a new elected Assembly in the province. The cease-fire ended in 1996 but talks continued. Under intense pressure from the British and Irish governments, the latter a Fianna Fáil–Progressive Democrat coalition led by Bertie Ahern, and with the active involvement of the American President, Bill Clinton, a new order of things began to seem possible. A crucial stage was reached in 1998 with the signing of the Good Friday Agreement by all parties in Northern Ireland. All pledged themselves to pursue their causes by political means. A ballot held in all thirty-two counties approved the Agreement by large majorities. Although unreconciled extremists on the Republican and Unionist sides continued to use violence, sometimes on a horrifying scale, including the killing of twenty-nine people by a car bomb in the centre of Omagh, the setting up of a new Northern Ireland Assembly began. On 2 December 1999 its elected members assumed power in an administration which included members of the Ulster Unionist Party, the SDLP, and, for the first time, Sinn Féin.

The progress of the Assembly was to be rocky, plagued both by entrenched mutual suspicions and by procedural disputes. David Trimble, the Unionist leader, and John Hume, the SDLP leader, were joint recipients of the Nobel Peace Prize in 1998; though Trimble hinted that that the award might be premature, both accepted in the interest of keeping up the momentum of the peace process. Both Trimble, elected as the Assembly's First Minister, and the Sinn Féin leader, Gerry Adams, had to carry with them a sceptical and potentially fissile band of district leaders and supporters. One of the elements of the Good Friday Agreement had been the Provisional IRA's agreement to decommission its weapons. Delays in the implementation of this caused recurrent crises, culminating in the Unionists' abstention from the power-sharing Assembly in the summer of 2001. In October of that year, Adams announced that the IRA had agreed to begin the process of decommissioning, and a few days later the international body set up to oversee the process confirmed that it had begun. The Unionists returned to their ministerial positions. Again, for the time being at least, the peace process was back on the rails. To one side, of course, peace and power-sharing represented, with varying levels of satisfaction, a sort of stasis; to the other side, with varying levels of urgency and commitment, peace represented the basis upon which further changes could be mooted and effected.

CHAPTER TWO

Legends

THE TAKING OF IRELAND

FROM the events of the first years of the third Christian millennium, in an Ireland with more than five million inhabitants, it is a huge step back to the days when the human population consisted of a handful of fur-clad hunters and their families. Yet the most fascinating aspect of Irish history is its continuity. Past and present remain intertwined in a manner that has a profound influence on the future.

Beyond recorded history lie the legends. Though nowadays it is accepted that the occupancy of the British Isles by speakers of Celtic languages goes back much further into prehistory than was quite recently supposed, the early inhabitants of Ireland preserved the traditional knowledge or belief that they had come, as a people, to Ireland from somewhere else.

The account of Irish beginnings, as we have it, is not an 'original' one. It has been heavily influenced by the need to adapt the traditional story, as it had been preserved up to the sixth century, to the demands of Christianity. In essence it is a genealogy, with some biographical and geographical details added. Like other such legends of early peoples, it traces the descent of the whole people, as a single kinship group, from a single ancestor of high prestige. In pagan times, this ancestor would have been a god (in the preserved Gaelic myths of the Ulster Cycle and others there is still plenty of evidence of pseudo-historical kings and heroes fathered by Celtic gods). With the adoption of Christianity, a heathen pedigree was no longer acceptable, and a satisfactory alternative had to be found. The learned men found their model in the Bible narrative of the *Old Testament*, which itself is, among other things, a genealogical document of the Hebrew kings. Their source was not so much St Jerome's Latin version, the *Vulgate*, completed in the late fourth century, as various commentators on the Bible, such as the third-century Christian chronicler Eusebius, and his successors (Orosius in the sixth century and Isidore of Seville in the seventh). Eusebius, a Palestinian bishop whose *Chronicon* set out to synchronise events in Christian and pagan history, was especially influential on the way in which the various forms of the Irish Annals were set out.

The earliest Old Irish texts do not survive, but many were still available in the twelfth century, when a collection of ancient documents by various writers from different periods was put together in the *Lebor Gabála Érenn*, 'Book of the Taking of Ireland'. The scheme of this book is based on six successive invasions of, or arrivals in, Ireland. The first is that of Cesair, granddaughter of Noah, sent to Ireland to escape the Flood. She is accompanied by her father, three other men, and fifty women. Their aim is to procreate and populate the land. Three hundred and twelve years later Partholón, also of Biblical stock, arrives. He and his people, the Partholonians, are descended from Magog. They settle in the east, but are destroyed in a plague. After a gap of thirty years come Nemed and the Nemedians, from the region of the Caspian Sea. They settle more successfully than their predecessors, but they encounter a ferocious sea-borne people called the Fomorians, noted as coming from the lands to the north of Ireland. The Fomorians establish their own colonies, doing battle with the Partholonians and the Nemedians. The fourth invasion is that of the Fir Bolg, the first people in the book to have a Celtic name ('men of Builg', a name probably cognate with that of the continental Celtic tribe of the Belgae), and said to have come many generations after the Nemedians. They are represented as short in stature and dark-haired. Thirty-seven years after them come the magic-endowed Tuatha Dé Danann, 'people of the god Danann' – the latter a name which is still not satisfactorily explained. The Tuatha Dé Danann defeat the Fir Bolg and the Fomorians and institute the era in which much of early Irish myth and legend is set.

The final invasion is that of the sons of Míl Espáine, literally 'soldier of Spain', and his eponymous followers, the Milesians. Despite his name, Míl's career begins in the East, in Scythia, as a military leader. Later in Egypt he commands the armies of the Pharaoh Nectanebo. He marries Scota, daughter of the pharaoh, and she bears him four sons, among them Éremon, progenitor of the Uí Néill of the north, and Éber Finn, ancestor of the Éogainacht kings of Munster. In fulfilment of a druidic prophecy, they leave Egypt for the unknown island of Ireland, but stop off in Spain, the land of his birth. There he dies and Scota (whose name can mean 'Ireland' or 'Irishwoman') carries on to Ireland. Míl himself is taken as the direct ancestor of the Irish–Scottish Gaels; and their kings' genealogies stem from him through his sons.

It was for a long time assumed that at the basis of this ancient legend lay the real fact of a migration or migrations from a far-off Eastern homeland which eventually came to an end in the new home in the furthest West. With the general abandonment by archaeologists of the idea of successive invasions, this assumption has in recent years seemed increasingly uncertain. There is a greater understanding of the way in which technology, belief, custom and language-change could gradually spread between peoples without the need to be imported in a highly specific or violent manner as the cultural baggage of warlike invaders. How then did the story of the invasions arise? The compilers

> Farfassa O'Mulconry, Peregrine O'Duigenan and Peregrine O'Clery, he
> assembled much material from ancient annals for a catalogue of Irish
> saints, and also compiled the *Annála Ríoghachta Éireann*, 'Annals of the
> Kings of Ireland', often referred to as the *Annals of the Four Masters*.

Cruithne, which, in *q*-Celtic form, is cognate with the Old Welsh *Priteni*. Both
terms originally meant an inhabitant of North Britain, and not specifically a
Pict. The Gaels knew of Cruithne before any of them set sail eastwards across
the North Channel. Sharing the north Ulster coastland with the Dál Riata was
a people known as being of the race of Cruithne, whose tribal name by the
sixth century AD was the Dál Araidhe. Although regarded as a subject-people
by the Ulster Gaels, the Dál Araidhe sometimes succeeded in possessing the
over-kingship of the province. There was also a group of the Cruithin established in Meath, in the centre of Ireland. These are generally understood to be
the same people as the Caledonian Picts, and to have entered Ireland at an
unknown time from North Britain (although it may have happened that they
entered North Britain from Ireland). There is a lingering account, found in
several different ancient sources, that the Picts came into North Britain from
the north, settling first in Orkney and spreading south from there. This does
not fit badly with the notion of a departure from the northern coast of Ireland.
Intriguing as these matters are, they have been shelved or ignored by historians for lack of convincing evidence to support any particular theory. Even the
language of the Dál Araidhe has a question mark over it. Was it Pictish? In
which case it was of the *p*-Celtic or Brittonic branch, not the *q*-Celtic or
Goidelic one. Had it been Pictish and been supplanted by Gaelic? What, if any,
were the relations between those Irish-located Cruithne and their Pictish
neighbours just across the narrow sea – the nearest being the Epidii of Kintyre,
identified by Ptolemy in AD 150 but unheard of since?

The question of language is important since, as the philologist Myles Dillon
made clear, the acceptance of long residence by Celtic speakers in Ireland and
Britain should mean acceptance of the view that the change in the Gaulish and
Brittonic languages from *qu-* to *p-* happened during the period when speakers
of a Celtic language were already living in Ireland. The Gaelic language of
Ireland did not undergo this change, and so Irish *ceann*, 'head', is matched by
Welsh *pen*; and *ceithir*, 'four' is Welsh *pedwar*. Dillon saw such speech innovations spreading from a centre on the continent and failing to reach as far as the
'lateral' areas of Ireland and Spain. But there is evidence of *p*-Celtic speakers
in Ireland from early times. How did the Gaels fail to adopt this change, if
they lived amidst people who did? Were the Gaels, or rather proto-Gaels,

somewhere else at the time? Was that somewhere else located in the Iberian peninsula (whose Celtiberian language is considered to have been *q*-Celtic)? Supporters of this view place considerable weight on the Míl Espáine legend. Such questions remain unanswerable, at least until further concrete evidence is produced in the form of comparable texts or word-samples.

The consensus among scholars today is that Celtic-speaking peoples have been resident in the British Isles for much longer than used to be supposed – a tenure reaching back into the 'Bronze Age', as long ago as 1600 BC and perhaps further. The notion of long-limbed, red-haired, iron weapon-wielding aristocratic warriors pushing their way ashore, in successive invasions, from about 700 BC, has been rejected. The only invasion still countenanced is from the immediate post-prehistoric period: the removal of many of the continental Belgae into South Britain, vouched for by Julius Caesar in *De Bello Gallico* around 54 BC. This does not imply that in the prehistoric period all the tribes were at a similar level of social organisation or cultural activity at any particular time, or that they were all from the same racial origin, or that there was no movement of population groups at all. Non-Celtic languages may also have been in use in certain areas, during some of that time. This was definitely the case in Spain, where Basque still survives and evidence of other non-Indo-European languages has been traced. The views first formed by Roman commentators have been justified: they wrote that the inhabitants of Britain believed that they had always been there. By these inhabitants they meant the *p*-Celtic speaking tribes who formed the Romano-British population of the province of Britannia, who were also closely related to the tribes of southern Scotland. But there is no reason to suppose that the Irish were different in this respect.

EARLY PEOPLES AND LEGEND

Influences affecting language, culture and politics came in from outside, unevenly, slowly. Even small population movements helped. It is likely that groups of diehard British warriors, as well as others from Gaul, came to Ireland to avoid Roman rule. Their contribution to social life may have been of a reactionary rather than a progressive nature, but the pattern of development is never likely to be uniformly in one single direction. Defeats and diseases also influenced ancient society, as (on a far longer time-scale) did climate and landscape change.

The first two 'invasions' of the *Lebor Gabála* have been dismissed by historians as too obviously concocted back-projections by later writers. But the Nemedians are thought to have traces of historical truth mingled in the highly coloured account of their battles with the Fomorians. And the latter, when stripped of mythological traits, and despite some anachronistic colouring by later scribes who knew the marauding Vikings, have been seen plausibly as inhabitants of the Hebridean Isles, which show many signs of prehistoric habitation. Professor T.F. O'Rahilly identified the Nemedians with a prehistoric people he called the Érainn, speakers of a conjectured *p*-Celtic language. In the *Lebor Gabála*, the Nemedians are seen as the ancestors of the (Irish) Cruithne and of the *Bretnaigh Cluada*, 'Britons of Clyde'. The tentative linking of the Fir Bolg with the Belgae need not imply a heavy traffic between the dunes of Flanders and the sandy bays of southern Ireland; other related tribal names are found separated by wide stretches of territory – Damnonii in southern Scotland, Dumnonii in south-west England, for example; as well as the Irish Brigantes listed by Ptolemy.

The semi-divine Tuatha Dé are harder to relate to any set of real people; they represent rather an idealised era which ends fittingly, in one tale anyway, when on their defeat by the Milesians they retreat to Tír na nÓg, the mythical land of the ever-young. In other versions they retreat underground, into the many barrows and raths of the Irish landscape, and their race becomes that of the fairy folk. The Milesians are the first overtly Gaelic-speaking people to be mentioned. Part of their story indeed is the creation of Gaelic, after the Biblical Tower of Babel episode, by Goídel Glas, on the instructions of his grandfather, Fénius Farsaid. Goídel Glas, his name later found as Gathelus, was the son of Niúl, and – like the later Míl Espáine – his mother was Scota, a pharaoh's daughter. In one of the clever inserted links which help to give the story plausibility, Goídel Glas's byname of *Glas*, 'green', refers to a mark left by a snake bite. He was cured of this in Egypt by Moses, who also prophesied that his descendants would one day live in a country where no snakes were to be found. And sure enough, Ireland is well known for its lack of snakes . . .

Also found at a later stage in the relation of the Milesian story, when they have reached Ireland, is their encounter with three goddesses, each of whom asks the Milesians to name Ireland after her: Banba, Ériu and Fódla. These names are closely identified with the land of the Gaels. Ériu is preserved in Erin. Not the least interesting aspect of the Milesian story is the implication that the speakers of Gaelic came to an Ireland which was Celtic-speaking, but of a *p*-Celtic language. In the words of Professor James MacKillop, referring to political power, 'Milesian hegemony spread to all corners of Ireland.' It has been noted by historians that the Roman conquest of Spain in 133 BC could have led to substantial displacement or emigration of Celtic language speakers from there.

The *Lebor Gabála* has been described as 'a laborious attempt to combine parts of the native teaching with Hebrew mythology embellished with medieval legend' (MacKillop). The bald outline of its story is greatly elaborated and complicated with sometimes contradictory or anachronistic events. Elements from it are found in many other sources, often with differences of detail. Impressive and suggestive as the ancient Irish legends are – one of the oldest literatures of Europe – there are few reliable facts that can be extracted from them. Only archaeology can establish definite knowledge of the prehistoric period.

CHAPTER THREE

Origins

THE EARLIEST INHABITANTS

No trace of human occupation has been found in Ireland from earlier than the end of the last Ice Age, though animal traces from interglacial warmer periods have been found. The first reliable evidence of human life comes from the Mesolithic period, the 'Middle Stone Age'. Flint tools have been found dating back six thousand years before the Christian era began. Although the main source of flints was in the north-east, Mesolithic people were established as far south as Cork. The arrival of the earliest people is so far undated, and the means by which they came is unsure. A land link, later submerged by rising sea levels, between Scotland and Ireland has been suggested, but they may equally well have come by boat. The relative density of very early sites in Ulster suggests western Scotland as a starting point.

The settlement of Mount Sandel, above the River Bann, has been dated to the seventh millennium BC. Its occupants lived in circular huts around 6 metres (nearly 20 feet) in diameter, supported by sapling stems, with central hearths, and were hunter-gatherers, living off the land and waters. Their camps were occupied on a seasonal basis, the people moving from site to site within an area of several square kilometres. Their way of life was practised for some 2,000 years, with gradual developments such as the use of heavier and more specialised stone tools. Two production sites for stone axes have been identified in the north, at Tievebulliagh in Co. Antrim, and on Rathlin Island, both places with outcrops of the polishable porcellanite stone which was preferred for axe-heads.

From around 4000 BC, new processes can be detected, the deliberate planting of crops and the domestication of animals. This heralds the Neolithic, or 'New Stone Age'. There was a long overlap and it is more probable that the new techniques were gradually learned than that a group of invaders arrived and put them into immediate practice. Undoubtedly there was trade, travel and contact among communities in the British Isles and perhaps beyond, from very early times. Forest clearance and the making of pottery are further evidences of the way in which Neolithic communities imposed themselves on the environment and enhanced their way of life. It was in this period that cattle, sheep and goats were introduced; wild pigs were already established. By the third millennium there is much evidence of human habitation, especially around the coasts. Houses were now rectangular, with mud walls on stone foundations, and thatched roofs supported by multiple wooden posts. As the Neolithic period wore on, there is evidence of a new style of pottery, the 'beaker'-shaped and decorated pots, again until recently assumed to have been brought in by a race of dominant invading people with greater technological skills. Most scholars have discarded this theory in favour of a gradual westward spread of ideas and techniques. This continuity theory is backed up by evidence that the new pottery styles were employed alongside older forms of tool-making.

HOUSES OF THE DEAD

In Ireland as elsewhere, the most imposing structural remains from prehistoric

NAVAN FORT

THE history of this site in Co. Armagh goes back to Neolithic times. During the late Bronze Age, a round house and circular stockade were erected, around 700 BC. One of the finds from that period is the skull of a Barbary ape, from Spain or North Africa, presumably brought as a gift to the ruler of the place. Major developments took place during the Iron Age. A great circular structure was erected, consisting of five concentric circles of timber uprights, the posts of each circle linked by planks, and with evidence of a very tall timber mast at the centre. The entire structure was probably covered by a conical roof. A few years after the building was completed, it was completely filled with close-packed stone to a height of around 2.8 metres (9 feet). The outer wall was burned and the entire circular mass of stone covered by turves. The purpose of this sequence of events is not known, though archaeologists assume that a special ritual or ceremonial was practised here. The site is identified with Emain Macha, ancient capital of the Ulaid, the Ulster people whose kingdom was one of the old 'fifths' of Ireland, and so with the legendary figures of Conchobar mac Nessa, Cuchulainn, and the episode of the *Táin Bó Cuailnge*, 'the Cattle-Raid of Cooley'. It was destroyed and abandoned in the late fourth or early fifth century. Like most other prehistoric sites, it lay neglected for centuries. Now the different concerns of academic archaeology, of official urge to preserve a historic site, and of the tourist industry's requirement to present and vividly demonstrate the country's 'heritage', have been reconciled in the high-tech Navan Centre for visitors which adjoins the site.

times are the houses of the dead rather than those of the living. More than 1,200 have been identified throughout the countryside. Ranging from the great restored mound of Newgrange in Co. Meath to obscure tumbles of stone, they testify to an economy that could spare the effort, man-hours and imagination to create structures using massive blocks of stone. Among the great megaliths are single stones weighing up to 100 tons.

Four kinds of tomb have been identified. Court tombs, mostly in the north, have an open courtyard leading to the tomb entrance. Portal tombs, mostly in the north and east, often referred to as dolmens, are distinguished by the great flat capstone placed above the supporting megaliths; originally a surrounding cairn of smaller stones and earth would have covered over this inner structure. Passage tombs, located in a wide strip between Co. Meath and Co. Sligo, are monumental mounds of earth and stone, with a narrow passage-way leading to the tomb chamber. Some, like 'Queen Maeve's Grave' on the ridge of Knocknarea, Co. Sligo, are placed in a location that dominates a whole tract of land. Newgrange, Co. Meath, is the best known, and its passage-way is situated so that the rising sun at the winter solstice shines straight along the passage and into the tomb chamber. This monument, with the similar ones of Knowth and Dowth close by, continued to play a role in new mythologies long after its original purpose was forgotten. It was considered as the home of the Tuatha Dé Danann, when they had retreated from the world; and it was also believed to be the burial ground of the earliest kings of Tara. In this way it remained as a cult site until the advent of Christianity. Wedge tombs, found largely in the west and south, are so called from the shape of the tomb gallery, whose walls and roof slope inwards. They are very numerous and have been taken to be a purely Irish type of burial site.

Stone carving, in its earliest forms simply ring and cup-marks, later more elaborate, often with spiral, lozenge and maze-like motifs, is found at various points at the entrances and in the interiors of tombs. Cremation appears to have been the preferred way of dealing with the dead, though many excavated funerary buildings also show evidence of unburned bones.

The careful construction, decoration, and sheer scale of the megalithic tombs have prompted a great deal of debate about the reasons for their presence, and about the communities that built them. The passage tombs of Ireland are usually grouped by archaeologists in an 'Atlantic' sequence that stretches from Brittany to the Orkney Islands, and that suggests a passage of cultural and artistic ideas, not necessarily one-way, over a great period of time. In recent years, theories about the great tombs have centred on their significance in land ownership. The relative meagreness of the 'grave-goods' found in the tomb chambers (though such places were always in danger of looting even soon after they were built) suggests that the real importance of the monument was not in the persons it contained, so much as its own massive assertion of an ancestral presence in, and a long-established possession of, the land around. If this explanation is correct, then it also implies anxiety about such possession, which could be brought on by competition for good land from other groups of people. Though it remains a

Funerary urn found at Knockneconra, Co. Carlow

theory, it also corresponds with the sense of close involvement and identification with the land which characterises the ancient legends and many very old traditions.

Also dating from the last thousand years of the stone age (up to around 1800 BC) are the earth-banked enclosures and stone circles, often found in proximity to burial mounds. In some places, like the Grange site by Lough Gur, there is a concentration of stone circles and individual standing stones. Substantial amounts of broken pottery appear to have been deposited at some of these sites. More than two hundred stone circles have been identified, though it is likely that many more existed. Beyond the assumption that such locations were used both for ritual purposes and perhaps for public assemblies of other sorts, their purpose and function are unknown.

ANCIENT CRAFTS

Around the time that Beaker pottery began to be made, or perhaps somewhat later, metal working began in Ireland. Copper deposits in the south-west were exploited from early in the second millennium BC, and prehistoric mineshafts from around 1500 to 1250 BC have been explored at Mount Gabriel, near Schull, Co. Cork. Extracted ore was smelted on site at the adit-head. The scale of the 'industry' is shown by the large number of surviving heavy are heads of copper. But the spreading knowledge of bronze, an alloy of 90 per cent copper to 10 per cent tin, giving a harder metal and a sharper edge, overtook pure copper work. Tin had to be imported, probably from Cornwall, and paid for. But Ireland had an even more valuable metal in the form of gold – of no value for practical purposes but everywhere prized for decoration and display, and for exchange. The gold came mostly from panning in the rivers of the Wicklow mountains and perhaps other areas like the Sperrins. It is from the Bronze Age that recognisable weapons first make their appearance and though some were clearly intended for display, and others for hunting, they also provide evidence that warfare between communities was not unknown. The cauldron or cooking pot, so often a feature of the later legends, was also made of copper, then bronze. Its manufacture required special skill in the hammering out of flat sheets, their reheating, or annealing, shaping and riveting. By this time it is also clear, from many examples of finely made harness-rings and bits, that the horse was widely in use. Elegantly curved bronze horns, their shapes influenced by natural bull's horns, have been found in different parts of the country. Twenty-four were found in the Dowris hoard, unearthed at Whigsborough, Co. Offaly. Such hoards as these have different possible origins. Dowris, with its range of musical instruments, spear-heads and axes, may have been a merchant's stock, or it may represent a set of offerings to a deity. Some were buried for safety; others represent what once was the scrap-heap of material for recycling by a craftsman.

The later Bronze Age, from around 1000 BC, is marked by clearer evidence of militarism in the form of the long-bladed, slashing sword rather than the rapier-like weapons previously made. Evidence of the nature of society at this

time is very scanty. But Peter Harbison notes that 'Together with the horns and cauldrons, the greatest glory of Ireland's Late Bronze Age is undoubtedly its gold-work.' Torcs (collars), necklaces, brooches and ornaments, often made with great fineness and precision, indicate the existence of a social level at which the possession and conspicuous display of wealth was customary. By this time, the era had begun when a Celtic form, or forms, of speech were in use in Ireland.

Gold earring found at Castlerea,
Co. Roscommon

THE IRON AGE

A deterioration in the weather pattern has been identified from around 600 BC, resulting in a reduction of cultivable land, a growth of forest cover, and the beginnings of the great coat of peaty bog that spread across so much of the landscape, often obscuring early settlements and structures. It is in this period that the beginnings of the Iron Age are to be found, an era of which Professor Michael O'Kelly remarked, 'This is probably the period in Irish archaeology about which there is least certainty and most speculation.' Professor Barry

Cunliffe notes that in Ireland 'from the beginning of the sixth century to the end of the second century BC there is little trace of any contact with continental developments, and indeed the dendrochronological [tree ring] evidence shows that over large areas forests were regenerating – an observation suggestive of a dramatic decline in population.' In an era when continental Celtic culture was reaching a high level, and when the Celts were beginning to be mentioned in the records of neighbouring peoples, it seems that Ireland was isolated figuratively as well as literally. The gold supply had dwindled and the kind of wealth that is shown by lavish burials in Europe and the Wessex region of Britain is not found in Ireland. One impressive gold 'hoard' was discovered at Broighter, Co. Londonderry, in 1896, including a model boat with seven oars on each side, a mast and yardarm, and a steering-oar. Peter Harbison suggests that this may have been brought, or made locally, by a refugee community of the Veneti people of Brittany, who monopolised seaborne trade between Gaul and the British Isles until they were defeated and harried by Julius Caesar in 56 BC. In general it seems that the islanders were slow to give up the use of bronze in favour of iron, despite fairly ample deposits of bog ore and plenty wood for charcoal. Such conservatism is typical of insularity, especially in an era of hardship.

Perhaps as a reaction to a more warfare-oriented society, the lake-house or crannog is found from the early part of the first millennium BC. It became one of the most common forms of dwelling, providing greater security than a house on land. At this point, domestic fortification was no more than a wooden palisade, designed to keep animals in (or out). Around the middle of the millennium, however, the ringfort became common. Its origins may still have been to enclose animals, but the enclosure was now made of stone, around a yard with a farmhouse and its associated huts. These ringforts or raths are found all over the country and were also built in Argyll in Scotland by the colonising Scots from the sixth century AD. In some areas unenclosed

Desmond Castle and rath, Limerick

based tribe of uncertain location was the Attacotti, recorded by Roman writers as a people of exceptional ferocity who later made good Roman soldiers. But for three hundred years, while the Roman colony flourished on the east side of the Irish Sea, events in Hibernia are hidden behind a green curtain. In that dimness loom heroic and semi-legendary figures. Conn of the Hundred Battles, whose name lives on in Connacht, is associated with Tara in the second century; in the sixteenth century, the Gaels would still refer to themselves as 'the race of Conn'. Niall Nóigiallach, 'of the Nine Hostages', founder of the long-enduring Uí Néill dynasty, who trembles on the verge of being a fully historical figure of the late fourth century, was said to be the first *ard rí* (high king), ruling from Tara. But the stories which record this still treat him as a magic figure whose copulation with an old hag turned her into a lovely young woman: a metaphor of winning the sovereignty of Ireland (and justifying the rule of his self-proclaimed descendants).

The Uí Néill were conquerors of Tara, replacing the dynasty that had previously ruled there, though it was with the usurpers that the high kingship began. Of all the kings linked with Tara, however, Cormac mac Airt, grandson of Conn, and to whom the Annals (written much later) ascribe a 40-year reign from AD 227 to 266, is the most celebrated in ancient writings. To his time the exploits of Fionn mac Cumhaill and the Fianna, and other episodes in the Fenian Cycle of legends, are ascribed. For long they were most popular and widely told set of traditional stories. In them Cormac is praised as a wise, just and generous king and law-giver, and he himself is the hero of *Echtrae Cormaic*, 'the Adventure of Cormac', but his actual existence is a matter of debate.

HEROES OF THE STORY CYCLES

Emain Macha was the centre-point of another great collection of legends, the Ulster Cycle. Its king then was Conchobar mac Nessa, a man even less easy to pin down to history than Cormac. Its principal palace was Cráebruad, the red-branch hall, perhaps so-called from its main beam, and the skill and exaggeration of the narrators depicts a place far greater than the archaeological evidence suggests. The great hero of the Cycle is Cuchulainn, the supreme warrior of ancient Ireland, who figures in many stories and whose character, deeds and life-story have a wide range of sources. As might be expected from its north-eastern setting, the Ulster Cycle makes frequent reference to Scotland, suggesting that there were close two-way links prior to the historical colonisation by the Scots. Cruachan too comes into these legends, notably in the *Táin Bó Cuailnge*, as the splendid palace of Queen Medbh and her husband Ailill, and representing Connacht as anything but the 'poor relation' of the other provinces that it was later to become.

OGAM

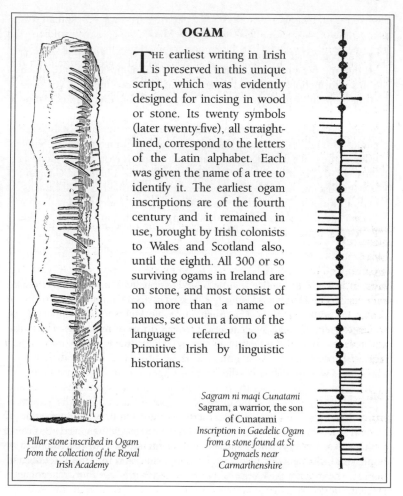

THE earliest writing in Irish is preserved in this unique script, which was evidently designed for incising in wood or stone. Its twenty symbols (later twenty-five), all straight-lined, correspond to the letters of the Latin alphabet. Each was given the name of a tree to identify it. The earliest ogam inscriptions are of the fourth century and it remained in use, brought by Irish colonists to Wales and Scotland also, until the eighth. All 300 or so surviving ogams in Ireland are on stone, and most consist of no more than a name or names, set out in a form of the language referred to as Primitive Irish by linguistic historians.

Sagram ni maqi Cunatami
Sagram, a warrior, the son of Cunatami
Inscription in Gaedelic Ogam from a stone found at St Dogmaels near Carmarthenshire

Pillar stone inscribed in Ogam from the collection of the Royal Irish Academy

As with the *Lebor Gabála*, historians have combed and compared the story cycles in the hope of establishing details that can be set against the archaeological evidence, with little effect. As with the historical legend, those who wrote down the texts we now have made their own additions and enhancements. Perhaps they also made their own deletions. It is notable that the surviving tales do not supply any creation myth, such as the Nordic and many other early peoples possessed. Perhaps the Celts did not have one, though their

---

PTOLEMY'S MAP

T HE geographer Ptolemy of Alexandria, in the second century AD, was the first person to set down place and tribal names of Ireland. Much of his information is believed to have been about two hundred years old at the time he compiled it. Some of it was probably even earlier, dating back to the Greek explorer Pytheas in the late fourth century BC. The names noted by Ptolemy bear little connection with later Irish place names, though his Isamnion has been equated with Emain Macha. Some tribal names, like the Brigantes located in the south-east, are the same as those of Celtic tribes in Britain. Others, like the Eblani or Gangani, remain obscure. A number of sites are simply identified as royal capitals, without a name. Two of these have been tentatively identified as Emain Macha and Cruachan, later the royal centres of Ulster and Connacht. But Ptolemy's names seem to predate the Heroic Age of Old Irish history.

---

worship of a sun-god suggests otherwise. Possibly such a story was censored out of existence by the monastically educated scribes who preserved so much else (in his book *The Irish Comic Tradition*, Vivian Mercier noted, however, the extent to which the bawdy element was toned down or removed). The magic world of Cuchulainn and Fionn had many elements that continue into the historical period. Champions fighting on behalf of their tribes; a warrior caste whose task was to attend on the king and fight for him; the importance of cattle-ownership; the necessity for the king or queen to be immensely rich and correspondingly generous; the presence of powerful satirists; the rivalry of provincial kings; the value of poetry and the tradition of oral preservation of law and story – all these were features of the early medieval society. But some of them may have been back-projected into the story, in order to create or emphasise links between past and present, or in order to import details and character types from the Greek epics, once these were known to the monastic communities of Ireland.

All these ancient royal locations were to be the venues of great fairs – social, literary, musical, athletic and commercial gatherings – in the medieval period, and probably earlier. Another such fair was held at Uisneach, in Co. Westmeath, whose hill was said to be the centre-point of Ireland and the place where the boundaries of all the provinces converged on the 'division stone', the Ail na Mirenn. The hilltop, which commands a wide view over the plains, has been a setting for beacon-fires from immemorial times.

CHAPTER FOUR

Saints and Scholars

THE COMING OF CHRISTIANITY

O GAM inscriptions, probably from the fourth century, give the names of some Irish people of that era. The only contemporary record, they tell nothing about their deeds or backgrounds. That cited by O'Kelly, the name *Grilagni maqi Scilagni*, is among the first known Gaelic writings, with its *maqi* the form still preserved as present-day Mac. The first historical name to be associated with action and events is that of Palladius, the bishop sent to Ireland by Pope Celestine in AD 431, to minister to a community or communities that were already Christian. The existence of such groups is more likely to be focused on trader families, in touch with the outside mercantile world, rather than the work of missionaries. Palladius's success and fate are both unknown. Ireland at that time was an overwhelmingly pagan country. The religious beliefs of the people were focused on nature, the seasons and specific places. The cult was administered by druids, a senior and venerated caste within the tribal structure. Druidic practices got a bad name from the Romans, but it is unlikely that the mass burnings and other barbaric human sacrifices that Roman writers of the early imperial era loved to deplore were being made in fifth-century Ireland.

The religion of the Irish was essentially passive; based very much on augury and ritual, it did not demand faith. Unlike Christianity, it was not a proselytising religion. Christianity had come to Britain through the arrival of soldiers and traders who had adopted its teachings, and from Britain, missionaries began to cross into Ireland. The most celebrated is of course Patrick or Patricius, a Romanised Briton who had been taken to Ireland as a teenage boy, captured in a slave raid. Having escaped after six years, and become a priest, he eventually returned as an evangelist. His own record, the *Confession*, and a letter addressed to a British chief, Coroticus, survive to provide details of his activities and the problems he faced. A great deal of myth later grew around Patrick, and his fame has overshadowed others who also brought the gospel to Ireland, at the same time and later. It was a lengthy business. In the sixth century, a hundred years after Patrick's time, Christianity was still only patchily established. But his writings bear witness both to his dedication and perseverance, and his pre-eminence as Ireland's patron saint, and that of his church

77

at Armagh as the religious metropolis, have never been in doubt since the eighth century, when the 'Patricians' established their claim over the supporters of St Brigid and her church of Kildare. St Brigid, whose death-year is recorded as 525, has left no authentication of her own existence, but by the mid-seventh century, her church was an important one, containing a shrine to her, and linked to a convent which produced a number of distinguished abbesses. Brigid's Christian powers were complemented by many of the attributes of the old Irish goddess Bríd, whose powers extended over fire, fertility, cattle and poetry. The writer Gerald of Wales, who came to Ireland with King John in the twelfth century, records that a perpetual fire was kept burning by the nuns at Kildare in honour of the saint.

THE EARLY KINGDOMS

The missionaries came to a country where there were more than a hundred kingdoms of varying sizes. These kingdoms were based on the kinship of a group of people, the *tuath*. The chief bore the title of *ri*, king. His functions combined those of war leader and law-enforcer with a priestly role, giving him a claim on his people's veneration as well as their loyalty. He was chosen, or emerged, from a small group who could claim royal descent within the *tuath*. The social stratification was a highly organised one, with an upper caste of druids and *fili*, the priests, bards, historians, lawmen and doctors. Other specialists, such as smiths, wrights, and other craftsmen, also enjoyed prestige. Wealth was measured chiefly in the possession of cows, and the warrior class were the owners of the livestock. Below them were the families who tilled the soil and looked after the animals, and who provided support for the warriors. All of these had specific rights, responsibilities and status. At the base were the slaves, prizes of war and raids, who had no rights. The Romano-British notion of a territorial bishopric could not be reconciled with such a society. Each *tuath* had to be converted separately, and once this had been achieved, each had to have its own church structure, in effect replacing the role of the druids. Priests, monks and bishops were mostly recruited among people who would otherwise have joined the ranks of the druids. (The early appearance of abbesses also suggests that women too could hold druidical positions.)

The *tuath* and its leading families could not ignore the neighbouring tribes. Partly for mutual security, partly herded by the larger or more aggressive kingdoms, they formed groups. The dominant king was the *ruire*, and he in turn, by the late fifth century at least, owed loyalty to the *ri ruirech*, or provincial king. Four original provinces whose origins are lost in time had to make room for a fifth, when the rising kingdom of Meath joined Ulster, Connacht, Leinster and Munster. A number of strong dynasties were established, based on provincial strength, and were frequently in contention. The somewhat shadowy position of high king, associated with the site of Tara, was the ultimate prize. This role, though unsanctified by tradition and not provided for in tribal law, carried immense prestige, and with tribute paid by all or most other kings, it also bestowed great wealth. In a society where prestige, status, and their display in as opulent a manner as possible, were of prime importance, the title of *ard rí* was worth fighting for.

COLONISING SCOTLAND

Perhaps the most important role of an over-king was in co-ordinating external attacks. By the fifth century, the Western Empire of Rome was beginning to crumble and the wealthy province of Britannia was vulnerable. Opportunist raids from Ireland became a regular thing, and Roman writers believed that there was collusion between the (Irish) Scots and the Picts in the heavy attacks made from 360 onwards. Although loot rather than conquest was the aim of these invasions, substantial colonisation took place in Wales, both north and south. But it was in south-west Pictland that the most significant Irish colony was established. The Dál Riata, a tribe located on the north Antrim coast, had probably settled on some of the Hebridean islands and part of the Pictish coast for some generations before the kingdom of Dál Riada was established, under the semi-legendary Fergus Mor mac Erc, in AD 500. The colonists brought with them the name of Scots, from a supposed ancestress of their people, Scota. For another few hundred years, this name would continue to refer to Irish people, or to Gaelic speakers, until the establishment of the Scottish kingdom completed its adoption to designate the subjects of the King of Scots. For almost a thousand years, Antrim, Argyll and the Hebrides formed a Gaelic cultural – and sometimes political – unit that was united rather than divided by the intervening seaways.

THE INFLUENCE OF COLUMBA

From the sixth to the ninth centuries, the pivotal point not only of this sea-linked region, but of the whole Irish Church, was the tiny island of Iona, of whose monastery Columcille (Columba) became abbot shortly after 563. He was not, as was once supposed, a great evangelist. But he was a great saint, whose example of piety, austerity, teaching and firm rule inspired a generation of missionaries in Britain and Europe. He was also the super-type of the Irish sort of abbot, a member of a royal family, someone who played a substantial part in secular as well as religious affairs. Making good use of his offshore base, and by force of personality and diplomatic skill, Columba imposed himself on kings and high kings. A poet himself, he is credited with saving the status of the bards, whose preservation of old pagan lore had earned them the enmity of the more rigorous Christian priests. There may have been a genuine crisis between bards and priests in his lifetime, but churchmen over a lengthy period preserved much from pre-Christian times, even if they often adapted and altered it in the light of their own times and their own preoccupations. As with Brigid-Bríd, many characteristics of older Celtic divinities were brought into the new religion, and helped to give Irish Christianity a more humane cast than that of the sin-obsessed Anglo-Saxons. It is to the monastic writers of the sixth and seventh centuries, who wrote down much that had formerly been preserved only in the oral tradition, that modern Ireland owes the survival of one of Europe's most ancient literatures.

THE EARLY CHURCH

This period was also the great era of the Irish Church, all the greater since it coincides with the eclipse of Christianity in much of Europe. The larger monasteries founded in the sixth century were the nearest thing to towns, and these communities of monks, lay workers and scholars numbered hundreds or even over a thousand. St Ciarán's foundation of Clonmacnoise, by the

COLUMBA'S COPYING

As a monk, Columcille went to the monastery of Clonard, where Finnian was the abbot. Finnian was the owner of a fine book, a Psalter, which he kept in his own study. Having been shown the book, Columcille admired it greatly, and wished he had a copy of it. But he knew Finnian was highly possessive of it, and so he began to visit the abbot's study in secret in order to make his own copy. He was caught, and Finnian demanded that he hand over the copy he had made. Columcille refused, saying that the book was Finnian's, but the copy was his own. The abbot appealed to his king, Diarmait, who gave a famous judgement: 'As the calf goes with the cow, so a copy goes with the book it is copied from,' he said. Columcille was obliged to hand it over. But the matter did not end there. Columcille returned to his own people, and stirred them up to make war on Diarmait. As a result the battle of Cúl Drebene was fought, in 561. It was said to be as a consequence of the blood shed here that Columcille, either exiled by the Irish Church or of his own will, left Ireland to reside in Scotland, ultimately becoming abbot of the monastery on Iona.

Clonmacnoise

Shannon, was perhaps the largest. Established in the mid-sixth century, it grew to its maximum size in the eighth. It possessed a school, a *scriptorium* or writing room, and a library, as well as numerous churches. The high crosses there, and many partly carved stones indicate that it was a centre of this great Irish form of sculpture. Bangor, founded at around the same time by St Comgall, and situated on the shore of Belfast Lough, enjoyed a similar level of prestige. From here St Columbanus set off on his long journey through Gaul and the Alps, that would finally end at Bobbio in Italy. Smaller communities and individual hermitages proliferated, not only on the mainland and inner islands, but on remote Atlantic rocks where the remnants of their 'beehive' stone huts still remain, as on Skellig Michael just off Valentia Island, but also on North Rona from where no other land is seen.

The Irish monasteries helped to preserve learning as well as the tenets of faith. Teaching was an important aspect of their work, and a high standard of literacy in Latin was maintained, which included the study of pre-Christian writers such as Virgil. They imported books from far-off centres of learning like Antioch and Alexandria, and also created books. In their *scriptoria*, monks wrote and drew on parchment sheets, using lichen and vegetable dyes to make their colours, and gold leaf for the most sumptuous or holy examples. Books such as these were holy objects, often used for curative purposes, and kept in special carrying-boxes. The *Book of Kells*, perhaps begun on Iona but completed at the monastery of Kells, Co. Meath (a place also celebrated for its high crosses), is the supreme example, still preserved as a national treasure in

Trinity College Library. The late eighth and early ninth century mark the high point of this art form, and the same artistic sense is found in metalwork, exemplified at its height by the superb Ardagh Chalice, of the eighth century, and by the first great period of the Irish carved high crosses in the ninth.

Whilst at the heart of the Irish Church was the personal concept of the *diserta*, withdrawal from the world of property and possession into a state of ascetic contemplation, the abbeys themselves were often well endowed by pious kings. Sometimes invited, sometimes testing their vocations by perilous mission-work, Irish monks brought their learning, art and faith into pagan areas. In Britain, where old Celtic kingdoms were shrinking in the face of Anglo-Saxon invasions; in Gaul, its Celtic kingdoms by now annihilated by Goths and Franks; in the Alpine regions inhabited by Alemannic tribes, Irish monks like Fursa, Aidan, as well as Columbanus and others, established monasteries and these in turn often set up daughter-establishments.

Christianity did not eliminate war, nor did it inhibit the warriors' custom of collecting and displaying the heads of their slain enemies. Although the Uí Néill, between its two branches, one in the north, one across the northern central area, had a firm hold of the high kingship, there was constant tension and aggression between the many royal lineages. In Munster the Eógainacht dynasty, with its base at Cashel, was predominant, and ambitious; but Edmund Curtis describes the high king's role in the eighth century as that of a 'president of a union of Irish states, which was now a heptarchy of Connacht, Meath, Leinster, Munster, Aileach, Oriel and Ulidia' – the last three indicating the fragmentation of the old province of Ulster.

For all its internal tensions, Ireland remained inviolate to invasion from outside. The Angles, Jutes, Saxons, Visigoths, Franks and other invading peoples from east and north stopped at the Atlantic seaboard, or were restrained by a buffer of the hard-pressed Celtic-speaking inhabitants of Britain and Brittany. To the north-east, the Gaels of Dál Riada kept their territory on both sides of the Moyle and joined in the internecine battles of the north. But the centuries of security were about to come to an end.

CHAPTER FIVE

Invasions

THE ARRIVAL OF THE NORSEMEN

IN the year 795, coastal communities on the east and west coasts were assailed from the sea by raiders, the first recorded one being on Lambay Island, Co. Dublin. The attackers were Norsemen. They were the first, and deadly, embodiment of the great upsurge of the Scandinavian peoples, which over the next three hundred years would wreak radical changes across the political map of Europe from Norway to Sicily and from Galway to Kiev. The first victims were aware only of blood-crazed killers and looters who appeared from nowhere and vanished again, in ships which could ride the open seas as easily as they could be rowed up shallow rivers. Virtually unguarded communities and open churches were an easy prey, and the pagan Vikings saw churches and abbeys only as treasure houses. By 830, Iona had to be abandoned. The novelty of the threat seems to have made the Irish kingdoms slow to react. Norse pressure on Scottish Dál Riada helped to push the Scots and Picts into the union which eventually produced a Scots-led Gaelic-speaking kingdom of Scotland, but the Irish provinces did not unite in the face of what soon became not only coastal attack but invasion of the interior.

By 840, Vikings were no longer 'summer raiders' but began wintering in Ireland. The Shannon, Bann, Boyne, and other rivers, and Lough Neagh, became highways for the marauding fleets. The invaders' numbers became ever greater, and in 845, one of their chiefs, Thorgest, made himself master of much of the north, and Armagh and Clonmacnoise, already much-battered, were both desecrated. At several points around the coast the Vikings established beach-head settlements behind walls, where ships could be repaired and stores kept. These were to be the nuclei of some important towns in times to come. An established enemy was easier to resist and counter-attack, and Irish kingdoms began to fight back. Thorgest was defeated and drowned by Máel Seachnaill, the Uí Néill King of Meath. But at an early stage, the dynastic rivalries of the Irish kings led them to make alliances with the invaders. Gradually, through the later ninth century and into the tenth, the nature of the relationships changed. By now, Norwegians and Danes were firmly established. The Hebrides and Man formed a maritime Norse state; its sea-kings controlled the Hebridean seaways, and constituted a formidable political and military force. The Irish, whose contacts with the outside world had long been primarily religious and cultural, apart from unreciprocated raids on Wales, were forcibly made to see themselves as part of a wider world in which no kingdom or island was safe, and where every state had to take account of potential threats from far away. One effect was to heighten contacts with

ROUND TOWERS

THESE are among the few uniquely Irish contributions to the western architectural tradition. The architectural historian Kenneth John Conant describes the round tower as 'the most poetic of the Celtic architectural creations. No towers are more graceful than these upward-pointing stone fingers of Ireland. There is no better example of the bravura of basically Northern design.' Conant dates the oldest ones back to the beginning of the ninth century, contemporary with the first Viking raids. Although the tower serves as a marker for church and graveyard, he notes that it was also designed as a practical place of refuge. The door is high in the wall, reachable by a ladder that could be drawn up. Loopholes make it possible to see what is going on and perhaps to toss out missiles. The round towers are often referred to as belfries, but they are such only in the sense that they were used as repositories for the small hand-bells, valuable for their saintly associations, which belonged to the adjacent church. Some 118 round towers can be identified, with thirteen still in a virtually complete state.

Ardmore Round Tower

Europe, where the Frankish empire was gradually enforcing stability. Many Irish clerics and learned men made their way to the court at Aachen. A pragmatic local response to raiding was to construct a round tower as a place of security both for treasures and people, and many of these ninth- and tenth-century structures remain intact.

DYNASTIC WARS AND THE RISE OF BRIAN BÓRUMA

As they became settlers, so the Vikings revealed themselves also as traders. Markets and currency came to Ireland through the growth of the Viking towns of Dublin, Wexford, Waterford, Cork and Limerick. Dublin became the seat of a king, in somewhat uneasy relationship with Norway, whose kings made periodic attempts to exert their supremacy over the Viking-controlled colonies. Irish and Norse traded, allied, and exchanged brides. At some times in the ninth century, the Norse colony was ruled by an Irish king. But the Norse urge to conquest was strong, and from 914 they began to consolidate their positions, reclaiming Dublin and fortifying the other ports. Two high kings, Niall Glúndubh of the northern Uí Néill in 919, and Domnall in 977, challenged them in vain. Between these events, the Norsemen also overran Cashel, and the Eóganacht kingship of Munster came to an end in 967.

It was from Thomond, in northern Munster, that a hitherto minor *tuath*, that of Dál Cais, came into prominence in the second quarter of the tenth century. Cennetig, King of the Dál Cais, and his family were prominent in the resistance to the expansion of the Limerick Vikings, and also by no means loyal to the provincial King of Munster. By 950 Cennetig was strong enough to require invasion by the Uí Néill high king, in an attempt to put down the upstart, and

Rock of Cashel

wipe out his centrally placed power centre. But in 963 Cennetig's son Mathgamain became king at Cashel. Four years later he defeated an army of the Limerick Norsemen with their Irish allies, and destroyed the town. Killed as a result of treachery in 976, the formidable Mathgamain was succeeded as King of the Dál Cais by his even more redoubtable younger brother, Brian. In 978 Brian took the kingship of Munster and in 973 also made himself master of Leinster. With the southern provinces securely his, he began to raid into Meath. The aim was a highly ambitious one, to overturn the long Uí Néill possession of the high kingship. Máel Sechnaill, King of Tara, was not to be easily toppled, however. After years of attritional war, for a time from 997 there was an agreement to accept each other's rights; and this consolidation of Irish power into northern and southern blocs for a time recalled the ancient legend of a division between 'Conn's Half' and 'Mogh's half'.

The Vikings were now at a disadvantage. Máel Sechnaill three times captured Dublin, imposing heavy penalties on the prosperous community. Brian's byname, Bóruma, 'of the tributes', speaks for his own capacity to impose penalties and taxes. The inevitable confrontation between north and south was initiated by Brian. Having put down a rebellion of the Leinstermen, in which the latter were assisted by the Dublin Vikings, in 999, he took possession of Dublin as its over-king. This itself was a challenge to Máel Sechnaill, but it was made unambiguous by an invasion of Meath. The venture was unsuccessful, and after losing a minor battle, Brian withdrew. His ambition was unchanged, and in 1002 he invaded again. On this occasion, in a way that suggests extreme diplomatic isolation, since no battle is recorded, Máel Sechnaill accepted Brian's supremacy. The scion of the Dál Cais, in an astonishing rise, paralleled among the Gaels only by that of Kenneth MacAlpin in Scotland, became *ard rí* of all Ireland.

Though he had himself described as *Imperator Scottorum*, Emperor of the Irish, Brian's legal authority outside his own kingdom was no greater than that of any previous high king. His power was a function of his military strength, his own personality, and, not least, of being in the right place at the right time – something impossible to accomplish all the time. He made an important state visit to Armagh in 1005, acknowledging its role as ecclesiastical capital and also showing his authority in such a significant – and northern – place. But he had to make nine military expeditions into Ulster before the last group to resist him, the remote Cenél Conaill, submitted in defeat in 1011. Although Brian's later reputation, fostered by O'Brien tradition, is that of a road-maker, church-builder and giver of books, it seems likely that he spent much of his time as high king in maintaining his position against threats of rebellion and actual defections from loyalty. The most serious of these came from Leinster and Dublin, which combined in resistance in 1013. Already there was trouble

Death of Brian Bóruma at the hands of retreating Norsemen after the Battle of Clontarf

in Ulster where the head of the northern Uí Néill, Flaithbertach, was struggling from 1012 to rebuild the dynasty's fortunes. Challenged from both sides,
Brian responded by mustering his forces. The crisis came early in 1014. On
Good Friday, 23 April, two armies met at Clontarf, just outside Dublin. Both
were composite forces, with Gaels and Norsemen on each side. Brian's
support from outside his own Munster territories was not great, though it
included Scots and Vikings opposed to Sitric, King of Dublin. Sitric, with Máel
Morda, King of Leinster, had the support of Sigurd, Earl of Orkney, with Viking
warriors from the Hebrides and Man. In a long, bloody and at first indecisive
struggle, Brian's army finally triumphed. But the High King himself, too old to
take part in the battle, and waiting nearby, was killed by retreating Norsemen.

IRELAND AFTER CLONTARF

Afterwards, Clontarf would stand for different things. It was a landmark battle,
which could be seen as a victory for Irish unity, or as a final defeat of Norse
ambitions in Ireland, or even as a victory of Christianity over paganism. None
of these entirely fits the facts. It was a product of Irish disunity. Norsemen
fought on both sides. By 1014, the Vikings were at least nominally Christian.
Yet after Clontarf, the concept of a single kingdom – as had emerged in
Scotland, Norway and England – was stronger, and the potential of a powerful
high kingship was more clearly seen and aspired to. The Norsemen did not go
away but it was no longer possible for them to dominate events. They gradually became the Ostmen, traders and burghers, their settlements becoming
merchant communities, with their own by-laws and civic structures, rather
than fortified camps. With their international mobility and connections, they
were useful in such limited import–export business as there was, largely
restricted to luxury goods and weaponry, and their towns, especially Dublin,
survived as ports and trading centres, under the rule of an earl. Their numbers
were too small to be of influence against the far greater numbers of the Irish,
and their contribution to language and culture was slight.

In one important respect the Ostmen of Dublin preserved their separateness.
As Christians, they aligned themselves not with the Irish Church but with that
of England. Until the mid-twelfth century, their bishop was consecrated by the
Archbishop of Canterbury.

Brian Bóruma's sons were unable to maintain his dominance of the Irish
kingdoms. In the years after Clontarf, the provincial royal dynasties regained
full control. The familiar pattern of internal rivalries between aspirant kings
and external struggles between rival over-kings resumed. A resurgence of
Leinster power, under Diarmait Uí Chennselaig, temporarily eclipsed Munster,
until the O'Briens asserted themselves in the person of Brian's grandson

GORMFLAITH

THIS Irish queen married first Olaf (Olath Cuaran), Viking King of Dublin, then Máel Sechnaill, King of Meath, and thirdly Brian Bóruma. She deserted Brian to plot against him with her son Sitric. She was clearly a woman who exercised great influence. The sketchy elements of her career serve as a reminder that Irish history, as written, has been very much not her-story. But powerful women are a recurrent theme, from the legendary exploits of Medbh, and of early woman-warriors, to St Brigid of Kildare, Gormflaith herself and such later figures as Grace O'Malley, the 'pirate queen' in the sixteenth century, and her contemporary Finola McDonnell. The rigorous exclusion of women from public life during many centuries means that their role in events is hard to trace and their influence hard to assess. But few would doubt that both were substantial. In the twentieth century, after a slow beginning – the Fianna Fáil women TDs of the 1930s were known as 'the silent sisters' – Irish women began to assume a more equal role, culminating in the election of two woman Presidents in the last years of the century.

Grace O'Malley's Castle

Turlough. After Diarmait's death he made himself the strongest man in the south and imposed himself also on Connacht. By 1080 he was the dominant king, but could not establish his authority in the north. On his death in 1086, power disintegrated once again. One of his sons, Muirchertach, painfully re-established much of the O'Brien hegemony, even over Connacht. The north, dominated by the Uí Néill King, Domnall MacLochlainn, was not waiting to be invaded: MacLochlainn pushed into Munster and obtained the temporary submission of Muirchertach.

During this period, there were events elsewhere in the British isles which would have significant effects in Ireland. In 1034 Scotland was united as a Gaelic kingdom under Duncan. In 1066, William, Duke of Normandy, invaded England and enforced his claim to its crown. With him came large numbers of knights and country squires, Normans, Bretons and Flemings, eager to benefit by land-grants from their feudal overlord, and to acquire titles – earldoms and lordships – to go with them. In Wales, a native prince, Gruffudd ap Llywelyn, had established his power over almost all its tribes and petty kingdoms. But only three years after his death in 1063, land-hungry Normans began to claim the most fertile parts of Wales for themselves.

In the confused situation that prevailed in Ireland, the sort of strivings and struggles that might have led towards a single state can be detected. But no

---

TAILTEANN GAMES

TAILTIU or Tailte commemorates the name of a queen of the Fir Bolg, whose husband Eochaid mac Eirc established a great festival in her honour, at the location still known as Teltown between Navan and Kells. The great fair was held, increasingly intermittently, from early times until as late as 1770. In the centuries prior to the Norman invasion, the holding of a Tailteann Games was the prerogative of the high king, and the ability to summon all Ireland to it was a mark of his authority. Athletic and artistic competition were at the heart of the Games, but they also provided a forum for all sorts of entertainment and social activity, including the 'Tailteann marriage' bond, which bound a man and woman for a year, after which they could amicably part if they wished. A revival was begun in 1924, under the auspices of the Free State government, and assisted by the Gaelic Athletic Association, without some of the more antique aspects but including motor-cycle racing. The effort to hold the Games at a four-yearly interval was dropped and the last Games were held in 1932.

one achieved sufficient strength or permanence to bring it about. All the king-doms shared common, or very similar, laws. They shared a language and an already ancient history (not only that, by now Irish historians were hard at work extending that history back into the events of the *Old Testament*). By no means least, they practised the same religion. In an era of emergent nation-states, and indeed also of a super-state in the form of the Holy Roman Empire, it would be remarkable if the Irish had failed to discuss the prospect and desir-ability of the same thing in their own land. In the end, the Church achieved for itself what none of the provincial monarchies quite managed to do, and became a national institution.

THE REORGANISATION OF THE CHURCH

This process, which happened through the later eleventh and the twelfth cen-turies, was aided by two powerful outside forces. One was the reform of, and the new enthusiasm for, monastic life. The great monastic orders of the middle ages had arisen, and Benedictine and Augustinian foundations were estab-lished in Ireland, first in the territories of the Ostmen. The other force was the growing strength and influence of the papacy. Practice in the Irish Church often fell short of the new rigour demanded by successive popes and preached and published by St Bernard. Its structure was still based on the old *tuatha*, with abbots as the most important figures. By the eleventh century, the abbot would often be a layman, a married member of the local aristocracy, whose position was hereditary, and whose religious duties had to be performed by a prior on his behalf. Monastic life was practised with varying degrees of auster-ity. Most monks were semi-secular figures who might even be married, though their wives did not reside in the convent. In the eighth century, with Máel Ruain, abbot of Tallaght, as its best-known exponent, the ascetic Céile Dé, or Culdees, 'the vassals of God' had a strong influence, perhaps reflecting a reac-tion against laxity. But by the twelfth century, the Céile Dé themselves had diminished in numbers, influence and rigour. The Church had lax marriage laws and an easygoing attitude to divorce. Despite ample evidence of piety and scholarship, the regime in Irish monasteries seemed far too casual and individ-ual to the reformists.

The minds of reformers were also concentrated by the attention paid to Ireland by the first Norman Archbishop of Canterbury, Lanfranc, who claimed superiority over the Irish Church in 1072. The reasons for this claim are not wholly clear: Lanfranc was as bold a snatcher of territory as his secular fellow-Normans; but it was perhaps founded in the orthodox Roman foundation of Canterbury compared to the home-grown and un-hierarchic structure of the Irish Church. Irish bishops, hitherto a somewhat obscure group, increasingly aware of their low status compared with those who ruled territorial dioceses elsewhere, began to assert themselves. Internally, the ambition of the O'Brien kings to establish themselves as kings of Ireland both assisted, and was assisted by, the centralising trend in the Church. A twelfth-century king needed to correspond with other monarchs in suitable style, and to be represented by ambassadors who could put his point of view forward with credit. The pool of talent for such scribes and emissaries was closely linked to the Church. The kings needed the churchmen; in turn the reformers needed a king of wide authority to convene and give security to the nation-wide meetings of clerics which gathered to consider the problems of the Church.

This new spirit revealed itself in architecture as well as in ideals of Christian behaviour, in lofty buildings whose bulk dwarfed the tiny stone churches of earlier generations. Cormac's chapel at Cashel was dedicated in 1134 and shows many signs of European influence, and many other buildings of distinctive Irish Romanesque style were to follow in the next hundred years. At the same time, there was a revival of the old art of sculpting high crosses. Many examples (many more than now) still stood from the eighth and ninth centuries, and the new school created larger figures, most often with the crucified

---

CLONFERT CATHEDRAL

ONE of the masterworks of Irish Romanesque sculpture is the west portal of St Brendan's Cathedral, Clonfert, Co. Galway, which dates from the mid-twelfth century. Its pilasters and arches are decorated with a rich variety of finely carved motifs and animal heads. But most visitors are arrested by the steep triangular pediment or gable that rises above the doorway. At each side of its peak are two carved human heads. Within the design are a further fifteen heads, placed in triangular or arched recesses. In his *Irish Churches and Monastic Buildings*, (vol. 1) Harold Leask notes of the heads in the pediment that 'each has the individuality which suggests a portrait.' Who they represent, or who carved them, is not known, but Leask hails it as 'this supreme example of Irish architectural art'. For the observer it is difficult to detach this spectacle from the recollection that the warriors of the Celtic tribes were head-takers far into Christian times. The trophy-frame of a tribal champion may have been not dissimilar in design. But the sculptor's genius, though it endows the pediment with a profound sense of the strange and archaic, relieves it of any sense of the gruesome. Almost certainly they are Christian icons. But it remains a monument to ponder over.

Christ on one side and the founding saint of the church on the other, as in the 'Market Cross' of Glendalough, with its founder, St Kevin.

Church reform began in the south but was then taken up by Armagh. In 1101, an Archbishop of Cashel was installed at a national synod, also attended by a papal legate, and King Muirchertach gave the Rock of Cashel to the Church. In 1105, Cellach became Abbot of Armagh. Although a member of the Sinaich family who had controlled the post for over a century, and a married man, he joined in the reform campaign, and took holy orders. In 1106 he also became a bishop. Such duality of posts, simony, was one of the practices frowned upon by Rome, but Cellach used his combined powers in the name of reform. Under royal auspices, a further significant synod was convened at Rath Breasail in 1111. Now the island was divided into two archdioceses, centred on Armagh and Cashel, and each of those was divided into twelve bishoprics. These dioceses were territorial, not tribal, their boundaries clearly spelled out.

Further progress towards reform is closely identified with the figure of St Malachy, born in Armagh in 1095. At the early age of 29 he was installed as Bishop of Down and Connor. A struggle with the old guard took place when on Cellach's death in 1129 he was named as Archbishop of Armagh. The Uí Sinaich had promptly installed a family member as lay abbot. It was 1132 before Malachy, with the backing of the papal legate and the reformist

Bangor Castle

movement, was installed. In 1137 he returned to Bangor, and two years later went to Rome, to receive from the Pope the *pallia*, or archbishop's collars, for Armagh and Cashel. He paused at Clairvaux, where St Bernard was building his abbey, and the two became lifelong friends and mutual supporters. From this meeting came the strong Cistercian tradition in Ireland, with their first monastery founded at Mellifont in 1140, by a party who had accompanied Malachy on his return. The Pope however would not grant the *pallia* unless the request were backed by a national synod. A further journey to Rome was necessary, in 1148, but Malachy died on the way, at Clairvaux. It was 1152 before another national synod was held, this time at Kells, and later at Mellifont, under the patronage of King Turlough O'Connor. At this the number of archdioceses was enlarged to four, with the addition of Dublin and Tuam; and the number of bishoprics from twenty-four to thirty-six. The inclusion of Dublin marks both the developing importance of the city, and the Church's eagerness to detach its metropolitans from their fealty to Canterbury. Papal approval of the synod was confirmed by the presence of a Cardinal-Legate, John Paparo.

STRUGGLES OF THE TWELFTH-CENTURY KINGS

The involvement of Turlough O'Connor is an indication that dominance had moved from the O'Briens, following Muirchertach's death in 1119, to the rulers of Connacht. Like all the high kings after Brian Bóruma, he was a *ri co fesabra*, a king with opposition, and though he enforced control on the reluctant and frequently rebellious provinces of Leinster and Munster, he had no say in the affairs of Ulster, where the MacLochlainns ruled in Tír Eógain. On Turlough's death in 1156, Muirchertach MacLochlainn claimed the high kingship, defeating Turlough's son Rory O'Connor. Though the high kings and their challengers were necessarily based on strong provincial positions and their headship of large and wealthy tribal groups, there was still room for an ambitious and active minor ruler to make an impact. Such a one was Tiernan O'Rourke, King of the petty state of Breffni, who mostly allied himself with the O'Connors and was able as a result greatly to enlarge his holdings. Tactical alliances and betrayals typified the behaviour of provincial and local kings. Leinster and Munster were subdivided on numerous occasions, each time a sub-king seemed to be getting too strong. Even though Turlough O'Connor ruled Connacht for fifty years, an exceptional reign, during which the functions, offices and support-systems of an over-king developed substantially, he could not prevail over the system, so long entrenched, of local kinship loyalties.

By the twelfth century, over-kings were granting land to monasteries and to loyal supporters, and written charters were coming into use rather than the spoken words and emblematic symbols of earlier times. Kings held councils, employed clerks and tax-collectors, and disposed of land in a way that shows, even before the arrival of the Normans, that the view of property was changing. Once upon a time the land of a *tuath* had been the property of the tribe. Now, increasingly, it was the property of the king. The frequent divisions of provinces and kingdoms, and the replacement of kings, carried out by the high kings who were concerned to maintain their own positions, also led to a detachment of land from people in many places.

A revolt of the Ulster sub-kingdoms, Oriel and the Ulaid, led to Muirchertach MacLochlainn's death in 1165. Rory O'Connor seized the chance to re-establish the Connacht dynasty as high kings. He took control of Dublin, easing his way in with the munificent bribe of 4,000 head of cattle, and established control of the kingdoms in Leinster, of Ossory, and Oriel. The King of south Leinster, Dermot MacMurrough, had been an ally of MacLochlainn. Now exposed to old enemies in the centre, and without hope of help from the north, MacMurrough saw his lands invaded and despoiled by a triumphant Tiernan O'Rourke.

Tacitus records that, centuries before, when Agricola had reached the Galloway shore, he been approached by an Irish leader who had sought Roman support in a war between tribes. Agricola had other things to do, however. The same plea was made, more successfully, by Dermot MacMurrough. In August 1166 he fled to south-west England, and looked for support among the Normans. The town of Bristol, his destination, was an established trading partner of Dublin, Waterford and Cork. In the hundred years since 1066, the 'Normanisation' of Anglo-Saxon England, and of Celtic south Wales, had been thorough. But the expansionist, acquisitive, opportunist spirit had not died down.

Ironically, the flight of MacMurrough marked the ascendancy of Rory O'Connor as a high king with no opposition. His dispositions covered every kingdom in Ireland. A great assembly at Athlone proclaimed him as high king and in 1168 he celebrated a Tailteann Fair, only the third since their abandonment in 926. By then, Dermot had already returned from his sojourn abroad, which had taken him to France as well as England. In Aquitaine he met Henry II of England, and swore allegiance to him. Henry provided him with a letter authorising any subject of the English king to assist Dermot to recover his kingdom. But the return to Leinster was inauspicious. O'Connor and O'Rourke moved rapidly to force his submission, despite his Flemish mercenaries, and his kingship was reduced to that of the old petty state of the Uí Chennsalaig. In May 1169, a band of some 400 Normans, of whom thirty were armoured knights, eventually landed at Baginbun, on Bannow Bay, Co. Wexford, in support of Dermot.

INVASION AND THE FALL OF THE CELTIC KINGS

'The fall of Celtic Wales heralded the fall of Celtic Ireland,' wrote Edmund Curtis. Pembroke in south-west Wales was already a Norman earldom in 1166. In fact the Fitzgeralds, Fitzgilberts, Fitzstephens and others who formed the first invading party were part-Welsh, but their instincts, training and methods were thoroughly Norman. In Wales they had established themselves by right of the sword, and they regarded Ireland as ripe for conquest in the same manner. Their patron was Richard, Earl of Pembroke, better known as Strongbow. His inducement was to succeed Dermot as King of Leinster, his status secured by a marriage to Dermot's daughter Aefe. He landed on 21 August 1170, with a more substantial army of a thousand men. Waterford was speedily captured, its Norse earl executed, and Strongbow married his Irish bride in the cathedral there. The seriousness of the threat was obvious, and Rory mobilised an army in defence of Dublin. But the invaders stormed the city from the south, while its Viking earl was still discussing terms, and took possession. No longer was Rory an undisputed high king.

On 1 May 1171, Dermot died, and Strongbow became King of Leinster. He fought off an attack from seaborne Vikings under Dublin's former earl, Asgall. More importantly, in a surprise sally from behind the walls, his men defeated the high king's besieging forces. O'Connor might have reflected that his army's fate was one shared by traditional forces all over western Europe. Even large numbers of foot-soldiers could not withstand mailed knights mounted on heavy horses. But the high kingship of Ireland went down as well.

Another king was taking a close interest in events. Henry II's licence to Dermot MacMurrough had not been intended to allow Norman barons of suspect loyalties to set themselves up as independent kings. It became known that he was preparing for a large-scale invasion of Ireland. Strongbow, who while under siege had offered his loyalty to Rory O'Connor in return for confirmation of his Leinster kingship (it was rejected: he was offered only the Ostmen's lands on the east coast) made haste to renew his vows to Henry. Henry granted him Leinster as a royal fief, and took the Ostmen's towns as his own royal domain. On 17 October 1171, accompanied by many of the nobility and a large army, he landed near Waterford.

Marriage of Stronghow to Aefe, daughter of Dermot MacMurrough

CHAPTER SIX

The Anglo-Normans

THE DOMINION OF HENRY II

Henry II's visit was a show of force rather than an invasion. No one was about to fight him. On the contrary, most of the kings and chiefs of Ireland came to offer him their submission and fealty. The twelfth-century historian, Gerald of Wales, who knew Ireland well, states that Rory O'Connor himself submitted. No charter existed to claim, no custom stated, that the King of England was overlord of Ireland. By their actions, the Irish kings themselves affirmed it; the only ones who did not attend on Henry were the rulers of Cenél Conaill and Cenél nEógain, in the far north. They may have felt inviolate – for the rest, it may have seemed dangerous to stand out. All sorts of rumours about Henry's intentions are likely to have been flying around. There is no doubt that he felt encouraged by the Pope's attitude towards Ireland. Despite the reforms brought about in previous generations, it was felt at the Lateran Palace that the Irish Church was still too lax in certain ways, both in its own practices and in its imposition of canon law on the people. Some elements in Ireland itself also encouraged Henry. There was still a reformist body among the clergy, and they hoped to draw the English king into their cause. The Ostmen hoped he would restore their rights.

Henry, who had still to appease the outraged Pope for the murder, which he had inspired, of Archbishop Thomas à Becket of Canterbury, directed his attention to the Church. The Ostmen's eastern towns remained an English Crown domain – in the case of Dublin, until 1922. By 6 November 1171, a synod was under way, sponsored though not attended by Henry, and summoned by the Archbishop of Cashel and the Bishop of Lismore, who was also a papal legate. The synod accepted the overlordship of Henry, and sent a report to Rome on the decayed state of the Irish Church, and on the steps the Synod had taken to bring reform. In May 1172, Henry II received Papal absolution for the Canterbury assassination.

The Irish kings may have hoped that when Henry left, things would return to something like the old order. But it was not to be quite like that. The Normans were too acquisitive to be easily accommodated, and they were intent on setting up their own systems. Men like Strongbow and Hugh de Lacy, Lord of Meath, were well aware that they sat where kings had preceded them. Their status in Ireland was higher than that of their peers in England and Wales. But to accept this pleasing aspect of life was also to let other aspects of Irish life exert their influence. The cultural differences of Ireland, so long entrenched, and its remoteness from the seat of Anglo-Norman royal power, gradually created a 'Hiberno-Norman' nobility, often – as with the families of Strongbow and de Lacy, both of whom had Irish wives – of Irish descent on the maternal side. None of this held them back from typical raiding, land-claiming, and building castles to defend the claim.

In 1175, Henry II confirmed Rory O'Connor as a tributary King of all Ireland except for Leinster, Meath, parts of Munster and the old Norse districts. These, the centres of Norman rule, had Henry II as their ultimate feudal lord. The disposition was not to last. The King of the Cenél nEógain, who had never acknowledged Henry II, struck southward into Meath; the Norman John de Courcy invaded Ulster and established himself east of Lough Neagh, and other struggles broke out. A new tactic was employed by Henry II when he named his son John as Lord of Ireland in 1177. John was only nine, and eight years passed before he arrived to inspect his domain. The intention was to install him as king, but this did not happen. Despite his having landed with a large army, neither Irish kings nor Norman lords came to pay homage during an eight-month stay. Though John could not enforce his personal authority, his period in Ireland laid the basis of a central English administration, based on Dublin, which was extended when he became King of England in 1199. Further notable families settled under his charters, including the Butlers and the de Burghs, often given estates on the basis that the land was theirs if they could hold it: the so-called 'speculative grant'.

COYNE AND LIVERY

COYNE is Irish *coinnmheadh*, 'guesting', and livery is the English word, related to 'delivery' and meaning fodder supplied for horses. Together, they had an unpleasant meaning for the tenants of an Irish or Anglo-Irish lord from the thirteenth to the fifteenth century. It was a means of billeting various members of the lord's retinue, together with their horses, at the expense of the unfortunate tenant. Such guests included the gallowglasses, or Scottish warriors, huntsmen, and other retainers. Indeed the tenant might be expected not only to house and feed men and beasts, but also to pay, or help to pay, their wages. The imposition was much resented. Parliament in 1297 tried to restrict it to domains in 'the land of war' or on the frontier. But coyne and livery was sometimes demanded even within the Pale.

In true Norman style, they made sure they held it, and took some more as well, to be doubly sure. The territory ruled by Irish kings was steadily pushed back. Meanwhile, the construction of Dublin Castle as a royal centre and depot established the *de facto* position of the old Viking town as the capital of English rule. Under that rule, English law was made to extend over Ireland, administered by a royal justiciar. Under this law, all land was held in the name of the English king, and granted by him to tenants-in-chief in return for specific services, civil and military.

THE NORMAN INFLUENCE

Writers on the Normans have commented on how life under them was organised around three institutions, the castle, the sheriff and the market. The shiring (formation of counties) was slow and few sheriffs were installed in Ireland, where in many parts it would have been difficult to build and even more so to hold the royal castles which secured their positions in England and Scotland. But the markets came, and with them the first coinages of Ireland, from mints in Dublin, and, for a time, also Limerick and Waterford.

Norman society required relatively intensive agriculture and a well-organised structure of service. Castle garrisons needed large and regular food supplies. Heavy horses needed ample pasturage and fodder. Mills had to be built to grind the grain. Armour and siege weapons needed tools and carpentry that represented the state of the art. Stone castles quickly replaced the first hastily built wooden structures, and needed not only expert stonemasons and joiners but the advice of military engineers. Religiously inclined as well as military, the new magnates also began to endow abbeys and churches, and once again looked for builders who could bring the newest styles to Ireland. The demand for good land and the need for money meant that Normans avidly sought the most favourable districts and had little interest in ownership of mountainous or unproductive territory.

The concept of the market was a clear one. It was a place where goods and products were exchanged, usually for cash, with a percentage finding its way to the lord who gave the market-town its charter. Some were royal boroughs, like Wexford and Waterford; others were set up by local magnates, like the de Lacy borough of Drogheda. These places began to assume the look of towns, with streets of merchants' houses congregated close to the protective castle. Unauthorised trading was forbidden. The concept of all this was quite different to that of the Gaelic community. Although that too had a head and a hierarchy, there was no cash-based economy. The social organisation was still akin to that of the ancient *tuath*, its grounds tilled by those who were at the lowest level of the kindred, and with hereditary specialists in law, medicine, teaching

St Lawrence Gate, Drogheda

and the skills of the bard, dependent on the chief or king for support and patronage. For all the 'local colour' taken on by the Normans, there were two nations in Ireland. The distinction became more strongly entrenched through the thirteenth century. The Gaels were forbidden to live within town walls, hence the 'Irishtowns' that developed. They were also officially classed as outside the common law of England and Ireland. Within their own communities, the brehon law could still be practised, but in any action against a settler, the Irish were at a serious disadvantage.

The Norman barons formed a kind of freemasonry, with well-established international contacts. It was as a result of a plot against him, backed by the

---

BETAGHS

FROM Irish *biatach*, a client or dependent of a chief, low in the hierarchy, whose function is to provide food supplies under a lifelong and hereditary obligation. In the Anglo-Norman domains, betaghs appear to have been more or less equated with serfs. Their service was to provide seasonal work on the manor lands, rather than to provide specific foodstuffs, and after the devastation of the Black Death, when labourers were in short supply, they were mostly able to commute this service for a rental payment; by the end of the fourteenth century, the term was becoming obsolete.

de Lacys, now Earls of Ulster (Hugh de Lacy having defeated de Courcy and sent him into exile), that King John returned to Ireland in June 1210. This time he did not scruple to use his army, and swept up the country from Waterford through Meath and into Ulster, exacting the pledges of fealty previously withheld. The campaign was wholly successful and was one of the few triumphs of John's unhappy reign. Thereafter, the Hiberno-Norman magnates remained

King John's Castle, Limerick

loyal to the Crown. In many cases, of course, families were represented both in England and in Ireland, and their loyalty could be more easily enforced. Of the important Irish kingdoms, only Connacht remained, though Donal Mór O'Brien held much of Munster, and married a daughter of his to the incomer William de Burgh, and Tír Eógain and Tír Conaill remained independent. But the claim of the O'Connors to any real high kingship was an empty one long before the death of Rory O'Connor in 1198. His brother Cathal succeeded him, but as King of Connacht only.

The combination of Norman entrepreneurship and the fertility of Irish soil produced strong economic growth in the thirteenth century. The population of the manors was increased by a flow of immigrants coming, or despatched, from England. Other members of these communities were Normanised Irish, who had taken English names and spoke the English language. This was done to avoid serfdom. Not only the betaghs, or lowest order of Gaelic society, but also independent farmers, were liable to be forced into serfdom, to maintain the basis of communal life on the Norman manor. With their estates established, wealth and security enabled the barons to leave the country and take part in crusades to regain the Holy Land from the Saracens. But Irishmen also participated. Muiredhach Albanach Ó Dálaigh, a poet, was one who went on the fifth crusade and refers to his experiences in verse that has been preserved. Banished from Ireland for some offence in 1213, he took service in Scotland after his return from the East. His nostalgia for the Celtic landscape was strong:

Help from Cruachan is far off
across the wave-bordered Mediterranean;
the journeying of spring separates us
from these green-branched glens.

Another Irish crusader of high rank was Aed mac Conchobhair Maenmuige, whose death is recorded in the Irish Annals in the year 1224, 'returning from the Jordan and from Jerusalem'.

The infusion of Norman settlers brought Ireland more into a pan-European setting than ever before. In effect it was part of an Angevin empire that also extended over Wales, England and large tracts of France. The buildings that went up confirmed these connections. Pointed-arch architecture in new churches and abbeys reflected an awareness of new styles, less 'insular' than the Irish Romanesque that had preceded it, created by master-masons who had learned their craft in England or France. Castles expanded from stone towers set on mounds to massively walled enclosures, designed to make a siege as difficult as possible, surrounding an inner bailey and with the original keep often the kernel of a larger block of towers and apartments. These embodiments of secular and religious power dominated the low huddles of thatched cottages which constituted most settlements.

THE THIRTEENTH CENTURY: WARS AND RUMOURS OF WARS

Even though much of Ireland's wealth was siphoned off by the royal exchequer, the barons were immensely wealthy. There was rarely peace among them; rivalry was high and they still had the spirit of frontiersmen, viewing Irish-held territory as open to acquisition. By the mid-thirteenth century there was little land left of interest to immigrants, and the pattern of landed families who would dominate life for the next five centuries was largely established. It was not a static pattern, but despite its instability, there was a fundamental coherence, just as there had been in the centuries before the Vikings came. Family alliances and power blocs, based in different parts of the country, replaced the roles of the old provincial over-kings, but the urge to dominance remained. Family feuds or leaders' deaths could equally well dissolve the power bloc and leave it in a vulnerable state.

The main groupings were those of the Geraldines and de Burghs. The latter dominated most of Connacht, and, from 1242, also became Earls of Ulster, their territory now extending far into the O'Neill lands of Tír Eógain, with the O'Neill King acknowledging the Earl as his overlord. By the end of the century, the Geraldines were firmly based in the centre of the country, with Kildare as their capital, but with wide holdings also in Munster, where the earldom of Desmond covered much of Cork and Kerry. Between these Geraldine regions stretched lands dominated by the Butlers, the earldom of Ormond at its centre and extending eastwards to Kilkenny. Within and between these great domains, smaller manors were controlled by dozens of other Anglo-Norman families. Normally owing feudal service to the earl, they would sometimes break ranks and ally themselves to a rival magnate. Although it is tempting to see this as a perpetuation of the old order, a kind of inevitable Irish *status quo*, it would be quite wrong. Certain vital factors were present that had not existed before the Normans' arrival. Firstly, there were the two nations. The Anglo-Normans might intermarry with the Irish royal families, and take on the glamour of Irish kings, but they would certainly have conquered and Normanised the entire country if they could. They were stopped from this by a combination of geography and the tenacity of the Irish inhabitants. Another vital difference was the controlling power of the English kingship, through the justiciar and the small but usually effective administration in Dublin. Particularly in the reign of Edward I, a military king constantly in need of funds, English tax gathering was pursued with great determination. A further factor, especially important in the north and west, was the was the involvement of Scots in Irish affairs. This would come to a peak in 1316 but from 1258 galloglasses (mercenary soldiers from the Hebrides and western Highlands) would be an important element in preserving the balance of power.

Deprived of the best land in the country, Irish kings still held their ground among the hills and mountains and on the rocky western coasts. Tír Eógain and Tír Conaill in the north were still O'Donnell and O'Neill strongholds, though O'Neill did homage to the Earl of Ulster. But Connacht was no longer an Irish kingdom, and the O'Connors clung to a small territory between it and Roscommon. The O'Briens were reduced to a part of Thomond. Throughout the vast possessions of the incomers, however, was a large Irish population, numbering among it many representatives of ancient dynasties that had once ruled in their localities and had not forgotten the fact. The Anglo-Normans were thinly spread, unassailable in their castles, but vulnerable outside them. An attempt by Brian O'Neill to revive his family's high kingship failed in 1260 when the Lord of Ulster's forces defeated him and his O'Connor and O'Brien allies at Downpatrick, but it showed that the Gaels had not lost hope of re-establishing suzerainty, if not of chasing out the Anglo-Normans. In 1261 the dispossessed MacCarthys of Cork rallied under Finghin, defeated a Norman army at the Battle of Callann near Kenmare, and restored control over much of their ancient kingdom, though not the town of Cork. For a brief time the Irish kings negotiated with the powerful Haakon IV of Norway, overlord of the Western Isles, as a potential high king, with the Ostmen's towns as a lure, but by 1263, Norse rule in the Hebrides was nearing its end. Haakon, worsted at Largs in Scotland in 1263, died on his way back to Norway. With him went the last chance of Norse involvement in Irish affairs. A new power arose in the southern Hebrides, that of the Macdonald Lords of the Isles, closely linked with their MacDonnell kindred in Antrim.

In 1264, de Burghs and Geraldines and their allies were at open war with each other. Richard de Burgh, Earl of Ulster, was captured by the Geraldines and held prisoner for a time. Whilst both Irish and Anglo-Normans were quite capable of internecine violence, the Irish were often also caught up in the incomers' struggles; and also sought support from them in their own disputes. The recurrent efforts to re-establish an *ard rí* show the Irish leaders' awareness of the perils of disunion, and also the strictly limited range of effectiveness of the justiciar, who was in effect the English king's Viceroy. Beyond the few shire counties, his edict did not run. In 1270 Aedh O'Connor, King of Connacht since 1265, defeated a de Burgh force at Ath in Cip, and regained control of much of the old kingdom. But in the south, the old kingdom of Thomond was granted by Edward I to Thomas de Clare, who speedily Normanised it from his new castle at Bunratty. Desmond was granted to Thomas Fitzmaurice, head of the Geraldines, who came to an accommodation with MacCarthy More, who continued to act as king in the far south-west. Edward I's justiciar, John de Wogan, established an Irish Parliament in 1297. The reason was the same as for all parliaments of the time, to facilitate the royal tax collections. In this case Edward I also sought to recruit troops from the Irish colonies, for his wars in Scotland and France. As a body the parliament represented only the Church, the lords and the landed interest, and was restricted to the counties already formed: Dublin, Louth (old Oriel), Waterford, Tipperary, Cork, Limerick, Kerry and Roscommon; and the 'liberties' (feudal estates with legal powers) of Meath, Wexford, Carlow, Kilkenny and Ulster. It was in no sense a parliament for the whole country, and its acts showed hostility and contempt both to the 'mere Irish', and the 'degenerate English' who adopted Irish modes of dress or hair-style.

SCOTTISH INVASION AND ENGLISH REPRESSION

In the weak reign of Edward II, the next power to be drawn into Ireland was the resurgent kingdom of Scotland, which had confirmed its independence by the battle of Bannockburn in 1314. Its king, Robert Bruce, was seen by the Irish kings as a possible high king, but he delegated the matter of Ireland to his brother Edward, a warlike figure but far less of a statesman. Edward's method was to ravage Ulster through 1315 and 1316, with a large army of six thousand men, whose demands stripped the resources of the countryside and caused starvation and misery to the people. On 1 May 1316 he was crowned High King of Ireland at Knocknemelan Hill, close to Dundalk. The Scottish invasion prompted other uprisings and unrest. In August 1316, Felim O'Connor, who had reclaimed the kingship of Connacht, was killed in a pitched battle against a Norman army led by William de Burgh and Richard de Bermingham, at Athenry. Robert I of Scotland came himself on campaign to Ireland in 1316–17. But Dublin was too strongly walled to capture, and no army could be mustered to meet him. He returned to Scotland. A notable victory was won by Muirchertach O'Brien at Dysert O'Dea, on 10 May 1318, when Thomond was reclaimed from the de Clares. Edward Bruce withdrew to Ulster. By now his strength was much reduced, and in a battle with an Anglo-Norman force at Faughart, near Dundalk, he was killed, on 14 October 1318. Though he cannot be said to have exercised the role, he was the last high king of Ireland.

It was a close-run thing. Conscious that Ireland was slipping from the English grasp, the Whitehall government sent Roger Mortimer as Lord Lieutenant in April 1317, equipped both with an army and with permission to make certain concessions to the Irish, one of which was their inclusion under English law, an old source of resentment. In those years much accumulated anger and suffering came to the surface. What ordinary people thought can only be guessed at, but a range of kings and chiefs put their names to a formal Remonstrance, sent to Pope John XXII at Avignon, charging both the English king and the 'middle nation' of colonists with violations of the rights of the Irish people and Church, acts of cruelty and oppression, and formally sundering their allegiance and transferring it to Edward Bruce. But Bruce's death ended the crisis for England.

A parliament at Dublin in 1320 renewed the rights of the clergy and people of Ireland under Magna Carta, but the full admission of all Irish to the

---

BERMINGHAM'S DINNER

PETER, or Piers, de Bermingham of Tethmoy in Offaly, whose death was recorded in 1308, was an Anglo-Irish magnate, whose family had first been granted land by Strongbow. A relative of his was archbishop of Tuam, another was lord of Athenry. Peter's fame, or notoriety, comes from an anonymous poem written in Middle English. One of the sixteen so-called 'Kildare Poems', it praises him for his action in entertaining thirty prominent O'Connors to a feast on Trinity Sunday, 1305. Once his Irish visitors were well-wined and dined, Bermingham ordered his men to attack them, and all thirty were murdered.

common law was not carried out. The laws of England were administered in the shires. The laws of Ireland were administered where the Irish kings still ruled. Between these were the feudal liberties and areas of disputed land where a hybrid 'march' or border law was practised, to the convenience of the local strong man, using elements from English and Irish laws as required.

THE BLACK DEATH

The fourteenth century brought the worst disaster to afflict the Irish people until the Great Famine occurred five hundred years later. The Black Death probably came to Ireland by way of Bristol, still the main port for Anglo-Irish traffic of all sorts. Its effects in the winter of 1348–49 were sporadic, but by the summer of 1349 it was ravaging the country, especially through the close-packed towns, the abbeys and the Norman manors. By contrast, the 'mountain Irish' appear to have suffered much less – an indication of the lack of contact between the two nations. On top of the destruction and wastage of warfare, recurrent outbreaks of plague more than decimated the population, killing perhaps one fifth in the years up to 1361. Agriculture was disrupted, crop production severely reduced, and economic life consequently brought to a low ebb. The strength of the Anglo-Norman lordships was greatly diminished.

THE BLACK DEATH

I BROTHER John Clyn, of the Order of Friars Minor and of the convent of Kilkenny, wrote in this book those notable things which happened in my time, which I saw with my own eyes, or which I learned from people worthy of belief. And in case things which should be remembered perish with time and vanish from the memory of those who are to come after us, I, seeing so many evils and the whole world, as it were, placed within the grasp of the evil one, being myself as if among the dead, waiting for death to visit me, have put into writing truthfully all the things that I have heard. And, lest the writing should perish with the writer and the work fail with the labourer, I leave parchments to continue this work, if perchance any man survive and any of the race of Adam escape this pestilence and carry on the work which I have begun.

To his text, documenting the effects of the plague, Brother John added two final words: *Magna karistia*, 'Great dearth'. Another hand made an addition, some time later: 'Here it seems that the author died.'

By this time, many of these lords were almost total absentees. Other land holdings in England or France drew them away, as did calls for royal service in the almost continuous wars of Edward III of England. Many preferred to be closer to the king and consequently to royal preferment. For these, their Irish holdings were simply a source of income. Their absence was resented by those lords who stayed and struggled in Ireland. Sixty-four lords holding land in Ireland were ordered to accompany Lionel, Duke of Clarence, when he was appointed Lieutenant in 1361. Married to the widow of the last de Burgh Earl of Ulster, Lionel held that earldom and the – at this time notional – lordship of Connacht. His efforts to thrust back the Irish from the advances they had made had a modest impact and were supported in lukewarm fashion by many of the resident lords. There was little glory or profit to be had in fighting in Ireland. Clarence left in November 1366, the main monument to his rule being the Statutes of Kilkenny, enacted by a parliament held in that town in February of the same year.

The thirty-six statutes, imposing a form of apartheid between the Anglo-Norman and Irish nations, show both the strength and the limitation of the

---

FOSTERING

ONE of the continuities of Irish life is seen in this form of child-rearing, whose origins go back into the pre-medieval period and which continued at least into the sixteenth century. It was done with both boys and girls. The child, usually from the age of six or seven, was sent to live with another family, usually part of the same kindred – the mother's side more often than the father's – but possibly linked only by obligation or political reasons. A fee was normally payable, particularly when the child was of higher status than its foster-family, and took the form of a prescribed amount of land or number of cows, depending on relative rank. The obligation on both sides was a substantial one. The fostering family were responsible for the appropriate education and upbringing of the child, its welfare and security; and could be held to account if things went wrong. The foster-child retained a commitment to the foster-parents, and had to contribute to their welfare in old age. The fostering bond was a strong one, between foster-brothers and sisters as well between parent and child; and might well take precedence over a closer blood-relationship. In some cases, with royal or very high-placed families, the dividing line between a fosterling and a hostage could be a very fine one.

---

colonising effort. The Kilkenny parliament firmly relegated everything Irish to second-class status. The inhabitants of 'the land of peace' (that is, the shires and feudal liberties) were not allowed to speak Irish, to intermarry with the Irish, to practise fostering, to use Irish law or to employ Irish bards. Such bans would not be made unless the proscribed activities were already widespread. Despite their colonialist tone, the Statutes showed, as the historian Edmund Curtis remarked, 'the failure of the Conquest of Ireland as it was meant to be, viz. a complete reduction of the whole island to English law and Norman lord-ship'. They showed a determination to hold the line, and preserve the 'land of peace' in its allegiance, and its tax contributions, to the English Crown. The implication of failure is perhaps one reason why hostility to the Irish expressed in the Statutes was so open and unabashed. In its preamble, the Irish are referred to as 'enemies'. The residents of the Pale, as the area in Dublin's hin-terland was beginning to be called, would cling to this legislation, and the Statutes would contribute to strife in the centuries ahead. Like some other regimes still to come, in this country and elsewhere, the Anglo-Irish parlia-mentarians appeared to have learned nothing, and forgotten nothing, in the two hundred years since their forebears had come to Ireland.

CHAPTER SEVEN

The Land of Peace and the Land of War

IRISH REASSERTION

B ETWEEN the land of peace and the land of war, where the Gaels ruled in their own style, was 'the march', the borderland, an area where two cultures and two sets of political institutions met and overlapped. Here lived 'degenerate English' who had adopted many Irish aspects of life and culture. They spoke Gaelic as well as, or instead of, English, were entertained by bards, and lived by 'march law'. Their allegiance to the English Crown was uncertain, and their military strength, backed up by Irish warriors, was considerable. The Kilkenny Parliament tried to keep them within the English camp. It could not place them beyond the law, as it had done with the independent Irish, and yet it could not enforce the Statutes upon them. Concessions were made, and they were acknowledged as 'captains of their nations'.

The Irish, whether they were a king or the most obscure betagh, were reduced to one and the same status, that is, no status at all. They could not obtain justice, talk their own language, wear their own clothes or even ride a horse in their traditional style, within the 'land of peace' (this last ban was so widely ignored by the settlers themselves that it had to be struck out of a later re-enactment of the Statutes). Within their own kingdoms, none of this was a problem, but the arbitrary removal of all legal protection by the supposed overlord was deeply resented. The kings – this term was still regularly used through the fourteenth century – and chiefs saw no bar to continuing their efforts to reclaim territory, and the sporadic moves towards a partial 'reconquest' continued. Old dynasties showed they still had vigour, as the O'Neills of Clandeboye clawed out a new dominion from most of the earldom of Ulster together with Irish-held territories of the MacDunlevys and the O'Flynns. In west Cork, Dermot MacCarthy established a lordship of Muskerry, adjoining the other MacCarthy lands of MacCarthy More and MacCarthy Reagh. In 1370, the O'Brien King of Thomond defeated the Earl of Desmond and took him prisoner. Leinster, the first province to have been conquered, was by the end of the century almost wholly in the control of the O'Byrnes and O'Tooles, except for the castles of Wicklow and Newcastle, and MacMurrough Kavanagh had a kingdom of Leinster worthy of the name. From 1372, the Dublin treasury paid him black rent of eighty marks a year to refrain from raiding within the Pale. Throughout the period since the Normans' arrival, the Irish had maintained the ancient inheritance system of the *derbfine*. While numerous Anglo-Norman estates were lost due to the ruling family line dying out, there was far less likelihood of that happening among the Irish. Furthermore, their system normally produced the most able – or at least the most ruthless and energetic – of the eligible kindred as king. However, the old system was in steady decline. The primogeniture method of the Normans became more and more attractive to chiefs; and the installation of a *tanaiste* until the chief's eldest son should come of age became common. Only in the absence of a suitable son could the old system be fully brought into action.

Among the Anglo-Normans, absenteeism of lords, a decline in numbers, and attrition of territory by the Irish, all served to bolster the positions of their greatest magnates. The Earl of Kildare and the Earl of Ormond controlled most of the old Fitzgerald and Butler territory. In Connacht, the de Burghs, though their name was now iricised into Burke, still ruled. But the extent of Irish reconquest was so widespread that a royal expedition was mounted in October 1394, when King Richard II arrived at Waterford with a large army, and the intention of regaining the lost lands, and restoring and regranting them to English lords.

RICHARD II

As on previous royal incursions, the presence of the English king seemed to work wonders. Richard spent Christmas in Dublin Castle and during his stay, which lasted until May of the following year, he received the submission of virtually every lord, chief or king. This was accomplished without warfare, with the major exception of heavy onslaughts on Art Oge MacMurrough, King of Leinster, made by an English force under the Earl Marshal, who had inherited a personal interest in Carlow. Art submitted in January 1395, binding himself to quit the land of Leinster with his vassals and fighting men. The others agreed to leave the land they had taken from the English. Among them was the King of Tír Eógain, whose ancestor had ignored Henry II. The credit for this relatively bloodless outcome lies with the Gaelic-speaking Earl of Ormond and with leading churchmen, such as John Colton, Archbishop of Armagh, who did a great deal to win over the Gaelic leaders. Throughout this period, there was no doubt that the Church sided with the Crown of England, in line with the papacy, against the 'Irish enemies'. A more subtle and intelligent king than most of his predecessors, Richard responded to the universal homage by admitting the kings' and chiefs' legal possession of the lands they had always

111

IRISH DRESS

THE costume of the native Irish was one of the things banned from the Pale in the Statutes of Kilkenny. There was nothing particularly 'Celtic' about their garb, and general modes of dress had changed more than once since pre-Viking times. In 1366 the English were taking exception to such things as the Irish male hair-style, which shaved the front of the head but let the hair grow long at the back; the Irish also grew moustaches and beards, whilst Englishmen tended to be clean-shaven. Both sexes wore thick 'rugg mantles' and most people normally used them as a coverlet at night as well. Men wore the Irish shirt, a long one which could be hitched up at the waist, and might often have been worn on its own, though tight woollen trews were usually worn. Irish clothes tended to be longer and more widely sleeved than the English ones – a wealthy Irish person dressed in the Irish style might well look more interesting,

Irish peasant dress, fifteenth century

indeed glamorous, in these flowing wool and linen garments, than the other inhabitants of the Pale. In the 1560s, the English topographer William Camden recorded that 'Most of the Irish go bare-headed . . . their hair flowing in long, curled locks, which they highly delight in, and are affronted at having pulled. They wear very wide linen shirts with wider sleeves and reaching down to their knees, and dyed saffron colour. They have very short woollen jackets, plain and very close breeches, and over all mantles of shaggy rugs.'

> The lack of a recognisably Celtic aspect to Irish dress troubled the aristocratic–antiquarian members of the Pan-Celtic cultural congresses which met regularly in different cities of the 'Celtic fringe' during the nineteenth century, and some of them sought to devise one, hence the saffron-coloured kilt that is sometimes worn by men or boys, usually in the context of a dancing *feis* (festival).

held. He made a distinction between 'Irish enemies', those who refused submission to England, and 'Irish rebels' whose disaffection could be cured and who might become like the 'obedient English' of the Pale. But the Statutes of Kilkenny remained in place. He left Ireland on 15 May 1395, well satisfied with his campaign. But it had in real terms resolved little or nothing. MacMurrough remained in Leinster, and no one had the power to remove him. Having sworn their fealty, the other kings and chiefs returned to pursue their former avocations. None of them restored territory to the Anglo-Normans.

The king's Lieutenant, Roger Mortimer, Earl of March, heir presumptive to the childless Richard II, had the task of implementing the dispositions made by Richard. He was struck down in the battle of Kellistown, Co. Carlow, fighting the men of Leinster. Richard II returned to Ireland in June 1399, intending to deal with Art MacMurrough, but by August events in his kingdom of England drew him back to where deposition and an obscure death awaited him.

GAELIC RESURGENCE

The dynastic wars in England between the houses of York and Lancaster distracted the English kings from many other issues, including that of Ireland. For most of the fourteenth century, events in Ireland were determined from within. It was an era of continued Gaelic resurgence, until fully two-thirds of the country was again under the rule of Irish kings and chiefs. Within the Pale, the Norman French speech of the original settlers gave way increasingly to English. Successive Lieutenants, some of them men of prowess and distinction like John Talbot, later to be Earl of Shrewsbury, were restricted in their actions by lack of finance and fighting men. The Irish leaders and the lords of the march were quite happy to affirm their homage when required to do so, but without making any concessions.

In such conditions, energetic men with a strong family power base could readily extend that power. From 1425 the earldom of Ulster was a title of Richard, Duke of York, as was the lordship of Connacht. But the real Lord of Ulster was Eógain O'Neill, inaugurated as its king in 1432; and in Connacht

Art Oge MacMurrough talking to officers of King Richard II about his
refusal to submit to the English King

the O'Connors had returned to virtual kingship, though it was split between the lines of O'Connor Don and O'Connor Roe. Leinster was ruled by the descendants of Art Oge MacMurrough, who had died undefeated in 1418. The far north-west was still a stronghold of the O'Donnells, and many lesser chiefs maintained their courts. Their Gaelic culture was strengthened by the sense of independence, and it was an era of classic scholarship and minstrelsy.

The great earldoms beyond the Pale had acquired a Gaelic tinge. Although the earls themselves chose Anglo-Norman or English brides, many of their junior kinsmen and followers took Irish wives, and, with far more Irish than English-speaking subjects, the leaders became Gaelic speakers and sometimes, like Gerald, third Earl of Desmond, Gaelic poets in their own right. They maintained their links with the king's Lieutenant, or Deputy, in Dublin, and with the faction-torn nobility of England. But the Geraldine earls of Desmond and Kildare, and the Butler Earl of Ormond, had their families, fortunes and future invested in Ireland. With their leading tenants and affiliated knights and small landowners, they were a strong though not united group. Among them a proud 'Old English' identity was retained. In the borderlands and debatable areas, a more mingled collection of local lords and chieftains, part Irish, part 'degenerate English', ruled over territories that sometimes were of considerable size. They did not possess the prestige either of the dynastic kings or of the Anglo-Norman earls, but in combination (rare and transient as this might be) they were a powerful grouping. Every ruler kept his band of fighting men, professional warriors who lived together or were quartered on the unwilling but hapless tenantry. Small towns and isolated abbeys with such gangs in the hills behind had to pay regular black rent to ensure their own security.

RICHARD, DUKE OF YORK

In 1449 a new Lieutenant arrived in Dublin, Richard Duke of York. Himself a great lord of Ireland by inheritance, his chief interest was to make the country into a strong base for his own side in its long dispute with the house of Lancaster. In this he was highly successful, despite the identification of the Butlers with Lancaster, which served to heighten the Yorkist enthusiasm of the Geraldines. Even when he was placed under attainder by the English parliament, and came to Ireland for his own safety, the Dublin parliament confirmed his position as Lieutenant in open defiance of Whitehall. In 1460, this brought the parliament to the position of declaring its supremacy within the country, and affirming that laws of the realm of England were not valid until 'held, admitted, accepted, affirmed and proclaimed' by the Irish parliament. Although this was simply a legal necessity to legitimise what they were doing

115

on behalf of the Duke of York, it marks an important change of attitude on the part of the lords, bishops and merchant burghers of the Pale and the feudal domains. Even for them, Ireland's interests could no longer be automatically aligned with England's.

The Yorkist victory of 1461 in England, and the accession of Richard's son as Edward IV, did not put an end to the struggle. The pro-Lancastrian Earl of Ormond was executed, but his brother Sir John Butler, claiming the earldom, invaded at Waterford with an English army in 1462. The whole south-east seemed likely to rise in rebellion, but at the battle of Pilltown, Butler was defeated by the army of the king's Deputy, the Earl of Desmond.

THE EARLS OF KILDARE

From this point, the dominance of the Geraldines was complete. The king's lieutenancy was nominally exercised for some time by the Duke of Clarence before he was executed (1478), but power was in the hands of the Earl of Desmond, and later the Earl of Kildare. Already by 1462 the fourth Earl of Desmond had established what was hardly less than an Anglo-Irish kingdom stretching from Waterford to Limerick, and in which Irish and English law operated, and the Statutes of Kilkenny were generally ignored. The O'Briens and the MacCarthy Mores were subordinate rulers to the earl. Thomas, fifth earl, maintained the style and strength of his father, to such a degree that serious alarm was caused in London. Although there is no evidence that he sought kingship, the degree to which power was becoming centred in Ireland troubled Edward IV as much as it had Henry II. Protests came from the Pale about Irish practices being forced on the inhabitants. In 1466 the Deputy was temporarily captured by the O'Connors of Offaly, after a skirmish, to the detriment of his authority and reputation. In 1467, a new Lieutenant, the Earl of Worcester, a man of culture but also a hard-boiled enforcer of the royal will, was sent across, with a firm commission to restore the status of the Crown. He called parliaments in Dublin and Drogheda to enforce this, and his position was strong enough to attaint the two Fitzgerald earls, Desmond and Kildare, for treason, and specifically for their 'alliance, fosterage, and alterage with the Irish enemies of the King'. Desmond was summarily beheaded; Kildare, released in the furore following the execution, later obtained a pardon. The shock of this judicial murder was great and pushed the Desmond earldom into opposition to England. But it was a brief disruption, before Worcester returned to England and 'home rule' resumed. Thomas, Earl of Kildare, was elected Deputy by the Irish Council in 1470. For more than sixty years the earls of Kildare would be effective rulers of Ireland.

Following his father's death, from 1478 to 1513 this rule was exercised by the eighth earl, Garret More Fitzgerald. By this time even the earls and their closest relatives were making Irish marriages, though careful to legitimise these by special acts of parliament, as with that of Garret More's sister to the son of the ruling O'Neill in 1480. Such marriages were usually political in purpose, and this one in particular made a bond between Kildare and the greatest family of the north. Firm alliance was also made with the O'Donnells under the long-lived Red Hugh O'Donnell. Opposition remained in the earldom of Ormond, cared for by James MacRichard on behalf of his Butler kinsman, the absentee earl.

With the seizure of the throne of England by Henry Tudor in 1485, the wars of the Roses came to an end, though this was far from being obvious at the time. In the early years of Henry VII's reign, the 'Great Earl' was left undisturbed in his complete dominance of the Irish parliament and of events in Ireland. There were extraordinary events in 1486–87, when the pretender Lambert Simnel, believed by many to be the rightful claimant to the throne, was crowned as King Edward VI of England and Ireland, at St Mary's Church in Dublin, with the full backing of the Earl and the Irish parliament. This was followed by an Anglo-Irish invasion of England, supported by German mercenaries, later in 1487. It failed to put Simnel on the throne, being routed by Henry's forces on 16 June 1487. But Henry had no choice but to give his disloyal Deputy a full pardon. Irish support was given in 1491 and again in 1495 to another pretender, Perkin Warbeck, who claimed to be the younger son of King Edward IV, though Kildare was more circumspect this time. At length Henry VII felt able to challenge the power of the Great Earl, and in October 1494 sent over a new Deputy, Sir John Poynings. Backed by a thousand soldiers with muskets (firearms were still a novelty and relatively rare in Ireland), Poynings' task was to reinstate English control. Poynings relieved the siege of Waterford being mounted by the Earl of Desmond, on behalf of Perkin Warbeck, and appointed English 'new men' as Chancellor and Treasurer and in other key posts. He summoned a parliament which was carefully packed with his, rather than Kildare's, clients and supporters, and the earl was charged with treason, and sent to London as a prisoner. 'Poynings' Parliament' formally annulled the acts of the parliament of 1460, and restored the supremacy of Westminster over Dublin. A new law, named after the Deputy, provided that no parliament should be summoned in Ireland until its purposes were approved by the English king and his council, and that no acts of the Irish parliament would be valid until licensed under the Great Seal of England.

Poynings' fourteen months in Ireland were a whirlwind of activity, intended to fortify the boundary of the Pale, to restore the royal revenues (sunk to virtually nothing) and to re-enact and enforce the Statutes of Kilkenny. With his departure in January 1496, these dispositions relapsed. But the Irish parliament remained neutered. With a stable monarchy now in England, not even the Great Earl could safely rewrite Poynings' Law. Nevertheless, Kildare was sent back to resume his dominance. In a famous phrase, Henry VII is said to have said: 'Since all Ireland cannot rule this man, this man must rule all Ireland.' This Kildare proceeded to do. Though he refrained from further interference in royal politics and remained a faithful subject of the Tudor king, he was effectively dictator of Ireland. Inevitably there was opposition, and not only from the eclipsed Butlers. Despite having made a political marriage to Kildare's daughter, Ulick Burke of Clanricard set himself up in opposition and made alliances with other chiefs of the west and Ormond. In a pitched battle at Cnoc Tuagh, near Galway, on 15 August 1494, Kildare won a complete victory.

Kildare has often been described as 'king in all but name' and his policy after 1496 has been much brooded over. If he had been able to engineer a Yorkist return to the English throne, an Irish kingship might have been his price. But a realistic assessment of England's long involvement with Ireland might have brought him to conclude that the strongest power in the British Isles, having seen off the last attempt at Welsh independence earlier in the century, and permanently irked by the independence of Scotland, would be unlikely to cede its claim to supreme control over Ireland. Poynings' Law was a significant indicator of this attitude. Garrett More had been in London, both as a prisoner and an honoured guest, and knew the English government better than most of his contemporaries. Even though he had a son admirably qualified to succeed him, he did not attempt the ultimate but possibly fatal step. His semi-independence remained like that of the Percys in Northumberland, a consequence of his remoteness from the seat of power, tolerated by the government because there was no better alternative. There was a revealing episode in 1478, when Richard III was forced to recall his designated justiciar, Lord Grey, since Kildare, holder of the office, refused to relinquish it. English governments rarely took such rebuffs lying down, but Kildare got away with it, as he did with much else.

TRADE AND CULTURE

With the large exception of the Burke rebellion, and for all the constant raiding and sieges caused by rivalries and feuds among chiefs, each with an army of sorts, the period of the 'Geraldine supremacy' was one of relative peace. The economic history of Ireland at this time is hard to trace. Parliament, with its effective remit restricted to the four counties of Dublin, Louth, Meath and Wicklow, was in no position to pass acts governing the trade of ports and places beyond its jurisdiction, nor was the Treasurer likely to collect customs dues from ports other than those of the Pale. Maritime piracy and landward cattle raids accounted for a substantial part of the economy of the Gaelic west. But by the late fifteenth century, European trade was extensive, both along the North Sea coasts and down towards the Mediterranean. In the middle of the century, the Fitzgerald earls were in communication with the banking and mercantile centre of Florence. Although Irish access to the North Sea trade was hampered by geography, there was no such constraint with regard to western France, Spain and the gates of the Mediterranean. After the terrible batterings of the fourteenth century, the fifteenth saw steady economic growth and an increase in population. Plague was still a recurrent threat, but not with the wholesale deaths of its first onslaughts. More ground was taken into cultivation. There was much new building and enlarging of old buildings.

Europe was experiencing the effects of the Renaissance, the rediscovery and re-interpretation of the classical past. There was a consciously modernising element in life, that showed itself in social behaviour, manners and customs as well as in the sciences and the arts. In Ireland, where the Gaelic language was dominant and indeed had increased in usage through the fifteenth century, an older civilisation was still vigorously entrenched. With Galloway and the Highlands and Islands of Scotland also, there was a large enclave of Gaelic culture. But it was in many ways an embattled one. Confident and proud as it was, it had long been inward-looking, when not on the defensive. Despite its long tradition, and high achievement in medicine, the oral arts and music, no one beyond the Celtic world took any interest in Celtic culture. And its tradition of knowledge, scholarship and poetry was a conservative one, not receptive to new ideas. The Celtic world had nothing to contribute to the climate of inquiry and experiment that was arising in renaissance Europe. This might be regretted as a loss, but it also reflects the remarkable still-enduring self-centred continuity of Irish life. The Renaissance did not wholly pass Ireland by, but its impact was limited, both on individuals and on certain aspects of life. When the Earl of Kildare endowed a library at Maynooth, he was doing what a great renaissance lord might well do. But he was also, probably quite consciously, following in a domestic tradition going back to Brian Bóruma.

The chief practitioner-guardians of this traditional culture were the bards. A bardic education and vocation were not things of chance. Bardic schools existed throughout the country and attracted students from Scotland also. The role of a bard was clear – to praise where it was due and to satirise likewise. The forms in use were traditional and few bards sought to change them. Most were content to rake through a capacious memory-stock of phrases, comparisons, names and events, in order to put together new verses for a patron's son's wedding, or successful raid, or other happening. They were normally well-rewarded. Satire was reserved for the patron's enemies, or for a niggardly donor. Often, the praise and the satire alike were skin-deep. The bards, long-haired, unctuous, jealous of their status, were often criticised for greed and were abhorred by the unadapted English as crude flatterers who sang for their supper. But they were appreciated as part of the fabric of a living and still vibrant society and their mystique was faithfully upheld: everybody knew that in 1414 Niall O'Higgins had killed the Englishman Sir John Stanley with a curse. The bards sang in the chiefs' halls of the deeds of legendary ancestors and planted none-too-subtle hints about the renewal of an Irish kingship and the ousting of strangers. The chiefs themselves, no longer calling themselves kings, had a more realistic assessment of the situation. But the bards served to maintain pride, spirit and, not least, the old concept of loyalty to the chief as head of the kindred. Their role was perhaps enhanced by the fact that the Church, at least in the persons of its prelates, was not aligned with the Gaelic Irish but with the Anglo-Irish and the residents of the Pale. Most of the Church's work among the people was done by Observantine friars rather than parish priests.

CONTINUED AUTHORITY OF THE KILDARES

The Great Earl travelled widely and made his presence known and felt throughout the country. As James Lydon points out in *The Making of Ireland*, Kildare's protection was not available free of charge. He derived a substantial income in protection money from the Irish chiefs whose lands were next to the Pale and even from individual religious houses. His rates went up when he held the post of Deputy. The remoter chieftains were less tractable and the O'Brien chief in particular, outside the web of marriage-relationships woven by Kildare, ruled Thomond as a separate enclave, even building his own bridge over the Shannon to avoid the tolls levied by the royal city of Limerick. But it was in a minor confrontation, with O' More of Leix in 1511, that Kildare received the musket wound that brought his death nearly two years later.

Young Gerald, 'Garret Oge', picked up the reins of government and was confirmed as Deputy. There had been a new king in London since 1509, Henry VIII, no stranger to Garret Oge, who had grown up at the English court. The new earl pursued the same approach that his father had so successfully followed, maintaining the Geraldine network of alliances, protection, extortion, rewards and raids. But the monarch was a very different one to Henry VII – a personality bursting with inner contradictions and characterised by a steadily increasing megalomania. The Tudor kings had an efficient information network, but aside from that, the Anglo-Irish subjects of the king were never slow to complain and protest about what was done by his Deputy. Kildare was summoned to London in 1519 to join in discussions on the troubled state of Ireland; and in 1520 a new Lieutenant was sent over, the Earl of Surrey, who had routed the Scots at Flodden in 1513. With insufficient men and money to face down the earls and chiefs, Surrey could do little, and was withdrawn in 1521. But in a pessimistic but realistic report to the king, he outlined the possibility of building new towns in Ireland and settling them with loyal colonists. The idea was not pursued, but nor was it lost sight of. Garret Oge was reinstated as Deputy, with his enemy Piers Butler, Earl of Ossory, as Treasurer: an effort to maintain balance that was doomed to failure. Geraldine and Butler factions fought in the streets of Dublin and across the countryside. As before, it became clear to London that however great the problems of Ireland with the Earl of Kildare in charge, they were a great deal worse when he was not. In 1532, Garrett Oge was still Deputy, with all his father's powers. But the years of wrangling and strife also underlined that he could not impose the desired peace, obedience and loyalty upon the population. And his ability to exercise his powers was restricted by a hostile council, whose leaders included the Archbishop and the Treasurer, both surnamed Alen, which was assiduous in sending back reports which maximised the Deputy's failures, shortcomings and misdeeds.

THE REFORMATION AND THE DOWNFALL OF THE KILDARES

In the decade before 1532, the Church in northern Europe was riven by the protests and teachings of Martin Luther and his followers. Sweden, Denmark, Switzerland and parts of Germany had broken with Rome and accepted Luther's Reformed Church. For decades before that, in Bohemia, the Netherlands, England and Scotland, Hussites and Lollards had attacked the corrupt state of the Church and advocated religious freedom. Ireland seemed remote from such advanced and heretical preachings. No one was excited by them; no heretics were burned or thrown from bridges. To the Pope and the papal government, Ireland had a dual status. It was a province with its own Primate and a long if often idiosyncratic history of adherence to the Catholic faith. But politically, it was a dominion of England. In the long power game played among Pope, Holy Roman Emperor, the most powerful monarchs of Europe, and the smaller states, the papacy had never even considered the possibility of treating Ireland as a separate political entity. Its status as a province of the Church was due to its history and not to any constitutional significance.

The Protestant movement in England became a royal cause when Henry VIII failed to reach agreement with the Pope in his wish to divorce his queen, Katherine of Aragon, and marry his mistress, Anne Boleyn. Like many other leading families, hers had Irish connections, in their case with the Butlers. After a long period in eclipse, that family's time was coming. The English Parliament of 1529 began the final breach between the English Church and Rome; by 1533 Henry was married to Anne Boleyn and had been excommunicated by Pope Clement VII. In 1534 Henry was proclaimed supreme head of the Church of England.

In February of that same year, Kildare was called to London. He was already a sick man, suffering the after-effects of a wound, as his father had done. Naming his son, Lord Offaly, known as 'Silken Thomas', as his deputy, he obeyed the summons. In London he was charged with the many offences listed by his detractors, and was denied leave to return. Sir William Skeffington was named Deputy in Ireland. The tide was turning against the Geraldines. Thomas learned that Skeffington – who had briefly been Deputy in 1530 before being undermined by Garret Oge – was commissioned to arrest himself and a number of his relatives and send them to England for execution. Perhaps prompted by a message from his father, for whom it would have been a normal reaction, Thomas declared open rebellion, in dramatic fashion, on 11 June, before the Irish Council. Thomas's declaration was not however the measured one that his forebears might have made. He denounced Henry as a heretic, and appealed to Irishmen to abandon their loyalty to the king. It was proclaimed that all Englishmen should leave Ireland on pain of death: this justified his supporters in killing Alen, the Archbishop of Dublin. Implicit in Thomas's stance was that Ireland was a domain of the King of England only as a fief granted by the Pope, and so, with Henry excommunicated, his right to Ireland was gone. This constitutional point went for nothing. In October Skeffington arrived with a large force and speedily took possession of Dublin.

In December, Garret Oge Fitzgerald, by now a state prisoner in the Tower of London, died. Now the Earl of Kildare, Thomas strove in vain to enlist other Irish magnates, or the Pope, or the Holy Roman Emperor, in his cause. With a royal army in the country, well-equipped with cannon and under a determined governor, the prudent baron or chieftain kept his head down and sent polite messages to Dublin and London. In March 1535 the Geraldine stronghold of Maynooth was captured; its surviving defenders slaughtered despite having surrendered, in what became known as 'the pardon of Maynooth'. By August, Silken Thomas's rebellion was finished. He surrendered, was sent as a prisoner to London, and after an interval to allow Irish passions to cool, he was hanged there, with five uncles, in February 1537.

CHAPTER EIGHT

Ireland's Elizabethan Wars

IRELAND UNDER HENRY VIII

THE Irish parliament met in May 1536 and confirmed that Henry VIII was 'Supreme Head in earth of the whole Church of Ireland'. Already, letters had been issued to authorise the suppression of certain convents. The parliament was a 'packed' one full of royal supporters; the new Archbishop of Dublin, Browne, had been sent to enforce the royal intention. Henry's reforms were designed to benefit both king and the state (with which he identified himself) and did not affect the doctrines or rituals of the Church. This may have eased matters for the bishops, who did not oppose the measure. The only clergy who did were the proctors representing the junior clerics in parliament: their parliamentary role was abolished. Nevertheless, people were disturbed by such evidence of Protestant zealousness as Archbishop Browne's destruction of a venerated relic, the 'Baculum Jesu' believed to have been St Patrick's crozier. Silken Thomas's appeal suggests that Henry's action was a source of grave concern to many people, but his rebellion was too obviously in the Geraldine interest for the attachment to it of the Church's cause to carry much weight. The other arm of Henry's policy, the dissolution of the monasteries, was accomplished at first only in the Pale and in English-controlled lordships. In Gaelic Ireland, the monasteries continued for a long time, some into the next century. But monasticism was by this time a shadow of its former self. The numbers of monks and nuns were small. Most abbeys were already effectively in the hands of laymen, commendators who siphoned off most of the income and paid a prior to maintain the religious life of the place. Anxiety about the future of the monasteries was most keenly expressed by the lords who feared that their profitable control might be taken away.

THE GERALDINE LEAGUE

Leadership among the 'Old English' was now exercised by Piers Butler, Earl of Ossory, while council and parliament were dominated by a group of 'new English' who were determined to seize the opportunity to reverse the steady diminution of colonial rule. Old laws were dusted off and re-enforced, including the statutes banning English–Irish marriage and fostering, the wearing of

Irish dress and the use of the Irish language. Ossory was not allowed to become another Kildare, however; although he made himself useful to the Tudor government, official policy was to keep the lieutenancy in English hands. The intention to push out the boundaries of English rule was plain to the Irish leaders. They responded by forming the 'Geraldine League', ostensibly for the protection of the sole surviving heir of the Kildares, a boy in his early teens, half-brother to Silken Thomas. In 1540, this young Gerald Fitzgerald was sent for safety to Florence. The League, organised by Manus O'Donnell of Donegal, united Irish lordships from south to north, including the Earl of Desmond and Conn O'Neill. Although they disposed of large forces, these were no match for the efficient regular troops commanded by Lord Grey, and after him Sir Anthony St Leger. A raid into the Pale by O'Neill in 1539 was pursued and defeated at Bellahoe. Grey's campaigns took him west as far as Galway and north as far as Dungannon and caused serious alarm among the leaders of the League. Various solutions were canvassed, including the offer of the Irish crown to King James V of Scotland, and leaders such as O'Neill made direct representations to Henry. Grey was removed in 1540, and his successor, St Leger, after an exemplary campaign in Leinster which obtained the submission of MacMurrough (ending their long kingship), O'More and O'Connor, followed a more constructive policy.

The formation and stability of the Geraldine League had shown that the Irish lordships could not be picked off one by one, and the existence of the Geraldine heir portended future trouble. The Tudor government had to find another solution than military suppression. At the same time, it was finding deep-seated resistance in Ireland to the Church of England's programme for the reform of worship. This hostility was plain at all levels of society, and was one of the elements that cemented the League. Strategic considerations also preoccupied the government. England and Ireland were placed between Catholic France and Spain, and still-Catholic Scotland. Ireland had to be secured against possible use as an invasion-base against England. For those opposed to him, Henry's claim on Ireland was an illegal one: if his predecessor Henry II had secured his claim to Ireland as a papal fief, then Henry Tudor had lost his right to it.

THE POLITICS OF CONTROL

With St Leger as its chief architect, a radical policy was implemented. As part of it, Henry VIII was unanimously proclaimed by the Irish parliament as King of Ireland, on 18 June 1541. Sovereignty was confirmed, on a hereditary basis, though not as a separate kingdom, but 'of this land of Ireland as united, annexed, and knit for ever to the Imperial crown of the realm of England'. Still,

Ireland now had a king, though he did not find it necessary to come and be crowned. The status of the inhabitants, whether English or Irish, changed. No longer were the Gaelic Irish beyond the law. Gaelic, formerly forbidden in the Pale, was used by the Earl of Ormond in the House of Lords to explain the proceedings to Irish and Anglo-Irish lords who had no English. But the general policy against Irish dress, speech, law and custom was maintained.

The presence of Irish chiefs at this parliament, and of others at specially convened sessions held at Limerick and Trim, bore witness to the success of another of St Leger's policies. This was the 'surrender and regrant' of lordships. By freely surrendering their traditional estates and possessions, the lords could receive them again from the king, in return for acknowledging him as lord. It was intended that this should be accompanied by the active anglicisation of the Irish nobility. The dream was of an Ireland where English-speaking earls and lords ruled their estates according to English law, lived according to English custom, attended parliament, and preserved the commonwealth as loyal subjects of the king. In its early years, this policy appeared to be working well. In an unprecedented way, Irish lords whose forefathers had been 'captains of their nations' and kings, took the oath, and accepted the role of parliament and council in managing the affairs of the country. The Earl of Desmond was reconciled to the Crown, and O'Neill (made Earl of Tyrone),

The Castle of Trim

125

O'Brien (made Earl of Thomond), O'Connor and Burke were among the chiefs who complied.

The period of harmony was brief. Too many tensions remained between the different groups of leaders. Too much history of strife and mutual contempt had piled up. A strong Lieutenant, with goodwill to and from both sides, might have been able to maintain the climate of reconciliation, but St Leger was succeeded by Sir Edward Bellingham, sent over by the 'Protector' Duke of Somerset on behalf of the young King Edward VI (Henry VIII had died in 1547). There was rebellion in the Irish lordships of Leix and Offaly, put down by Bellingham, who sent the O'Connor and O'More chiefs as prisoners to London. Somerset was an active supporter of Protestant reform, but it was becoming ever more clear that there was virtually no appetite for this in Ireland. The Archbishop of Armagh led the churchmen in opposition to his colleague in Dublin. A small but vocal group of New English in the council, led by the vice-treasurer, Sir William Brabazon, was keen both for church reform to be pushed through, and for a return to a more coercive policy within Ireland. Such views found a ready response from the Somerset government, and even when St Leger was reinstated, he found himself presiding over a disintegration of Irish and English interests, and also obliged to maintain the aggressive policy towards the Irish which had been instigated by his predecessor.

The situation which had seemed so promising in 1541 was now sliding into chaos. The Irish leaders, seeing the O'More and O'Connor lands under grant to new English tenants, were once again concerned for their traditional rights and status, though nothing as strong as the Geraldine League arose. The 'surrender and regrant' policy was abandoned. It had not gone down well in the Irish lordships, where the lawmen, bards and other upholders of traditional practice were scornfully critical of the new earldoms accepted by chiefs of ancient lineage. Of course there was an element of job-preservation present in the brehons' attitudes, but it did not go unnoticed that the landowning status of an English-created earl was different to that of an Irish king or chief. It was personal, and hereditary by primogeniture – quite different to the trusteeship of the Irish ruler in lands which had once been those of the *tuath*.

A CATHOLIC INTERLUDE

In 1553 Henry VIII's elder daughter, Mary, became queen, the first ruling queen of Ireland. Mary had remained a member of the Catholic faith and her accession saw a return to Catholic forms of worship. Archbishop Dowdall of Armagh, who had exiled himself in Europe, returned to Armagh, and the Protestant Browne was deprived of the see of Dublin. At this time Gerald, the new Earl of Kildare, was allowed to return, but the white hope of the Geraldine

League was to prove an inoffensive subject of the English Crown. A return to Catholic practice did not mean a change in other attitudes, and in 1556 the Earl of Sussex was appointed Lord Lieutenant. The counties of Leix and Offaly were declared Crown lands, renamed as King's and Queen's counties, and two-thirds of their territory, on the eastern side, was made open to 'English subjects born either in England or Ireland'. The inevitable result was warfare between the resident Irish and the government-backed incomers. Although the government had cleared its path legally, it found enforcement another matter, particularly as the size of holdings, and their boundaries, were hard to define. Faced with this messy situation, the architects of 'plantation' as a policy did not give up, but they revised their methods.

ELIZABETHAN IRELAND

The resumption of Catholic worship came to an end in 1558 when Mary Tudor died and was succeeded by her half-sister, Elizabeth. A parliament of 1560 confirmed the new queen as Supreme Head of the Church, and an Act of Uniformity required the use of the new *Book of Common Prayer* by all the clergy. Non-attendance at the official Church was punishable by a fine. But in the course of Elizabeth's reign, a substantial degree of toleration was given to those who did not attend, or who balked at acknowledging a secular ruler (and a woman at that) as head of the Church.

Elizabethan England was an aggressive, dynamic, mercantile society, one of the strongest Protestant powers of Europe, with a piratical attitude to other countries' possessions and a fiercely acquisitive approach to unclaimed or contestable ground. By now, England had been forced out of its last continental possession, Calais, and, as it faced the superpowers of the time in Spain and France, a new and belligerent spirit of nationalism was evident. To the royal government, Ireland was full of running sores. In north-east Ulster, Macdonalds and Macdonnells lived as part of a semi-independent Hebridean–Irish set of lordships that took little account of Edinburgh or Dublin and none at all of London. Large numbers of Scots had settled on the Irish side, and pursued their avocation of mercenary soldiers for any chieftain who cared to hire them. The efforts to plant settlers in the midlands had produced endemic warfare. The population as a whole was resistant to Protestant reform, as were most of the clergy. Many of the Irish lords were in a state of actual or potential rebellion; and as government spies duly reported, were seeking help in France and Spain to drive the English out. The Anglo-Irish lords were another suspect group, most of them Catholic, most of them reliant on the loyalty and service of Irish tenants and soldiers, most of them embroiled by marriage ties with the Gaelic 'Irish enemy'.

127

THE MAC-AN-IARLAS

THE *Mac-an-Iarlas*, or sons of the earl, were the brothers Ulick and John Burke, sons of the Earl of Clanricard in the 1560s and 70s. Their father was not a man of action, but the sons were prominent in the opposition to the English presidency of Connacht. By now their family, originally de Burgh, was quite Gaelicised, and it was the privileges and style of the Gaelic aristocracy that they fought to maintain. Returning from Dublin in 1576, having made submission to the government, they did not wait until they were out of sight of Athlone Castle before they 'shook off their English clothes in the Shannon and resumed Irish dress'. In that year they attacked Athenry, and, as the Lord Deputy Sidney reported, 'In this town was the sepulture of their fathers and their mother was also buried there; the chief church of which town they most violently burned, and Ulick, being besought to spare the burning where his mother's bones lay, blasphemously swore that if she were alive and in it he would burn the church and her too rather than any English churl should inhabit or fortify there.'

But there were also opportunities. The island was large, fertile, potentially rich. If controlled by loyal English lords, with a loyal English tenantry, then there would be a happy state. The lords would be rich, their tenants prosperous, and the strategic threat would be neutralised by a loyal militia which could cope with any invasion from Europe. Not least, a massive drain on the English treasury would be stopped. As previous English governments had discovered, the cost of maintaining an army in Ireland was immense, much too great to be borne by the government's Irish revenues or even by taxing the ever-protesting inhabitants of the Pale, most of whom were in favour of a military solution but had no wish to pay large taxes to support it.

During the latter half of the sixteenth century, the English government, through its representatives and potential beneficiaries, set out to complete what the Normans had begun four hundred years before. There was even a degree of the same method of 'if you can conquer it, it's yours', as when Sir Nicholas Bagenal was granted the lordship of Mourne and Newry Abbey. But a much tighter central control was exercised, and newer methods were also employed. It had also to be borne in mind that in the kingdom of Ireland, all were now subjects under the law. But once it had been established that the landholder was guilty of treason to the Crown, it was possible to procure a jury to declare the lands forfeited. An Act of parliament could then ratify the decision, and the confiscated territory could then be re-tenanted by suitable people. The 'native' population could be expelled to resettle themselves else-where, in areas not under English control.

A NEW SCHEME FOR CONTROL

Under the lieutenancy of Sir Henry Sidney, from 1566 to 1571, the military effort was stepped up. A new defender of Irish liberty had risen to prominence, in the person of Shane O'Neill, son of Conn Bacach who had accepted the earldom of Tyrone. Conn had died in 1559 but the government balked at rec-ognising Shane and awarded the earldom to his nephew. O'Neill disputed this both through legal process and by force of arms, though his true ambition was to be recognised as Earl of Ulster. His remark to government envoys, 'My ancestors were kings of Ulster and Ulster is mine and shall be mine,' was perhaps the first of many ringing and unequivocal phrases to come from that province, and O'Neill fought for supremacy over the O'Donnells and the Scots of Antrim, defeating the latter at Glenshesk in 1565. Sidney invaded O'Neill's country, but O'Neill was killed in 1567 by the Antrim Scots, following his defeat in battle with the O'Donnells. He was succeeded by the equally inde-pendent-minded Turloch Luineach, and for a time the government left Ulster to its own affairs. Sidney had a programme for administration as well as for conquest, and began to put this into effect by installing provincial 'presiden-cies' in Munster and Connacht. The presidents and their councils were intended to introduce civil government. There was some success in Connacht, where new shires were created and by 1577 a new system of annual rent was agreed, replacing all former exactions, obligations and taxes imposed by lord or government. Sidney's aim was to reduce the authority and military power of regional and local warlords. In Munster, though MacCarthy More abandoned his kingship to become Earl of Clancarty, the attempt to establish a presidency collapsed, partly under pressure of the continuing Desmond–Ormond hostil-ity, and partly because of the activities of incoming 'planters'.

The long tradition of the absentee landowner received a sharp twist with the arrival of the English Sir Peter Carew, from Devon, who appeared in Munster with the claim of being heir to Fitzstephen and the original Carews of Ireland. This was harking a very long way back. Carew's claim, covering most of Carlow and large extents of the old MacCarthy kingdom, was accepted despite the protests of Kavanagh and Butler, who currently held most of the disputed ground. Carew was the most successful of a band of 'gentleman adventurers' who arrived in Ireland around this time, among them Sir Walter Raleigh and Sir Humphrey Gilbert.

The Earl of Desmond was imprisoned in London in 1567, on suspicion of treason. The following year, his kinsman, James Fitzmaurice Fitzgerald, was elected Captain of the Geraldines, and took up arms, ostensibly to safeguard the earl's rights. He was joined by Sir Edmund Butler, who was still enraged about the Carew judgement. The upstarts proved to be as ready as the old Normans to defend their gains, and the revolt was put down without mercy. The wholesale killing of surrendering garrisons, which had provoked immense outrage at Maynooth, was by this time an almost routine feature of warfare. Fitzmaurice fled to Europe.

THE CROWN AND THE CATHOLICS

In 1570, Queen Elizabeth was formally excommunicated. Up until then, the papacy had maintained her rights; now once again there was a difficult clash of allegiances for the Catholic Irish and Anglo-Irish. To Catholic Europe, the true queen should be Elizabeth's distant cousin, Mary I of Scotland (who had fled her own country and was an English prisoner). A sense of profound unrest spread through the Anglo-Irish community. Most of them wished to combine loyalty to Elizabeth with the freedom to practise their Catholic faith. But this latter was something the government was less and less inclined to grant.

The hierarchy of the Church in Ireland was now almost wholly appointed from England, and was wholly committed to implementing Protestant rites and methods. On their progresses through the country, presidents and governors destroyed all statuary and decoration of churches, sent monks packing, and evicted priests who still practised traditional Catholic forms. The religious dispute deepened. On both sides a more dogmatic and doctrinal approach sharpened attitudes. The success of the Counter-Reformation, begun at the Council of Trent in 1545, instilled a new discipline and sense of purpose among Catholics. By the mid-1570s, an Irish Church-in-Exile was effectively in being, with its own bishops, and retaining the loyalty of almost all sections of the population apart from those who were committed to Protestantism. The Anglican clergy had the power of the state behind them but did not have, and did not seek, the support of the people. In England, Catholics were a small minority by now, and men such as Archbishop Loftus of Armagh may have felt that the same thing would happen in Ireland.

A CRUSADE AGAINST THE CROWN

Meanwhile, James Fitzmaurice Fitzgerald and others were actively working for support from the Catholic powers for an invasion of Ireland, which would drive out both the heretic religion and the government which was imposing it. But if the Anglicans miscalculated their spiritual support, so did the Catholics overestimate their secular backing. On 18 July 1579, Fitzmaurice landed near

Dingle, with a very small Spanish force and a papal Bull from Gregory XIII which deprived Elizabeth of both her kingdoms. Fitzmaurice's appeal for support was answered by the brothers of the Earl of Desmond, but actively opposed by many others. In a skirmish at Barrington's Bridge, near Limerick, with the Burkes of Castleconnell, Fitzmaurice was killed. In 1580, some 800 more Italian and Spanish troops landed, and there were uprisings in Munster and even in the Pale, where two prominent Anglo-Irish families, the Eustaces and Nugents, made alliance (once unthinkable) with the O'Byrnes of Wicklow. A royal army was defeated in Glenmalure before the rising was stamped out. The campaign in Munster was one of siege and scorched earth, which laid waste much of the province. The papal invasion force never got past the fort, Dun-an-oir, at Smerwick cove, from where it surrendered and, having laid down their arms, its men were massacred. It was far into 1583 before the government forces, led by Lord Grey, with the active assistance of the Earl of Ormond, again had the situation under control. The Earl of Desmond had entered the rising late, failed to give it new impetus, and was killed in Kerry by Ormond's men on 11 November of that year.

THE FIRST GREAT PLANTATION

The English government's nightmare had happened, and even though the invasion itself was of no account whatever, the atrocities committed by the queen's forces clearly showed the force of the reaction. The south-west had borne the brunt of the fighting, and Munster was reduced to a wasteland. The savagery of the campaign left the country subdued, though restive, and from mid-1586 the government set in motion its programme of plantation in Munster. Although more than half a million acres of the best land was expropriated for the purpose, this first large-scale attempt at settling a new breed of loyal colonists was only partly successful. Attempts to survey the 'seignories' into which the land was divided were soon abandoned, and prospective tenants left to argue, take recourse to the law-courts or to fight for what they considered theirs. Many Irish land-holders also appealed to the courts against the taking of their lands. Although Sir Walter Raleigh was said to have acquired 40,000 acres, some of the other 'undertakers' lost much of the land they had been granted. Instead of the dreamt-of loyal colony there was an uneasy mixture of newcomers, Old English and Irish.

THE SPANISH THREAT AVERTED

With England and Spain moving towards war, the authorities kept an iron hand on Ireland. The Deputy, Sir John Perrot, fought several campaigns in

Ulster, and succeeded in procuring the submission of the MacDonald chief, Sorley Boy (*buidhe*), by a form of submission and regrant, in 1586. Sir Richard Bingham, president of Connacht, was particularly active and ruthless. In July 1586 he put down a Burke uprising in Mayo and pursued and attacked a body of around 1,500 Scots mercenaries who had been summoned by the Burkes. On 22 September, with a smaller force, he routed them in a surprise attack and killed almost all of them, massacring also a similar number of their womenfolk and children, one of the worst actions of a bloody time. By the time the Spanish Armada set sail in 1588, the government's aim was achieved. Ireland was pacified, and the authorities were on the alert against any invasion. In fact there was no plan to invade Ireland. The Spanish invasion fleet, battered by the English and then by a great storm, was under orders to keep well clear of the Irish coast. Many failed to manage this. Bingham reported that twelve ships were wrecked off Connacht, and the total was twenty or more. On coasts where piracy and wrecking was a way of life, there was looting and stripping of survivors, but in most cases, officials or a compliant local chief were soon on the scene. Most of the Spaniards were summarily hanged. Those who landed in Ulster were the luckiest, with around 3,000 of their number conveyed to neutral Scotland and safety by the O'Donnells and O'Neills.

THE CLANS OF ULSTER

Such independent action by the Irish chiefs of the north-west underlines the degree to which Ulster remained outside the control of the English government. Efforts to colonise large tracts of it, like that of Walter Devereux, Earl of Essex, in 1573, in Clandeboye, had led only to failure after murder and massacre (including that of the entire population of Rathlin Island in July 1575), and left a legacy of bitter anti-English feeling. Of its greatest men, Turloch Luineach, ruler of a major O'Neill sept, and claimant of the title of The O'Neill, was friendly towards the government so long as he was left alone. The O'Donnell chief, Hugh, was on good terms with the government. Hugh O'Neill, heir of the first Earl of Tyrone, had been made Earl of Tyrone in 1585 as an earnest of the goodwill between himself and the Crown. The Maguires of Fermanagh were a formidable nation, the largest of a number of lesser groups which also included the O' Cahans, MacMahons and Magennises. In the north-west were enclaves of MacSweeneys, once Scottish galloglasses. On the north-east coast, the Macdonalds, led by Sorley Boy, remained strong, despite decades of effort to repel them by the Clandeboy O'Neills as well as the English government. The MacQuillans, another Scottish clan, had also established themselves in the district known as the Route. In County Down were outposts of English settlement, the Savages and the Whites.

GALLOGLASS

IRISH *gallóglach* means 'foreign warrior', or perhaps 'warrior from *Innse Gall*', as the Hebrides were known from the time of their Viking occupancy. In the Gaelic commonwealth that existed between the eleventh and sixteenth centuries, embracing north Connacht, Ulster, the Hebrides and Argyll, the galloglasses were an important element. As professional soldiers they formed the backbone of the army of any important chief, and played an important part in staving off English settlers' penetration to the north and west. They wore the Highland plaid and were called 'Redshanks' by the English. In battle they usually wore armour and were most formidable as a defensive force.

Since the collapse of the earldom of Ulster, no one had been overall ruler of this collection of wasps' nests. The writ of Dublin did not reach here, and Catholic priests openly went about their duties. It was a prosperous region, particularly where the land was good, and the government of Deputy Perrot hoped that the policies of surrender and regrant, and the imposing of a royal army in the province, to be maintained by the exacting of food, accommodation and other contributions from the inhabitants, would stabilise life in the province. The existence of this force was intended to maintain the peace, and to bridge over a transitional period in which the chieftains would divest themselves of their armies and make a 'composition' with the government for the right to receive rents and other services from their people.

This strategy was wrecked by the internal stresses and strains of Ulster itself. Among the O'Neills, the sons of Shane vied with the Earl of Tyrone as to who should become The O'Neill after Turloch. Among the O'Donnells, there was rivalry between the chief's heir, Domnall, and the chief's second wife, Finola MacDonnell, who sought the position for her own son, Hugh Roe. There were many other family and inter-family dissensions. And a whole class of Gaelic society, the warriors who formed the chief's escort and army, and maintained his prestige, saw in the process of 'composition' their own dissolution. For the time being, however, they remained essential. Every chief was busy augmenting his own forces, arming his peasantry and recruiting from western Scotland. Scotland was also the source of arms and ammunition. The armies required food and action, and cattle raids were common. The factionalism among O'Donnells and O'Neills set up crises of loyalty among the smaller groups, especially when a chief died and had to be replaced.

The policy of Perrot's successor as Deputy, Sir William Fitzwilliam, was to allow some kind of balance of power to establish itself among these conflicting interests, with his English garrisons as guarantors of overall stability. To this end, he released Hugh Roe O'Donnell, who had been kept under arrest by Perrot. With little support from the freeholders of Tyrconnel, but with a large Hebridean force provided by his formidable mother, Hugh Roe needed a cause, and found one by reasserting the old O'Donnell claim to Sligo. He found an ally in Hugh Maguire, another Gaelic dynast at odds with many of his own leading men. In 1592 he assumed the chieftainship of O'Donnell, and by 1593 he was at open war with the government.

HUGH O'NEILL'S WAR

Hugh O'Neill's aims and tactics have been much discussed. Unlike his warlike namesake Hugh Roe, he was a diplomat and tactician by nature. In 1593 and 1594 he was opposed to the O'Donnell–Maguire revolt, though his military participation against them was half-hearted. He had been developing his own position against the sons of Shane O'Neill and against Turloch Luineach. He intended to make himself the master of a strong power base in the north, from which he could act as mediator between Gaelic Ireland and the English Viceroyalty. But Hugh O'Neill was no more able to dictate the pace and nature of events than was the Deputy. Once he had acceded to Maguire's request, and put himself at the head of the revolt, he tried to contain it, and steer it, keeping Ulster as the focus, and rejecting all efforts to extend the war into the rest of the country. He also kept open lines of communication with the government, even when he was proclaimed a rebel and traitor. In a manner that carried echoes of Kildare, he wanted to present himself as the indispensable man of Ireland. A victory over a royal army at Clontibret in 1595 confirmed the impetus of the revolt. In 1596, O'Neill and O'Donnell began negotiations with Spain and made an appeal to the Munster lords to join them, resulting in an extension of the war there. In Wicklow, Fiach MacHugh O'Byrne rose again, bringing the war very close to Dublin. Though he was killed in 1597, the allies won an important victory at the Battle of the Yellow Ford, near Armagh, in 1598.

Whether he had willed it or not, O'Neill's war took on a national character, and uprisings broke out across the country. But it was a Gaelic war. The 'Old English' did not rally to O'Neill despite his claim to be defending 'Christ's Catholic religion'. Faced with the most serious challenge for more than a century, the English government first made a botched effort by sending as Lord Lieutenant, the Earl of Essex, who achieved nothing and went back in disgrace, then in 1600 it began the process of clawing back its control, through a long, hard, bitter and professional military campaign led by Lord Mountjoy as Deputy, assisted by Sir George Carew, President of Munster. The

Irish were supported by shipments of arms and ammunition from Spain, and only a 'Protestant wind' in October 1596 prevented a Spanish invasion force from landing.

When a Spanish force did land, on 21 September 1601, at Kinsale, the tide of events was already moving against the Gaels. The easy anchorage of Lough Foyle was in English hands. In Munster and Leinster English armies were carrying out a policy of devastation and scorched earth. The landing had been made in the south-west because Munster had risen against England; but now the English were back in control of the province. O'Neill and O'Donnell were in Ulster, and the Spanish force of some 2,500 was promptly put under siege. O'Donnell set off southwards, but delayed in Tipperary while his men went on raids. During November, he smartly evaded Carew who was sent to head him off. O'Neill meanwhile was making a slow and circuitous progress south. Under an able commander, Don Juan de Aguila, the Spaniards held out in Kinsale and even made some sorties against the besiegers. Aguila sent anguished messages, reproaching his allies for their dilatory behaviour, but in O'Neill case at least, the delay was quite probably deliberate. He was no longer looking for victory, but preparing for the consequences of defeat. In that scheme of things, an attempt to relieve Kinsale was not a consideration.

Events moved on. English cannon picked away at the crumbling defences of Kinsale, but Mountjoy's army was suffering severely from exposure, various infectious diseases, and lack of provisions. Meanwhile, a Spanish supply squadron arrived at Castlehaven at the beginning of December. The English Admiral Leveson sailed to destroy it but was forced to retire, and the Spanish established themselves in the strong points around Bantry Bay. By 6 December, O'Neill's forces were at last in the area, and Mountjoy's besiegers were caught between the Irish and the Spanish. O'Neill did not want to force the issue, still preferring to play a waiting game, but O'Donnell's fighting spirit prevailed. On 24 December, their plan already given away to the English by treachery, their battle order undermined by argument over precedence, O'Neill and O'Donnell were defeated by Mountjoy's smaller but resolutely commanded and well-deployed force. O'Donnell left on a Spanish vessel, to seek further help, leaving his men under the command of his brother Rory. O'Neill retreated with his own men. Aguila negotiated an honourable surrender, accomplished on 2 January 1602. Kinsale was a notable English victory, and despite the efforts of Hugh Roe O'Donnell to obtain further help, it was not forgotten in Spain that their invading force had been left to struggle on its own for several weeks.

At the time, Kinsale seemed less of a milestone for the English, and they pressed on through the winter, to eliminate or neutralise what remained of rebel forces. Rumours of a Spanish return persisted, adding to the tension. By summer of the following year Mountjoy was in the heart of O'Neill's land, and O'Neill fired his own castle of Dungannon as the Deputy's army approached. Queen Elizabeth had taken an intense interest in the campaign, and now urged her Deputy to show mercy to subordinate chiefs but not to pardon the 'Arch-traitor'. Despite one last small victory over royalist forces in Connacht in 1602, the ten-year-old war was effectively over. O'Neill, bereft of his castles, with most of his supporters now in the queen's peace, was ready to submit. The ailing queen, seeing in O'Neill's surrender the end of the war, authorised the Deputy to offer terms (which he did not altogether willingly). And so, ironically, a few days after Elizabeth I's death, but unaware of it, O'Neill surrendered. The Deputy – who knew of the queen's death and was technically without authority as a result – accepted the submission. When he learned that the Queen Elizabeth was dead, Tyrone wept. The Deputy's secretary, Fynes Morison, cynically ascribed the reason to chagrin: 'For, no doubt, the most humble submission he had made to the Queen he had so highly and proudly offended much eclipsed the vainglory his actions might have carried if he had held out till her death.'

IRELAND UNDER JAMES I AND VI

The new King of Ireland was James Stewart, King of Scotland since 1565, and a remote descendant of Robert Bruce. Though half his nation spoke Gaelic, he had no love for the Gaels, and had written of the Hebrideans as savages. The triumphant Mountjoy had announced to King James that Ireland was now 'capable of what form it shall please the king to give it'. The new dynasty did not change government attitudes in the slightest, and widened the policy of encouraging the vassal septs to claim independence under the Crown, thus weakening the hold of the Irish lords. The surviving leaders were benignly treated. Rory O'Donnell was made Earl of Tyrconnel in 1603. O'Neill, pardoned and restored, had a friendly relationship with Mountjoy, now made Earl of Devonshire and retaining his title of Lord Lieutenant though resident in England. But Mountjoy died in 1606, fallen from royal favour.

By 1605 Ulster, hitherto the least anglicised of the four provinces, was divided into nine shires, was garrisoned by English troops, and was being brought speedily under English law. Its inhabitants had been proclaimed as owning their allegiance only to the king, and not to any lord. Attendance at Protestant services was compulsory, and priests and members of such counter-Reformative orders as the Jesuits were proscribed. Despite their submission, the Spanish links maintained by the chiefs aroused suspicion in Dublin and London. O'Neill's son was the commander of a Spanish regiment; O'Neill himself received a Spanish pension. He was in dispute with Donal O'Cahan, his son-in-law, over some land. Three years before, O'Cahan was his vassal and the question, if it arose, would have been settled by force. Now in August 1607 he was called to London for arbitration on the matter. The fate of Kildare had not been forgotten. O'Neill and the other chiefs felt highly, and increasingly, insecure, never certain whether they might be accused, rightly or wrongly, of conspiracy. In September, the two earls and almost a hundred lesser chiefs, together with their immediate families and retainers, left Ireland for a voluntary exile in Europe

THE DESERTION OF THE NOBLES

Many a son of Ireland, from Columcille and the wandering monks on, had turned their backs on their native land and followed their destinies elsewhere. This was different – no destiny beckoned. These earls and chiefs were stepping into oblivion. Any hope they had of mustering enough aid to restore themselves in the old manner were soon dashed. But it is a unique gesture. In almost every other country of Europe, from the Balkans to the Highlands of Scotland, the native nobility put as its first priority its own struggle to maintain power. For such as these, to withdraw from power, not as the result of some catastrophic defeat, not because they were put under compulsion, would have been unthinkable. But the Irish nobles saw things differently. Their defeat had been long and slow. They had held it at bay a long time, and finally made a great effort to fight it off. But the order of things was changing. The cultural and economic web that cradled the Celtic chieftaincies was collapsing. There was no going back to the old style, and the alternative – accepting an English title and losing the grandeur, precedence and homages of the past – was of little appeal. Even for O'Neill, brought up in English style, the life of an English earl – particularly for an ex-rebel – under a whimsical and arbitrary king, was not an appetising prospect. A certain poignancy can be seen in their withdrawal, as if they were members of some legendary race, retreating beyond the horizon to a Tír na nÓg where ancient glory could be maintained for ever. In fact they went to Madrid or Rome and died of drink and nostalgia. For those of their loyal people who remained, unable to afford or contemplate a life anywhere else, the mass exit of their leaders was a dreadful blow. The class of bards and historians, ever ready to complain on their own behalf, spoke for many more than themselves when they condemned the selfishness of the departure. Many did not give up hope of O'Neill's return until they heard of his death, blind and short of money, in 1616.

CHAPTER NINE

The Stewart Kingdom

IRELAND AT THE BEGINNING OF THE
SEVENTEENTH CENTURY

ALMOST ten years of warfare, with the vastly expensive deployment of men, guns, ships and all the resources to support them, and a long catalogue of burnings, deaths and destructions, had finally resulted in a complete English hegemony in Ireland. For the first time, the king's Viceroy could impose his will from Donegal to Cork. The Deputy was Sir Arthur Chichester, and in three out of four provinces he could report relative peace, the presidential system and the garrisons creating a basis for control which turned Irish chieftain and Old or New English lord alike into landlords rather than warlords. The towns were in a bad way, their trade much reduced and the population afflicted by recurrent plague. Economic life was generally at a low level. Much trade went on by barter. There was a lack of coinage, and the Irish coins minted under the Elizabethan regime had been debased: alloy mixed with their silver until their value sank far below their nominal worth. The country estates had been raided and re-raided by armed bands looking for food or loot. Few Irish lords would have the resources or the security to build the kind of big-windowed, unfortified country house by now often found elsewhere: the stout, almost windowless walls of tower houses were still a necessary protection. But artillery fire and siege techniques had wrecked many of them, as well as larger castles. Much of the countryside was reduced to wasteland and scrub, and wolves were a hazard. The mass of people were still Gaelic-speaking, living in turf cabins and practising agriculture in a traditional form, with seasonal movements of cattle and sheep, and a somewhat basic method of tillage which often involved attaching the plough or harrow board to the horse's tail.

The Catholic faith had to be followed increasingly furtively. Developing their country's role as one of the Protestant powers of Europe, the English government maintained a hard line, especially after the 'Gunpowder Plot' incident of 1605. But officious attempts actively to persecute Catholic 'recusants' were firmly discouraged by London. The Anglican Church showed no missionary zeal towards the population. The bishops were English, without interest in or sympathy for their Irish flocks. Many churches were in a state of great dilapidation. The distance between the official Church and the people made it easier

ARCHBISHOP USSHER

JAMES Ussher (1581–1656) was born in Dublin, into a long-established Anglo-Irish family. Educated at Trinity College, he took holy orders in the Church of Ireland, and stayed on to become Professor of Theological Controversies. In 1621 he was made Bishop of Meath and in 1625 was promoted to Archbishop of Armagh. One of the cleverest men of his time, he was a careful scholar and a sound administrator. His computation of the age of the world, at 4,406 years, was based on meticulous study of the Bible text, and was accepted as correct well into the nineteenth century. Though it has left Ussher as something of a figure of fun today, such a judgement is unfair in the context of his time.

for the Catholic priests, trained at various centres on the continent, not only to minister to the faithful, but to keep a whole Church structure in being. Although Ireland was at comparative peace, there was plenty of opportunity for fighting men in Europe, where the minor wars were flaring that would result in the conflagration of the Thirty Years War. Irish mercenaries abroad frequently faced one another from opposing sides. The country had a large reserve of 'swordsmen', the armed retainers of chiefs and magnates, and enough of these remained at home to cause the government some anxiety. Army garrisons were maintained at strategic points, particularly in Ulster.

COLONISATION

In Ulster, following the flight of the earls, there was a vacuum of power and Chichester moved to fill it, with the assistance of the energetic Sir John Davies, as solicitor- and later attorney-general. The absent Earls of Tyrone and Tyrconnel were attainted for treason, and their lands made forfeit to the Crown. Little was heard now about freeholders' rights in the vast areas now under the Deputy's control, but Chichester's original proposals did embrace settlement grants to the already established Irish inhabitants. An uprising in August 1608 by one of the remaining Irish chiefs, Sir Cahir O'Doherty of Inishowen, in which the town of Derry was burned down, brought about a change in this policy. Two further Irish leaders, Niall Garbh O'Donnell, and Donal O'Cahan, were accused, without supporting evidence, of complicity with O'Doherty, and, after a Dublin court failed to convict them, were sent to the Tower of London. Their lands, along with Inishowen, were included in a more extensive and drastic scheme of settlement now proposed, severely restricting the amount of land available to the 'deserving' natives, and opening up great tracts for colonisation. As with earlier schemes, the business was entrusted to 'undertakers' who would bring in settlers and establish townships where these would live and which would be defensible against attack. Church lands were left in the Church's hands, but the bishops were as keen as anyone to see their assets profitably developed. Colonists were sought in both of James's other realms, England and Scotland. Many came from the Borders, where a long-established warlike way of life had been eliminated by the Union of the Crowns in 1603.

The City of London, already a great mercantile centre with investments in transatlantic colonies, joined in the exploitation of this new and nearer one. Its merchant companies formed a formed a joint-stock business to develop the county of Coleraine and its two main towns, Derry and Coleraine. The progress of colonisation was sporadic and slow, and, despite Chichester's intentions, many Irish tenants were accepted by undertakers and Church land agents, who preferred any tenant to none. Furthermore, they had to invest less in housing and defence for Irish tenants. A more intensive Scottish settlement took place in the old lands of Clandeboye, where two Scottish lairds, Hamilton and Montgomery, made an agreement with Con O'Neill, its proprietor. Antrim's northern Scottish enclave, of Gaelic-speaking Macdonalds, was preserved, with Sorley Boy's son named as Earl of Antrim, and his domain now included the MacQuillan country of the Route. In south Antrim and reaching into Down there quickly became established a population of Scottish Lowland farmers, most of them Presbyterian in their religious views. Old Dalriada, which had seen the departure of the Scots to Argyll in the sixth century, was

---

THE ROYAL SCHOOLS

PART of the arrangements to help make the plantation of Ulster permanent was the setting up of five free schools under royal patronage, at Armagh, Cavan, Coleraine, Dungannon and Enniskillen. Each was endowed with land to provide it with income and all were in action by 1625. In 1629 further royal schools were set up on Crown territory at Banagher in King's County and Carysfort in Co. Wicklow. Perhaps the most successful was the Enniskillen one, surviving as Portora Royal School. A French visitor in 1796 noted that the headmaster's income was a very substantial two thousand pounds a year – 'a sort of bishopric'. The heads were Church of Ireland clergymen. Portora's best-known alumni are Oscar Wilde and Samuel Beckett, neither of whom was at all typical of the generality of pupils.

---

now, more than a thousand years later, settled by Scots of a different sort, who spoke their own form of English, and regarded the Gaels with hostility and incomprehension.

THE PARLIAMENT OF 1613

In 1613, for the first time since 1585, the Irish parliament was convened. Much legislation was needed in the new scheme of things, including the confirmation of attainder of the Ulster earls, but the government was greatly concerned to ensure that the new assembly should not have a Catholic majority. The thirty-three counties returned two members each, of whom the majority were likely to be Catholic, and the same applied to the forty-one boroughs. In six months between December 1612 and May 1613, forty new parliamentary boroughs were created, all of them certain to return a Protestant member. Many of these places were scarcely worthy of being called a town at all, though some, like Newry and Enniskillen, later became important centres. With Protestant bishops and new boroughs, the government engineered a majority in both houses. The recusants protested, vainly, about 'miserable villages by whose votes extreme penal laws shall be imposed on the King's subjects'. Objecting to the election of Davies as Speaker, they withdrew their representatives first from the Commons and then from the Lords. After four days of tumult, the parliament was prorogued, and did not reassemble until October 1614, by which time some steps had been taken to attend to the recusants' grievances. The government's majority in the Commons was reduced from thirty-two to six, and proposed anti-Catholic legislation was dropped. But it was clear to the Catholic Party – formed almost entirely of the Old English gentry and the burghers of the towns of Munster and Leinster, with very few Irish members – that their likely role in determining affairs was as a permanent opposition, at best. The form of the Oath of Supremacy, necessary for all holders of public office, which asserted the king's position as supreme head of the Church, kept them out of judgeships and other offices in the royal gift. After 1615, there was to be no further parliament until 1633. Simultaneously with the parliament, there was a Convocation of the Church, and this drew up the articles defining the creed of the Church of Ireland. The Calvinist nature of these not only ensured the continuing opposition of the recusants, but was to bring the Irish Church into collision with its Anglican parent.

THE ANGLICISATION OF IRELAND

For the administrators of Ireland, one of the lessons of the parliament was that plantation must be pushed forward, not only in Ulster but in other provinces.

Since peace meant a lack of opportunity for rebellion, confiscations were not as easily procured as before, and in order to create tracts of good land for settlement, the government resorted to dubious and contested methods. These included the ferreting out of ancient charters, sometimes going back as far as the time of Richard II, to prove that the Crown had title to ground occupied by an Irish chief. Serious trouble arose in Wexford, where many small proprietors found themselves ousted, but the policy was forced through. This caused concern to Old English landholders, some of whom were vulnerable to a similar claim. Increasingly, as the Irish chiefs accepted English law, and abandoned old traditions of Irish dress and even of speech, they were moving towards a fusion with the Old English nobility.

Another vital concern for the rulers was that their dominion was failing to be self-supporting. There was a continuing call for resources from England. This was despite evidence that fortunes could be made in Ireland, the most conspicuous example being Richard Boyle, an immigrant adventurer whose flair for capitalism developed smelting and weaving industries in the south, and who became Earl of Cork in 1620. King Charles I, who acceded in 1625, had considerable sympathy for the Catholic Church and his own High-Church beliefs ensured that the anti-Catholic laws continued to be lightly enforced. But Charles had his own troubles with an increasingly Puritan-dominated parliament in London. In his quest to ensure adequate funds without recourse to parliament, he negotiated the 'Graces' with the Catholic lords and bishops in 1627. For a payment of £120,000 over three years, it was promised, among other things, that the oath of supremacy would be replaced by one of allegiance, and that titles to land going back sixty years would be honoured. A parliament was to confirm the agreement. But the parliament was never called, and the Graces not put into legal effect. Having paid their money, the recusants felt they had been tricked.

WENTWORTH'S GOVERNORSHIP

In 1632, Lord Wentworth was sent by the king as Lord Deputy. His brief was a dual one, to make Ireland into a net revenue-earner, and to keep it secure for the Crown. Despite Charles's treatment of the Catholics, he knew himself to be their best hope. The main focus of Wentworth's activity was to be not on them, but on the old guard of the Irish Council, and the new men of the plantations. Between them these two groups controlled the economic life of the country, and the administration was responsible for tax collection and remittance to London. Each year there was a shortfall, which London had to make good. Wentworth, raised to the Lord Lieutenancy in 1639 and created Earl of Strafford, made a determined attempt to convert the mixed elements of his dominion into a regulated Stewart commonwealth. 'Thorough' was the code-word for the royal policy, and Wentworth lived up to it. With the Catholics, he attempted a stick-and-carrot approach, holding out the offer of further Graces or implementation of those that had already been paid for, but also requiring further donations to royal funds as an alternative to enforcing the anti-Catholic laws. He was as ready as Chichester to identify estates to which the Crown had a historical claim, and outraged the Old English by supporting a campaign to promote plantation in Connacht. But he visited similar treatment on the more recent landowners and the undertakers. Most of them had failed in some way – some of them in virtually every way – to honour the obligations they had purchased. To Wentworth, the fact that the purchase prices had been scandalously low was another incentive to act. There had been a good deal of corruption in the business of acquiring land.

At opposite ends of the country, he assailed the strongest of the new plant-ers. The Earl of Cork found himself divested of former Church lands that he considered his own and which he was in the process of developing, and was fined £15,000. 'A most cursed man to all Ireland, and to me in particular,' noted Boyle of the Lieutenant. The powerful London merchant companies, whose progress in Ulster had been slow, were fined £70,000 for failing to carry out their charter obligations, and the charter itself was cancelled. Typically for his time, Wentworth's Viceroyalty also made him a fortune: he kept a substan-tial proportion of what his measures earned for the Crown. But under his rule, the Irish contribution to England's exchequer increased substantially. The reclaimed Church lands were returned (to the Church of Ireland). The action against the Derry planters was also a stroke against the City of London. In both of these cases, Wentworth, while carrying out his duties, was also furthering the general policy of his royal master, to support the Church, and to resist the City, which was wholly pro-parliament in the growing power-struggle which would lead to civil war in England.

The doctrines of the Church of Ireland, drawn up in 1615, were unaccept-able to the king. Wentworth enforced the acceptance of the thirty-nine articles of the Church of England, at a convocation in 1634. This removed the Calvinist element from the official Church, and estranged many Protestants, particularly in Ulster, as a result. Prior to that, they had co-existed peaceably within the Church structure, but now a Presbyterian movement began to gain strength, stimulated by events in Scotland, where opposition to Anglicanism was coming to a head. Several of the more outspoken ministers were deprived of their livings and took refuge in Scotland. In 1634–35 Wentworth also called a parliament, something the Stewart monarchy only did when it needed to ensure its financial support; and succeeded in raising large sums, £100,000 to pay off the accumulated deficit in addition to payments which would eliminate the annual shortfall in Irish revenue. The parliament was not wholly biddable, however, and made trouble for the Deputy over the failure to implement the Graces. The pressure came from Protestant as well as Catholic members, and Wentworth took fright. He resolved matters partly by granting some minor reliefs to the Catholics, and partly by building on the fears and hostilities among the Protestants, to ensure their majority could be deployed. Despite his exhortation to the parliament not to divide between 'Protestant and papist', his policies in fact helped to maintain separate factions. Indeed, they depended on balancing the different forces against one another.

In the six years' effort to establish a royal absolutism in Ireland, Wentworth achieved, for the first time, the rule of civil government across the entire country, even if the laws were applied or not at 'His Majesty's pleasure' rather than due process. When he was recalled by the king in 1639, it was as a successful governor whose methods had turned around the situation in Ireland, and might yet save the situation in England. As Mountjoy had been, he was named Lord Lieutenant, with a Deputy installed in Dublin. But within two years Wentworth was impeached and executed, his enemies in Ireland and England combining to bring him down. The Presbyterians of Ulster had been greatly excited and enthused by the National Covenant subscribed to by the Scots in March 1638, which promised resistance to the king's efforts to impose English religious forms and structure. To counter this, Wentworth compelled all males over sixteen to swear a deeply resented 'black oath' of loyalty to the king. When the London parliament attacked Wentworth, an alliance of virtually all elements of the Irish political-religious community provided a torrent of evidence to assist in his impeachment.

Wentworth's confidence in his control of Ireland was not illusory, and it enabled him in 1640 to raise a substantial army in Ireland on the king's behalf, and to have its maintenance paid for by the Irish parliament. It was under the command of an Old English grandee, the Earl of Ormond, who was a Protestant, but it was largely manned by Catholic troops, and Presbyterian propaganda seized on this to damn it as a papist army to be sent against Protestant citizens. The army, several thousand strong, was never put into action, and after Wentworth's execution in May 1641 it was disbanded.

PARLIAMENTARIANS AND ROYALISTS

Charles I's policies had led to disaster for him in England and Scotland. His third kingdom, which he had never seen, seemed to hold out hopes of support that might yet help him retrieve control. Under Wentworth it had seemed a bastion of loyal support. Control of the administration was now in the hands of two Lords Justices, Borlase and Parsons, both of them appointed by the king, but with considerable pro-parliament sympathies. Many in Ulster supported the alliance between the Scots and the English parliamentarians. The New English, mostly Anglican, and often with Puritan sympathies, were mostly disposed towards the parliamentary side. For the Old English, however much they mistrusted the king, there was little choice but to support him. The Puritan zeal of the parliamentarians had an inevitable message of threat to Catholics. That was clear to the Irish, but some of them also perceived an opportunity in the situation. A royalist, Catholic Ireland could be established, under the king. The king himself made tentative approaches for military support to the earls of Antrim and Ormond in the summer of 1641, but these came to nothing.

THE REVOLT OF 1641

At the same time, intense discussion was happening among some Irish chiefs and leading members, military and religious, of the Irish in exile. The moving spirit was the Leinster chief Rory O'More. Action came in October, with uprisings in Leinster and in Ulster. The aim in Leinster had been to take Dublin Castle, but that was foiled when one of those in the know drunkenly blabbed. In Ulster, however, the insurgents, led by Sir Felim O'Neill, swept across the province. Massacre, rape, torture, burning, looting and destruction followed. The leaders of the revolt could not stop their followers in this; the peasantry had seized the chance to fight their own war against those who had for decades ousted them from their land and treated them with contempt. The number of deaths has never been quantified, but the undoubted atrocities committed against civilians inaugurated a new phase of warfare that was even more undiscriminating in its brutality and savagery than the battles of the previous century, and was to culminate in the horrors of Drogheda and Wexford in 1649.

O'Neill claimed to be acting on behalf of the king, which did nothing for Charles's cause in England, though he vehemently disowned Sir Felim and his associates. After the Dublin setback, O'More won a victory over a small government force at Julianstown in November 1641. Borlase and Parsons appointed Ormond in charge of the army in Ireland, but restrained him from a major campaign. As the rising spread, there was a complete collapse of identity between the New English and the Old English. Mutual suspicion not only over the religious question, but over the newcomers' covetousness of the broad acres held by the descendants of the Anglo-Normans, could not survive the crisis caused by the revolt. By the end of the year, the Old English were throwing in their lot with the Irish, and fighting for their concept of a royal, loyal Catholic Ireland – ironically, against the king as well as his parliament.

145

CONFEDERATES AGAINST THE CROWN

The uprising was nation-wide, and great tracts fell under the control of the rebels. In March 1642, proposals to form a provisional government in the king's name were discussed at Armagh, and in May, an assembly of clergy and lay leaders – 'the lords and gentry of the confederate Catholics' – met at Kilkenny. A supreme council and an assembly were nominated here, though the assembly did not meet until October.

The confederates had an army, or at least a group of armed forces, led by experienced soldiers: Owen Roe O'Neill in Ulster, Thomas Preston in Leinster, and Garret Barry in Munster. So did the king, still in control of the Dublin government, with Ormond as his general. So did the London parliament, now at open war with the king's party. This latter army, under the Scot Robert Munro, landed at Carrickfergus in April 1642. For the time being, Ormond and Munro fought separately against the confederates, in north and south, rather than against each other.

In September 1643, after almost two years of indecisive military action, a one-year truce was agreed between the confederates and the king, represented by Ormond, who was now made Lord Lieutenant and given the title of marquis. This did not mean a cessation of fighting, as the Ulster Scots were still at war, and the O'Brien Lord Inchiquin, like Ormond a Protestant member of a Catholic family, was fighting for the parliamentary cause in Munster. The

Parliament House, Kilkenny

king now opened communication with the confederates, through the Protestant Earl of Clanricard and Ormond. Despite its loyalty, the Kilkenny assembly demanded substantial concessions before agreeing any alliance with the royal forces. The English parliament had punished the confederates with the Adventurers' Act of 1642, which deprived them of all title to their estates and threw the land open to anyone of Protestant credentials who could take and hold it. The confederates wished to do away with any claim of the London parliament to legislate for Ireland, and the king was asked to confirm the independence of the Irish parliament. The Old English were determined to secure their own positions and to end anti-Catholic discrimination.

Even in a beleaguered situation, Charles I was unlikely to grant away the very things he was fighting for: his own supremacy as king was closely bound in with the structure of his Church. The discussions dragged on for two years. The Kilkenny assembly brought a new element into its deliberations. The Irish clergy had always been part of the council of a chief or king and they were represented in strength here, with Archbishop O' Reilly of Armagh as president. But the papacy was taking an interest, and papal envoys involved themselves in the debates. The most notable was Giovanni Battista Rinnucini, Bishop of Fermo, who arrived as papal nuncio in October 1645, bringing with him a supply of arms and money for the confederate cause. As a standard-bearer of the Counter-Reformation, Rinnucini took a hard line. A draft treaty that had been finally worked out between Ormond and the confederates in 1646 was dismissed, and its supporters threatened with excommunication, as its terms did not specifically restore the full rights of the Catholic Church. The nuncio was not alone in his view that hints and promises from the king were not to be relied on, and that concessions must be fully spelled out and agreed without ambiguity. Charles's earlier failure to enact the Graces had had its effect. But many of the Old English leaders believed that the treaty was the best they could get, and should be accepted. Rinnucini's intransigence effectively derailed the whole cumbersome process of negotiating with the king.

The nuncio's influence extended to the real action in the field. In June 1646, O'Neill defeated the Scots at Benburb. Munro's army was broken, but O'Neill did not consolidate his victory, instead marching south to put himself at Rinnucini's disposal. The nuncio's role as paymaster may have contributed, but Owen Roe was an ardent Catholic; and belief in the guiding or punishing hand of God was by no means confined to the Presbyterian camp (on his defeat, Munro had commented, 'For aught I can understand, the Lord of Hosts had a controversy with us'). With an army to support him, the nuncio took complete control of the confederate council. An assault on Dublin was planned, but was abandoned because of the rivalry between O'Neill and

Preston. In early 1647, negotiations with the king, via Ormond, were resumed. Ormond, still holding Dublin, was sceptical of procuring terms that would satisfy the nuncio, and began to negotiate with the English parliament for it to take over Dublin. For a loyal servant of the king, as Ormond was, it may seem odd to prefer the king's declared enemies to his self-proclaimed friends, but Ormond was hostile to Catholicism, and felt that the confederates were setting too high a price on their loyalty to Charles. By the summer of 1647, all of Ormond's garrisons had formally surrendered to parliamentary forces, and the earl himself had left the country. Dublin was under the command of a parliamentary officer, Michael Jones.

The confederacy had great strength, but its own internal rifts and rivalries, and its inability to produce a leader who could transcend these, caused its collapse. Its motto, *Pro Deo, pro Rege, pro Patria Unanimis*, 'united for God, King and Country' had a hollow ring. Rinnucini was a dictator with a mission, but devoid of policy to achieve it. The chief generals had been rivals when both served the King of Spain, and rivals they remained. Preston's army was routed when he tried alone to take Dublin. Inchiquin had virtually all of Munster in his control, and a somewhat depleted Kilkenny assembly, attended largely by Old English members, decided to make a truce with him. This was condemned by Rinnucini, but by now the Old English at least had done with him, though the Irish were with him, and the confederation was at odds with itself. O'Neill made an effort to capture Kilkenny, but eventually withdrew northwards. Inchiquin, having devastated much of Munster on behalf of the parliament, switched his loyalties to the king in April 1648 and prepared to burn out those of his former supporters who had not followed suit.

At the beginning of 1649, the confederates, Inchiquin, and the king's party agreed the terms of an alliance, with Ormond as its leader. Time had run out for Charles I, who was executed by the victorious English parliament in January, but his heir, Charles II, was immediately proclaimed king by the royalists. The confederation, already dismembered, dissolved what was left of itself, and the king's government was nominally entrusted to twelve commissioners under Ormond. Inchiquin and Ormond went on the offensive, but O'Neill, back in Ulster, was temporising with the parliamentary forces and the Scots, and did not join in. The royalist army under Inchiquin took Dundalk and Drogheda from the parliamentary forces, but Ormond's intended attack on Dublin was forestalled by Jones, who came out and routed him at Rathmines on 2 August.

Two weeks later, Oliver Cromwell, with 3,000 troops of his 'New Model Army', cannon and siege machinery, arrived in Dublin, and the balance of power in Ireland shifted decisively.

IRELAND UNDER CROMWELL

Cromwell, architect of victory in the English Civil War and undisputed leader of the parliamentary party, knew exactly what he wanted to achieve. Ireland was to be pacified and put under the rule of the Westminster parliament. If he did not intend also to punish the Irish for the atrocities committed in Ulster, his troops certainly did. Within three weeks of his arrival he retook Drogheda from the royalists, the surrendered garrison was put to the sword, and in the rampage many clergy and civilians were also killed. Cromwell saw the blood-bath as 'a righteous judgment of God upon these barbarous wretches, who have imbrued their hands in so much innocent blood'. Just as the Protestants had seized on, and magnified, the already sufficient record of cruelties and deaths in Ulster, so the massacre of Drogheda would become a recurrent theme in the exhortations of Irish nationalists. Both sides made the most of the grisly actions in a pamphlet war of propaganda that went on alongside and long after the military campaign. In October there was another scene of carnage in Wexford, when the parliamentary troops went out of control and, as their general himself noted, 'put all to the sword that came in their way'. In the course of the winter and spring, a succession of garrison towns in the south were captured, with only Waterford, which had always prided itself on its royal allegiance, offering stiff resistance. Kilkenny yielded in March.

Cromwell's Fort, Drogheda

149

Massacre of civilians at Drogheda by Cromwell's troops

Ormond still had large numbers of men at his disposal, and after Drogheda O'Neill renewed alliance with him, but in November Owen Roe died. Yet again the morale of the royalists was severely shaken, and Ormond did not attempt any substantial action after Rathmines. Cromwell left Ireland in May 1650, leaving his son-in-law, Ireton, to complete the pacification campaign. A further blow was dealt to the royalists when Charles II, making a deal with the Presbyterian Scots in order to secure their military support, turned on the Catholics and promised to enforce all anti-Catholic legislation, branding those who had fought for his cause as 'bloody Irish rebels'. In December, Ormond left Ireland for France. Clanricard took over as Lieutenant in the king's name, but he was no general, and no other leader appeared. Despite the presence of as many as 30,000 armed men on the opposing side, Ireton and his successors were able to proceed steadily with a succession of sieges that brought the remaining fortified towns under English control, the last being Galway in May 1652; and to procure the surrender of all the royalist forces.

ORGANISATION UNDER PARLIAMENTARY RULE

The eight years of parliamentary rule brought enormous changes. At the start, merely to restore order was a daunting task. The country was in a worse condition even than it had been in 1603. Many small towns had been virtually destroyed. Law and order had collapsed. Armed bands moved at will through the countryside, living off what they could find. Great numbers of people, ousted from their homes, or losing their breadwinner, were reduced to vagrancy and begging. Deaths from malnutrition, exposure and recurrent waves of plague probably far outnumbered those caused directly by warfare. Thousands of homeless people were transported to the West Indies where they were put to work as indentured labourers, in conditions hardly better than slavery. Cows, horses, other animals, and seed corn were all in desperately short supply, and the money to buy them was equally scarce. In Ulster, and other areas where plantation had occurred, more than half the colonists had fled home. Once again, large tracts of once-cultivated land had gone back to heath and scrub. Even after the last 'official' surrender, outlaw groups remained, and the designation 'Tory' appeared as a name for a renegade Catholic.

With relatively few supporters outside the bigger towns, and none at all among the country nobility, the parliament had a free hand, and, in contrast to previous settlements, no effort was made to rehabilitate the existing power structure. Four regional commissioners were appointed to put the country's affairs, religious, political and economic, in order, and set about establishing local government under military support. It was necessary to start a tax-collecting system as soon as possible. The army of occupation had to be paid for.

Confiscation and redistribution of land was carried out on a scale far greater than anything seen before. More than half the territory of Ireland was forfeited. An Act of Settlement in 1652 provided the basis for this. It imposed penalties on almost everyone who had been involved in activity hostile to the parliamentary cause. Heading the list, and named for execution as well as expropriation, were 104 men identified as leaders, such as Ormond, Inchiquin and Rory O'More. Four classes of person were also declared as beyond pardon: they were those who had taken part in the first phase of the rebellion in 1641; all Roman Catholic priests who had aided the rebellion; all who had been responsible for killing civilians, and all civilians who had killed English soldiers; and all persons still in arms who failed to submit within twenty-eight days of publication of the Act. For others, the penalties were to be applied according to the degree of 'delinquency', and involved the loss of from one-fifth to two-thirds of their property. Their remaining land might also be taken in exchange for land elsewhere.

Beneficiaries of the situation included those who had taken advantage of the 'Adventurers' Act' of 1642, and many soldiers of the parliamentary army, who accepted farms in lieu of payment. There now was a returning tide of colonists to Ulster and other existing plantations. In September 1653 an 'Act of Satisfaction' passed by parliament provided for how the confiscated lands would actually be allotted. Connacht was to be a sort of Irish reserve where delinquent proprietors would be resettled. Forfeited lands in ten counties of the other three provinces were divided between the Adventurers (by now

THE DOWN SURVEY

DR WILLIAM Petty (1623–87) was one of those seventeenth-century polymaths whose skills knew no bounds. He first came to Ireland as physician-in-chief to Cromwell's army, in 1649. From 1654 he was put in charge of surveying all the land which, after the collapse of the confederate rising, was confiscated for redistribution. His survey, called the 'down survey' because its results were literally set down on maps and plans, was the first really scientific one in Ireland. From it, Petty produced an atlas of Ireland, *Hiberniae Delineatio*, in 1685, which remained the basis of Irish cartography until the Ordnance Survey began work in 1824. Petty was the first president of the Dublin Philosophical Society, and also wrote *The Political Anatomy of Ireland*. Knighted and granted lands in Kerry by King Charles II, he set up an ironworks and experimented with fishery improvements.

clamorous to get their reward) and parliamentary soldiers. Remaining forfeited lands would be allocated at the government's discretion. The same action was taken with urban property, and a great deal of business was transferred from the recusant merchants and traders into the hands of Protestants, at the same time ensuring that civic government was also under Protestant control.

Implementation of this, though by no means as complete as the Act proposed, was effective enough to show that the government was able to enforce its will. Thousands of ousted small land-holders trekked with their stock and possessions to new land across the Shannon. Tenants of sound Protestant credentials moved into the vacated farms. Although the government's intentions had been otherwise, large numbers of Irish labourers, of both sexes, remained behind: the newcomers insisted that they needed workers. As allocations were made, a land-market developed. Many soldiers were ready to sell their land-allocation without even waiting to see it. For the Adventurers, the reward was often a disappointment. Overgrown fields, undrained soil, the lurking presence of cattle-thieving outlaws in the hills, a sullen Gaelic-speaking workforce – this was often the reality that awaited them, and many sold out. Waiting to buy, at low prices, were that section of society once known as the 'New English', who had arrived in Ireland before the events of 1641 and after, and who remained largely Protestant, though many had been royalist in sympathy.

THE PROTESTANT ASCENDANCY

From 1654 Ireland sent thirty members to parliament in Westminster, in the first full triple union of England, Ireland and Scotland. Elected on a very limited franchise, many of them army officers, they played little part either in the parliament or in Ireland. By 1654 the country once again had a Deputy; in 1657 it was Henry Cromwell, representative of his father, who was now established as 'Lord Protector'. Civil rule was restored, though troops of the standing army were garrisoned throughout the country. The four courts of Dublin were re-established, and sheriffs and justices of the peace re-appointed in the shires. A cadre of officials staffed the administration of justice and the economy; men who had no specific loyalty other than to government, and who would make an easy transition when the restoration of monarchy came in 1660.

Although the commonwealth allowed religious freedom, there was a major exception, which fell heavily on Ireland. The mass was forbidden and Roman Catholic clergy not allowed to practise or to be in the country. The official semi-tolerance that had formerly been the norm vanished completely in this period. Priests, if found, were liable to be executed, deported or sent to the West Indies. Informers were rewarded. The commonwealth's policy was to propagate the Puritan form of Protestantism, and to this end a parish structure was renewed, with the aim of having an approved minister in every parish. The Church of Ireland was disestablished, its prayer book was banned, and its few surviving bishops deprived of all authority. Although some Church of Ireland ministers, and Ulster Presbyterians, proved acceptable, there was always great difficulty in attracting suitable parish ministers. Meanwhile, often in disguise, and leading furtive lives, some Catholic priests remained, and others were sent in from the Irish seminaries on the continent. They had the inestimable advantage of having been taught Gaelic, and their links with the people remained strong.

The 'Protestant Ascendancy' was now in place, as a separate layer above the bulk of the population, sealed off by self-interest, religious affiliation and its links with government and society in England. Its leaders in the final stage of the commonwealth were Lord Broghill and Sir Charles Coote, both of them former royalists who had come to terms with the commonwealth. Henry Cromwell resigned in June 1859, nine months after Oliver's death, and though some hard-line soldiers sought to establish a British republic, briefly holding Dublin Castle, Broghill and Coote were already in touch with Charles II in his Dutch exile. A national convention was called in Dublin in February 1660, and was attended by the new landed interest. Broghill and Coote, themselves holders of large areas of forfeited land, persuaded this assembly that a restored monarchy was the best way of preserving what they had gained, and the convention's acceptance of this was influential on opinion in England. The convention, its members drawn from the old constituencies, and a parliament in all but name, also raised a poll-tax to pay off remaining arrears of payment due to the parliamentary army.

IRELAND UNDER THE RESTORATION

On 14 May 1660, Charles II was duly proclaimed as King of Ireland in Dublin, six days after his restoration in London. Broghill and Coote were early visitors to London, as delegates of the Dublin convention. They were particularly anxious that a parliament should be formally called. As representation was based on property, such an assembly would be very similar in composition to the Dublin convention.

In his Irish policy, Charles II had to consider this fact, among other demands and obligations. There was some irony in his settlements. The faithful Ormond was made a duke and restored to his estates, and so was General Monk, the Cromwellian turned royalist, who became Duke of Albemarle and Lord Lieutenant of Ireland. Broghill and Coote were made earls of Orrery and Mountrath respectively. The Church of Ireland was re-established and given its

ORMOND AND DUBLIN

APART from its two cathedrals, Dublin had few buildings to boast of until the eighteenth century. Its castle was described by one seventeenth-century Deputy as 'the worst castle on the worst site in Christendom'. James Butler (1610–88), twelfth Earl and first Duke of Ormond, three times Lord Lieutenant, laid out St Stephen's Green and saved Phoenix Park for the city in Charles II's reign (the king had it destined for one of his numerous mistresses). Ormond, the first of his line to be brought up as a Protestant, was also responsible for the building of the Royal Hospital at Kilmainham, setting a trend for distinguished neo-classical architecture that was to be followed for more than a hundred years.

lands and privileges back, and the various sorts of Protestant sectary were lumped in with papists in a proclamation which banned them all from holding meetings; but despite the efforts of the Bishop of Down and Connor, the Presbyterians, now strongly entrenched in the north-east, were allowed to maintain their organisation (from 1672 they would receive an official subvention, or *regium donum*). Monk soon resigned his lieutenancy to Ormond, who returned to Ireland in July 1662.

Charles had the usual Stewart antipathy to parliaments, but it was essential to summon one, both to establish his own Irish revenues, and to consider the land question. It duly met in May 1661. By far the largest element in the population, the indigenous Irish people, now to a great extent leaderless or enrolled in the service and rent-books of new and alien landlords, were not represented at all. Only in Connacht did something like the former state of affairs exist. Their former leaders, the Old English and Irish lords and chiefs, were mostly dead or exiled, and those who might be considered 'innocent papists' in the new political climate were debarred by religion from attending, though they pleaded their cause energetically at court in London. There was a strong representation of the Protestant royalists, who had nothing to fear and much to hope for. The strongest group were the commonwealth landlords and burgesses who had taken over so much forfeited territory. Most of them had been supporters of the English parliament in the Civil War, and all of them had colluded with its officers. They were an anxious group, but their anxiety was largely to do with retaining their gains. Charles had already, in April 1660, proclaimed a general amnesty for the parliamentarians. In November of that year he also confirmed the possessions of the adventurers and soldiers as held on 7 May 1659, though with a clause reserving the rights of 'innocent papists' to get their confiscated land back. In fact up to three-quarters of the soldiers had probably already sold their land, though that left some nine thousand who had set up as farmers and small landlords – a potentially troublesome group.

Irish courts would not accept any grants of Charles's until they were confirmed by Irish statute. The Irish parliament, dominated by the new landowners, and the royal council in England argued for a year before a Bill satisfactory to both could be framed. This was the Act of Settlement, and seven commissioners were appointed to hear claims for reinstatement or compensation. Only a fraction of these were ever considered, and those who were accepted found it very hard to assert their rights against the refusal of the occupants to leave. Even so, an attempt at a coup was made in May 1663, by disgruntled ex-soldiers under Colonel Thomas Blood, and they briefly held Dublin Castle. Ormond, who had had his own estates restored, sponsored a compromise settlement in the Bill of Explanation, which was complete by August 1665. Its most contentious measure was to expropriate a third of the land granted to Adventurers and soldiers, so as to provide room to accommodate those who had been granted decrees of innocency, plus a number of other named persons. None of the contending groups was satisfied but the Bill was passed. The effect was still to keep landowning in Ireland heavily dominated by Protestants. The recusants now owned little more than a fifth of the land, and had little influence left in the towns.

THE ECONOMY UNDER THE RESTORATION

No other parliament was summoned in Charles II's reign, and the government of the country stayed in the hands of the Viceroy and his council. Despite bandits on land and pirates on the coast, and innumerable local flare-ups on the land ownership issue, the general peace allowed agriculture and trade to be safely practised once again, and further pockets of manufacture to be developed. By 1671, the Irish accounts showed a modest surplus instead of the time-honoured deficit. At last, perhaps, Ireland was turning out to be that jewel of productivity of which English rulers had dreamed in vain for so long. Unfortunately, this prospect made Ireland suddenly inviting to many people who might otherwise have shunned any association. The king, an unprincipled opportunist himself, did not lack for advisers who wanted to show how they could improve Ireland's profitability to the Crown (and themselves). Ormond's political rival, the Duke of Buckingham, wrecked the burgeoning trade in Irish cattle by forcing restrictions through the London parliament, purely to frustrate Ormond. The corrupt practices of the tax farmers employed by the Crown to collect and pass on the various revenues meant that many government bills were not paid, and army pay and maintenance fell into serious arrears. It was an era of monopolies, when the old mercantile trading economy was giving way to an early form of capitalism, with few models or rules to be followed.

The economy might have grown faster and bigger if Irish farmers and merchants had not discovered that though they might share a king with England, there was an economic price to be paid for even a modest degree of political independence. As a satellite state, Ireland was not entitled to trade freely with England, or its colonies, or to share in the trade monopolies which bodies like the East India Company enjoyed and enforced. English wars, like those with Holland, the greatest mercantile power of the time, also struck at Irish trade, but despite these drawbacks, there was growth. Restrictive English regulations were often evaded, particularly in the transatlantic trade. Greater wealth began to be reflected in the building of town and country houses by the rich. No longer were the old thick-walled, almost windowless tower houses, of which so many had been built in the previous two hundred years, sufficient to reflect the status and opulence of their owners, or able to hold the amount of furniture now considered necessary. The market towns grew in population and wealth, none more than Dublin, which rivalled Edinburgh in population and was bigger than any English provincial city.

Cattle, beef, butter, tallow, grain and hides were the main exports. The import list grew in range and cost – tea, coffee, textiles, manufactured articles, books, wine, coal. Such items as these were consumed primarily by the small proportion of wealthier inhabitants. In the 1670s, Sir William Petty estimated that six out of seven of the Irish people lived at subsistence level. Inhabiting traditional-style turf-roofed houses, they grew their own food, wove their own coarse cloth for clothes, paid the rent in kind rather than in cash, did much trade by barter for necessary items like salt, and rarely dealt in coins other than copper ones. By now, the potato, introduced in the late sixteenth century from North America, was increasingly becoming a staple item in the people's diet.

RELIGIOUS ANXIETIES

The people of north-east Ulster, once closely linked in culture with Gaelic Scotland, now had closer ties with the south-western Scots of Ayrshire and Galloway, a region racked by guerrilla warfare between the supporters of a Presbyterian form of worship and the government's efforts to impose Episcopal forms by force. This conflict reached across the narrow sea, and many rank-and-file Ulster Presbyterians responded to the fierier doctrines of the Scottish Cameronians and other extreme sects. Their ministers, enjoying a semi-established status with the *regium donum*, rarely shared this covenanting enthusiasm. Ormond, restored as Lieutenant in 1677, kept substantial numbers of troops in the north as a precaution against any rising in support of the Scottish insurgents.

The relative degree of peace seemed precarious. The land question, officially closed, was still unofficially disputed in many places. The Catholic population was resentful of the official discrimination it suffered. Although a declaration of Indulgence suspended the penal laws for a time in 1672–73, and any enforcement after that was rare, the oath of supremacy (of king over church) was still required for office-holders, and kept them out of positions of authority. A crisis in late 1678 disrupted this climate of comparative tolerance, with the uncovering in London of the supposed 'Popish Plot' against the king's life. In Ireland, all the Protestants' fears about living alongside a Catholic majority surfaced in a brief panic, which Ormond's government did its best to play down. But despite Ormond, the Catholic Archbishop of Armagh, Oliver Plunkett, was officially claimed to be implicated in the plot, was arrested, and, when it was clear that no case could be sustained against him in Ireland, was brought to London, tried, convicted on fabricated evidence, and executed in 1681.

It was not lost upon the Catholic population that Charles II had no legitimate heir and that his brother, Duke of York and heir-presumptive, was a practising Catholic. Surely a Catholic nation could reasonably expect a restoration of its liberties from a Catholic king? In February 1685, James II duly succeeded his brother, and expectations ran high. Ormond was recalled to London. The army in Ireland, by now already officered and manned to a substantial degree by Catholics, was under the control of the Catholic Richard Talbot, a close associate of the new king, and made Earl of Tyrconnell. The question of religious discrimination seemed all but answered, and attention focused on the land question. When Ormond's replacement, the Protestant Earl of Clarendon, was in turn replaced by the Earl of Tyrconnell in 1687, anxiety among the Protestant community reached a new pitch. There had been no Catholic Lieutenant since the Reformation. Although the royal policy of removing religious discrimination was a balanced one, its allowance of freedom to dissenting Protestant sects was of little significance in Ireland. Within two years, many Catholics were appointed to official posts, and by dint of careful electoral management, a Catholic majority was returned in the Dublin parliament. Tyrconnell made no secret of his frustration over the Protestant domination of land ownership, a 'damned thing' in his opinion. Many Protestants took fright and left Ireland, either selling out or becoming absentee landowners. Military officers deprived of their posts left to seek service elsewhere, or stayed to make trouble. In a short time, a self-exiled Protestant émigré community was voicing its resentments in London and at the court of William of Orange, James II's son-in-law, in Holland, just as their Catholic compatriots had done in Spain, France and Rome.

HUGUENOTS AND PALATINES

WHEN the Edict of Nantes ended the toleration of Protestantism in France, in 1685, around 10,000 Huguenots (French Calvinists) migrated to Ireland, encouraged by the parliament with financial grants and advantageous leases. There had been a small colony of them in Dublin since 1665. Freedom to practise their form of worship was what attracted them, and they brought a wide range of skills and crafts, notably in linen-making and in weaving, and their own strong 'work ethic'. Many were military veterans, and rallied to King William in the war of 1690. One of their larger settlements was at Portarlington, Queen's County (now Co. Laois), where some 'Huguenot-style' buildings remain. Others, including the linen-making pioneer Samuel Crommelin, settled near Lisburn, Co. Antrim. Altogether they congregated in over twenty centres. Over four or five generations, they became largely assimilated into the Protestant population, mostly adopting the Church of Ireland, though French churches remained in a few locations into the nineteenth century.

A smaller immigrant community was that of the Palatinate Germans, again displaced by French religious intolerance. Some three thousand in number, they came to Ireland in 1709 and settled in Limerick, Kerry and Tipperary. They did not integrate as successfully as the French, and by 1760 many had departed for North America. The Germans retained their own communal identity more than the Huguenots, but they responded positively to Methodism (itself heavily influenced by German Moravian pietism). Even they, by 1800, were almost wholly English-speaking. As relatively prosperous, and Protestant, farmers in largely Catholic areas, they were often victims of night raids. David Hempton, writing in *The People of Ireland*, comments that 'the Palatines still retained subtle elements of their . . . Germanic origins until well into the twentieth century.'

THE GLORIOUS REVOLUTION

To Tyrconnell and the king, the re-establishment of a Catholic Irish kingdom seemed feasible as well as proper; after all it was a separate realm, inhabited chiefly by Catholics. But the Irish policy was observed with close attention by the king's opponents, and it was assumed, with considerable reason, that James would try to do the same thing in England. England, at least in its ruling and influential landowning and mercantile classes, had become an overwhelmingly Protestant nation; and the Civil War, not yet a lifetime away, when the king had been forcibly called to account, was increasingly remembered. When two regiments of Tyrconnell's army were summoned over to England in 1688, attitudes hardened. In November, at the invitation of James II's opponents, William of Orange landed in England. By 24 December, James had fled to France. The 'Glorious Revolution' was taking place.

In Ireland, however, Tyrconnell as Lieutenant held out for James II, with the support of most of the nation. He met serious opposition only in Ulster, where first Londonderry and then Enniskillen refused to admit his new garrisons. In January, the Presbyterian leaders of Ulster formed county associations and declared for the new sovereigns, William and Mary. Tyrconnell led an army into Ulster in March and defeated them in the 'Break of Dromore' on the 14th, after which many people fled either to Scotland or within the walls of Londonderry and Enniskillen, which still held out against Tyrconnell. In the same month, James II landed at Kinsale, supported by a small French force, and came north to lead the advance on Londonderry (only the emergency need for Irish support could procure the first visit by a king since that of Richard II). The governor's willingness to surrender was overruled by the townspeople, and a siege began. With inadequate artillery and no siege equipment, James's army could only try and starve the defenders into submission, a tactic which looked likely to succeed in a town over-filled with refugees. Starvation and disease took a heavy toll. On 28 July, however, two relief ships finally succeeded in breaking through the boom laid by the besiegers across the Foyle. Three days later, the 15-week-old siege was abandoned.

During these operations, in May 1689, the parliament, heavily dominated by the Old English, accepted a Bill which repealed the post-commonwealth Acts of Settlement and Explanation, leaving the way open for a new wholesale redistribution of property. This lost James a great deal of the support which the Protestant population had previously offered him. The parliament also restated Ireland's independence of legislation made in England, though James stopped short of assenting to the repeal of Poynings' Law. A new name entered the public vocabulary at this time, that of the Jacobites, or supporters of James.

THE BATTLE OF THE BOYNE

The forces at King James's command were substantial, and well-provided with French munitions. But a Jacobite army under Justin MacCarthy, Lord Mountcashel, on its way to attack Enniskillen, was defeated by a Williamite one from Enniskillen on 31 July at Newtownbutler. With this, Ulster was effectively lost to the Jacobites, and the supporters of William had a substantial base to build upon. But the campaign was a hesitant one at first. That the fight was to decide who was King of Ireland was incidental: Ireland was the chosen arena for deciding the future governance of England. And there were reverberations even beyond England, since William of Orange was not (unlike his distant descendant, George I) motivated simply by ambition to occupy the English throne. Control of England was part of his strategic plan to isolate and defeat the French monarchy. Under the 'Sun-King', Louis XIV, France was threatening to engulf the Low Countries and dominate Europe. William's appointed general, Marshal Schomberg, refused a battle with the Jacobites in September 1689, and, after a winter without initiatives, William himself landed at Carrickfergus to take charge of the campaign in June 1690. Now Ireland had two kings on its soil. In March, James had exchanged five regiments of Irish soldiers for 7,000 French troops led by the Comte de Lauzun. A battle was now inevitable. James was at Dundalk, moving north on Ulster when news of William's landing was confirmed. Reverting to defensive action, he chose to station his army on the south side of the River Boyne, throwing up earthworks to make attack more difficult.

On the morning of 1 July, the battle began. This was contemporary-style warfare, and by no means simply an affair of ill-armed Celts against disciplined ranks of musketeers; both sides were commanded by professional officers with a large nucleus of trained soldiers. But James's had a higher proportion of untrained men, volunteers or forcibly recruited. Both armies were large,

Site of the Battle of the Boyne

though William's numbers were substantially greater, around 36,000 to James's 25,000. James's decision to stand his ground rather than take the offensive, though tactically sensible, was not perhaps the best use of his infantry, who gave way before the persistent oncoming pressure of the Williamites along the whole front. Perhaps with a retreat in mind, James had already sent much of his artillery back towards Dublin. Ferocious charges by his cavalry under Tyrconnell could not change the issue. The Jacobite army was defeated, though the late deployment of the French troops, held in reserve, enabled a fairly orderly retreat to be made, and it was not a rout. It was enough for James II, however. He left Ireland a few days later, appointing Tyrconnell as his Lieutenant.

The victory of the Boyne meant that Dublin was open to William's army, and the Jacobite forces regrouped in the west, leaving the capital to be taken over. On the wider European scale it confirmed the thrust of William's policy (indeed the defeat of the Catholic James was welcomed by the Catholic rulers of Madrid and Vienna, coalition partners in William's Grand Alliance against France). In Ireland itself, the matter of which side would ultimately win was still far from decided. Though the significance of the campaign had reverted to the domestic level, there was hard and bitter fighting ahead. William left Ireland at the end of August, with Tyrconnell securely in possession of the fortified points of Limerick and Athlone, and all the territory west of the Shannon. The Dutch general Ginkel took command of the Williamite forces.

THE END OF THE CAMPAIGN

On the Jacobite side, the most prominent campaigner was Patrick Sarsfield, a member of a landed family from the Pale. He took Connacht from the Enniskillen Protestants, inflicting their first defeat; and a successful attack on William's siege equipment helped in the holding of Limerick. Through the winter of 1690–91, both sides engaged in sporadic raids and skirmishes while preparing for a major campaign. Once again, rural life was badly hit. With around 50,000 men under arms, there was immense pressure on all food supplies, and both armies requisitioned ruthlessly. The civilian population in the countryside suffered most, and again there was starvation and disease on a wide scale. For both sides, it was seen as a war of survival. Though William and Mary initiated a regime of religious tolerance in Great Britain, the need to keep their Ulster allies on side prevented them from extending this to Ireland. To the Ulstermen, toleration could only mean Catholic dominance and they were determined to resist it. A new French general, the Marquis de St-Ruth, with supplies of arms and money, landed in March, and took command of the Jacobite army, though he was very soon on bad terms with Tyrconnell and with

Site of the Battle of Aughrim

Sarsfield. The latter had been made Earl of Lucan by James II and was himself often at loggerheads with the Lieutenant. Disunity at the top was a bad augury for a campaign against the slow but thoroughly professional Ginkel with his army of 20,000 men. The Williamites took Athlone on 30 June 1691 and the Shannon was no longer a barrier. Against the wishes of his Irish colleagues, St-Ruth marshalled his forces for another pitched battle, and at Aughrim, near Ballinasloe, on 12 July, the Jacobites were heavily defeated. Unlike the Boyne, there was great loss of life at Aughrim, though very much more on the Jacobite side. St-Ruth was killed and estimates of the Irish dead were around 7,000. This was a crucial defeat. The Jacobite forces were left in disarray, and in a short time, Galway and Sligo were surrendered. Limerick was put under siege. With even the bellicose Sarsfield accepting that there was no hope of a Jacobite recovery, negotiations between the two sides took place, and culminated in the Treaty of Limerick, signed on 3 October. This marked the end of the war. On 22 December, a French fleet took Sarsfield away from Ireland, with 12,000 troops.

THE TREATY OF LIMERICK

The Treaty was a contentious one. Sarsfield, a soldier not a politician, was chiefly concerned with getting terms for extracting his forces as a fighting unit. For those Jacobites and Catholics who remained, the terms did not seem unsatisfactory. Religious freedom 'consistent with the laws of Ireland' was granted, and the oath of supremacy was not to be required from Catholic office-holders. Catholics were given security of possession of their estates, or their right to practise trades and professions. The leniency of the terms outraged many Protestants, whether they wanted the fruits of victory or to prevent a further Jacobite rising. When parliament – restored to a substantial Protestant majority – met to ratify the treaty, in 1697, references to religious freedom and to the oath of supremacy were omitted. Meanwhile, the laws of Ireland had already been modified in 1695 to include some of the penal or 'popery' laws which would remain in force through most of the eighteenth century. The first of these prohibited Catholics from bearing arms, other than the nobles and gentry who were specifically allowed to do so under the Treaty of Limerick; a more potentially damaging one refused Catholics permission to go abroad for educational purposes, while also banning Catholic schools at home.

In fact, though further Jacobite risings would occur in the Scottish Gaeltacht, with some Irishmen involved, there were no more in Ireland. With a substantial army presence, Government-paid spies, and a watchful and suspicious Protestant population, it would have been difficult if not impossible to mount an armed rebellion. The existence of the Irish Brigade in France, based on Sarsfield's evacuated army, also drew off many potential fighters. Possibly James II's brief stay in Dublin, which enabled his Irish subjects to get the measure of the man, did not help his cause. He died in 1701, but a commitment to the Stewart dynasty remained strong among some members of the Protestant as well as the Catholic community. Their influence on events in Ireland was minimal. The main strength of Jacobitism in Ireland lay in the continuing support of the papacy, which meant that nominations to the Catholic Church hierarchy were made through the Stewart court, based first in France, then in Rome. The power of patronage (maintained up to 1766) was the only instrument of influence that the impoverished court-in-exile possessed.

CHAPTER TEN

The Ascendancy Rules

MEASURES AGAINST CATHOLICISM

YET another war had left the country in a bad way. The longer-term effects were mostly in the west, where the larger towns, Sligo, Galway, Limerick, took a long time to recover from the physical, social and economic effects of the battering they had taken. The west was to remain a relatively undeveloped region compared to other parts of the country. Remoteness from the capital, and a higher proportion of mountain land partially accounted for this, but the much greater extent of Catholic land ownership was also responsible. The penal laws begun in 1695 were extended in 1704 by the Act to Prevent the Further Growth of Popery. This forbade Catholics from buying land or inheriting it from Protestants, and from taking out long leases. On the death of a Catholic landowner, his estate had to be shared among all his male heirs. Such measures made it increasingly difficult for Catholic landowners to manage or develop their estates. One of the consequences was the preservation of the Irish language and traditional popular culture in Connacht, together with the maintenance of traditional methods of agriculture.

THE DECLINE OF GAELIC CULTURE AND LANGUAGE

Classic Gaelic culture, dealt a shattering blow by the flight of the earls, had declined steadily through the seventeenth century. The bardic structure, led by the *ollamh*, and the bardic schools, required the support of an aristocracy which paid and sustained the poets in return for their compositions. To have in his retinue a celebrated bard was a prestigious thing for any chieftain, whose praises would be duly sung and magnified. By the late sixteenth century, however, the tradition had become distinctly ossified, and the high culture of the bards had degenerated into fulsome flattery for anyone rich enough to make a good present to the poet. The drastic reduction in aristocratic patronage and the collapse of traditional Gaelic society meant that poets had to find new styles and new songs in order to survive. The high-flown literary language of earlier bards was discarded in favour of a more direct use of language, aimed at the people rather than the lords, and with a wider range of subject-matter. Satire and complaint remained prominent in the poetic repertoire, however.

public office in the boroughs they had controlled, unless they took an unacceptable oath. In Scotland, with which their ties were very close, their co-religionists formed the official and established Church, which increased their sense of injustice.

The tide of Anglicanism waxed and waned, according to the changes of power in London, but Dublin maintained the sanctions even at times when London dropped them. Under them, the validity of Presbyterian marriage could be challenged, and respectable persons accused of having illegitimate children, with important repercussions for inheritance of family property. A Toleration Act, passed in 1719, did little to answer the Presbyterians' grievances, since it merely allowed them to do what they had been doing anyway – holding their own services and organising their own Church. They remained liable to tithes and to being summonsed by church courts. Many Presbyterians and other Protestant dissenters emigrated to the North American colonies, a process that had begun on a small scale in the seventeenth century, but which now grew considerably. The sense of oppression nurtured during this time helps to explain the militancy which Ulster Presbyterianism later adopted.

Catholics continued to constitute more than two-thirds of the population. By the early 1700s they had almost a century's experience of how to evade, mitigate or neutralise the effects of hostile legislation. Often the penal laws were enforced lightly or not at all, depending on the officiousness of those in authority in particular districts. Except at times of anti-Catholic scares, it was possible for priests to operate quite openly. The seminaries on the continent continued to provide a regular supply and it has been reckoned that during much of the eighteenth century, there was a priest for every 1,000 members of the Catholic population (estimated at 1,750,000). It remained possible to be baptised, live and die as a Catholic. But exclusion from political and official life was rigorous. Even if he qualified in terms of property-holding, a Catholic was not allowed to vote, far less stand for office. The great majority of the Catholic population were farmers, peasantry, artisans and labourers, whose exclusion from the franchise was shared with Protestants of the same income level. Apart from what the churchmen might provide by way of guidance, it was a leaderless community. The day of the great Catholic landowners, Irish or Old English, was long gone. Unlike their Protestant peers, the Catholics of the labouring and peasant class were regarded by the Ascendancy leaders as a race apart: uncouth, even savage people living in squalid accommodation. Ignorance, and an element of fear underlay this contemptuous attitude. Many Irish youths still left to join continental armies, and it was known that if the professional Irish soldiers returned home *en masse*, they would make a highly formidable army.

EIGHTEENTH-CENTURY GOVERNMENT:
PATRONAGE NOT PARTY

The government of Ireland continued to be exercised through the office of Lieutenant, through the council, the courts and the parliament. Increasingly vice-regal rather than military in its primary role, the lieutenancy was a major source of patronage. In the eighteenth century, it did not seem strange to award a well-paid job – often involving minimal work – to a close relative, or friend, or supporter. That was how government worked. It could also work by financial transactions. In 1722 an Englishman, William Wood, acquired the profitable concession to mint copper coins for Ireland. The resultant protests were less about the system that allowed this to happen, even though Wood had obtained his patent by paying the vast bribe of £10,000 to the king's mistress, the influential Duchess of Kendal, but because there had been no prior consultation with Dublin, and Wood's profit was considered excessive.

The Lieutenant was responsible to the king, but the old royal prerogatives were gradually being absorbed by the form of British government which was established following the parliamentary union of England and Scotland in 1707. Whigs and Tories, not long before hardly better than swear-words as descriptions of politico-religious factions, now formed the two dominant political parties; and a Whig government would certainly expect to install a Whig Lieutenant in Dublin. But the Dublin parliament did not divide on Whig–Tory lines: the position was rather like that of the one-party state of some countries in later times. The part played in government by parliament was small. It had no control over the executive or over official appointments. Still trapped by Poynings' Law, it could not initiate or enact legislation on behalf of Ireland, without reference to English interests. For its members, whether bishops or earls in the Upper House, or landed gentry in the Commons, the Lieutenant and the British connection remained the guarantees of their status and condition; and, as with the sacramental test issue, their opposition to government initiatives almost always arose from a reactionary desire to protect their position.

Loyal as the Ascendancy was, it was not entirely the Lieutenant's creature. Partly taking its cue from its London counterpart, the parliament often contested British government policy towards Ireland. Its interest was never more than that of the community it represented, but on several occasions between 1692 and 1720 it made efforts to assert its legislative independence – one of the most notable being made by William Molyneux, member for Dublin University. In 1697 he wrote a pamphlet, *The Case of Ireland's Being Bound by Acts of Parliament in England, Stated*, which went back through the parliament's archives to justify the claim that it alone had the right to legislate for Ireland.

As in all serious issues between the Ascendancy and Britain, there was an economic cause, in this case an English parliamentary effort to ban Ireland from exporting wool, which was seen as a threat to the important English woollen trade. In 1720, the British parliament passed an Act, the notorious Sixth of George I, for 'The better securing the Dependency of the Kingdom of Ireland upon the Crown of Great Britain'. This affirmed that the House of Lords in the Westminster parliament was the final court of appeal for Irish questions. Intended to put the Irish parliament firmly in its place, the Act achieved its aim, but at the expense of creating a widespread sense of anger and dissatisfaction. In 1721, Ireland was excluded from the East India trade, except for goods sent and received through English ports. In 1733, Irish participation in trade with the West Indies was banned. Such efforts to sustain English monopolies were hard to enforce; they could be ignored by boldness or circumvented by bribery, but they made it difficult for Irish traders to operate on a large scale, and were a constant reminder that Ireland was considered a second-class state.

During the eighteenth century, successive Lieutenants practised and perfected an informal system of parliamentary management, using their great incentive of patronage. A whole range of well-paid posts, from judgeships and commissioners of revenue, down to sheriffs' clerks and local revenue men, were in the government's gift. It was never hard to find parliamentary managers who would undertake to keep parliament on side with the government, in exchange for a share in the distribution and receipt of such power and influence. William Connolly was the first of a line of such 'undertakers'. A parliament managed in this way was unlikely to be the source of constitutional reform. Before such a movement did emerge, however, there were many issues which stimulated controversy and debate outside parliament. Anger, hope, argument and despair were all vented in a torrent of pamphlets, pasquils, open letters, cartoons, slogans and other forms of publicity. Among these, the most influential and lasting are the contributions of Jonathan Swift, whose fine scorn could rise far above the general level of rhetoric and abuse, and whose anonymous *Drapier's Letters*, written against Wood's coinage (and provoking official fury) stand with the *Modest Proposal* (that the poor should eat their children) as evidence that Irish satire could still carry a dangerously sharp edge. The *Drapier's Letters* were published through 1724, and helped to raise the protest to such a peak that the British government first reduced, then in September 1725 finally cancelled Wood's patent. Swift was anything but an Irish nationalist, but in the generation after his (he died in 1745), opposition to British dominion was not restricted to Catholics or Jacobites. Gradually, among some of the Protestant community, London's claim to superiority was provoking a reaction in the direction of Irish independence.

THE ECONOMIC PYRAMID

England's problem with Ireland had always been how to exploit its actual and potential wealth, without the effort costing more than the result. Now, with the entire island pacified, shired and under the control of the English government, seemed the time for this problem to disappear. Fortunes could be made in Ireland. Stately homes in the country and streets of fine town houses were built for those who were near the top of the economic structure. A great amount of money left the country each year in rent payments to absentee owners: Thomas Prior in his *List of the Absentees of Ireland*, compiled in 1729, estimated this at £325,000. Such a siphoning-off of capital was a brake on improvements to farming and fisheries as well as on investment in manufacturing. Certain industries made the same kind of progress that was generating the 'industrial revolution' in Britain and northern Europe, notably the linen industry of the north, developed by Huguenot immigrants from France with the Irish parliament's active encouragement. But the opposition of British manufacturers did much to stifle commercial development, whether in manufacture or trading. The land and its produce remained at the basis of economic life.

Signs of wealth were visible in such things as the building of the new parliament House in Dublin. Other public buildings, including the Four Courts, went up in the capital, giving it a townscape to rival that of Copenhagen or the 'new town' of Edinburgh, with broad new streets and great squares laid out by the 'wide streets commissioners'. Trinity College was enlarged. These grand projects were paid for out of the public purse, or, in the case of domestic housing, by developers who knew they had a ready market among the officials, merchants and landed gentry.

The wealth to sustain this flowed upwards from the land. But the people at the lower end of the economic structure had very little share in it. Land tenure was exercised through several stages of tenancy and sub-tenancy, so that large estates let on long leases and generous terms ended up in a multiplicity of smallholdings, often on short or insecure leases, at disproportionately high rents. Hundreds of thousands of families, living at a subsistence level, working the land, supported the opulence of the ruling class. Beyond them was a numerous class of the semi-destitute, living as day-labourers, street entertainers, beggars and vagrants – people who had lost their homes and land through debt, illness, insolence to important people, inability to cope, or sheer rejection of an intolerable existence. In the bigger towns, and close to military barracks and to harbours, prostitution of women and children formed another aspect of the hidden 'black economy'. Isolated and unprotected individuals were at risk of being snatched and kidnapped by gangs operating a 'white slave' traffic to the American plantations.

Nevertheless, the population, living mostly on a monotonous but sufficiently nutritious diet of which potatoes, oatmeal and buttermilk were the
main constituents, continued to grow in numbers. No census was attempted
in the eighteenth century, but a reliable estimate of the population suggests a
growth through the hundred years from around two and a half million to
almost four million. This expansion was slowed by years of bad harvests, as in
1727–30, and again in 1740–41, and 1756–57, when food prices soared and
famine, with its accompanying epidemics of disease, struck at individual areas
or across the whole country. Its impact was also reduced by a steady flow of
emigration, chiefly to the North American colonies.

Despite severe law enforcement, including whipping, branding, transportation (first to the West Indies, later to Australia) and capital punishment for a
wide range of offences, poverty inevitably gave rise to much petty crime.
Among the Ascendancy, the 'native' Irish were regarded as thievish and brutal
by nature. Such characteristics, combined with an inability to speak the
English language, made it possible for them to be seen as a subject race for
whom squalor was natural and hardship desirable, since the possession of
money would lead only to drunkenness and debauchery. In this way, an
Ascendancy family could not merely enjoy its superior lifestyle but feel virtu-
ous about it.

By no means all the Catholic Irish lived at this level of economic deprivation
and social disesteem. Many were farmers or country merchants, often on the
same economic level, and friendly terms, with their Protestant neighbours. In
the eighteenth century they conformed to the dress, language and general style
of the Ascendancy farming family, and were distinguishable only by their lack

---

THE WILD GEESE

Some time around 1725, this phrase arose to describe those who left
Ireland to serve in foreign armies. Its author is unknown, but it is
found in an official letter of 1726, used as if it were a current phrase.
With it, a touch of romance is applied to the condition of exile and the
business of being a mercenary soldier. It was employed most memorably
by W.B. Yeats, in *September 1913*:

> Was it for this the wild geese spread
> The gray wing upon every tide . . .
> Romantic Ireland's dead and gone;
> It's with O'Leary in the grave.

---

of attendance at the Anglican Church. But they remained unenfranchised, ineligible for public office, and at the mercy of the penal laws.

EIGHTEENTH-CENTURY POWER BASES AND THE PATRIOT MOVEMENT

From the 1730s on, the two most important men in Ireland, in terms of government, were the English Archbishop of Armagh (appointed 1724) and the Speaker of the House of Commons (Henry Boyle from 1733 until 1755). A succession of archbishops, with close connections in England, beginning with Hugh Boulter in 1724, managed the House of Lords and were influential in the placement of Englishmen in official posts. Boulter also procured the removal of Catholic voters from the franchise, in 1727. Boyle, in alliance with the Lieutenant and the council, managed the House of Commons and ensured a government majority. During his long tenure he achieved this with such effect that the Dublin Castle authorities began to fear that the Speaker was altogether too powerful.

It was around the middle of the eighteenth century that the term 'patriot' began to become a familiar one in Irish politics. The concept of the *patria* or fatherland had been one that rallied Catholic supporters in the later sixteenth century, but these latter-day Patriots were members of the Protestant community. In the parliament, they were a fluid group, their numbers waxing and waning depending on particular issues, or on the degree to which Boyle could buy them off. From 1747, a new archbishop, George Stone, opposed Boyle and allied himself with another group of members ready to 'undertake' the government's business, led by John Ponsonby, of Bessborough, Co. Kilkenny. In 1751 the Duke of Dorset, a former Lieutenant, was reappointed, with a brief to restore power to the administration. To shore up his own position, Boyle determined to demonstrate his power. The initial focus of confrontation was the old cause of Irish parliamentary independence, which flared up again in 1750–53. In both of these years the Irish revenues achieved a surplus of income over expenditure, part of which was assigned by a vote of parliament to reduce the Irish national debt. The Act providing for this was approved by London, but with a clause inserted to specify that the Crown had agreed to it. This was to emphasise that the Crown's permission was essential: the Irish parliament was not free to decide what to do with the surplus. The Irish parliament accepted this amendment in 1750 but, led by Boyle in stormy debate, refused to do so in 1753. The majority was a narrow one, 122 to 119, but it showed the weakness of the government when the 'undertaker' system went awry.

Popular opinion hailed the vote as a victory for Ireland and the members who supported it were praised as 'patriots'. Patriot clubs were formed. A large segment of the Ascendancy showed itself as being in favour of Irish parliamentary independence, not only from Westminster but from the Viceroy. It was far from being a coherent movement, but it represents a substantial shift in general attitude, to the point where the Patriots had to take their stand on being Irish. In another phrase of the time, 'the Protestant nation' was being forced to define itself. In the parliament itself, matters were smoothed over by 1755. Boyle relinquished the speakership for the earldom of Shannon and a pension, and Ponsonby became Speaker and chief undertaker. As blatant a piece of political fixing as the century could show, it caused anger and derision among those who had supported the Patriots, but patriotism had never been Boyle's motive.

ECONOMIC PROTEST: WHITEBOYS AND OTHERS

This was peaceful, loyal protest, though a foretaste of the 'No taxation without representation' cry which would soon come from over the Atlantic. Ireland had no representation at Westminster. From 1759, however, a more dangerous and subversive form of protest struck at the Ascendancy landlords themselves. For some decades, the amount of ground under pasture had been increasing at the expense of ground under tillage. This was a commercial consequence in the trade of beef, tallow and hides, and was resented by the cottagers whose land was often taken away by the landlord to extend the cattle pastures. In 1759, this process accelerated considerably as a result of the lifting of the ban on exporting beef on the hoof from Ireland to England (whose population was beginning to increase dramatically). Protests began around 1760 in Tipperary, where the white-shirted *Buachaillí Bána*, or 'Whiteboys' came out by night to throw down fences and walls, and to kill and maim cattle belonging to the enclosers.

The activities spread into the adjoining counties, and soon other long-standing grievances were added to the list, notably the tithe levied on the potato crop. Inevitably, too, the most hated of the landlord class were attacked personally, with deaths and injuries resulting. Parliament passed 'Whiteboy' acts prescribing the death penalty for those caught, but a pattern of agrarian protest was firmly established. Such developments were not unique to Ireland, and there is little doubt that news of direct action in one area influenced events elsewhere. Anonymous, spontaneous, midnight violence to property, animals and people was the recourse of a section of the community who felt increasingly insecure and who had no other way of protecting their own interests. The Catholic Church did not condone their actions, and the bishops advised the cottagers to use the law. While this was both natural and expected, it indicates also the desire of the Church not to inflame country life in a way which would bring down a harsh enforcement of the penal laws. For their part, the Whiteboys and other protest groups were just as keen to modify the often pressing demands for money made upon them by the Catholic clergy.

Whiteboy-type action spread even to Ulster, which was, in its north-eastern corner at least, the most prosperous province and one in which wealth was distributed more evenly than elsewhere. The established 'Ulster Custom', generally practised though based on no law, gave tenants a degree of rights and security not found in other parts of Ireland. 'Tenant right' had a market value, which a tenant could sell on to a successor, or, if evicted, could be claimed from the landlord at full value. Tenants had thus more incentive to improve the property, and there was more co-operation between tenant and landlord.

A Linen Board had been established in 1711, intended to develop the industry on a nation-wide basis, but Ulster soon became the focus of activity, both in the growing of flax and the processing of the crop. In 1713 the province produced a million yards of linen cloth; by 1796 the amount was forty-seven times more. Families of smallholders could be involved at all stages, and growing, carding, spinning and weaving were all cottage industries. Bleaching, finishing and marketing – the latter through Dublin rather than the still small town of Belfast – was in the hands of larger businesses who bought the raw cloth from the weavers.

CANALS

CANAL building in Ireland predates that in England. The first canal to be cut in Ireland was the Newry Navigation, begun in 1731 to transport coal from the east Tyrone field. Also coal-connected was the Tyrone Navigation, begun two years later. Government money was granted lavishly to canal projects in the eighteenth century, supervised by a set of commissioners from 1752, but the longest canals were completed in the nineteenth. The country was bisected in 1803 by the Grand Canal, which linked Dublin to Shannon Harbour, near Banagher, and another cross-country waterway linked Belfast via Belleek to the Upper Shannon. The Royal Canal, from Dublin to Mullingar, and again with an extension to the Shannon, completed twenty years after the Grand, was always a poor relation. In 1837, the Grand Canal carried over 100,000 passengers, the Royal only 46,450. Freight traffic on the canals, never in great bulk, was hit by the railways. But it was not until 1961 that Coras Iompair Éireann, the national transport board, withdrew services on the Grand and Royal Canals.

Householders in central Ulster formed the 'Hearts of Oak' association in 1763 to protest against compulsory labour demanded in the building of new roads and bridges. The grand juries, recruited from the larger property-owners, which formed the county administrations, were determined to get their improvements as cheaply as possibly. In the face of such opposition, the grand juries backed down, but in 1770 a new popular movement known as the 'Hearts of Steel' arose, in protest against the increased rents charged on the vast Donegall estate in Antrim, and quickly spread, gathering other causes to it as well, all of an economic sort.

It was also a time when food prices were rising steeply. When one 'Steelboy' was imprisoned in Belfast, a band of 500 marched into the town and forced his release. This was an exclusively Protestant organisation, but the unrest caused by high rents, evictions from long-held land, and rising prices was common among small tenant farmers throughout the country. All became aware that by uniting, acting together, and enjoying or enforcing the silent loyalty of their communities, they created a popular force that could give them at least a negative control over local events, and give the authorities a very difficult time:

> . . . with Hearts of Steel
> Bravely resolved in mutual league unite
> To keep Possession, and support their Right.

Organised and determined activity of this kind, at a local level, was a new phenomenon. Reaction by the government and landowning class was typical in its inability to read, or to come to terms with, the signs of change. Though repressive action by government and landlords, some of whom formed armed posses to patrol their districts, greatly reduced Whiteboy activity in Munster in 1765, there were further outbreaks in the 1780s, by the 'Rightboys' of Cork, and others. The Whiteboy tradition of direct action remained active for another hundred years.

CHAPTER ELEVEN

The Age of Revolution

POLITICS AND POWER IN THE EIGHTEENTH CENTURY

B Y 1757, the triumvirate of Boyle (now Earl of Shannon), Speaker
Ponsonby and Archbishop Stone had resolved most of their differences.
They were now the Lords Justices, charged with management of affairs
in the Lieutenant's absence (at this time the Lieutenant resided in Ireland only
when parliament sat, perhaps eight months in each two years). Parliament
again took the initiative: Ponsonby in his consultations with the Lieutenant or
the council in effect telling them what would and what would not be allowed,
within the limits of the parliament's jurisdiction. In consultation with the
Ascendancy magnates, the Lords Justices exercised much of the power and
patronage of the government. The parliament remained committed to a reactionary conservatism, and much of the reason for its occasional fits of patriotism was a fear of excessive liberalisation being introduced from London.

Beyond the pillars of the stately new Parliament House (completed in 1739),
discussion ranged far more widely. There were several constituencies of
people, of whom only one, the Anglican–Protestant land-owning Ascendancy,
was fully represented in parliament. There was also a substantial Anglican–
Protestant group of tradesmen and artisans, shading off towards the labouring
class – an element most prominent in Dublin, where they furnished the
numbers for the city's volatile, and patriotically inclined, mob which took to
the streets when feelings ran high. The disparate range of the others, the
Presbyterian–Protestants (mostly in Ulster), the smaller groups of Methodists,
Baptists and Quakers, and the wealthier Catholic merchants and landowners,
had little say in national affairs but a strong vested interest in national stability
and economic security. The anti-Catholic penal laws, though still on the
statute book, were not being enforced. The fourth and by far the largest group,
unrepresented and with little sense of security or stability, was a reserve of discontent that occasionally erupted into local violence, but that had little in the
way of political aims or direction.

'Patriotism' could be found among all these groupings, though as a political
handle it could be affixed to a variety of different vessels. The basic tenet was
that Ireland was a separate kingdom under the British Crown, and as such
should be independent in its law-making and its institutions. Added to this

Scots–American privateer-commander John Paul Jones, in capturing a Royal Navy ship in Belfast Lough in 1778, was regarded somewhat equivocally, but served as a reminder of Ireland's long and relatively unprotected coastline. The anxiety was answered by the formation of a volunteer militia. Created and officered by the Protestant Ascendancy, uniformed and armed at its own expense, the Volunteers numbered over 40,000 by 1779.

The Volunteers were the darlings of the Protestant nation. If they were animated by anti-French feelings, they were just as full of patriotic sentiment also. Their formation had been sanctioned by the Lieutenant, who could not have done otherwise. But now, as if by magic, the Patriot cause had acquired an army. Flood, who true to his word, had retained his Patriot convictions while pocketing his guineas, spelled it out: the Volunteers were there to exact Ireland's rights from England, and to remain on foot until they were secured. It was a somewhat unreal-seeming situation. The Lieutenant, the Earl of Buckinghamshire, had seen events pass completely beyond his control. But there was no suggestion of a *coup*, no word of treason – he was not under threat. He frankly admitted he was out of his depth, and London had no advice to offer him. Grattan, Flood and the other leaders, together with the vast majority of their smartly clad militiamen, were not revolutionaries. As constitutionalists, they looked to the parliament to achieve their aims.

TRADE REFORMS AND AN INCREASE IN WEALTH

Parliament responded strongly to the mood. With the Catholic population no longer seen as a threat to the state, the more liberal-minded elements in the Protestant Ascendancy were prepared to accept their Catholic fellow-citizens as co-campaigners in the same cause. Catholics were still forbidden to carry arms, but an Act of 1778 went a great way towards repealing the disabling legislation which affected their rights to lease and bequeath land. Only Patriot support pushed this through, against intense hostility from the more conservative Protestant camp. Throughout most of 1779, Lord North's Tory British government contrived to ignore the crisis in Ireland. The parliament due to convene that autumn had the Patriot wind full in its sails. The loyal address to the king, prepared by the council, had a forceful amendment added: 'That it is not by temporary expedients but by a free trade alone that this nation is now to be saved from impending ruin.' What they sought was the lifting of restrictions on Irish trade, imposed by Britain for the benefit of British shippers and merchants, and the placing of Irish trade under the sole control of the Irish parliament. As the Patriot leaders well knew, they had the backing of the Whig opposition in London. In December, North put forward a sweeping set of trade reforms for Ireland that conceded all the Patriots wanted. His motive was at least as much to undermine the Whigs as it was to pacify the Irish, but it was a triumph for the Patriots, who pressed on with further demands.

The Irish economy began to benefit from the relaxation of trade restrictions, and also by measures passed in the Dublin parliament. This body showed a shrewd economic sense in its support of a variety of industrial initiatives undertaken by, or invested in by, its own members. The Corn Law Act of 1784 was perhaps the most important of a number of measures designed to protect and improve agriculture, industry and trade. In 1783 the Bank of Ireland was established by royal charter and with the substantial initial capital of £600,000. Its first Governor, David La Touche, was a scion of an immigrant Huguenot family which had been involved in banking since the 1690s. A substantial amount of capital was directed towards the building of the Grand Canal and other canal systems, and the urban splendour and outward growth of Dublin increased rapidly. Hundreds of country landlords were able to build 'Georgian' houses and surround them with wooded demesnes.

The increase of wealth was deployed and enjoyed by a very small section of the population. Living standards for them rose dramatically, and improved also for the stratum of society that supplied them with equipment, services and materials. Despite the contempt for tradesmen affected by the typical Ascendancy squire, the line of distinction between him and the better-off merchants was becoming increasingly blurred. Little benefit worked its way downwards to the great mass of the peasantry. Visitors to Ireland remarked on the tattered rags worn by the cottiers, and their primitive dwellings: 'the most miserable looking hovels that can well be conceived' wrote an English traveller, Arthur Young, in the 1770s. They were equipped with hardly any of the furnishings and fittings that even the cottagers of England were by now accustomed to. But despite their lack of adequate clothing and furniture, which emphasised their absence from the cash economy, the country people experienced some advantage over other peasant communities of Europe. Their diet, if monotonous, was nutritious, consisting very largely of potatoes, supplemented with oatmeal and buttermilk, and it promoted physical growth and health. Cormac Ó Gráda notes that 'the key to the relative tallness and longevity of the Irish poor is probably that, thanks largely to the potato, they were relatively well fed.' One consequence of this was that the overall population was growing with great rapidity.

THE CONSTITUTIONAL ISSUE

National wealth and an economic surplus brought a sense of confidence to the ruling class which helped the Patriot cause. If this was to be advanced, parliament had to play its part, but the Patriot leaders knew that only a strong continuing tide of public opinion could compel parliament to action. Buckinghamshire and his Secretary, Heron, had done what they could, by the usual methods, to assure the compliance of members before the assembly met in April 1780, but the orators and journalists of the opposition had been active in promoting the Patriot argument throughout the country. Pamphlets, speeches, songs, inspired rumours, all helped to bring public opinion to a feverish level. A late government concession, removing the sacramental oath for Protestant dissenters, did nothing to curb the fervour. In parliament on 19 April, Grattan led for the Patriot side. His resolution moved that 'the King's most excellent Majesty, and the Lords and Commons of Ireland, are the only power competent to enact laws to bind Ireland.' The efforts of the Lieutenant's members managed to get the matter indefinitely adjourned, but it was plain that it was not going to go away.

Under a new Lieutenant, the Earl of Carlisle, an Act of Habeas Corpus was passed, but otherwise the government held the line against reform; and the Patriots did not take advantage of the British humiliation at Yorktown in 1781, which resulted in the establishment of the United States of America. It was once again outside parliament that the next move took place. A convention of the Volunteers met at Dungannon on 15 February 1782, with Charlemont, Grattan and Flood (who had lost his official position) determined to use the strength of the movement by reiterating its aims, the chief of which remained legislative independence. Among the resolutions that were passed with acclaim was one put forward by Grattan, 'that as men and as Irishmen, as Christians and as Protestants, we rejoice in the relaxation of the penal laws against our Roman Catholic fellow-subjects.' After Dungannon, indefinite adjournment of the constitutional question was no longer an option. But in parliament a week later, it was again postponed. Then at the end of March the government of Lord North in London fell, the Whigs under Lord Rockingham came into power, and after speedy consultation between the new administration and representatives of the Patriots, the matter came before parliament again on 16 April. Once again Grattan led the debate, but this time he knew he had won even before the vote:

> I am now to address a free people: ages have passed away and this is the first moment in which you could be distinguished by such an appellation . . . Ireland is now a nation; in that new character I hail her, and bowing to her august presence, I say, *Esto perpetua*.

It was grandiose oratory for a moment that appeared indeed historic, and stamped that parliament as 'Grattan's parliament' for the generations to follow. It voted him a sum of £50,000 in recognition of his achievement. But

Grattan in Parliament demanding Irish independence

the victory was incomplete. The Irish government was still in the hands of the Viceroy, with all the powers of patronage. There was no Prime Minister, no Irish cabinet. Parliament remained an assembly of Protestant magnates and their agents, and as such, remained open to influence, pressure and purchase. Just as the Patriots had no intention of renouncing the English king, so the British government, whether Whig or Tory, had no intention of relinquishing Ireland, and London began to drag its heels on framing legislation to confirm what the Dublin parliament had agreed. Flood led the continuing agitation that finally resulted in Britain passing the Renunciation Act in April 1783, conceding the Irish parliament's exclusive right to legislate for Ireland – but even then Poynings' Law remained in force. Ireland might be a kingdom but its parliament was not sovereign.

The government of the youthful British Prime Minister, William Pitt, tried in 1785 to establish a new and more equitable trading relationship between Britain and Ireland, but intense opposition from English trading interests effectively wrecked the original plan. The political concessions demanded from Ireland in return would have wiped out much of the control of trade which had been gained in 1782. In August 1785, Pitt's watered-down 'twenty proposals' were savaged in debate and the majority in favour of letting them go forward to become a Bill was so small that the government simply dropped the matter. Although the parliamentary Patriots of Dublin and the Whigs of England would remain allies, it was always an uncertain alliance, of fluctuating warmth, with each side as eager to use the other as it was to help it – a relationship whose stresses would eventually wreck the British Liberal Party, almost a century later. A degree of disillusion with the political process set in, and among the Volunteers, brought to such a high pitch of expectation in 1782, the more radically inclined now turned away from Grattan.

REFORM OR REVOLUTION?

Sixty thousand strong in 1782, the Volunteers as a whole were not a revolutionary force, but nor were they the tools of any politician. They embraced the full spectrum of Protestant life. Their titular head was the Duke of Leinster, who apparently saw no inconsistency between constitutional reform and the retention of his own very considerable rights of patronage. But among the officers and the rank and file there were men of a more radical persuasion. Volunteer meetings could provide political education as well as military drill, and, especially in Dublin, there was a strong popular element within the movement. The leaders of this element, men like James Napper Tandy, Dublin activist and commander of the Volunteer artillery, followed the progress of the democratic movement in France, hailed the Revolution of July 1789, and studied such documents as the Constitution of the United States and Tom Paine's profoundly influential book *The Rights of Man*, published in 1791. The French Revolution created at least as much excitement as the American one. The *Belfast Telegraph* wrote in the autumn of 1789: 'The French Revolution acted as a spell on the minds of Irishmen . . . their sympathy was roused to a state of excitement almost painful, and that longed to find relief and indulgence, in re-enacting such spirit-stirring scenes . . . Twenty-six millions of our fellow-creatures (nearly one-sixth of the inhabitants of Europe) breaking their chains, and throwing off almost in an instant the degrading yoke of slavery, is a scene so new, so interesting, and sublime . . .'

The newspaper noted the height of public feeling in 'the liberal and enlightened town of Belfast, the Athens of Ireland', and how the Volunteers paraded in salute to the revolutionary French. Building on this radical enthusiasm, and the American and French examples, the generation following that of Grattan and Tandy was more inclined to take direct action.

SECTARIAN AND NON-SECTARIAN GROUPS

Though many wealthy Catholics contributed funds to the Volunteers, the general attitude among their ranks towards the movement was a cautious one. Few in the Patriot Party spoke up for complete emancipation of the Catholics, although the more far-sighted, including Grattan, realised that the political and economic independence which they sought would be fatally damaged from the start if the exclusion of Catholics was maintained. The growing *rapprochement* was marred by sectarian violence in Ulster. This had an economic origin. From the mid-1780s, rivalry in Co. Armagh over land ownership and competition in linen-making had developed between Protestants and Catholics to a point where some of the Protestants, following Steelboy tactics, and known as the Peep o' Day Boys from their dawn raids, began to harass Catholic farmers and burn their houses. The Catholics responded by forming armed groups known as the Defenders, which quickly spread into other provinces. Leading Catholics still retained a deep mistrust of the Dublin parliament, but among the 'middle-class' commercial families, growing in numbers, wealth and influence, there was an increasing sense of frustration with the gradualist approach of the Catholic Committee. This could point to some successes: Catholic Relief Acts were passed in 1778, 1782 and 1793; but the relaxations prompted the feeling that more concessions were possible as well as reasonable, and by 1791, a more militant spirit had grown in the Committee, with the merchants John Keogh and Edward Byrne as its leaders. A split followed, with the more cautious members, led by Lord Kenmare, forming their own body.

and Republican movement. In that year the Dublin branch of the Society was officially suppressed. An Anglican clergyman, the Rev William Jackson, who had adopted the Republican cause, came to Ireland from France to enquire as to the possibilities of a French invasion being supported. Betrayed by a friend in government pay, Jackson was tried for treason and poisoned himself in the dock; Wolfe Tone was sufficiently embarrassed by the business to leave the country for America, by agreement with the Dublin Castle authorities, even though there was no direct evidence against him. The United Irishmen became an underground movement, meeting in secret, neurotic about infiltration by spies (which was endemic) but increasingly resolved on taking drastic action. Meanwhile, through all the available media, newspapers, broadsheets, songs and pamphlets, libertarian propaganda continued to be diffused across the country. The United Irishmen's Belfast newspaper, the *Northern Star*, was widely read. The government passed an Insurrection Act in 1796, making the administration of unlawful oaths punishable by death, and introduced further emergency measures, including search powers and the suspension of habeas corpus. The militia, of suspect loyalty to the state, was complemented by a force of yeomanry, part-time soldiers recruited from the Protestant community and led by Ascendancy officers.

In December 1796, a substantial French military force left Brest, commanded by Lazare Hoche, a revolutionary general, and bound for the invasion of Ireland. It was an unseasonable time for such a venture, and the 'Protestant wind' which had upset Catholic plans in the past now blew a furious gale on the forces of rational materialism. Though some ships assembled in Bantry Bay, they returned to France without being able to effect a landing. Tone, who had gone from America to France, was on one of the vessels. Thoroughly alarmed, the government embarked on a campaign to disarm what was seen as the most militant province, Ulster. The number of United Irishmen estimated to be in the province was almost 118,000. Under General Lake, a ruthless and thorough search for weapons was undertaken, with the militiamen inflicting whippings and torture in order to force confessions. Its haul of weapons included muskets, bayonets and pikes, many of them antiquated. A martyr was found in William Orr, a Protestant farmer hanged for administering the United Irishmen's oath of secrecy – 'Remember Orr' became a rallying cry. *'Hapless nation,'* wrote the United Irishmen poet, William Drennan, in an ode on Orr's death:

> hapless land!
> Heap of uncementing sand!
> Crumbled by a foreign weight:
> And, by worse, domestic hate.

Bantry Bay

The violence of the government's action undoubtedly helped to stir up a popular reaction. Arms searches of equal violence to those of Ulster were carried out in Munster and Leinster, in districts where the Defenders were well established. Grattan and the moderate Patriots of parliament were helpless spectators; in May 1797 Grattan withdrew from the House of Commons after the collapse of an attempt to introduce a new Reform Bill. Lord Edward Fitzgerald, son of the Duke of Leinster, and a more radically minded Patriot than his father, had quitted parliament in the previous year and aligned himself with the United Irishmen. Neither side was troubling itself about the parliament now: a general election held in the summer of 1797 aroused scant interest. Having infiltrated the United Irishmen network with a substantial network of spies and informants, including the turncoat Samuel Turner, who had been on the executive committee, the authorities were as well-informed about the revolutionaries' plans, and their negotiations with France, as the leaders themselves. Whilst the official terror campaign went on, with the intention of removing both the will and the means for revolt, the leaders were left to develop their plans, until, on 12 March 1798, the government pounced, arresting all but three of the 'directory' or governing council.

THE SUPPRESSION OF THE 1798 RISING

Those who remained free managed to bring forward the date for a rising to 23 May, though the movement was thrown into great disarray. On 19 May, Lord Edward Fitzgerald (whom the government would have preferred to quietly to England than it had been at the start. At one level, this had much to do with the emigration of the cleverest and most articulate scions of the Ascendancy. Men like Burke, Sheridan and Goldsmith were absorbed and appreciated by the English political and literary community just as Wilde, Moore and Yeats would be a century later. Members of the nobility, like Robert Stewart, Viscount Castlereagh, moved easily between their country estates, Dublin and London.

Familiarity of a different and often more patronising sort was assisted by a more numerous class of immigrant to Britain, that of Irish labourers and servants, often first-generation English speakers. They were often brought over by landlords who owned property in both countries. As industrialisation got under way in Scotland and the North of England, larger numbers were drawn across by advertisement, rumour and the activity of factory agents. England was by far the largest market for Ireland's produce, and Ireland in turn was a major importer of English goods.

At this time, the population of Ireland, at around five million, was almost half of that of England, and nearly three times that of Scotland. To many people, a full parliamentary Union seemed to be the obvious way to cope with the Irish 'problem'. Among them was Adam Smith, the father of political economy, who noted that: 'By a union with Great Britain, Ireland would gain, besides the freedom of trade, other advantages more important, and which would more than compensate any increase in taxes that might accompany the union . . . Without a union with Great Britain, the inhabitants of Ireland are not likely to consider themselves for many ages one people.' Smith foresaw a social and political disintegration within Ireland, unless it were contained within the structure of a larger unit. He recommended either Union or complete separation, as did Lord Camden, the Lieutenant until June 1798, who wrote: 'Ireland is like a ship on fire, it must be either extinguished or cut adrift.' As far as Camden was concerned, the alternative was purely rhetorical – the British government never entertained the thought of Irish separation. There was far too much at stake – history, investment, profit, prestige, security. For Prime Minister William Pitt, confronting the rising power of Napoleon Bonaparte as post-revolutionary France moved towards Empire, Union became an imperative.

THE ACT OF UNION

Under a new Lieutenant, the soldier Lord Cornwallis, and with the management of Lord Castlereagh and Lord Clare, the business of arranging the Union was taken firmly in hand. In 1759, even the suggestion of a Union had been enough to bring the Dublin mob surging into the parliament building in furious protest. Forty years later, the will of the people, even of the Protestant people, was scarcely a consideration. The task was to persuade the Ascendancy parliament to abolish itself. It was not an easy one. The first attempt, in January 1799, was lost by five votes. Grattan, returned to the political arena, and the moderate Patriots were allied in opposition to the proposal with conservative Ascendancy members whose motives were very different. There was intensive canvassing and pressurising of individuals. Everyone holding an office under the Irish parliament had to be bought out. Virtually everyone who had a position of influence had to be persuaded, or bribed, into relinquishing it.

On 24 January 1799 the House of Commons, buoyed up by popular feeling, especially in Dublin, voted against Union. The government pressed on, using bribes, promises, threats and cajolements. It was the blatant fixing techniques employed at this time that did much to cast a shadow over Castlereagh's subsequent career. Among those who felt the pressure were the bishops of the Roman Catholic Church. Pitt had genuinely desired that Catholic emancipation should accompany the Union, but dropped this element when it became clear that even among pro-Union Protestants its retention might jeopardise their support. Instead, assurances were given to the bishops. Catholic emancipation, once the Union was accomplished, would be swiftly brought into law. On the other hand, there was no question of the government ever supporting an Emancipation Bill in the Dublin parliament. In this way the support of the Catholic Church for Union was assured, and with it the bulk of the more prosperous Catholic population. Among those who resisted was the 25-year-old lawyer, Daniel O'Connell, scion of a Catholic landowning family in Kerry, already a formidable debater. His repugnance to bloodshed had kept him out of events in 1798, but he maintained a stout belief in religious freedom, political radicalism and Irish independence.

Meanwhile, the London parliament approved the proposal for Union. The indefatigable Castlereagh used every opportunity of the patronage system to install Union-minded men in public office, and it was made clear that the British government would not climb down on this issue. In January 1800 the parliament reconvened. Grattan, who had resigned in 1797, was re-elected and – again dressed in his Volunteer uniform – spoke passionately against Union. But a year's interval had made a big difference. Both sides had made strenuous efforts to influence and deploy public opinion. But London was prepared to will the means as well as the end. The cost was colossal, with over £1,250,000 spent on buying out the rights of proprietors of rotten boroughs and occupants of parliamentary posts. Many members resisted Union on principle right to the last vote, but the graft and jobbery which had so long sustained the Dublin parliament in the end undid it, at the expert manipulation of

Castlereagh and his assistants. Enough members were bought, or coaxed, into providing a majority of 153 to 88 in the final debate on 7 June, and on 1 August 1800, the Bill for Union received the royal assent and the Irish parliament ceased to exist. The United Kingdom of Great Britain and Ireland came into being, with its parliament in London, where a hundred Irish members sat in the House of Commons, with four bishops and twenty-eight peers in the House of Lords. The bishops, of course, were of the Church of Ireland, now united with the Church of England. The stately parliament building was now redundant, until the Bank of Ireland occupied it, but the Castle remained busy, and the position of Lieutenant, or Viceroy, was retained, with its Privy Council.

Grattan's last speech in the Dublin parliament seemed to see Ireland as a Snow-White who had eaten the poisoned apple:

I see her in a swoon but she is not dead; though in her tomb she lies helpless and motionless, still on her lips is the spirit of life and on her cheeks the glow of beauty.

CHAPTER TWELVE

Union

OPTIMISM – AND DISAPPOINTMENT

WITH Union achieved, the reaction of most people seemed passive. There were no disturbances, and daily life went on as usual. A few people had become extremely rich out of it, most of them having been wealthy already, like John Foster, Speaker of the Dublin parliament, and the Marquis of Downshire, both of whom received large proportions of the compensatory cash. The terms of Union gave Ireland equal trading opportunities and also some protection of its own linen industry. The Irish legal hierarchy remained intact. The Bank of Ireland, chartered in 1783, retained control of currency, issuing its own notes: the two currencies were not combined until 1826. For Irish trade and industry, especially with a European war on, the prospects looked good. The building or extending of fine town and country houses went on, and there was extensive construction of roads, bridges and harbours. Many people at the time expected a rapid growth of manufacturing industry, on the lines of what was occurring in Scotland, Wales and England. An interest in surveying for mineral deposits, helped by the new science of geology, began among landowners, hopeful of discovering wealth lying beneath acres of unproductive land.

Within a year of the Union, it became plain to the Catholic population and their priests that emancipation was not, after all, to be part of the package. Pitt and his associates may have been sincere, but they had promised what they could not deliver. George III, still on the throne after forty years, despite bouts of lunacy, clung obstinately to the view that his coronation oath made it impossible for him to accept Catholic emancipation. King George's power under the constitution made this an effective block. Pitt was compelled to resign, and Cornwallis and Castlereagh went with him. To the Irish Catholics it was a flagrant betrayal of trust. For those with a sense of history, it was not the first time that their goodwill had been exploited and cheated by English authority. As time went on and it became ever more apparent that their cause had become simply a political football tossed about between Whig and Tory factions at Westminster, their latent or open hostility to the Union grew greater, and the influence of those who had opposed it from the start was increased.

PROTEST AND PROSELYTISING

The rumbling discontent found other ways to express itself. The most important was anti-tithe protest. In the preliminaries to Union there had been much talk of commutation of this burden, which fell most heavily on the poorest – and largest – section of the population. Their anger was increased by the fact that many of the Church of Ireland clergy were absentees, or were pluralists with several different livings. Since they did not require its ministry, Catholics and Presbyterians alike were even more aggrieved at having to pay for non-existent services. Tithe reform was regularly discussed but for twenty years after the Union, no government managed to achieve it.

Meanwhile, both Presbyterians and Catholics experienced a sense of revivalism; a strongly evangelistic movement among the former emphasised the individual's involvement with the Gospel. The Catholics began to build new churches, chapels and schools. Monastic houses were formed, or re-formed, and benevolent societies were established. Here too there was an evangelistic spirit, and wealthier lay people donated money to have religious books printed and distributed among the poor. A certain rivalry developed between the two movements, though neither gained many converts from the other, and for a time public disputes between rival clerics became fashionable. Huge numbers of religious tracts were printed and distributed free. In between these highly active and engaged groups, the Church of Ireland remained largely comatose, though some of its clergy were involved with the evangelical movement or otherwise energetic in their pastoral duties.

RURAL POVERTY

Dwellers on the land had other reasons for complaint apart from tithes. The agrarian system of the time, particularly outside Ulster, has been described by the historian R.B. McDowell as 'an economist's nightmare. Agriculture being the sole industry of any importance, the landlord had almost a monopoly of the means of existence, so rents tended to be high and the conditions of tenure hard, the tenant, who was usually left to carry out all improvements, having no rights to compensation for his labour when his lease expired.' Small farms were subdivided and sublet again. The labouring, cabin-dwelling families were the broad base of a social structure whose shape resembled the spire of a Buddhist temple rather than the conventional vision of a pyramid – wide at the base and rapidly tapering to narrowness and a fine point. Burdened by rents and tithes, by the charges made by the Catholic clergy, the cottagers maintained the traditions of self-defending or self-avenging secret societies, and groups with such names as the Threshers, the Whiteboys, the Ribbonmen, and others, went on midnight rides bent on arson, beatings-up or murder. Most often the victims were not the landlord or land agent, but other small farmers who had taken up an evicted tenancy: it was a community forced to be at war with its own members.

The potato crop was the vital and virtually the sole source of sustenance for the majority of country dwellers. The low standard of living, with large families in cramped accommodation, encouraged early marriage, and further large families. Despite a high rate of infant mortality, endemic diseases such as dysentery, and a steady emigration, the growth in population was turning into a great spurt. From around five million in 1800, it reached over eight million by 1840: 'a vicious increase' commented one British parliamentarian in 1822. Many observers were concerned by the population explosion. In an age when it was accepted that children too were workers, there was little work for these increased numbers. After the victory over Napoleon in 1815, with peace in Europe, the demand for soldiers and sailors fell drastically, as did the requirement for cloth, rope, victualling and supplies of all kinds for the armed forces.

Cottiers, as the cabin-dwellers were called, divided and subdivided their already small patches of land to accommodate greater numbers, and struggled to pay rents and tithes. Only the potato could provide a substantial enough yield from small patches of earth, and the dependency of the country people on this one crop became ever greater. The universal fuel in most of the country was turf, eked out by furze and firewood. In *Ireland: A New Economic History*, Cormac Ó Gráda estimates that a million families depended on turf as fuel on the eve of the Great Famine – well over half the population. To cut and transport a year's supply was the equivalent of two weeks to a month's work for a labourer, and the cost of purchase was anything from fifteen shillings to two pounds – from fifteen to forty times a labourer's daily earnings (and many cottiers lived almost wholly outside the cash economy). Large farms were growing grain for milling on an almost industrial scale, destined for consumption in the towns and by the more prosperous elements, and for export, while others continued to rear and export black cattle. Bread and beef, requiring a cash purchase, were usually beyond the means of the cottiers.

EARLY NINETEENTH-CENTURY SOCIETY

Some of the large farms were well managed and run on improved lines, and the value (not quantity) of agricultural exports doubled between 1800 and 1820. Others were inefficiently run by owners or tenants without the money or will to invest in drainage, land improvement, machinery or stock. Many landowners were absentees. Among those who lived on their estates, the prevailing ethos was rarely one of enterprise. To quote McDowell again: 'The Irish landed gentry, the descendants of successful soldiers, pioneers, land speculators and Gaelic dynasts, were distinguished by their reckless high living and unthinking extravagance.' Most of them were in debt and their rents often went largely to pay off mortgages and loans. Obligations of this kind made it difficult for them to agree to rent-abatement, even if they felt a sympathy for their tenants' difficulties. The by now long-established 'gentlemanly' lifestyle, with its riding and hunting, its informal clubbishness, its leisurely meals and legendary drinking, reflected the highest aspirations of a majority of Irish squires.

Expectations of industrialisation were not fulfilled. There were big businesses and factories in Ireland, but they were mostly based on traditional produce and activities – brewing, linen-making, flour-milling. Cotton spinning and weaving, using cotton imported from the slave plantations of the American South, also became important for a time before being priced out of the market by the bigger Lancashire industry.

The social pattern, always in the process of subtle or gradual change, reflected some of the new aspects of life. The removal of the parliament meant a change in the status of Dublin, which though remaining the centre of commerce and law, lost its annual influx of country gentry for the parliamentary season. Still the second-largest city in the British Isles in 1800, it was soon to be overtaken in population by the industrial centres of Glasgow, Manchester and Birmingham. The aristocracy retained their links with England or Scotland, but the squires became more embedded in the Irish countryside, and those who had had Dublin houses usually sold them off.

The Ascendancy still exercised wide powers in the administration of the shires, through the grand juries and in such posts as justices and road commissioners. Agriculture, landowning and their attendant businesses and local industries, from smithies and mills to carriage and boat builders, were supported early in the nineteenth century by a somewhat ramshackle structure of local banks, some of which were hardly more than grocers issuing promissory notes. In 1804, Skibbereen had twelve such banks, while Youghal had twenty-three. In the post-war slump of 1815–16, a number of banks failed, and again in 1820 there were significant collapses, leading to widespread disruption of trading. The lines of social division between the smaller country landowners and the country town merchants became increasingly blurred. The squires took shares in mills, fertiliser works, local banks, often as 'sleeping partners' but sometimes as active participants. While paper money circulated widely in the three southern provinces, in denominations as low as sixpence, in Ulster there was far greater reliance on coin, based on the gold guinea.

The surge of population growth had its greatest effect upon the Catholic community, always by far the largest element. Whilst it undoubtedly greatly increased the numbers of the poor, it also increased the numbers of those

THE ROYAL BELFAST ACADEMICAL INSTITUTION

By 1814 Belfast was a substantial and growing town of around 28,000 people, the largest in Ulster. In that year the Belfast Academical Institution was founded, in order to provide a college education for future Presbyterian ministers. Previously, students from the Presbyterian community had to go to Scottish universities, as many continued to do. However, there were theological reasons why this was not always seen to be desirable, apart from the feeling that the Ulster Presbyterians were wealthy and numerous enough to support their own college. Nevertheless, government money was also sought and provided. This was despite the fact that one of the founders, William Drennan, was a prominent former activist of the United Irishmen. The town's old radical tradition was on the wane, but its spirit infused the college's early years. So did theological discord, as a dispute over the nature of Christ (going back to fourth-century Arianism) shook the Presbyterians. The Institution awarded its own degrees, but with the inauguration of the non-sectarian Queen's College in 1845, it ceased to do so. In its handsome city-centre building, it remains as a flourishing grammar school.

eligible, under the 'forty-shilling freehold' terms, to vote in parliamentary elections. In many counties they were emerging as the majority element of the electorate (bribery or threats to the limited numbers of electors continued to be rife, encouraged by the vote being public). These more prosperous members of the Catholic community were free to practise their religion, to engage in trade and commerce, and to acquire land. But they were still almost wholly excluded from holding any kind of public office.

More and more, the language of the entire country was English. A sense of separation grew between English and Irish speakers, and the concept of the Gaeltacht, districts in the further west and north where monoglot Gaelic was still the norm, became common, and in the eyes of the rest of the country tended to be equated with the most backward aspects of peasant life. The old Irish language had few defenders. Bad roads, bad inns, and the poverty and squalor of overcrowded country areas kept romance at a distance. Despite the interest among literary folk in other countries, the reserves of poetry, legend and folk-history held in these communities were generally ignored by the English-speaking populace for whom the songs and melodies of Thomas Moore provided an Irish–English ambience in the most tasteful contemporary style.

THOMAS MOORE

BORN in Dublin, Moore lived from 1779 to 1852 and was one of the first Catholics to study at Trinity College, from 1793. He intended to be a lawyer, but a keen interest in music and in traditional song triumphed, and he became a song-writer, author and ballad-maker. He made his reputation first in London, and rarely resided for long in Ireland. His first book was dedicated to the Prince Regent, and, becoming the recipient of an English sinecure, he did not follow his Trinity friend Robert Emmet into the field of political action. Between 1808 and 1843 he produced ten volumes of *Irish Melodies*, including such enduring favourites as 'The Last Rose of Summer', and the patriotic 'The Harp that once through Tara's halls'. Moore derived much of his music from Edward Bunting's pioneer collections, begun in 1796, and when challenged about his borrowings and alterations, was defiant: 'Had I not ventured on these very admissible liberties, many of the songs [tunes] now most known and popular would have been still sleeping with all their authentic dross about them in Mr Bunting's first volume.' Bunting, from his second collection, also set down the Irish texts, but Moore had no interest in the original words and composed his own lyrical and often sentimental words to the tunes he borrowed.

AN UNEASY UNION

All historians of Ireland have noted that the Union was flawed from the start. Indeed, having been conceived and brought about chiefly for the purposes and convenience of the British government, it could hardly have been otherwise. The continuing presence of a Lieutenant and his administration – something not found necessary either for Scotland or Wales – indicated an acceptance that the governance of Ireland was something different to that of the other countries of the United Kingdom. The failure to implement Catholic emancipation alienated a large proportion of the population. But as J.C. Beckett noted: 'The survival of a separate administrative system for Ireland had another, and a deeper, significance: it was both the symbol and the instrument of a continuing Protestant Ascendancy . . . In every department of government, central and local, the Protestant landlords, their allies and dependants, remained in control.' Nevertheless there was an important difference, brought about by the parliamentary Union. To preserve its power and status, the Protestant Ascendancy no longer had its own parliament: the guarantor of its position was the Imperial parliament in London. They were welded to the

Union, just as their Catholic fellow-countryfolk, rebuffed in their aspirations by the Union, were disaffected from the beginning.

ROBERT EMMET'S RISING

The first notice of serious dissent was served by the brief insurrection led by Robert Emmet in the summer of 1803. Emmet had been among the United Irishmen of 1798, and his attempt, with other veterans of the movement, to take Dublin Castle was the last gesture by the United Irishmen. The struggle lasted less than a day, fifty people were killed, including the Lord Chief Justice, Lord Kilwarden, whose carriage was set upon by the insurgents. Emmet fled, was caught in the Wicklow Hills, tried, and hanged in October 1803. His eloquent self-defence at his trial became a nationalist text:

> Let no man write my epitaph; for as no man who knows my motives dares now to vindicate them, let not prejudice or ignorance asperse them. Let them rest in obscurity and peace; my memory be left to oblivion and my tomb remain uninscribed, until other times and other men can do justice to my character. When my country takes her place among the nations of the earth, then, and not till then, let my epitaph be written. I have done.

Twenty-one others were executed, including Thomas Russell, one of the founders of the United Irishmen. Emmet's abortive effort has been criticised, but it was a considerable achievement to have organised it, so soon after the crushing of revolt in 1798, and with a large deterrent military presence. Emmet's hope of sparking off a general insurrection was a forlorn one. Many opponents of Union denounced the rising, including Daniel O'Connell, and it lent strength to the opponents of Catholic emancipation.

THE CATHOLIC EMANCIPATION ISSUE

The disenchantment of Catholics with the Union, and their continuing exclusion from public life, could not fail to create an unstable society. The very fact that Catholic citizens, especially of the wealthier sort, were neither fish nor fowl, able (if adult males) to vote yet unable to assume any position of leadership, made for a sharper dissatisfaction than the old penal laws had generated. Their impatience and resentment took the form of action groups, petitions, complaints and pamphlet campaigns, but the campaign was at first both hesitant and discordant. Grattan, briefly in the London parliament as a member for an English constituency, through Whig support, and as a Dublin member from 1806 until his death in 1820, spoke up regularly for Catholic emancipation. As

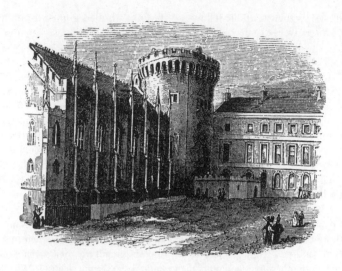

Bermingham Tower, Dublin Castle

had happened before with the Catholic community, it was its aristocratic members who first took on the leadership, their sense of *noblesse oblige* encouraged by the bishops, since neither spiritual nor temporal lords had any wish to see the 'popular' element take control. A Catholic Convention was founded in 1810. But the impatience of the middle-class Catholics – lawyers, merchants, small landowners – led to the formation of a more widely representative Catholic Board in 1811. The arrival of a new Chief Secretary, the Tory politician and future Prime Minister, Robert Peel, in 1812, was a further depressant to the Catholics, as Peel was not only opposed to emancipation but was a politician and administrator of great ability, well able to cope with opposition. On his advice, the Conventions Act, still conveniently in force and preventing any meeting of an extra-parliamentary representative assembly, was used to declare the Board illegal, and it was suppressed. (Indeed the whole martial law apparatus of 1798 remained in force for the first three decades of the new century, giving the government far greater powers of civil control than obtained in the other parts of the United Kingdom.)

DANIEL O'CONNELL AND THE CATHOLIC ASSOCIATION

There was intense debate over whether, if the Church allowed the government to have power of veto over the appointment of bishops, this would be enough to allay the opposition to emancipation. Vetoists and anti-vetoists argued and bickered, but despite Vatican support for the veto policy, the bishops and the popular leaders found themselves united in opposition to it. By the second decade of the century, Daniel O'Connell had established himself as the most vocal, and one of the most intransigent, leaders of the emancipation movement. But it was not until 1823, by which time three emancipation Bills had failed in parliament, that O'Connell began to establish an effective organisation. In 1824 his Catholic Association, founded in the previous year, was made open to anyone who could subscribe a penny a month. The venture was hugely successful, and the Association became the first means, other than violence, by which the unenfranchised Catholic peasantry could play a part in influencing events. They saw the Association as a method of resolving all their grievances. O'Connell's prestige among the people rose high, and he cultivated it in large public meetings, where his oratory enthused the audiences and alarmed the government, whose agents provided full reports of the fiery speeches made by 'the Counsellor'. An attempt to prosecute O'Connell for incitement to rebellion failed, but the government suppressed the Catholic Association. It was impossible to suppress the movement, however. The name was changed, and the penny 'Catholic rent' was still paid to provide a fighting fund, to sustain the campaign and assist victimised members.

Several elements combined to make the movement coherent and effective. The active support of most priests was vital. Also significant was the presence of thousands of returned soldiers and seamen, many of them non-commissioned officers, influential figures in their own communities. Legal skills were readily available and the movement was well financed. Soon its effectiveness on a local basis was made clear in parliamentary elections, where the Catholic freeholders began to secure the election of pro-emancipation candidates. These were necessarily Protestants, until, in the Clare by-election of June 1828, O'Connell announced that he would stand in person, though he would not, if elected, take the oath of allegiance, which would have required him to denounce his own Church as impious and idolatrous: 'I would rather be torn limb from limb than take it.' He won a decisive victory, and was cheered across the country on his return from Ennis to Dublin. It was the first time a member of parliament had been elected, having declared he had no intention of taking up his seat; but the example would often be followed in later years.

After almost thirty years, the government could no longer ignore or prevaricate on the issue. Ireland was in a ferment. The Prime Minister, the Duke of Wellington, accepted that there was no alternative to Catholic emancipation and persuaded the reluctant King George IV of its necessity. Intense thought was given to how the effects might be mitigated, and the 'veto' scheme was raised again, as was a proposal to pay government salaries to the bishops and

O'Connell refuses to take the oath of allegiance after being elected to parliament in the Clare by-election

priests. But such 'legitimisation' of the Church of Rome, even if acceptable to the Catholics, was not to be tolerated by those who spoke for the Protestants. On 13 March 1829 the Emancipation Bill became law. Outmanoeuvred and defeated, the government consoled itself by abolishing the Association and empowering the Lieutenant to suppress 'any association deemed to be a danger to the public peace'; and the forty-shilling qualification for country voters was raised to ten pounds, substantially reducing the Catholic freeholders' voting power. A number of petty restrictions remained in place. But nothing could conceal the fact that a major victory had been won, and the triumph was O'Connell's.

ANTI-UNION AGITATION

For the tens of thousands – perhaps as many as a quarter of a million – who had sustained the Catholic Association, the political victory was merely an earnest of what they still demanded – relief from tithes and the rack-renting system. Virtually the only legislation relating to land tenure passed in the previous thirty years had been to make it easier for landlords to procure the eviction of tenants. All the old grievances remained, and the peasantry looked to their leaders to continue the campaign. There was a further issue, too. Buoyed up by what had been achieved, for many in the Catholic Party a new great aim emerged: the repeal of the Union. O'Connell, an opponent of Union from the start, formally made this a principal aim of his party.

During the period of Reformist Whig government in the 1830s, repeal found some support among Irish Tories, despairing of what seemed an unholy alliance between the Whig government and O'Connell's substantial band of parliamentary supporters. Suffering what R.B. McDowell described as 'the ludicrous and pathetic spectacle of propertied persons in a panic', they foresaw, accurately enough, the decline of the Ascendancy, and felt that, with an Irish parliament restored, they could re-establish their old position. In every place where their numbers allowed it, they struggled to consolidate their position. Although there were many secret and semi-secret societies, often transient in nature, on the same lines as the Whiteboys and Ribbonmen, the Orange Order was most important in this: by 1835 there some 1,500 branches throughout the country, though the great majority were in the north. It was a social as well as a political–religious organisation, providing its members with some security against illness or loss of employment. Its strength in Protestant communities was so great, and its influence so pervasive, that the Whig-dominated House of Commons appointed a select committee in 1835 to investigate it; and for ten years it kept a low profile, though continuing its activities both public and private. Even moderate Protestants felt some concern at the possible outcome of events.

O'Connell had mobilised the Catholic community, given it self-expression, confidence and freedom – to many he was now 'the Liberator' – and aroused its expectations. At the same time, especially after 1829, he made special efforts to reassure the Protestants of Ireland that they were not threatened simply because social justice needed to be done to their Catholic fellow-citizens. Many disbelieved this and thought it a sop to O'Connell's Whig allies in England, but O'Connell was sincere. He believed in civil rights and in the separation of government and religion. For him there was no reason why any man should 'be compelled to support another man's clergyman any more than he would another man's lawyer or doctor'. In his reformist views on society he was ahead of his time and far ahead of the Irish Catholic bishops, who deplored many of his views and policies. Yet he could not help equating Ireland, in his oratory, with 'Catholic Ireland'. His speeches, and those of his more outspoken supporters, did a great deal to discourage non-Catholics from identifying themselves with the Nationalist movement.

THE LICHFIELD HOUSE COMPACT

O'Connell's enthusiasm for repeal was heightened by his experience of the Westminster parliament. Even with a sympathetic government, it was plain that the great majority of British members were ignorant of, bored by, and prejudiced about Irish issues. In 1835, some 60 out of 105 Irish members of the Commons were 'O'Connellites', but that was a mere 10 per cent of the House. The House of Lords was even more opposed to the nationalist–reformist spirit in Ireland. Repeal of the Union would not happen by parliamentary means. But reforms were still possible, as well as vital in order to reduce the simmering state of popular discontent. By the informal 'Lichfield House Compact' of 1835, Lord John Russell, the Whig leader, secured O'Connell's parliamentary support in return for the Irish leader's participation in plans, decisions, and appointments relating to Ireland. A variety of measures were implemented, helped on by an energetic Under-Secretary, Thomas Drummond, from 1835. They included the formation of the Royal Irish Constabulary (RIC). Part of the attempt to reduce the high levels of violence against individuals and property, it also centralised management of the police force and took the responsibility for appointing constables away from the local justices. But it was Peel whose name was preserved in the by-name of the police, as in a radical, parson-mocking shaft of 1831:

> Brave peelers march on with the musket and sword,
> And fight for my tithes – in the name of the Lord.

Drummond's determinedly even-handed approach was criticised by Protestant spokesmen, who saw it as pro-Catholic; but he was backed by the Chief Secretary and the Lieutenant, Lord Mulgrave, and the number of Catholic magistrates, jurors, and other local functionaries gradually increased, while remaining a small proportion of the whole. A number of stipendiary magistrates were employed, and in 1838 there was a purging of the ranks of justices of the peace, removing almost a third of them.

EDUCATION, POOR LAW AND TITHE REFORMS

From 1831, a National School Board had been formed to develop education. This provided money for local schools, provided textbooks and teachers, and supervised the system. Money also had to be raised locally, but the result was a rapid spread of elementary education with a consequent general advance in literacy. The literacy was in English, and the advance in many communities was made at the expense of Irish, which still had few friends in authority. The Board was carefully composed to represent the religious denominations, and its syllabus tried to separate secular and religious education. Children of different denominations were to receive religious instruction separately. But it was felt that some generalised religious instruction should be given, and the form of this did not escape religious controversy, with the Presbyterians, Church of Ireland and Catholic Church all finding fault for different reasons. Each body also complained at the inadequate degree of its own involvement in the national education system, and the Church of Ireland in 1839 set up the Church Education Society to provide its own parochial schools. Wrangles

---

O'CONNELL AND PEEL

A SHARP personal rivalry existed between Daniel O'Connell and Sir Robert Peel, quite apart from their opposing political stances, which in Peel's case earned him the sobriquet of 'Orange Peel' from O'Connell: '. . . a raw youth, squeezed out of the workings of I know not what factory in England . . . sent over here before he got rid of the foppery of perfumed handkerchiefs and thin shoes'. Peel dismissed O'Connell and his associates as 'a band of mischievous demagogues'. In 1815 Peel, always a prickly character, challenged O'Connell to a duel, which was narrowly averted. Duelling was becoming a somewhat archaic, and officially deprecated, way of resolving personal disputes, and O'Connell did not accept further challenges. But the personal animosity remained.

---

about schooling between the churches and the government were a rehearsal for the later storms over university provision.

A Poor Law system was introduced, with 130 designated 'unions', combined districts in which a Board of Guardians supervised the lives of the destitute. Each was required to construct a workhouse – a stern work ethos for the lower classes was fundamental to Whig philosophy, as a later decade would more plainly reveal. Daniel O'Connell was a sharp opponent of this policy, preferring to trust to charitable works and even recommending emigration. In his eyes, the problems of the country were political rather than economic, and political reform would produce economic benefits for the rural poor. These were extremely numerous: a government commission reported in 1836 that there were 585,000 labourers without employment for thirty or more weeks of the year. A Board of Works was set up to plan and oversee such projects as the Shannon navigation. Town administration was modernised from 1840, with a wider electorate – 'the lowest rabble of the boroughs will be the burgesses', grumbled the Duke of Wellington from the opposition benches – and O'Connell became Dublin's first Catholic Lord Mayor for more than two centuries. Many town halls date from the Whig decade.

Progress in matters of tithes and rents was slower, though a number of Church of Ireland bishoprics were abolished. From 1831 a tithe war was waged in many districts, with people banding together to refuse to pay, or to make collection as difficult as possible. In 1838, a Bill for the commutation of tithes was finally passed. Under this, the tithe was changed into a regular sum of money and responsibility for paying was transferred to the landlord, who of course recovered the cost from the rent of his tenants. But the poorest tenants were relieved of the burden of contributing. It was less than the reformers had hoped for, but enough to end the tithe troubles. Rents and land tenure, however, remained a serious problem: still nothing was done to improve land law. The Whig government and its supporters were sustained in their actions by the belief that Ireland was in a process of transition from the subdivided smallholding and the potato-patch economy to one of large farms with a regular workforce. In fact this was happening only on a very limited scale, and even there it did not solve the problem of there being more workers than work.

IRELAND'S FIRST RAILWAY

By this time, technological advance had produced the steam railway, and the first line in Ireland, the Dublin and Kingstown, was built in 1836. Drummond proposed a national railway system, to be built under government auspices, believing that efficient transport would bring social and economic benefits.

Remarkably, this was approved by parliament, though never put into effect. The railway system developed in piecemeal fashion.

O'CONNELL'S LAST CAMPAIGN: THE DRIVE FOR REPEAL

In 1841 a Tory government, under Peel, was elected to power. While it disappointed its Irish supporters by maintaining the reforms of the previous administration, it did not undertake further reforms, and the basis of its Irish policy was to damp down and circumvent the repeal movement. The campaign for repeal of the Union, which had been to some extent tuned down during the Whig years, had now been taken up with renewed force. The Repeal Association had been founded in 1840. O'Connell, aged sixty-six in 1841, was still the foremost advocate of repeal and the undisputed leader of popular opinion among the Catholic population. All the techniques that had brought the emancipation campaign to victory were brought into use again. Members were enrolled at various levels of payment; a flood of pamphlets, newspaper articles and books was released. Key influences on popular opinion and feeling, especially among the priesthood, were cultivated and encouraged. There were active supporters even among the traditionally cautious bishops. O'Connell himself travelled the country, addressing huge public gatherings with all the old forcefulness of his oratory. The effort built up through 1842 and the surge of popular response was such that O'Connell proclaimed that 1843 would be 'the year of repeal'. His hope was that the momentum of pro-repeal feeling would be so strong that despite both the Tory government and the Whig opposition being wholly against it, they would have to cave in as Wellington had done in 1829.

O'Connell's view of repeal was always to reinstate the status that had obtained with Grattan's parliament – domestic self-government: 'for Irish administrative functions the Irish parliament would have control within Ireland . . . for all other administrative functions the British parliament would have control,' was his reply to an enquiry from an English radical supporter in September 1843. The composition of such a parliament would of course be very different to that of the 1790s, and for that reason, within Ireland a very solid and substantial body of opinion was firmly opposed to repeal. Apart from the small number of political radicals, there was little interest in or enthusiasm for repeal in Britain. As 1843 wore on, it became clear that the government was not going to yield, and O'Connell, who was committed to constitutional methods, was in danger of painting himself into a corner. Half-anticipating armed repression by the government, he had hinted that his followers would rise in self-defence, but the government, despite much tightening of security and strengthening of garrisons, did not attempt to strike.

The confrontation, when it came, was anti-climactic and turned on a legal nicety. A mammoth meeting of the repealers had been planned at the historically resonant site of Clontarf, for 8 October. The notices advertising it could be implied as suggesting the meeting would have a military character, which was illegal. Although the government knew that the meeting was to be no different in kind to its predecessors, it took the chance to ban it, at three days' notice. O'Connell obeyed the ban, and the great gathering, intended to be the climax of the campaign, was abandoned. Though constitutionalists praised him, it was a blow to the Liberator's prestige among the rank and file, which was partly redeemed by the government going on to prosecute him and some of his associates on charges of conspiring to excite disaffection. O'Connell rose to the occasion. The trial was a transparent fix, from its all-Protestant jury to its judge who inadvertently displayed his own partiality. Though found guilty, and sentenced to prison for a year, the accused men had their sentences quashed on appeal to the House of Lords. It was another triumph for O'Connell, with a splendid *Te Deum* in pro-St Mary's Cathedral to mark 'the deliverance of the beloved Liberator', but also his last, apart from the extraordinary gathering in Dublin which paid posthumous tribute when the foundation stone of his statue was laid in the street which bears his name. Ill health overtook his robust physique, and he took a gradually less active role. From 1845, the catastrophe of the Great Famine overshadowed his political aims. In 1847, feeling his death to be imminent, he set off on a visit to Rome, but died on the way, at Genoa.

THE LEGACY OF O'CONNELL: YOUNG IRELAND

For more than twenty-five years, O'Connell had been a predominant figure. He had set the agenda, the pace and the style of politics. Like a chief, he kept a close household of associates and admirers; he dispensed patronage as cheerfully as any Ascendancy magnate; his son John was taking a prominent position in the movement. But by the mid-1840s, though still venerated, he was beginning to be seen as a man of a bygone era, and his autocratic style was open to criticism, as was the behaviour of his entourage, who, in the words of one critic, wanted 'the uncensured handling of public money in their gluey claws'. The movement he had nurtured and led was developing a momentum, and exploring new directions, of its own. Young men who had never known pre-Union life, children of the nineteenth century, were starting to question his aim, his tactics, and his whole approach. 'Too low, too timid, occasionally too sectarian, and on the whole much too lawyer-like,' was how the *Nation* newspaper summed up the great man's repeal campaign. The *Nation*, which for a time outsold the older *Freeman's Journal*, was the mouthpiece for a radical group who emerged around 1842 and who outflanked O'Connell in their ideas – clever, articulate and high-minded young men, products of Trinity College, and among them Thomas Davis, Charles Gavan Duffy, and John Blake Dillon. As a group they were known as 'Young Ireland' with a degree of patron-isation: Davis was thirty in 1844 and died the following year, Duffy was twenty-eight and lived into the next century. Although paying great respect to O'Connell, they somehow managed to adopt different postures to him on a whole range of issues.

Young Ireland were committed to the repeal campaign, but they had the vision of a fully independent Ireland, sharing a king with England but in every other way a sovereign nation. In their nationalism there was also a strong cul-tural tinge: in a way typical of the time throughout Europe, they invoked the legends and heroes of the past, to give a historical and national quality to the agitations of the present. James Clarence Mangan and Samuel Ferguson were their poets; Ferguson, trained as a lawyer, became a considerable expert on Irish antiquities. With Catholics and Protestants in their number, they formed one of those groupings that from time to time tried to establish a non-denominational middle ground in which the country's discordant elements could operate unitedly. Davis in particular was a keen advocate of non-sectarian education. When in 1845 the Peel government, combining a genuine sense of need and duty with its desire to find non-political ways of pacifying the Catholic population, passed a Bill to establish three 'Queen's Colleges' in Belfast, Cork and Galway, there was immediate controversy over the plan to make them non-sectarian. For the church parties, this equated to 'godless', and there was widespread protest, particularly expressed by the Catholic Archbishop MacHale of Tuam. As with the National Schools controversy, an underlying suspicion of each party's motives clouded the debate: all sides knew the importance of education in forming opinion and belief. By 1849 the colleges were in being, but Catholic students were strongly deterred from entering. The only college to be an immediate success was Queen's College, Belfast (now Queen's University) where there was a large potential intake of students from the Presbyterian community, who had previously had to go to the Scottish universities for their higher education. Davis and the other Young Irelanders, keen supporters of the government plan, were at odds with O'Connell, who supported MacHale and the Catholic hierarchy.

The Young Ireland men were not practical politicians and had none of O'Connell's vast influence and popular appeal. Their attitude, and their writ-ings, were to be important for the next generations, however. They left two sig-nificant legacies. Firstly, they summoned the Irish past to help redress the Irish present. The spirits of Cuchulainn, of Niall Noígiallach, of Brian Bóruma, even of Míl Espáine, were called forth, and continued to play a part in Nationalist mythology. Secondly, they firmly, if implicitly, accepted the probability that violence would be necessary to secure independence. In a famous response to the question, 'What is the *Nation's* tone to be?' the answer was 'Wolfe Tone'. This view was anathema to O'Connell, whose memories of 1798 were real and bloody, not romantic and imaginative, and in 1846 he cornered the Young Irelanders with a set of resolutions which committed the Repeal Association to 'moral force' only – purely constitutional means of action. They resigned, or were expelled, and in January of the following year established their own Irish Confederation, formalising the split in the Nationalist movement. The Association remained under the aegis of the ailing O'Connell, and after him, his son, John, proving not after all to fit his father's shoes, it dwindled away. It was also in 1846 that Charles Stewart Parnell was born, and until he came to political maturity, the Nationalist movement would have no really commanding figure again.

It was also the year in which politics and every other aspect of life were overshadowed by a natural disaster on a horrifying scale.

CHAPTER THIRTEEN

Hunger

POTATO BLIGHT

AROUND fifteen million tons of potatoes were being grown in Ireland, of which between six and eight million tons formed the basic diet of around three million of the population. A large part of the crop was exported, part was retained for seed, part (mostly unfit for human stomachs) was eaten by pigs, and the better-off section of the population also consumed their share as part of a more varied diet. A typical peasant family, with two adults and five children, relying wholly on the potato, would need about 4 tons of the vegetable, requiring at least an acre of soil for cultivation, to last through the year. Even then the 'hungry months' of July and August would have to be supplemented, usually by bought-in oatmeal and herrings, which had to be saved up for somehow. The fungal disease of *Phytophthora infestans*, potato blight, moving westward from Belgium and Holland, had reduced the harvest of 1845 by about 40 per cent, in a particularly wet autumn. As a result, hardship and hunger had affected many rural households. Poor harvests and food shortages were nothing new: they had occurred seriously in 1800–01 and again in 1816–18, and contributed to the continuing, underlying pattern of discontent among the peasant population. Until the establishment of the Poor Law in 1838, any kind of relief from destitution was a matter of private or local charity. Now there was a greater sense of official responsibility, if only because each district had its union board. In the summer of 1846, it became clear that the potato crop was almost wholly blighted.

In 1845–46 the Tory government, still headed by Sir Robert Peel, took some remedial action, organising the purchase of maize meal ('Indian meal') from America for distribution at low prices to the worst-affected areas through a relief commission, set up in November 1845. (The gruel made from the often poorly milled meal was known as 'Peel's brimstone'.) But the measure helped to keep food prices down, and, combined with the consumption of most of the pig population, averted actual starvation. In July 1846 a new Whig government came into power, with Lord John Russell again as Prime Minister, just as it was becoming clear that the year's potato crop was an almost total failure. With a large part of Ireland's population deprived of its normal food, and unable to pay for an alternative, action was necessary. In charge of the provision of

---

CONACRE

T HIS was the term for land rented for the production of a single crop, most often potatoes. It was the means by which most members of the labouring class got land on which to plant the crop which provided the great bulk of the family food for a year. Conacre rents could be paid in cash, but for many thousands the rent was deducted from the already modest amount of payment due for their labour on the landlord's or tenant's ground. The system worked – though often the cause of agrarian disturbances – until the potato crop failed, when it accentuated the disaster of the Great Famine.

Famine relief was Charles Trevelyan, Assistant Secretary to the Treasury, an able and hard-working administrator. His ideas coincided closely with those of the new government. They managed the affairs of the richest, most technically advanced, and – as they saw it – most humane country in the world, of which Ireland was constitutionally an integral part. A human catastrophe of huge proportions was upon them.

GOVERNMENT RESPONSE

The grudging inadequacy of the government's action has been put down to its preoccupation with the 'laws' of political economy. These set the preservation of property rights and of free trade as top priorities. For a long time, liberal opinion in Great Britain had condemned the selfish inactivity of Irish landlords (though without undertaking land reform) and it was felt that Ireland's resources should now be used to remedy Ireland's disaster. There was no mechanism for such a policy to be implemented, even if it had been practicable. But the government's attitude was firm. 'It must be thoroughly understood that we cannot feed the people,' wrote Russell in October 1846. Stories of distress soon began to pour out from Ireland, and charitable relief funds were set up and were well supported in Britain and America. Voluntary help was provided by private groups, who set up food distribution points and soup kitchens: prominent among these were the Quakers, whose contribution was out of all proportion to their numbers in Ireland. The Quakers asked for nothing, but folk memory long recalled that some Protestant charities demanded religious conversion as the price for their soup. Under Trevelyan's supervision, a programme of public works was set up, its aims and effects limited by a refusal to spend state funds on projects that might bring profit to private persons. The rates of pay were very low, and when applied as 'piece-work' even these were often beyond the powers of a malnourished and weakened workforce to earn.

Behind the government's insistence on self-help, and Trevelyan's frequently expressed alarm about the dangers of the Irish people becoming dependent on – or taking advantage of – official doles of food, other and more sinister spectres danced. In the eyes of many people, the country was grossly over-populated; a state of affairs made worse by the fact that around a third of the people had 'nothing to do' other than grow potatoes, eat them, and produce children. Those who saw the Great Famine as an inevitable natural occurrence, or as divine intervention, had a ready-made excuse to deplore matters without doing anything to improve the situation. The victims were the rural Irish – in many minds an 'only' crept in here – and it was possible to achieve a certain detachment from their plight. The Lord Lieutenant, Lord Clarendon, wrote to the Prime Minister in August 1847, remarking that they should be equally blamed for keeping the people alive or letting them die: '. . . we have only to select between the censures of the Economists or the Philanthropists – which do you prefer?' Officious persons were quick to point out any instances of people benefiting unduly from relief: '. . . in "breaking of stones" the stones are frequently measured several times . . . The consequence of this is that men are sometimes receiving £1. 4s. per week; I say receiving for it is quite impossible that they could *earn* that amount by such kind of labour.' Quoting this, Cormac Ó Gráda wryly points out that had such rates been typical, Ireland would have been inundated with workers from Great Britain.

In March 1847 the Board of Works was employing over 700,000 people: by far the biggest employer in the country. The average wage paid was around a shilling a working day. But the cost even of subsidised food for a family was at least twice that amount. Turf was still needed. And landlords still required a rent from those who could remain in their cottages. Inability to pay rent forced out very many families, as did a condition in the relief provisions which refused public assistance to anyone holding more than a quarter-acre of land. During that year, the government was forced to accept that there was no alternative to feeding the people. Soup kitchens were set up throughout the country, and around three million people received at least one helping a day. The establishment of these cost money, and many people had to walk some distance to reach them; but it was felt that the provision of cash or food tokens would lead to misuse. In 1847 the potato crop was unaffected by blight, but it was a much smaller harvest than was needed. Lack of seed potatoes, lack of cash to buy them (the price had quadrupled since 1845), human exhaustion and disease – all had put severe limitations on planting in the early part of the year. But it enabled the government to declare that the problem was over, and in the autumn of 1847, the soup kitchens closed down. Charitable donations from Britain and America, which had been at a high level in 1846, diminished as endless repetition of distress stories began to dull the edge of sympathy. The workhouses were left to cope with the problem. But in the areas most affected, the Poor Law unions were bankrupt and a reluctant Treasury had to advance funds to keep them struggling along.

STARVATION, DISEASE AND MISERY

The problem was a national one, although the areas most drastically affected were in Connacht and Munster. Of the 130 Union districts, only 26 had less than 20 per cent of their population on food rations in July 1847. The great majority of these less-affected zones were in the mixed-farming areas of Ulster, where tenants' rights also prevailed. But the places unaffected by hunger were not always spared by disease. Refugees from the stricken countryside brought a typhus epidemic to Belfast in the autumn of 1846.

As the winter of 1847–48 wore on, the effects of continuing destitution and disease became ever more apparent. The workhouses were packed and despite a high death rate among the inmates, they could scarcely begin to cope with the level of mass destitution. At least, it was believed, the potato blight had gone away. But in the summer of 1848 it was clear that the blight had returned. The crop was again a failure. After the years of disaster, it was a dreadful blow. For the Irish peasantry, their country had become a place of horror and despair. By the end of 1848, Ireland was in a state of devastation greater than any war had caused and probably greater than that left by the horrendous visitations of the Black Death four hundred years earlier. Starvation, malnutrition, exposure, exhaustion and the accompanying range of diseases had dramatically accelerated the death rate. Sober estimates of the number of deaths accountable to the Great Famine stand at around a million people. During the years 1846–50 a further million left the country. The census of 1851 recorded a population of 6,550,000. The Famine years set the pattern for a process of mass emigration which reduced the population from its peak of around eight and a half million to less than five million by the end of the nineteenth century.

In a hard irony which did not go unnoticed, agricultural produce continued to be exported through the period of the Famine, even from Kerry. Those who were not dependent on the potato crop continued to eat and drink, though food prices rose, and there were varying degrees of hardship experienced. On an individual basis the peasant and labouring class, which was the only one to be seriously affected, was almost outside the cash economy. Nevertheless, their numbers were so large that their effective removal from economic production could not fail to have an impact. Rents to sub-landlords and big landlords declined, dramatically in the worst-hit districts, and consequent problems affected tradesmen, banks and merchants. The circulation of bank-notes fell by 40 per cent between 1845 and 1849. Some small social groups were hit hard in a more permanent way – the mortality rate of doctors, medical workers, and priests doubled or trebled in the Famine years.

Expenditure by the British government on Famine relief in Ireland has been calculated as £9.5 million. The economic historian Joel Mokyr has pointed the comparison between this and the £69.3 million found to fight the Crimean war, between 1854 and 1865. But even at the time, the official action was branded as inadequate. O'Connell's last campaign was against a government which could find £20 million to compensate former slave owners but would not reach far into its 'British' funds to relieve the stricken Irish. Official statistics inevitably recorded an increase in crime at this time, the greatest being in robbery (up 4.6 times between 1844 and 1849) and stealing of sheep and cattle (a more than 9-fold increase in the same period). It was believed that many committed crimes in the hope of being transported to Australia, though most robberies were the result of sheer desperation. Anger and unrest spilled into the political arena, and helped to widen the breach between the Repeal Association, still committed to 'moral force' and the more intransigent Irish Confederation.

THE REBELLION OF 1848

The Nationalist and politically reformist views promoted by Young Ireland were sharpened by events. Not only their reaction to the Famine, but also the rise of an insistent radical spirit elsewhere, notably in France and among the Chartists in Britain, helped to spur John Mitchel, founder of a new journal, *The United Irishman*, in 1847, the land reformer Fintan Lalor, and others to a new attempt at direct action. Mitchel, William Smith O'Brien and Thomas Francis Meagher were charged with sedition, and Mitchel was sentenced to transportation. Well-informed, as ever, of developments in revolutionary circles, the government prepared for trouble, suspending habeas corpus on 21 July 1848 and making it illegal to be a member of a confederate club. But the insurrection was a minor affair. O'Brien, persuaded to take the lead, tried to raise the peasants of Kilkenny and Tipperary, but if he and his colleagues had hoped that the Famine would increase the readiness of the people for armed revolt, they were wrong. Dispirited and deeply worried by the way the very soil seemed to have turned against them, the country people were not in a mood for heroics. Repeal, never mind a republic, seemed irrelevant compared with real events. The Catholic Church condemned the rising. Apart from a skirmish at Ballingarry, Co. Tipperary, between a group of about a hundred rebels and a band of police, there was no bloodshed, and the rebellion lasted little more than a week. Minor, even pathetic, as it was, it offered the anti-Irish elements in England a stick which was duly waved. 'Ingratitude' and 'Savagery' were blazoned on it. Some of the leaders fled to America, but O'Brien and Meagher were caught, and tried for treason; the death penalty was pronounced, though later commuted to transportation.

But the failure of 1848 did nothing to reduce the enthusiasm of those who had planned or supported the rising. And, as the immediate impact of the Famine receded in 1849 and after – though its effects would linger on in various ways for many decades – it left a profound sense of difference and separateness among the Irish people, which was not at first articulated into any particular political form. They had endured a terrible collective experience which had brought huge numbers of them to wretched premature death, and forced huge numbers of others to leave the country, with few resources, in order to survive. The scale and nature of the disaster, of a kind that seemed to represent a recurrent vindictiveness of the natural world, left a deep impression on those who lived through it, or escaped from it. Those who did survive the wasteland of hunger and disease felt little reason for gratitude to anybody. For the many who suffered little or no privation during the Famine years, it was discomforting to contemplate what had happened to their less fortunate fellow-citizens. To blame what many considered an alien government – behaving no worse than they might have expected – for its insufficient response did not perhaps entirely answer the matter. The individual and social traumas left by the Famine have not yet been adequately explored.

CHAPTER FOURTEEN

The Winning of the Land

DEPOPULATION AND EMIGRATION

A LTHOUGH economists debate whether the Great Famine was the cause, or whether it simply accelerated and accentuated trends that had been latent or gathering pace since the slump of 1815, there is no doubt that its legacy ran deep into economic life, politics and society, and could be read in the landscape itself. More than 200,000 smallholdings were wiped from the face of the countryside, and the amount of ground under tillage was greatly reduced. This was partly caused by the drop in population, but also by the repeal of the Corn Laws, carried out by Peel's government in 1846 and ending the price-protection of Irish corn. Imported corn was cheaper than the home-grown crop, and farmers turned more and more to stock-rearing. Despite the fall in population, there was still economic hardship, which drove people to keep up the flow of emigration. And a generation of Famine orphans was growing up in the workhouses, and in the houses of relations and friends. As they reached their teens, there was nowhere for them to go but out of the country. Between 1850 and 1914, some four million people left Ireland: a rate of emigration larger than any other country's. The figure is probably an under-estimate, since many travelled unrecorded to Britain. The great majority of emigrants were young, aged between 18 and 25, and a substantial proportion were female. The steady reduction in population was assisted by a trend, again more marked in Ireland than anywhere else, to late marriage or to lifelong celibacy. In 1851, of the 45 to 54-year-old group, 12.1 per cent of men and 12.6 per cent of women remained unmarried. By 1911 the percentages were 27.3 and 24.9 respectively, having increased decade by decade. The consequences of population loss were felt much more in the countryside than in the towns, and the proportion of urban inhabitants grew rapidly, in Ulster reaching 38 per cent of the total population by 1911.

EXPANSION IN EMPLOYMENT

As conditions came back to normal, the human toll of the Famine, and the continuing drain of population through emigration, created a new labour market. Many members of the potential labouring class were absorbed into railway building, or left the country to swell the much larger gangs of 'navvies' operating on railway and canal construction in Britain and Europe. In many areas, demand for labourers exceeded supply, and wages began to rise. Though prices also rose, there was a gradual improvement in the standard of living. The range of possible occupations was steadily widening. The spread of the railway system not only created a variety of jobs but it also unified time across the country. In 1849, Dublin and Cork were linked; in 1851, the Dublin–Galway line was opened, and by 1855 Dublin and Belfast were joined by rail with the completion of the lofty viaduct over the Boyne at Drogheda. A network of minor branch lines and light railways was also developing, and the demands of timetabling meant that communities which had always lived by sun-time now invested in clocks, to the benefit of the Dublin and other town clockmakers.

Mechanics, builders, glaziers, carpenters, printers, gasworks engineers and stokers, and postmen, were needed all over the country. Inevitably the greatest range of employment was in the bigger towns. Cork and Waterford, as well as Belfast, built iron steamships, with all the ancillary trades required, though in the second half of the century Belfast left the others behind to grow into one of the largest shipbuilding centres of the world. In 1846 Ireland had 118 breweries, most of them quite small; by the end of the century the number was 39, with the bulk of production centred in Dublin and Cork. Improvements in transport and production made brewing an important export industry from the 1840s. The introduction of the power loom in linen-making, from 1850, helped to make Belfast the world's main linen centre, and the industry was given a major boost by the fall in cotton production brought about by the American Civil War in the mid-1860s. Food processing, particularly bacon and fish curing and butter production, was important, and both Belfast and Dublin developed a considerable tobacco industry, boosted by the greatly increasing popularity of cigarettes. Improved transport was a problem as well as a help to Irish industry: better distribution enabled British-made goods to penetrate the Irish market more easily, and competition was often stiff. Manufacturers of consumer items early learned the value of 'national' brands to fight off imports.

The relative smallness, and declining numbers, of the population, and a lack of natural mineral resources, limited the extent of industrial development. Shipbuilding apart, heavy industry was rare and, like the Dundalk and Dublin locomotive works, it existed almost wholly to supply internal demand. Coal deposits had long been known to exist in certain districts, and sporadic efforts were made to create a mining industry, its most continuous development being the Arigna field in Leitrim and the workings at Coalisland in Co. Tyrone. But the coal seams were difficult to mine and the price of Irish coal was easily undercut as the huge expansion of Welsh and Scottish mining got under way

BIANS

THE first mail-coach services began in 1789, from Dublin to Belfast and Cork. In 1808 a Belfast–Armagh coach was started. But the great development came from around 1815. Carlo Bianconi (1786–1875) was born in north Italy and came to Dublin to work as a travelling pedlar for a print-publisher. Later he became a shopkeeper in Clonmel. His experience of padding the roads from town to town had convinced him that there was a good opportunity for a reliable transport system in the provinces, where there was virtually no cross-country transport. Bianconi set up his first service from Clonmel to Cahir in 1815. The time was right – mail traffic was increasing. Horses were cheap in the post-war slump; and a carriage tax encouraged many people to give up their own carts. Business expanded and by the 1840s, the 'Bianconi' or just 'Bian' was a byword for an open car operating from town to town (often run by another operator). Bianconi soon had competition, and Bourne and Purcell were among others who made fortunes out of horse transport in the pre-railway era. The speeding-up and easing of transport also encouraged the growth of tourism, and there was a gradual spread of good, or at any rate, better inns in the west and south-west to cater for this new traffic. Bianconi remained a shrewd businessman, buying shares in the new trunk railways and using his cars to provide connecting services.

after the 1850s. In 1900, 125,000 tons of coal were mined, compared to 20 million tons in Scotland.

SOCIAL AND ECONOMIC EFFECTS

There were some paradoxical developments as living standards slowly rose. The diet of the country people, with potato consumption greatly reduced, was actually less nutritious, despite a greater variety. Tea, usually well-sugared, became the main beverage, replacing buttermilk or water. In the countryside, housing standards improved, and the once-typical one-roomed cabin with scanty furniture was inhabited only by one per cent of the population by 1900. But expansion in the towns led to a drop in housing standards, and many old houses were turned into multi-family tenements with inadequate sanitation. The situation was particularly bad in Dublin, though reflected in proportion in other towns. Typhoid and tuberculosis were endemic diseases in these

WILLIAM DARGAN

BORN in Carlow, Dargan (1799–1867) was the father of Irish railways. Having trained as an engineer and surveyor in England, he returned to Ireland and set up as a road-building contractor. In 1831 he began building the Dublin–Kingstown Railway, Ireland's first, and was involved in most subsequent railway construction, often accepting shares as payment. Other business interests included canal barges, packet ships, linen mills and farms. Dargan became immensely wealthy, one of Ireland's few industrial magnates, and was the prime mover in the Irish Industrial Exhibition of 1853. Subsidising this, together with other philanthropic work, and the failure of his textile business, lost him his wealth, and by 1866 he was bankrupt. Dargan declined the offer of a baronetcy from Queen Victoria, but had the unusual pleasure of seeing a statue put up in his honour during his own lifetime.

congested warrens (Belfast was a notable exception, with its outward spread of artisans' terraced houses). As a result, the life expectancy of country dwellers was better than that of the urban poor; but overall, the average rose from below 40 years in the era immediately preceding the Famine to 50 years by the 1870s, and continued slowly to improve.

Great fluctuations marked the trends towards economic and social improvement. Poor harvests were normally the root cause. Three bad harvests in a row between 1859 and 1863 caused a serious economic depression and raised the workhouse population from 46,000 to almost 67,000. In 1879–81 there was an even more serious repetition, and during the 1870s famine conditions reappeared in Mayo, where the potato had regained something close to its old dominance in the rural diet.

A new Ireland was emerging, with an emptier countryside, bigger towns, connected by railways and the telegraph system, informed by nationally distributed newspapers and magazines, and in touch – through the emigrants – with a wider world. Its language, except for the remoter western recesses, was English. Writing in 1936, Edmund Curtis was able to note: 'Those who have talked with aged survivors of the time before the Famine understand what a change then took place in the numbers that spoke Irish and in the purity and richness with which it was spoken and the poetry and folklore that was embedded in it.' Like every other issue, language could not be detached from religion. When during the 1840s the Church of Ireland's evangelising element began to use the Gaelic language in an attempt to gain converts, the Roman

FATHER MATHEW

THEOBALD Mathew (1790–1866), of the Capuchin Order, and based in Cork, was connected with a prominent Catholic landed family of Co. Tipperary. A temperance movement had existed before his time, directed chiefly at excessive drinking among the gentry. But the consumption of cheap and often illegally distilled whiskey was creating serious social problems at all levels of society. Father Mathew's great achievement was to make Temperance a mass campaign. Some estimates put the number of those who signed the pledge to abstain from alcoholic drink as high as five million by 1842. It was an era of enthusiasms – O'Connell and the Catholic rent had shown what a popular movement could do; and Mathew put a strong religious as well as social message into his campaign. This tapped into a belief, widespread at that time, that the Second Coming of Christ was imminent, and that it would be as well to have one's soul in good order. Politically, too, it seemed as if a new order was on the way, with the establishment of the Repeal Association, and this helped promote a sense of social responsibility among the Catholic–Nationalist population. Father Mathew became a popular hero, which did not endear him to the hierarchy of the Catholic church; in addition, to the discomfort of his fellow-priests, he was warmly supported by many Protestants. His teetotalist campaign, like much else, was lost to sight in the course of the Famine years, but its effects continued, and even at the end of the twentieth century, the proportion of total abstainers was around 20 per cent of the adult population.

Catholic Church, not a great supporter of Irish in the nineteenth century, strongly discouraged people from its use.

THE LAND REFORM ISSUE

Political life changed also. The old issue of repeal was gone with O'Connell and the Famine. Because of the great thinning in the ranks of the cottiers and labourers, there was a new, keen interest in the land – how it should be owned and worked. The landowning class had emerged from the Famine period with no credit, and its actions after 1850 increased popular hostility towards it. Eviction became a scandal. Of the remaining smallholders, very many were cleared out. Police figures record the eviction of 117,000 families between 1846 and 1887, affecting some 600,000 people. The average size of a holding grew considerably, and the emphasis of agriculture moved towards stock-rearing. Tensions and hostilities between tenants and landlords remained at a high level. To the Irish tenantry, land reform was an urgent matter, and many of the more radically minded in the English Liberal Party (as the Whigs now identified themselves) agreed. But among other Liberals and even more so among the Conservatives (as the Tories now were named) the sanctity of land ownership remained an untouchable thing. Even some of those who thought reform was desirable for Ireland resisted it, in case Irish implementation should encourage tenants in England to make demands for greater security.

Many landowners were mortgaged beyond all hope of repayment, and in an effort to free land for the market, legislation in 1848 and 1849 made it easier for such encumbered estates to be sold. But instead of being bought, as was hoped, by new landlords willing to invest in improvement, they were largely bought up by speculators who sought to squeeze the maximum rental for their investment and the situation was exacerbated. No other land reform seemed likely, and local tenants' associations began to be formed, with a national Irish Tenant League appearing from August 1850. The three 'Fs' were the League's aim: fair rents, fixed tenure and free sale. This last 'F' was the old but still prevailing 'Ulster custom', which Ulster tenants were keen to see made into law. An ex-Young Irelander, Charles Gavan Duffy, still editing the *Nation*, was one of the leaders, and like Young Ireland, the League sought to embrace the religious divide.

As before, sectarian altercations on other fronts made this unity very hard to sustain. Fervent Protestants were currently expressing outrage over the 'Papal aggression' by which a re-established Catholic hierarchy of England sought to take territorial titles for its diocesan bishops, and the government passed an Act in 1851 to forbid this. There was some optimism following the general election of 1852, in which a considerably enlarged electorate returned forty (out of the hundred) Irish members pledged to work for land law reform. They formed an Independent Opposition Party in parliament, but their own internal splits, and their failure to impose themselves or achieve anything was one of the sources of a gradual resurgence of political nationalism. In 1855 Gavan Duffy left Ireland to restart his life in Australia (with considerable success, becoming Premier of Victoria and accepting a knighthood). The Independent Opposition, much reduced, remained the parliamentary voice of tenants' reform until 1866.

JAMES STEPHENS AND THE IRISH REPUBLICAN BROTHERHOOD

For a time, during the 1850s, with post-Famine economic recovery becoming more apparent, and with political activity at a low ebb, those members of the

English government who liked to think that Ireland would eventually become reconciled to the Union might have felt they were being proved right. Ireland's first Cardinal, Paul Cullen, Archbishop of Armagh and then Dublin, was in favour of maintaining the Union. But even those of Unionist sympathies in Ireland itself would have been unlikely to agree that assimilation was taking place, being far more aware of the extent of latent hostility to the Union and deep frustration at the government's inability to achieve land reform. The political ebb would be followed by a Nationalist, not a Unionist, tide.

In 1857 Jeremiah O'Donovan Rossa, then twenty-five, founded the Phoenix Society in Skibbereen, where the talk was of republicanism and revolt; and in 1858 a secret revolutionary movement was started in Dublin by James Stephens, a 34-year-old veteran of the 1848 rising who had fled to and returned from the USA, and associates, which eventually acquired the name of Fenians, a recalling of the legendary Fianna. It was also known as the Irish Republican Brotherhood (IRB); and its members tended simply to call it 'the Organisation'. Much of the ardour, ideology and funds of the movement would be pumped in from the United States, where a handful of political refugees leavened the much larger number of economic migrants in the ever-growing Irish communities of New York and Boston. Paris too was a centre for Nationalists whose beliefs and proposed tactics could not safely be aired in Dublin. Some of the Fenians had been Young Irelanders, and like that organisation they included both Protestants and Catholics, and kept a certain distance from the churches (as the churches did from them), but not much of the Young Ireland philosophy came with them, other than a commitment to armed revolt. Tenants' rights were something that could be speedily achieved after an independent republic was secured; Home Rule was a contemptible half-way house: their credo was a sovereign Ireland and their text was 'Soon or never'.

Rather reluctantly, Stephens, in 1863, started up a newspaper, the *Irish People*, to help promote the Fenians' ideas. It was so much simpler to launch an insurrection than to persuade an indifferent or otherwise-inclined population. But several years of stumping the country had shown him that constitutional nationalism was far from dead; even his old commander Smith O'Brien (pardoned in 1854 and back from Tasmania) condemned secret societies; Cardinal Cullen, whose nationalism fell short even of Home Rule, thundered against them. Stephens's associate, the journalist and novelist Charles Kickham, wrote: 'If the people were submissive to the clergy in politics there would be no Fenian Brotherhood. Ireland would be allowed to perish without a hand being raised to help her.' The Fenians' sense of immediacy was further diluted by the American Civil War which, from 1861, had diverted the attention of the Irish Americans, who were enlisted in large numbers on both sides.

235

On the positive side for the Republicans, the end of the American Civil War in the spring of 1865 released from service a large number of battle-trained Irishmen who were sympathetic to the Fenian cause.

Somewhat in the manner of O'Connell and Repeal, back in 1843, Stephens determined that 1865 should be 'the year', and once again, as plans began to be made in Dublin, indiscretion, treachery and espionage meant that the authorities became aware of what was intended. In September 1865 they swooped: the *Nation* was suppressed, and among other Fenian leaders, John O'Leary, joint editor of the *Irish People*, and Kickham, were arrested at once, Stephens being caught a few weeks later. Across the country, known Fenian sympathisers were rounded up and arrested, habeas corpus again being suspended in early 1866. The brief invasion of Canada by a substantial IRB army in June 1866 ensured even greater government vigilance. Regiments which might harbour Fenian sympathies were transferred from Ireland. Stephens escaped to the USA, and tried to organise a rising for March 1867. Although some of the leaders were arrested in February, the attempt to mobilise the Fenians' support went ahead. But though on the night of 4–5 March armed groups assembled in many places, including several thousand on Tallaght Hill just west of Dublin, they dispersed with hardly a shot being fired.

THE FENIANS IN BRITAIN

The Fenians had already established one new tactic, which was to take their campaign into Great Britain. February 1867 had seen a failed attempt to raid an arms depot at Chester Castle. In September a police van was ambushed in Manchester, in an effort to free two Fenian prisoners. A police sergeant was killed, and in November three of the raiders were hanged. The fate of the 'Manchester Martyrs', Allen, Larkin and O'Brien, aroused feelings similar to those which would be expressed after the executions of 1916, though on a lesser scale. But the young Parnell made his name in 1876 by rising in the House of Commons to interrupt the Chief Secretary for Ireland, who had referred to the 'Manchester murderers', and declare that neither he nor the Irish people considered the executed men to be anything other than martyrs. The Fenians had found two strong weapons, one of them inadvertently: terror tactics in Britain, and the cult of the sacrificial hero in Ireland. The first time civilian deaths were caused in Britain, in December 1867, as the unintended result of an explosion intended to release an IRB prisoner in London, however, the Fenian leadership expressed a genuine sense of horror and indignation at an action committed in its name. Despite their failure to galvanise the Nationalist population into rebellion, they remained a potent semi-hidden force in social and political life. Many moderate Nationalists campaigned to have imprisoned Fenians released.

GLADSTONE'S REFORMS

In 1868 the Liberal politician, William Ewart Gladstone, became Prime Minister of the United Kingdom. He was already known to Irish voters as the man who in 1853, as Chancellor of the Exchequer, had introduced income tax to Ireland and raised the duty on spirits, but in 1868 Gladstonian Liberals won 66 of the 105 Irish seats. 'My mission is to pacify Ireland' was his comment on taking office. The events of 1866–67 had convinced him that reform in Ireland was vital, and his first major response was to provide for the disestablishment of the Church of Ireland. The census of 1861 had shown that of a population of five and three quarter million, four and a half million were Roman Catholics, 700,000 were members of the Church of Ireland, and another 550,000 were in other churches, mostly Presbyterian. It was not the statistics, but political choice, that dictated Gladstone's move. An Act of 1879 removed the links between the Church of Ireland and the state: now it was a church in Ireland, on the same basis as others, and it retained only around half of its vast endowments. At the same time, the *regium donum* payments to Presbyterian clergy and the Maynooth grant were terminated, with final lump sum payments. A long-standing source of resentment to Catholics and Presbyterians was thus removed, though the ancient cathedrals were not, as some of its adherents had hoped, restored to the Catholic Church. To members of the Protestant Ascendancy, it was a heavy blow, and many of them, with the Conservative Party, saw it as a dangerous crack in the Union.

Further upset awaited them when Gladstone followed with a Land Act in 1870, which gave 'Ulster custom' the status of law, and in other provinces allowed for tenants to be recompensed for improvements they had made, when their leases ended, and also to be entitled to payment for 'disturbance' if evicted (unless evicted for non-payment of rent). For various reasons, including the problem of defining 'Ulster custom' in individual cases, the Act was less successful and popular than its authors had expected. The Tenant League had wanted much more than this back in 1850. But it was as much as any British government could deliver in 1870. Also in that year the Fenian prisoners were released. After the years of inaction, these measures restored faith in the possibility of reform by constitutional means. One of the government's aims, to defuse the Fenian movement, was largely achieved, though the Republican–revolutionary spirit was not appeased and the movement remained as a secret society with strong links to the Irish Americans. Ironically for the Liberals, the revived interest in parliament meant a heavy defeat for them in 1874, when in the first general election to be held by secret ballot, sixty members were returned as 'Home Rule' supporters, and only ten Liberals.

THE HOME RULE LEAGUE

From now until 1918, the 'Home Rule' phalanx of Irish MPs would be a significant force at Westminster, often, as now, holding the balance between Liberals and Conservatives. Its first leader was Isaac Butt, then sixty-one years of age, a conservative-minded Protestant barrister who had debated against O'Connell as a young man, and whose Home Rule views had been acquired in 1865, when he had defended the Fenian leaders on trial. In 1870 he had formed the Home Government Association, which had a strong minority contingent of disaffected Tories and Ascendancy members, and whose aim was similar to that of earlier federalists, with an Irish parliament for Irish matters, and Irish representation in the Imperial parliament. In 1873 it was replaced by a Home Rule League, still a broad-based coalition of different groups, including some Fenians, whose revised constitution of that year bound them to 'moral force' only, in times of peace; and to await the decision of a majority of the Irish people 'as to the fit hour of inaugurating a war against England'. The province least responsive to the Home Rule League was Ulster. In 1874 it returned only two Home-Rule MPs, both from Cavan. Elsewhere in the province unionism was strong, and closely identified with the Protestant section of the community.

Neither the growth of commerce and industry, nor the gradual extension of democratic rights, had prevented the hardening of opposition between two religious communities in Ulster, of broadly equal size. Where and when they impinged on each other, riots and fights were inevitable, and sometimes happened on a large scale. The Presbyterians had been no friends of the Ascendancy, but they saw the Ascendancy's losses as the Catholics' gains, and clung firmly to the Union. Indeed the Union, essentially political and economic now that the Church of Ireland was cleft away, appealed to them more than it had before. The Protestants who led or joined the Home Rule League were from the centre and south, not from the north.

CHARLES STEWART PARNELL AND THE LAND WAR

Isaac Butt died in May 1879. His natural conservatism and moderation had not made him a strong or effective leader of the parliamentary group. A splinter group, with Charles Stewart Parnell, MP for Meath, as a leading member, had taken up disruptive tactics in debate, which Butt had deplored. It was Parnell, then aged thirty-three, who emerged as the leading figure. In May 1880 he was elected leader of the parliamentary party, and with him, a new sense of purpose was instilled into the Home Rule members. His authority and prestige would rise to match O'Connell's, but in most respects Parnell was a

---

RESIDENT MAGISTRATES

THE office of resident magistrate (RM) was created in 1822, though stipendiary magistrates had appeared in Dublin since 1795, and had also been appointed to some especially disturbed districts. Initially recruited from ex-officers or civil servants, and responsible to the Chief Secretary, the RMs were expected to be even-handed in their administration of justice. They had to live in their districts. Whilst the majority of them had an affinity to the Ascendancy, they also marked a stage in the removal of local power from the landowning class. The well-known *Some Experiences of an Irish RM*, by Edith Somerville and Martin Ross (1899), gives a humorous fictional account of an English RM's adjustment to rural Irish society. In 1912, there were sixty-four RMs in office. The Free State replaced them with the post of district justice, but resident magistrates remain in Northern Ireland, although they now require legal training and qualification.

---

very different character. Like O'Connell he came from a well-off landowning background, but his was Protestant, from Avondale, Co. Wicklow; and his mother was the daughter of an American admiral. Not a natural orator, he never developed the flamboyant, rambling manner of his predecessor, but achieved an incisive, almost clipped style that commanded attention. His personality was remote and austere rather than bonhomous and fiery. But he was a leader beyond question, and one of his gifts in this respect was his ability to represent his aims in a way which made them seem reasonable to a wide range of fissile opinion both in the parliamentary party and in the country.

In 1879, Parnell accepted the presidency of the Irish National Land League, founded in that year by the Fenian Michael Davitt, whose father had been an evicted tenant and who was a passionate land reformer. His Fenian activities had already earned him seven years of jail between 1870 and 1877. The distress in Mayo, where famine conditions reappeared in the 1870s, gave new impetus to the tenants' unrest and the League's activity spread quickly into Munster and Leinster. Large numbers of tenant farmers could not afford to pay the rent in what was a period of poor harvests and economic recession, and the number of evictions soared. For those in arrears of rent, no 'disturbance money' needed to be paid on eviction.

From the original aim, which had been to secure reductions or abatements of rent, the campaign grew to become an overtly anti-landlord one, which became known as the Land War. The League encouraged tenants to withhold all rent payments if a reduction could not be negotiated. If a tenant were then evicted, the League employed the tactic which Parnell called 'moral coventry' and which became became known as boycotting after it was applied to Lord Erne's Mayo estates, managed by Captain Hugh Boycott. The pressures of ostracism were a strong deterrent to anyone taking up the land or work of an evicted tenant. Boycott brought in workers from Ulster, members of the Orange Order, but a police force 1,000 strong had to be deployed for their protection. The League leaders were careful to keep within the law, but the stormy speeches of Parnell and other leaders stoked the sense of determination among their followers, and there was an increase in violence throughout the countryside. 'Captain Moonlight' and his boys were out, picking up on what was by now a long tradition of intimidation, destruction and localised terror. Even before the League was formed, the Earl of Leitrim, an unpopular landowner, was shot dead in 1878, but such assassinations were rare, and most violence was between tenant groups and the police, or rival tenants. Other tactics, greatly detested by the sporting landlords, included the sabotaging of hunts, the disruption of local race meetings, and the killing of game that was being preserved for shooting parties.

THE LAND ACT

Gladstone, out of office since 1874, was again Prime Minister from 1880. Though the government took on additional powers to prevent intimidation and mob assembly, it also set up an inquiry, under Frederick Ponsonby, Earl of Bessborough, into the causes of the unrest. In 1881 a new Land Act was passed, conceding much of what had been demanded in the past. The 'three Fs' were now granted, and a Land Commission was formed, with power to adjudicate on disputed rents, and to purchase estates with a view to reselling them to tenants by means of a loan. The Commission was rapidly inundated with claims, and its stance was generally pro-tenant. With its work began the great transfer of land ownership from landowners to working farmers, which continued into the twentieth century. Gladstone and Parnell were execrated by the landlords, many of whom suffered a considerable loss of income, or had to sell up. But the Act was not immediately welcomed by those whom it was intended to benefit.

The passing of the Act did not mean that the Land War was over. Its political leaders had always had a wider aim than the reform of land tenure. Davitt and his associates, including the strongly influential John Devoy, based in New York, had never lost sight of the Fenians' ambition. Their tacit alliance with Parnell, which had underlain the success of the Land League, had been called 'the New Departure', but their agenda remained far more extreme than

Parnell's. He was adroit in avoiding a too-close identification with the IRB. He himself fiercely criticised the Land Act for not going far enough, and did so in such strong terms that in October 1881 the authorities imprisoned him under the provisions of their special powers, and declared the Land League an illegal organisation. A spell in Kilmainham Jail for the man who already to many was 'the Chief' could only enhance his prestige, and turmoil in the countryside increased. Continued rent strikes, boycotts and outbreaks of violence followed through the winter, and by April 1882, the government accepted that concession was necessary. Parnell was equally keen to come to some agreement, before the revolutionaries might take control of the situation, and the 'Kilmainham Treaty' established a joint understanding between himself and the authorities. Further concessions were made to the Land Act, the special powers were withdrawn, and Parnell was released.

HOME RULE AND THE NATIONAL LEAGUE

This compounding with the authorities effectively ended the 'New Departure', which was no longer of value to either party. Parnell used his influence to promote the Land Act, and by the end of the year the Land War was effectively at an end. When a secret band calling themselves 'the Invincibles' murdered the new Chief Secretary and the Under-Secretary in Phoenix Park, Dublin, on 6 May 1882, he was horrified, as indeed were many Fenians. The group was hunted down and five men were hanged. They were not generally accorded the status of martyrs, but the assassinations were a reminder that within the Republican–revolutionary movement there was always an element which was not prepared to wait for the majority of the people to announce the 'inauguration of war with England'. Between 1883 and 1885, the American Clan na Gael organisation funded a bombing campaign on British soil, which spread some alarm about 'Fenian terror'. In October 1882 Parnell replaced the Land League with the National League, thereby switching the focus of action from the land question to the national question. The National League had a national network of support, though the Protestant counties of Ulster largely ignored it. Continuing electoral reform, steadily enlarging the electorate, also strengthened his hand. The general election of November 1885 returned 86 Parnellite members to parliament. Earlier that year Parnell had shown that the Irish were in no party's pocket when he switched support from Liberals to Conservatives and brought down the government. In the brief Tory administration that ensued, a significant improvement to the system of land purchase by tenants was passed.

His long travails with the affairs of Ireland had convinced Gladstone, again Prime Minister, that Home Rule was necessary. With a majority of 86 seats in the Commons, there seemed to be no bar to achieving it (though the Lords might be problematic). A Bill was duly introduced in 1886, and supported by Parnell despite some reservations; he took a view essentially similar to that enunciated by Michael Collins in 1922, that it would provide 'freedom to achieve freedom'. Despite Gladstone's eloquence and authority, however, the Bill was rejected. The Conservatives unanimously opposed it, and his own Liberal Party split rancorously over the issue. Gladstone resigned, and the ensuing general election returned a Conservative majority.

Even in Ulster, seventeen of its thirty-three members of parliament were Parnellites in 1885. Though opposition to the Home Rule Bill had been fiercely expressed there, the rock on which the Bill foundered was lodged in London rather than in Belfast. Dissident English Liberal imperialists and old-style Whig defenders of property rights united with the Tories. But there was no doubt about the virtually united opposition to Home Rule among the Protestant population. In the north-eastern counties of Ulster, where they formed a demographic majority, the population was mobilised from its aristocratic and industrialist upper class to its large proletarian working class, with all the sectors in between. 'Ulster will fight, and Ulster will be right!' the Conservative leader Lord Randolph Churchill had proclaimed, after visiting Belfast. In the event, this was not put to the test. But mass demonstrations led to confrontations, riots and widespread sectarian fighting, quelled only by military intervention.

PARNELL'S STRUGGLE, REPUDIATION AND COLLAPSE

Home Rule went off the political agenda at Westminster, though not in Ireland. For the government, an Irish policy was vital in the climate of frustrated expectation which now prevailed among the majority of the population, but the new Chief Secretary, Arthur Balfour, another future prime minister, fell back on an old staple and reintroduced and re-enforced repressive legislation. There was a strange episode in 1887–88 when the London *Times* published a series of articles which sought to implicate Parnell and other nationalist leaders in murders committed during the Land War, culminating with the facsimile of a letter, allegedly written by Parnell, linking him to the Phoenix Park murders of 1882. Parnell sued, and an official inquiry found the whole thing was trumped up by a journalist, Richard Pigott, who committed suicide. Parnell was wholly vindicated, and his authority and prestige were unscathed.

Renewed agitation among tenants in 1886, following a bad harvest, was backed by the National League, which developed the 'Plan of Campaign', a scheme for tenants on larger estates to combine in offering rents they felt to be fair. If refused, the rents were paid into a fund which would help those evicted.

League money was also put into the fund, and such practical action kept the League relevant in the eyes of the people. Parnell, carefully managing a parliamentary alliance with the Gladstone Liberals, maintaining the discipline and effectiveness of the League, still nursing links with the Irish Americans, did not actively endorse the 'Plan of Campaign', which was the brain-child of his Lieutenant, William O'Brien. He seemed to be a man waiting for his moment, the inevitable hour when Home Rule would come. But Captain William O'Shea's decision to sue for a divorce in 1890 turned the moment into something very different.

For some years O'Shea, at one time a Nationalist member of parliament,

Charles Stewart Parnell

had been complaisant with the sexual liaison of his wife Katherine and the Irish leader; now for personal and political reasons, he went public, naming Parnell as co-respondent. Public interest was intense and the case was copiously reported in the press. Parnell offered no defence and was duly identified as the guilty party. His position in Ireland hardly seemed affected, and he was re-elected chairman of the Irish Parliamentary Party, and a large public meeting endorsed him. But to some of his Liberal allies he was now tainted by immorality and scandal, a man unfit to hold public office. Gladstone felt unable to maintain support for Home Rule with Parnell as leader of the Irish Party. This altered the view of most of Parnell's colleagues. With many others, they argued and pleaded for at least a tactical resignation, which could be followed by marriage to Mrs O'Shea and a return to public life. Parnell refused absolutely. A certain hauteur and distantness which had always characterised him, and enhanced his authority, was now perceived as obstinacy and an urge to cling to power at all costs. The 'moral question' dogged him, and the Catholic clergy were aligned against him. On 6 December 1890, after a series of highly charged meetings, the parliamentary group split, with only twenty-seven remaining to acknowledge Parnell as their leader.

In his struggle to retain control, Parnell had repudiated the alliance with Gladstone, and condemned the Liberals' Home Rule policy as inadequate. Only he, this stance proclaimed, could take the country forward to its proper

243

place among the nations. Through 1891 he traversed the country, addressing meetings, rallying those who still backed him, heckled and sometimes pelted with mud by persons who had once adulated him. Under intense and continuous strain, his health collapsed, and he died in Brighton on 6 October 1891. The huge crowd which attended his funeral procession to Glasnevin bore witness to a stunned sense of loss. In the words of Edmund Curtis: 'He was . . . followed to the grave by a vast concourse of mournful followers or repentant foes, who for the last time united in honouring the fallen Chief. The dramatic exit of the heaven-born leader left the national cause for thirty years to wander in the wilderness.'

This was a strong statement. But when Gladstone, in his fourth and final term as Premier, introduced his second Home Rule Bill in 1893, it passed the Commons but was rejected by a huge majority in the House of Lords. Had Parnell still held both his commanding position in Ireland, and the esteem he had enjoyed in Britain, the political context would have been very different, and the lords a good deal less certain of themselves. The Nationalist movement remained split between Parnellites, led by John Redmond, and anti-Parnellites. Though the latter were greater in numbers, their leaders, Tim Healy, William O'Brien and John Dillon, were disunited and after the failure of the 1893 Bill, a kind of political apathy set in among the public at large.

THE AFTERMATH OF FAILURE

The energy that had accumulated around the Home Rule issue was channelled partly into other manifestations of separatism. In 1893 the Gaelic League was established, with Eoin MacNéill as a leading spirit, and Douglas Hyde as its first President. The teenage Patrick Pearse was an early member. The League was intended to be non-political, and while its focus on the regeneration and reintroduction of the Irish language inevitably gave it an attraction for Nationalists, it also included men like Standish O'Grady, author and journalist, who believed that the Ascendancy should adapt and renew itself to spare the country from 'a shabby, sordid Irish Republic, ruled by corrupt politicians and the ignoble rich'. Official opinion was still reflected by the attitude of the famous Trinity don, J.P. Mahaffy, who considered the Gaelic Revival movement as a return to the Dark Ages. The Gaelic Athletic Association had been established by Michael Cusack in 1884, and was closely identified with the Nationalist movement from the beginning, though for a time during the 1890s it dropped its bar on members playing or watching 'alien games', or being in the police or military.

Below the surface of public life, the Republican activists took their own interpretation of the situation. Home Rule was a lost cause, and the only way towards independence was a military one. 'Military' was the right adjective: they were not advocating indiscriminate use of gun or bomb, but envisaged a real confrontation, as soldiers of the Republic, with the army and police of the Imperial power. The 'soon or never' spirit which had animated the first generation of Fenians was absent, however.

A NEW TACTIC AGAINST HOME RULE

Conscious of the dangers, the Conservative government of 1895 resolved on a positive Irish policy, summed up in a phrase of the new Chief Secretary, Gerald Balfour: 'to kill Home Rule with kindness'. To a degree this meant introducing the same reforms to Ireland that were being made in Britain, including the establishment of county, urban and district councils. This removed the last rung from the Ascendancy's gradually dismantled ladder. The grand juries, nominated from among the counties' landed gentry, which had controlled local affairs since Anglo-Norman times, were replaced by democratically elected councils. Although they kept a role in criminal proceedings until 1948, their composition became very different. For the no-longer dominant Ascendancy, there was further bitter irony in seeing even a Tory administration appoint Catholic and Nationalist persons to the kind of official posts once reserved for themselves. The government also continued to encourage the transfer of land ownership from tenancies to owner-occupier farmers. The Irish aristocracy had little reason to support Home Rule, and, apart from some wilful eccentrics, opposed it as vigorously as they could. Outside Ulster, however, they were by now a section of society that spoke only to themselves. In Ulster, where solid support for Union linked all classes in the Protestant population, the Marquess of Londonderry and the Duke of Abercorn could still preside over anti-Home Rule gatherings and lend their names to declarations, even though they were figureheads rather than the prime movers in the popular Unionist movement, whose real leaders were from the wealthy middle class.

AN AGRICULTURAL MARKETING INITIATIVE

In the 1890s, with the growth of the Australian and South American grain and meat trades, Irish agriculture felt the effect of heavy price competition. Based as it was on relatively small units, it was still reliant on a system of local markets and resale through a series of dealers, each taking a percentage. From 1894, energetically promoted by Horace Plunkett, at that time a staunchly Unionist landowner, who had learned much from American methods, the Irish Agricultural Organisation Society (later Irish Co-operative Organisation

THE KILLEEN CIGAR

ONE of Horace Plunkett's ideas was that tobacco could be grown in Ireland, and become a valuable addition both to agriculture and to manufacturing industry. A few people tried to grow it, including the Earl of Fingall on his estate. His countess sold a Killeen cigar to King Edward VII at an Irish fair in London in 1903, but little other economic success is recorded. The processing of imported tobacco was a major industry, however, with Gallahers of Belfast at one time the largest tobacco producers in the world.

Society) was set up to co-ordinate the work of some 800 local rural co-operative schemes and provide a central marketing and distributive framework. From 1899 Plunkett was also appointed Vice President of a state-run Department of Agriculture and Technical Instruction, set up to educate farmers in the most up-to-date practice.

IRISH SOCIETY AT THE TURN OF THE CENTURY

As the nineteenth century drew to an end, Ireland seemed a workaday sort of country, more concerned with the business of making a living than with idealist politics. In many ways it was integrated into the United Kingdom. A sense of this was particularly strong in north-east Ulster, where unionism was dominant in politics and there were close industrial links in the Belfast–Glasgow–Liverpool triangle. Under the dynamic rule of William Pirrie, Harland and Wolff of Belfast were building giant liners for the White Star Line and other international shipping companies. A telephone cable was laid from Donaghadee to Portpatrick in Scotland in 1893. Red-painted pillar boxes with

ANGLO-IRISH?

STEPHEN Gwynn, once a well-known and prolific author, and also a Home-Rule MP (he represented Galway from 1906 to 1918) protested about the rise of the term 'Anglo-Irish' to describe people like himself: 'I was brought up to think myself Irish without question or qualification, but the new nationalism prefers to describe me and the like of me as Anglo-Irish.'

Queen Victoria's monogram stood in every main street. Irish regiments garrisoned distant territories of the Empire. In London, Lancashire and central Scotland, large working-class Irish communities had become established during the century, with much travel to and from old and new homes.

Following an older tradition, writers like Oscar Wilde, George Moore, Bernard Shaw and W.B. Yeats, emerging from the no-longer ascendant Protestant community, looked to London as the place to make their reputations, whilst drawing heavily on their differing Irish backgrounds, from landed gentry to poor-but-genteel Dublin bourgeoisie. Irishmen served in the Imperial parliament and administration. In 1900 Edward Carson was Solicitor-General, and Roger Casement a distinguished member of the consular corps. A vigorous social life was still played out in the houses of the aristocracy, new and old, whose inhabitants liked to entertain young officers from the army and navy, and moved easily within a network of marriages and relationships that extended on both sides of the Irish Sea.

Oscar Wilde

Great contrasts and social gulfs existed. The visitor to Dublin could see the full range of it on the streets, from the shiny new chauffeur-driven motor of a Guinness baron, to the tram-cars crowded with city clerks, clerkesses and workmen, to the donkey and cart come plodding in from the country with a load of farm produce or turf. No single individual could encompass all those multifarious aspects of life, but one who perhaps comes closest is George Russell, 33 years old in 1900. Born in Lurgan, Co. Armagh, he was not conventionally religious but had intense mystical experiences from his boyhood onwards. In Dublin, he was a fellow-student with W.B. Yeats at the Metropolitan School of Art. Having to earn his living, he became a draper's clerk in 1890 and published his first book of verse, under the mystical pen-name AE, four years later. Horace Plunkett employed him in the Irish Agricultural Organisation Society, of which he became Assistant Secretary, and

247

READING ROOMS

THE provision of reading rooms in provincial towns and villages had been part of unofficial national campaigns since the eighteenth century. There a wide range of people could have access to the pamphlets and books published for the cause, whether it was political, religious, or other – the temperance movement for example. The reading room was also a place where discussion and education could happen. In the post-Parnell political doldrums of the 1890s the notion was revived, this time with the intention of encouraging interest in Irish writing, past and present, through a National Literary Society. It was proposed that a range of books should be reissued. Many people involved themselves in this, often with somewhat conflicting aims, and there was a substantial clash of ideologies and egos. The veteran Fenian, John O'Leary, saw the reading rooms as part of the war of ideas that must be waged to instil an actively nationalist spirit. Douglas Hyde, elected president of the new Society, was chiefly concerned with the preservation and revival of Gaelic. W.B. Yeats also took the literary line, but, not himself an Irish speaker, believed that English was the best vehicle. His ideal was 'a national literature that made Ireland beautiful in the memory, and yet had been freed from provincialism by an exacting criticism, a European pose'. Yeats was also keen to be the selector of the books to be published or reissued. Others were equally keen to make sure he had nothing to do with it. In the end the 'safe' choice was made of the elderly Sir Charles Gavan Duffy, returned from his Australian sojourn, to be the selector. The network of libraries and reading rooms did not come about, and only a few of the books were reissued, but the Literary Society played its part in the trend towards a wider recognition of the value of Irish culture: a far from uniform trend, in fact formed by the actions of a variety of often discordant and mutually hostile factions and personalities.

editor of its magazine *The Irish Homestead*. His home became one of the centres of Dublin's literary and intellectual life. In the early years of the new century he would take part in the struggles to found a national theatre, and also emerge as a champion of the striking transport workers, writing a majestic denunciation of Martin Murphy, the autocrat of the tramways. AE was to be a regretful exile in his last years, but at this time he was a moving spirit in Irish life, typical of many less prominent or gifted people in his ability to respond to both its mundane and spiritual aspects, the daily round and the eternal vision.

c120
- Ireland appears on Ptolemy's map of the known world. Seven rivers and five towns are marked.

c300
- Irish pirates begin to raid Roman Britain.

c350
- Ogam, the first written form of the Irish language, appears on gravestones and inscriptions in Ireland and western Britain.

c400
- The Dál Riata of northeast Ulster plant their first settlements in western Scotland.

c425
- Emain Macha (Navan Fort), ancient capital of Ulster, is destroyed by the Connachta.

431
- Palladius is sent from Rome as 'Bishop to those in Ireland who believe in Christ.'
  Starting date for *The Annals of Ulster* (written later).

432
- St Patrick arrives in Ireland.

433
- St Patrick lights the Paschal Fire on Slane Hill (tradition).

441
- St Patrick spends Lent on the summit of Croagh Patrick (tradition).

447
- St Patrick makes Armagh the ecclesiastical capital of Ireland.

c450
- Niall 'of the Nine Hostages', founder of the Uí Néill dynasty, dies.

467
- St Benew of Kilbennan, disciple of St Patrick, dies.

470
- Tara is established as the capital of the Uí Néill dynasty.

c484
- Enda founds a monastery on the Aran Islands, according to tradition the first monastery in Ireland.

493
- The death of St Patrick (tradition); some sources give 461.

500
- The beginning of the 'Golden Age' of the Irish Church. Over the next century, monasteries are established throughout Ireland.

- Written Irish develops an alphabet based on Latin letters (Archaic Old Irish period).

521
- The birth of St Columcille at Gartan, Co. Donegal.
- Buite, Abbot of Monasterboice Monastery, dies.

524
- The death of St Brigid of Kildare (traditional date).

527
- Emly Monastery, Co. Tipperary, founded by this date.

530
- The death of Enda of Aran.

537
- Eogan, King of Connacht, is killed by his rival, Guaire, near Sligo.

540
- Dermot of Inchleraun founds a monastery on Lough Ree, Longford.

543
- St Columbanus is born in Leinster.

545
- Glasnevin Monastery, Co. Dublin, is struck by an epidemic of the plague which kills its abbot, Berchan.

546
- St Columcille founds the Monastery of Daire Calgach on the site of modern Derry.

547
- St Ciarán founds the Monastery of Clonmacnoise on the River Shannon.

548
- The plague epidemic claims many lives. It continues until the end of the next year.

549
- Abbots Tighernach of Clones Monastery, Ciarán of Clonmacnoise Monastery and Colum of Terryglass Monastery die, possibly from the effects of the plague epidemic.

551
- Nessan the Leper founds Bangor Monastery.

559
- St Brendan founds the Monastery of Clonfert.

c560
- The *Vulgate* Bible of St Jerome reaches Ireland from Italy.
- Latin becomes established as the language of the Irish Church.

561
- St Columcille is censured at the Synod of Tailtíu.

563
- St Columcille sails to Scotland and establishes a monastery on the island of Iona.

575
- Assembly of Druim Cett. The King of the Uí Néill claims sovereignty over the Dál Riata. St Columcille prevents a plan to expel the poets of Ireland.

577
- The death of St Brendan of Clonfert, also known as 'the Voyager'.

587
- St Columbanus leaves Ireland on a missionary journey to the continent of Europe.

c590
- St Columcille writes the *Cathach*, the earliest Irish manuscript of any importance.

591
- St Columbanus establishes a monastery at Luxeuil in Gaul.

597
- The death of St Columcille.

c600
- 'Insular Latin' emerges as the language of the Irish Church.
- The monk, Asprorius, writes the first Latin grammar in Ireland.
- The death of Canice of Aghaboe, founder of Kilkenny.

610
- St Columbanus travels to northern Italy and founds the Monastery of Bobbio.

615
- St Columbanus dies in Bobbio, Italy.

c618
- The death of Kevin, founder of Glendalough.

624
- The birth of Eunan of Raphoe, author of *Vita Sancti Columbae* (Life of St Columba).

626
- The death of Aedán of Ferns.

630
- The Synod of Magh Léna is held to settle the date of Easter.

635
- St Aidan begins a mission to convert the Northumbrians. He founds the Monastery of Lindisfarne.

636
- St Carthage founds the Monastery of Lismore.

637
- Congalo Claen, King of the Dál Riata of Antrim, is killed at the Battle of Mag Roth.
  The Uí Néill gain dominance in Ulster.

649

- The death of Ragallach mac Uatach, the first documented king of the Uí Briúin dynasty of Connaught.

c650

- The treatise *Hisperica Famina*, an eccentric Latin grammar, is written in Ireland.
- The death, in France, of the missionary monk, St Fursu. He was buried in the Irish Monastery at Péronne.

658

- The death of Dimma, Bishop of Connor, Co. Antrim.

663

- Thousands are killed by a new outbreak of the plague. It lasts for several years.

664

- In England, the Synod of Whitby rules against Irish monastic practices.
- Colman, Irish Abbot of Lindisfarne, resigns his office. He returns to Ireland with his followers and founds a monastery on Inisboffin.
- Bede's *Chronicle* comments that many English have gone to Ireland for religious study. He praises the generosity of the Irish people.

667

- The plague outbreak ends after causing widespread devastation.

c670

- The first mention of St Patrick's Day (17 March), in *The Life of St Gertrude of Nivelles*.

c675

- *The Book of Durrow* is illuminated (now in Trinity College, Dublin).

679

- Eunan of Raphoe is appointed Abbot of Iona.

c680

- *Antiphonary of Bangor* written.
- Scholars compile the Brehon Law Code, Leth Moga.

689

- St Kilian, a missionary abbot, is martyred at Würzburg, Germany.

c690

- Muirchú writes his *Life of St Patrick*, the basis of all later accounts. He describes the saint as 'Bishop of all Ireland'.

697

- The Synod of Birr is convened.
- Adomnán's Law, also known as 'the Law of the Innocent', places women, children and clergy under protection in time of war.

c700

- The beginning of the Classical Old Irish linguistic period.
- The Moylough Belt Shrine is made by Irish craftsmen.

714
- The Kilnassaggart Pillar Stone is carved in Co. Armagh. It is the oldest dated monument in Ireland.

716
- The monks of Iona accept the Roman Church date for Easter.

c720
- The *Collectio Hibernensis* – a compilation of Irish Canon Law – is written on Iona.

c725
- Irish craftsmen make the Ardagh Chalice.

c730
- The *Senchas Mor* ('great old knowledge') – a compilation of Brehon laws – is written.

740
- The ascetic Culdee ('Servants of God') movement develops in Munster in response to the increasing secularisation of Irish monasteries.

747
- The death of Ferdáchrich of Dairinis, who was the teacher of the Culdee reformer, Máelrúain.

753
- The death of mac Oige of Lismore, one of the first Culdee abbots.

c755
- The stone high crosses at Ahenny in Co. Tipperary, are sculpted in a style inspired by earlier wood and metal crosses.

760
- The Clonmacnoise and Birr Monasteries go to war.

763
- The first record is made of the Culdee monastery at Finglas, one of 'the two eyes of Ireland'.

764
- Durrow Monastery suffers 200 dead when it fights a pitched battle with the monks of Clonmacnoise.

c770
- Monks at Bangor, probably inspired by the works of the chronicler, Eusebius, compile an *Irish World Chronicle*.

774
- The King of Leinster grants Máelrúain land to build Tallaght Monastery, second of 'the two eyes of Ireland'.

780
- Dublittir of Finlas presides over the Assembly of Tara.

792
- The death of the church reformer, Máelrúain of Tallaght.

795
- The first Viking raid in Ireland is made on the monastery at Lambay Island, Co. Dublin.

796
- Death of Dublittir of Finglas, one of the leaders of the Culdee reform movement .

c800
- *The Book of MacRegal of Birr* is illuminated (now in Bodleian Library, Oxford).
- A high cross is raised at Moone, Co. Kildare. It is one of the earliest high crosses to portray scenes from the scriptures.

802
- Vikings attack and plunder Iona.

c805
- *The Book of Kells* is illuminated by this date, probably in Iona.

807
- Monks fleeing from Iona found the Monastery of Kells, Co. Meath.
- Heláir of Loch Cré, a Culdee abbot, dies.

816
- Vikings plunder the monastery on Scattery Island, Co. Clare.

820
- Feidlimid mac Crimthain becomes King of Munster.

823
- Bangor Monastery is raided by Vikings. Many monks are killed.

c825
- The Irish scholar, Dicuil, writes a world geography for the King of the Franks.

830
- At least 26 monasteries have been plundered by Vikings since 795.

834
- Clonmacnoise is plundered by Vikings.

837
- A fleet of 65 Viking ships from Orkney and Norway lands in Dublin Bay.

840
- The Viking army winters in Ireland for the first time, initiating a transition from raiding to attempts at colonisation.
- Feidlim, King of Munster, advances as far as Tara and kidnaps Gormflaith, wife of Niall, the reigning Uí Néill king.
- The death of Maeldíthruib, the last of the reforming abbots, marks the declining influence of the Culdees.

841
- The foundation of Dublin as a Viking settlement when a long-phort is situated on the River Liffey. Another longphort is established at Annagassen, Co. Louth.

845
- The Viking chief, Thorgest, desecrates Clonmacnoise and places his wife on the high altar.
- Johannes Scotus Erigena appointed to the royal school at Laon.

846
- The Viking chief, Thorgest, is captured and drowned by Máel Seachnaill, King of the Uí Néill.

c850
- A Viking cemetery is established at Islandbridge, Dublin.

851
- Danes from Northern England, led by Ivan of York, attack Ireland.

853
- Olaf of Norway lands with his army and assumes control of the settlement at Dublin.

861
- Aed Finnliath, King of Ailech, allies with the Vikings of Dublin against the High King.
- King Cerbhall of Ossory defeats Viking raiders at Grangefertagh Monastery, Co. Kilkenny.

862
- Aed Finnliath is inaugurated as High King at Tara.

863
- Viking raiders plunder prehistoric Boyne Valley passage graves.

866
- Aed Finnliath drives out Viking raiders from Donegal to Antrim.
- Ivan returns to the Kingdom of York.

871
- Ivan of York returns and establishes his claim to Dublin.

872
- The death of Ivan of York, described by Irish annalists as 'King of the Norsemen of all of Ireland and Britain'.

876
- Viking activity declines, and there is very little raiding or new settlement for 40 years.

877
- Flan, High King of Ireland, is defeated by King Lorcan at Magh Adhair, the inauguration place of Thomond.

900
- The peak of Viking power in Ireland has passed.
- The beginning of the Early Middle Irish linguistic period.
- Latin scholarship is in decline with the increasing secularisation of the monastic system.

902
- The Irish destroy the Viking colony of Dublin. Many of its inhabitants move to the Kingdom of York.

908

- Flan, King of Tara, defeats and kills Cormac, King of Cashel, at the Battle of Ballaghmoon.
- Cormac bequeaths three ounces of gold and a satin chasuble to the Monastery of Mungret.

c910

- The resumption of Viking raids and settlement.

911

- Vikings establish a settlement at Drogheda.

914

- Vikings found the city of Waterford.

916

- The accession of High King Niall Glúndubh of the Uí Néill, founder of the O'Neill septs of Ulster.

917

- The death of King Tathal Ua Muiredaig, ancestor of the O'Tooles of Leinster.

919

- Danish Vikings defeat the Leinster Irish and establish the town of Dublin.

c920

- The high cross of Muireadach, one of the finest in Ireland, is sculpted at Monasterboice, Co. Louth.

922

- The town of Limerick is established by Vikings.

925

- Sitric, King of Dublin and York, converts to Christianity.

928

- Vikings massacre a thousand Irish in the Dunmore Cave, Co. Kilkenny.

934

- The Dál Cais dynasty begins to rise to power in what is now modern Co. Clare.

941

- Muircheartach of the Leather Cloaks, King of Ailech, circuits Ireland on a great raiding expedition.

944

- The reign of Olaf, chief founder of the Kingdom of Dublin, begins.

948

- Vikings destroy the Monastery of Slane, Co. Meath

950

- Dublin is developing as a trading city, noted for its trade in slaves and luxury goods.

951

- Vikings plunder St Mullins Monastery, Co. Carlow.

967

- The Viking city of Limerick is plundered by the Dal Cáis.

968
- Domnhall, King of Tara, expels Vikings from Monasterboice.

969
- Tuamgraney Church in Clare (thought to be the oldest Irish church still used today) is rebuilt.

972
- Vikings occupy Scattery Island, Clare.

973
- The death of Conchobar mac Teig, ancestor of the O'Connors.

c975
- The monastery at Metz is founded by Catroe of Armagh.

976
- Brian Bóruma succeeds his murdered brother, Mathgamain (Mahon), as King of the Dál Cais.

978
- Brian Bóruma claims the Kingship of Munster.

980
- Máel Sechnaill defeats the Dublin Vikings at the Battle of Tara. He is inaugurated High King.

981
- Máel Sechnaill captures the town of Dublin.

986
- Brian Bóruma captures Limerick.

989
- Máel Sechnaill captures Dublin again.

995
- Máel Sechnaill captures Dublin for a third time and amongst his plunder he seizes the 'Ring of Thor'.

997
- Máel Sechnaill and Brian Bóruma agree to divide Ireland between them.

999
- Brian Bóruma defeats combined armies of Leinster and Dublin at Glenmama, Co. Wicklow.
- The first Irish coins are minted in Dublin by King Sitric Silkenbeard.

1000
- Brian Bóruma conquers Dublin. King Sitric Silkenbeard submits.
- Icelandic records praise the quality of goods on a vessel from Dublin.

1001
- Brian Bóruma attacks the territory of the Uí Néill.

1002
- Máel Sechnaill concedes the High Kingship to Brian Bóruma.

1003
- Reginald the Dane builds a great tower in Waterford.

1005

- Brian Bóruma gives 20 ounces of gold to the Church. He recognises the Bishop of Armagh as Primate of all Ireland

1006

- Brian Bóruma carries out a royal circuit of Ulster unchallenged.

1007

- *The Book of Kells* is stolen from Kells Monastery (but recovered two months later).

1013

- Gormflaith, the estranged wife of Brian Bóruma, encourages her brother, Máel Morda, King of Leinster, and Sitric, King of Dublin, into rebellion against the High King.

1014

- Brian Bóruma defeats the Vikings of Dublin and Orkney, and the Irish of Leinster, at the Battle of Clontarf. He is slain in his tent by retreating Norsemen. His body is taken to Armagh for burial.
- Máel Sechnaill resumes High Kingship.

1022

- The death of Máel Sechnaill. The authority of the high kingship effectively lapses.

1028

- King Sitric Silkenbeard of Dublin makes the pilgrimage to Rome.

1029

- King Sitric Silkenbeard's son is kidnapped by the Irish. He is ransomed for silver, 2,000 cattle and 120 British horses.

c1030

- Dúnán becomes the first Bishop of Dublin.

1037

- The Church of the Holy Trinity (later Christchurch Cathedral) is founded in Dublin.

1046

- The Synod of Sutri initiates the Gregorian reform of the Church.

1049

- An Irish monk, Aaron of Cologne, is consecrated Bishop of Cracow, Poland.

1050

- The beginning of Late Middle Irish linguistic period.

1064

- The death of Donnchada, son of Brian Bóruma and titular High King. Turlough O'Brien accedes as first of the 'kings with opposition'.

1068

- The sons of Harold, the Saxon King of England, are slain by William the Conqueror, who attacks Bristol with a fleet supplied by the Vikings of Ireland.

1073
- The last known Abbot of Castledermot Monastery in Co. Kildare dies.

1074
- The Bishopric of Dublin falls under the authority of the Norman Archbishop of Canterbury.

1075
- The Irish cleric, Marianus Scottus II, is granted the Church of St Peter at Regensburg, Germany.

1076
- Murrough MacFlann, claimant to the high kingship, is murdered in the round tower of Kells Monastery.

c1080
- The beginning of a flourishing period in ecclesiastical metalworking inspired by a mixture of Irish and Norse artistic styles.

1088
- Ulstermen destroy Mungret Abbey, Limerick.

1092
- Monks on Leane Island, Killarney, begin to compile *The Annals of Inisfallen*.

1095
- The Church of St Michan (Dublin) is founded.

1096
- Malchus is created Bishop of Waterford by the Archbishop of Canterbury.

1098
- There are many casualties when Munstermen burn down the monastery at Lusk, Co. Dublin.

c1100
- Craftsmen make the Shrine of St Patrick's Bell, one of the earliest Irish examples of the Viking-inspired Urnes style.

1101
- The first Synod of Cashel.
- The Rock of Cashel, capital of Munster, is granted to the Church by King Muirchertach, son of Turlough O'Brien.
- The Grianan of Aileach – capital of the O'Neills – is torn down by the army of Munster.

1102
- King Muirchertach marries one of his three daughters to Arnulf of Montgomery, a powerful Norman lord who sends Gerald of Windsor to Ireland as his envoy.
- St Anselm of Canterbury urges the reform of the Irish Church.

c1105
- *The Book of the Dun Cow* is compiled at Clonmacnoise by Maol Mhuire. It includes *The Táin*, the earliest long literary text in Irish.

1111

- The Synod of Rath Breasail is attended by 50 bishops, 300 priests and 3,000 clerics.
- Ireland is divided into two arch-dioceses – Armagh and Cashel.

1120

- Turlough O'Connor revives the Feast of Tara, emphasising his claim to be High King.

c1123

- The Cross of Cong is made for Turlough O'Connor, King of Connacht.
- St Malachy is appointed Abbot of Bangor.

1124

- The round tower at Clonmacnoise Monastery is built.
- St Malachy is made Bishop of Down and Connor.

c1130

- *The Book of Leinster* is compiled from earlier sources. It includes a diagram of the banqueting hall of Tara.

1132

- St Malachy is installed as Archbishop of Armagh.

1133

- Cattle herds are decimated by a bovine epidemic lasting for two years.

1134

- Dermot MacMurrough accedes as King of Leinster.
- The Clonmacnoise round tower is struck by lightning and badly damaged.

1135

- Cormac's Chapel is completed on the Rock of Cashel.

1137

- Dermot MacMurrough joins Connor O'Brien, King of Desmond, in a siege of the Viking port of Waterford. In return, O'Brien accepts MacMurrough as his overlord.
- St Malachy establishes the Augustinian Priory of Downpatrick.

1139

- St Malachy, en route for Rome, leaves four monks to train at the Cistercian Abbey of Clairvaux.

1140

- Mellifont Abbey – the first Cistercian monastery in Ireland – is founded.

1148

- St Malachy dies at Clairvaux on a second journey to Rome.
- Dermot MacMurrough invites Cistercians from Mellifont to establish Baltinglass Abbey, Co. Wicklow.

1150

- Bective Abbey, Meath, is founded by the Cistercians.

1151

- The Battle of Móin Mor. Turlough O'Connor and Dermot MacMurrough defeat Turlough O'Brien, the King of Munster. Annalists claim that over 7,000 of the Munster army were killed.

1152

- Dermot MacMurrough abducts Dervilla, wife of Tiernan O'Rourke, King of Breffni.
- Paparo, first papal legate sent to Ireland, presides over the Synod of Kells. He divides Ireland into the archbishoprics of Armagh, Cashel, Dublin and Tuam.
- Mellifont Abbey now has seven daughter houses in Ireland.
- Owen, an English knight, gives the earliest documented personal account of a pilgrimage to Patrick's Purgatory.

1153

- Dervilla is returned to her husband, Tiernan O'Rourke.

1155

- Pope Adrian IV issues the Bull Laudabiliter, granting King Henry II permission to go to Ireland in order to reform the Church.

1156

- Muirchertach MacLochlainn becomes High King but with opposition. His rivals are Rory O'Connor and Tiernan O'Rourke.
- Kells Monastery is burnt by raiders.

1157

- The Cistercian church at Mellifont is consecrated with great ceremony.

1158

- Jerpoint Abbey is established for the Benedictine order by Donal MacGillapatrick.

1161

- Cistercians from Mellifont establish Boyle Abbey in Co. Roscommon.

1162

- The Synod of Clane reaffirms the Primacy of Armagh and rules that lectors in Irish churches must be trained in Armagh.

1163

- Laurence O'Toole, Abbot of Glendalough, is appointed Archbishop of Dublin.

1166

- Rory O'Connor becomes High King. He captures Dermot MacMurrough's castle at Ferns and drives him from the Kingdom of Leinster. MacMurrough flees to England seeking military help to regain his kingdom.

1167

- Dermot MacMurrough enlists the help of Richard de Clare, the Anglo-Norman Earl of Pembroke (Strongbow). He returns to Ireland with a small detachment of Flemish mercenaries and re-establishes himself in Ferns.

1169

- Anglo-Norman forces invade Leinster at the urgent request of Dermot MacMurrough.
- Some 400 men, under Robert Fitzstephen, land at Bannow Bay, Co. Wexford (May 1). Maurice Fitzgerald lands near Wexford town with about 140 men. Wexford is occupied by the Anglo-Norman forces.
- The building of a cathedral on the Rock of Cashel is initiated.

1170

- Strongbow lands near Waterford with 200 knights and 1,000 foot soldiers (August 23).
- The combined Anglo-Norman armies capture the fortified towns of Dublin and Waterford.
- Sixty-three religious houses now observe the Augustinian rule, many of them reformed Irish monasteries.

1171

- Strongbow marries Aefe, daughter of Dermot MacMurrough.
- Dermot MacMurrough dies (May), leaving Strongbow as his heir and King of Leinster.
- High King Rory O'Connor and Haskulf, King of Dublin, lay siege to Dublin. The Anglo-Norman garrison of Dublin destroys O'Connor's camp at Castleknock and the Norse/Irish army is dispersed.
- King Henry II of England lands at Crook, near Waterford, with a large army and establishes his headquarters in Dublin. The Kings of Leinster, Breffni, Ulster and Airgialla submit to Henry II.
- The second Synod of Cashel is held.

1172

- Henry II establishes his overlordship of Ireland. Dublin is granted a royal charter.
- Hugh de Lacy is granted the Kingdom of Meath – he builds a motte and bailey at Trim.
- Pope Alexander III writes to the Irish kings, advising them to recognise Henry.
- There are now 15 Cistercian daughter houses to Mellifont Abbey.

1173

- Pope Alexander III writes praising Henry II on his Irish conquest.

1175

- Rory O'Connor submits to Henry II in the Treaty of Windsor.

1176

- The death of Strongbow leaves his daughter, Isabella de Clare, a minor, as heir. Meath passes into the hands of the Crown, to be administered until Isabella comes of age.

1177

- Prince John, son of Henry II, appointed Lord of Ireland at the age of nine.

- John de Courcy invades Ulster and builds a castle at Downpatrick.

1179
- Balla Monastery, Mayo, is destroyed by fire.

c1180
- John de Courcy starts construction of Carrickfergus Castle, Co. Antrim.
- Cistercians from Baltinglass replace the Benedictines at Jerpoint Abbey. Cistercians from Monasternagh found the Holy Cross Abbey, Tipperary.
- Cormac's *Missal* illuminated (now in the British Library, London).

1185
- Prince John is sent to govern Ireland. He grants unconquered Irish lands to Norman lords and builds castles at Lismore and Ardfinnan.
- John de Courcy asks Jocelin de Furness to write a life of St Patrick.

1186
- The Irish assassinate Hugh de Lacy after he erects a castle on the site of Durrow Monastery.

1189
- William Marshall receives Strongbow's Irish estates when he marries Isabella de Clare.
- Donal Mór O'Brien builds Clare Abbey for the Augustinian canons.

1190
- Malachy of Armagh is canonised.

c1191
- Giraldus Cambresis writes the first version of his account of Ireland, *Expugnatio Hibernica.*

1192
- Founding of St Patrick's Cathedral, Dublin.

1193
- Augustinians from Bodmin, Cornwall, establish the Priory at Kells, Co. Kilkenny.

1197
- Limerick is granted a royal charter from King John, affording it all the liberties of Dublin.
- Rory O'Connor, the last High King of Ireland, dies and is buried at Clonmacnoise.

1199
- Dublin is established as an administrative county.

1200
- The Irish Exchequer is established.
- William Marshall founds Tintern Abbey, Co. Wexford, with monks from the great Cistercian Monastery of Tintern in South Wales – in fulfillment of a vow made during a stormy crossing of the Irish Sea.
- The Classical Modern Irish linguistic period begins around this time.

1202
- King John's castle at Limerick is completed.

1203

- Gerald Fitzgerald builds a castle at Maynooth, Co. Kildare – in later centuries the seat of the Earls of Kildare.

1204

- Clonmacnoise is burnt down for the 26th time in its history.

1205

- Hugh de Lacy is granted all the land of Ulster.
- William Marshall founds the Cistercian monastery at Graiguenemagh.

1206

- The See of Meath moved from Clonard to Newtown Trim.

1207

- The counties of Cork and Waterford are established. Irish coinage is minted bearing the symbol of the harp.

1210

- King John returns to Ireland and drives the De Lacys out of their lordships of Meath and Ulster.
- John de Grey builds a bridge over the River Shannon at Athlone.
- Theobold Walter begins building a round keep at Nenagh.

1211

- The counties Tipperary and Limerick are established.

1212

- An Anglo-Norman army allies itself to Scots invaders in a concerted attack on the Irish of Ulster.
- The Archbishop of Dublin initiates the building of Dublin Castle.

1213

- King John submits to Pope Innocent III and receives England and Ireland as a papal fief.

1214

- Glendalough is joined to the See of Dublin.

1215

- At this date, only a quarter of the Irish bishoprics are held by Englishmen.
- A royal charter grants the citizens of Dublin possession of the Liffey fisheries up to Islandbridge.

1217

- William Marshall issues a charter to Callan, Co. Kilkenny. The Irish Treasury is established.

1220

- The multiangular keep of Trim Castle is completed by William Peppard.

1224

- The St Mary Magdalene Dominican Friary is founded at Drogheda by Luke Netterville, Archbishop of Armagh.

1227
- Richard de Burgh is granted the whole land of Connacht for an annual fee of 500 marks.
- Jerpoint Abbey affiliates itself to Fountains Abbey, Yorkshire.

1228
- The Abbot of Mellifont resigns after a papal examination of abuses in the abbey.

1230
- Thomas Fitzmaurice is granted estates in Co. Limerick – his castle at Shanid later becomes the 'chief house' of the Fitzgeralds of Desmond.
- Ireland's only Trinitarian monastery is founded in Adare, Co. Limerick.

1231
- Richard de Burgh builds a castle at Galway.
- The Franciscan friars establish their first Irish religious house at Youghal.

1233
- The counties of Louth and Kerry are established.

1234
- Richard Marshall is murdered at a truce meeting on the Curragh, allegedly at the request of King Henry III, after a quarrel.
- The full military muster of the English colony invades Connacht.

1237
- Walter de Burgh builds castles at Loughrea and other strategic points in Connacht.
- The De Barrys establish Ballybeg Augustinian Friary, Co. Cork.

1240
- The Cistercian Abbot of Knockmoy, Co. Galway, is censured for having his hair washed by a woman.

1250
- The Anglo-Normans now dominate most of Munster and Leinster and have penetrated Connacht and the eastern parts of Ulster.
- Robert de Muscegros erects a castle at Bunratty, Co. Clare.

1251
- A mint is opened in Dublin.
- Buttevant Franciscan Friary is founded and dedicated to St Thomas à Becket.

1257
- The Anglo-Norman advance, northwards from Sligo into Ulster, is stopped by the O'Donnells at the Battle of Credan.

1258
- The Princes of Thomond and Connacht acknowledge Brian O'Neill of Ulster as King of Ireland.

1260
- The joint armies of Connacht and Ulster are defeated at Downpatrick and Brian O'Neill is killed in battle.

1261
- The MacCarthys of Kerry defeat the royal army at Callann, killing many of the leading settlers in Desmond.
- Norman expansion into west Munster ends and does not resume.

1262
- Irish chiefs ask King Haakon IV of Norway (who is wintering with his fleet in Scotland) to lead them against the Normans.

1263
- Walter de Burgh is made Earl of Ulster.

1265
- New Ross is walled.

1269
- Robert de Ufford builds Roscommon Castle.

1270
- The Irish check the expansion of the Anglo-Normans into Thomond and Roscommon at the Battle of Ath in Cip.

1271
- Walter de Burgh dies after a short illness.

1272
- By now there are 38 Cistercian monasteries in Ireland.

1277
- Stone Castle is erected at Bunratty by Thomas de Clare.

c1279
- The Walls of Galway are completed at a cost of 46 pounds.

1280
- The De Clares build Quin Castle, Co. Clare, as part of an expansion into O'Brien territory.
- St Canice's Cathedral, Kilkenny, is completed.

1286
- Richard de Burgh succeeds to the Earldom of Ulster – he becomes known as the 'Red Earl'.

1290
- The first mention in Irish annals of *gallowglass* or 'foreign soldiers', mercenary axemen hired from the Scottish Highlands and Islands.

1292
- County Roscommon is established.

1297
- An Irish parliament is established in Dublin – with representatives from the 'liberties' (feudal estates) and counties.

1300
- Ballymote Castle, Co. Sligo is built by Richard de Burgh.
- The Dominicans have by now established 25 friaries in Ireland.
- Towns are represented in parliament for the first time.

1301
- An Anglo-Norman contingent is sent from Dublin to aid Edward I in his war against Scotland.

1302
- Elizabeth de Burgh, daughter of the Red Earl, marries Robert Bruce of Scotland.

1305
- Richard de Burgh builds Northburgh Castle (Greencastle) at the mouth of Lough Foyle, Co. Donegal.

1306
- County Carlow is established.

1308
- The O'Kellys destroy the town of Roscommon and capture its castle. John le Decer, Mayor of Dublin, has the aqueduct supplying the city's drinking water repaired.

1310
- A parliament is held at Kilkenny. The government legislates that the heads of Irish clans should be held responsible for the actions of their dependants.
- Felim O'Connor is inaugurated as King of Connacht.
- Native Irishmen are barred from joining Anglo-Norman religious houses.

1315
- Edward Bruce claims the crown of Ireland. He lands at Larne with a large Scottish army, attacks the Anglo-Norman colony and causes widespread devastation.

1316
- Edward Bruce is crowned King of Ireland at Knocknemelan Hill, near Dundalk.
- St Patrick's Cathedral, Dublin, is badly damaged in a fire.

1317
- Edward Bruce is joined by his brother Robert, King of Scotland.
- Anglo-Norman castles and towns in Limerick and Tipperary are destroyed by the Scottish army.
- Donal O'Neill of Ulster writes to Pope John XXII requesting him to recognise Edward Bruce as King of Ireland (the Irish Remonstrance).
- A general pardon, granted to rebels in Co. Cork, indicates that many members of the Anglo-Norman Condon and Roche families have already been Gaelicised.

1318
- The Scots invasion and bad harvests, cause famine in the country.
- Edward Bruce is killed in a battle at Faughart by John de Bermingham.
- The O'Briens defeat the De Clares at the Battle of Dysert O'Dea.
- Anglo-Normans abandon Bunratty and other Thomond castles north of the River Shannon.

1320

- Parliament is held in Dublin. The Archbishop of Dublin opens a short-lived university in the city, with four masters.
- The Church of St Nicholas of Myra is built in Galway about this time.

1323

- Dame Alice Kyteler is convicted of witchcraft in Kilkenny – she escapes but her maid, Petronella, is executed.
- *The Book of Kildare* is compiled about this time.

1326

- The Red Earl of Ulster dies, leaving a young heir.

1327

- Robert Bruce invades Ulster for a second time but he returns to Scotland by winter. In the aftermath of the wars, Connacht has passed out of English control.

1329

- Maurice Fitz-Thomas is created first Earl of Desmond and granted the county of Kerry.
- The Anglo-Norman Earl of Louth takes Irish harpers and poets into his service.

1330

- A new belfry tower is erected at Christchurch Cathedral in Dublin.

1332

- Walter Burke (de Burgh) is starved to death in Northburgh Castle by order of the Brown Earl of Ulster.

1333

- The Brown Earl is murdered at Le Ford (modern Belfast), in retaliation for Walter Burke's death .
- Norman possessions in Ulster beyond the River Bann are lost to the Irish.

1334

- The Aran Islands are raided by Sir John Darcy, Lord Justiciar of Ireland.

1335

- A force of 1,500 men are sent from Ireland to aid Edward III in his Scottish war.

1336

- There are concerted attacks on Anglo-Norman settlements in Leinster.

1339

- *The Dublin Annals* state there is 'general war throughout all Ireland'.

c1340

- Eamonn and William de Burgh establish territories in Mayo and Galway.

1341

- The Irish parliament criticises the English administrators for their mismanagement of Ireland.

1346
- Relics of St Canice are lost after his church at Aghaboe is destroyed.

1347
- The government decrees that English settlers may not marry anyone Irish without its express permission.

1348
- The Black Death arrives in Ireland, with many deaths in Dublin.
- The Fitzgeralds of Desmond acquire Askeaton Castle, Co. Limerick.
- Edward III seizes Dunbrody Abbey because its monks refuse to give alms to the poor or receive guests.

1349
- The plague spreads throughout Anglo-Norman areas. The Bishop of Armagh estimates that two-thirds of the English colony have been killed by the Black Death. Eight friars die in one day in the Dominican church in Kilkenny.

1350
- The Black Death sweeps through Irish-held areas.
  John O'Byrne, new Lord of the O'Byrnes of Wicklow, is paid to keep his subjects at peace for two years.
- Sir Thomas Rokeby is appointed as justiciar and ordered 'to establish the peace of the land'.

1351
- Rokeby instructs English settlers to avoid contact with the Irish.
- Brehon law is banned in areas under royal control.
- William de Burgh founds the Ross Errily Franciscan Friar in Co. Galway.

1352
- Rokeby defeats the MacCarthys of Cork and Kerry and pacifies Munster.

1353
- The O'Kellys found a Franciscan friary at Kilconnell, Co. Galway.

1354
- A royal army is defeated by the O'Byrnes in the Wicklow Mountains.

1355
- The death of the first Earl of Desmond.

1357
- Thomas Rokeby dies four days after concluding a campaign against the Irish of Leinster.

1358
- Art MacMurrough raises war in Leinster and threatens Dublin.
- Gerald Fitzgerald succeeds as the third Earl of Desmond. A renowned poet, he introduces the love lyric to Gaelic literature.

1360

- English colonists petition King Edward III for help against the Irish.
- The death of Richard Ledrede, Bishop of Ossory, who tried to ban secular songs in Ireland.

1361

- Lionel of Clarence (third son of Edward III) is appointed as justiciar.
- The seat of government is transferred to Carlow.
- There is a second outbreak of the Black Death.

1366

- The Irish parliament passes the Statutes of Kilkenny, banning the use of Irish language, customs and dress by English and loyal Irish subjects.

1367

- Administrative documents in Dublin begin to refer to 'Irish enemies' and 'English rebels'.

1370

- The O'Briens and MacNamaras burn down Limerick and capture the castle.

1375

- The important trading centre of Kilmallock in Co. Limerick is walled.
- At this date, the Franciscan friary at Ennis, Co. Clare, has 350 friars and 600 pupils in its renowned school.

1379

- Edward Mortimer, Earl of March, is appointed the King's Lieutenant in Ireland (he dies in 1381).

1392

- Richard II appoints the Duke of Gloucester as his Lieutenant.

1394

- Richard II arrives in Ireland.

1395

- Art MacMurrough and other Leinster chieftains submit to Richard II near Carlow (February).

1398

- The death of Gerald 'the Poet', third Earl of Desmond.
- Roger Mortimer, Earl of March, is slain by the O'Byrnes at the Battle of Kellistown, Co. Carlow.

1399

- The second visit of Richard II to Ireland. He leaves Prince Hal (afterwards Henry V) and Humphrey, Duke of Gloucester, in Trim Castle for safekeeping.

1400

- The fine for killing a 'man of learning' in Connacht is 126 cows.
- The O'Neill Harp (now in Trinity College, Dublin) is made about now.

1402

- The Dublin militia, under their mayor, kill 500 O'Byrnes in a battle at Bray, Co. Wicklow.

1405
- First documented reference to Irish whiskey.

1411
- Laurent de Pasztho, a Hungarian knight, gives one of the most detailed medieval accounts of the pilgrimage to Patrick's Purgatory.

1414
- The bard, Niall O'Higgins, is alleged to have killed Sir John Stanley by means of a malediction.

1416
- *The Great Book of Lecan* compiled.

1418
- The death of Art MacMurrough, chief opponent of the English colony in Leinster.

1423
- The death of Turlough O'Donnell, Lord of Tyrconnell, noted for fathering 18 sons by 10 different women and having 59 grandsons.
- The first Irish house of the reforming Augustinian Observant movement is established at Banada, Co. Sligo.

1425
- Dominican Observants found a house at Portumna, Co. Galway.

1429
- Building grant of ten pounds offered to landowners who will build defensive towers in the area that is to become known as 'the Pale'.

1430
- This year sees the beginnings of a revival in monasticism.
- Irish and Gaelicised lords establish Franciscan, Dominican and Augustinian friaries throughout Ireland during the next 80 years.

1431
- Foundation of the Choir of St Patrick's Cathedral.

1433
- Franciscan Observants are established at Quin, Co. Clare, in a friary built on the ruins of an abandoned De Clare castle.

1435
- Landowners in the part of Ireland under English control are forbidden to employ Irish bards and rhymers.

1440
- Tower-houses are built in large numbers from about this date.

1443
- A great festival of Gaelic poets and musicians is held at Killeigh and over 2,700 attend.

1445
- A native-born prelate is appointed as the head of the Irish Franciscans for the first time.

1446
- The word 'Pale' is first used to denote the counties around Dublin still under the control of the Dublin administration.
- Cormac Laidir MacCarthy builds Blarney Castle, Co. Cork.

1448
- Muckross Franciscan Friary, Co. Kerry, is founded by the MacCarthys.

1449
- Richard of York is appointed Lord Lieutenant of Ireland – he stays only a short time before returning to England to fight in the Wars of the Roses.

1452
- The White Earl of Ormond dies at Ardee Castle.

1459
- The Duke of York takes refuge in Ireland after the Lancastrians are victorious at the Battle of Ludlow.

1460
- The Irish parliament held at Drogheda declares its right to be the sole legislator for Ireland.
- Yorkist and Lancastrian factions in Ireland are led by the Fitzgeralds of Desmond and Kildare and the Butlers of Ormond respectively.
- Moyne Franciscan Friary is founded by the MacWilliam Burkes of Mayo.

1461
- Edward IV of York defeats the Lancastrians at Towton in England.

1462
- Thomas Fitzgerald, son of the fourth Earl of Desmond, defeats the Earl of Ormond's army at the Battle of Pilltown – establishing the supremacy of the Fitzgeralds in Ireland.

1463
- Thomas Fitzgerald succeeds to the earldom of Desmond on his father's death. He is appointed as Lieutenant by Edward IV.

1465
- About this time, silver groats are minted in Waterford.
- The MacCarthys found Kilcrea Franciscan Friary, Co. Cork.

1466
- The defences of Meath are permanently weakened when the O'Connors of Offaly defeat the Earl of Desmond.
- The Franciscan friary at Adare, Co. Limerick, is completed.

1467
- John Tiptoft, Earl of Worcester, is sent to govern Ireland as the new Lieutenant by Edward IV.
- Thomas, fifth Earl of Desmond, is seized and summarily executed whilst attending parliament at Drogheda.

- Bunratty Castle, Co. Clare, is completed by Seán Finn MacNamara.

1474
- The Guild of St George – a small standing army of 120 archers and 80 men at arms – is established in the Pale.

1476
- Brehon law has totally replaced common law in County Waterford.

1478
- Garret More Fitzgerald succeeds as the eighth Earl of Kildare – he dominates Ireland for the next 30 years and becomes known as the 'Great Earl'.

1484
- St Nicholas Church, Galway, acquires collegiate status.

1485
- Richard III defeated at the Battle of Bosworth Field in England.
- Henry VII founds the Tudor dynasty.

1487
- Lambert Simnel, pretender to the English throne, is crowned Edward VI at St Mary's Church in Dublin.
- Waterford, the second city in Ireland, asserts its loyalty to Henry VII.
- Lambert Simnel invades England with an army including Irish Yorkists and German mercenaries and is defeated at the Battle of Stoke.
- First recorded use of firearms in Ireland, when a soldier is shot dead at a siege in Donegal.

1491
- Perkin Warbeck arrives in Cork, claiming to be Richard of York, younger of the two sons of Edward IV. He is accepted by the Earl of Desmond and other Munster lords.

1493
- The Mayor of Galway hangs Walter Lynch, his own son, for murder.

1494
- Sir John Poynings is appointed Lord Deputy with orders to reassert royal authority in Ireland. He calls a parliament in Drogheda.
- Poynings' Law is passed, asserting that no parliament may be called in Ireland without the express permission of the English king and his council. This marks the end of the Middle Ages in Ireland and the beginning of the Modern Era.

1495
- Waterford is unsuccessfully besieged by followers of Perkin Warbeck.
- It is decreed that the Constable of the strategic Carlingford Castle, Co. Louth, must be an Englishman.

1496
- Henry VII re-appoints the Great Earl to Lord Deputy, saying 'Since all Ireland cannot rule this man, this man must rule all Ireland.'

1500
- A fire in Galway destroys large parts of the city's residential area. *The Book of Lismore* is written around this date.

1501
- The O'Connors capture Sligo Castle in a surprise attack.

1502
- Bad weather causes famine and disease in many areas.

1503
- Garret Og Fitzgerald, heir to the Great Earl of Kildare, returns home from England, where he has been in custody.

1504
- The Battle of Knockdoe. The Great Earl's army defeats an alliance led by his son-in-law, Ulick Burke of Clanricard. The Great Earl receives the Order of the Garter from Henry VII.

1505
- Red Hugh O'Donnell, King of Tyrconnell, dies after a reign of 44 years.

1507
- Thomas O'Farrell begins building the last medieval Dominican friary in Ireland at Ballindoon, Co. Sligo.

1508
- The O'Donnells capture Enniskillen Castle from the Maguires.
- The last medieval Franciscan friary in Ireland is founded at Creevelea, Co. Leitrim, by Owen O'Rourke.

1510
- The Earl of Kildare leads a campaign against Irish rebels in Munster. He recaptures several castles but is defeated by the O'Briens of Clare near Limerick .

1511
- Hugh Dubh O'Donnell, the Great Earl's principle ally in Ulster, is knighted by Henry VIII.

1512
- O'Donnell raises a mercenary army. He defeats the Burkes of Connacht and then forces the submission of Art O'Neill of Tyrone.

1513
- The death from gunshot wounds of Garret More, the Great Earl of Kildare, the 'best and foremost of all the Galls that had ever arisen for power, renown and dignity' (*The Annals of Connacht*).

1514
- At this time, there are reported to be 60 Irish and 30 English descended 'chief captains' ruling over independent lordships outside of royal authority.

1515
- James and John Fitzgerald, rival sons of the Earl of Desmond, fight for the control of the Geraldine fortress at Lough Gur (Limerick).

1516
- Piers Butler is appointed the eighth Earl of Ormond.

1517
- Dundrum Castle, Co. Down, is recaptured from the Irish MacGuinness sept.

1519
- Garret, Earl of Kildare and Lord Deputy since 1513, is ordered to England on charges of malfeasance.

1520
- The Earl of Surrey, Henry VIII's new Lord Lieutenant, arrives in Dublin.
- He brings with him orders to subdue Ireland by persuasion rather than violence.
- The Corporation of Galway bans Brehon jurists from representing clients in its law courts.

1521
- The Earl of Surrey ravages the territories of the O'Connors, the O'Mores and the O'Carrolls.
- The German artist, Albrecht Dürer, sketches a pair of Irish mercenaries.

1522
- English warships are sent to prevent mercenaries crossing over from Scotland to Ireland.
- The Earl of Ormond is appointed Lord Deputy.

1523
- The Earl of Kildare returns home after four years' detention in England.

1524
- The Earls of Ormond and Kildare make peace – Ormond marries Kildare's sister.

1525
- The Archdeacon of the Diocese of Leighlin assassinates his Bishop; he is later executed along with his accomplices.

1526
- Garret Oge, Earl of Kildare, is committed to the Tower of London on suspicion of treason.
- Rory O'Tunney carves the tomb of Piers Fitz-Oge Butler at Kilcooly Abbey, Tipperary.

1527
- Garret Oge is cleared of all charges and released.

1528
- A long-standing dispute between the English and Irish branches of the Butler family is finally resolved when Thomas Boleyn accedes as the Earl of Ormond.

- A gale hits the west of Ireland on the Friday before Christmas, sinking many ships and destroying the chapter house of Donegal Abbey.

1529
- James, Earl of Desmond, receives Gonzalo Fernandez, the chaplain of Emperor Charles V.

1530
- William Skeffington is appointed Lord Deputy.
- The death of George Brann, the miserly 'Greek' Bishop of Elphin. He is called 'a stumbling block to humanity' in *The Annals of Connacht*.

1531
- Skeffington campaigns in Tyrone and Donegal.

1532
- English forces demolish Dungannon Castle, the main seat of O'Neill of Tyrone.

1533
- The Irish parliament confirms the supremacy of the See of Armagh over Dublin.

1534
- Garret Oge, Earl of Kildare, is arrested for treason and dies in Tower of London (September). 'Silken Thomas' Fitzgerald, his son, rebels against Henry VIII and attacks Dublin Castle.

1535
- William Skeffington captures Maynooth Castle, chief seat of the Fitzgeralds of Kildare, and massacres its garrison.
- Silken Thomas Fitzgerald's rebellion is crushed by Lord Grey's army.

1536
- The estates of the earldom of Kildare are confiscated. Lord Grey is appointed Lord Deputy.
- The 'Reformation' parliament takes place in Dublin.
- Several large Irish monasteries are ordered to be suppressed and their properties confiscated.
- George Brown is appointed as the first Protestant Bishop of Dublin.

1537
- Silken Thomas Fitzgerald and five of his uncles are executed at Tyburn, London.

1538
- The O'Connors of Offaly submit to Lord Deputy Grey.
- The dissolution of All Hallows Priory, Dublin (site of the future Trinity College).
- St Patrick's Staff and other Irish relics are publicly burnt in Dublin.

1539
- Lord Deputy Grey defeats the combined forces of the O'Neills and O'Donnells at Bellahoe on the borders of the Pale.

- The Irish government is ordered to suppress all religious houses. Gracedieu, one of the few Benedictine convents in Ireland, is closed along with its famous girls' school.

1540

- Henry VIII's 'surrender and regrant' policy offers titles and favourable terms to Irish and Gaelicised English lords who submit to English authority.

1541

- The Irish parliament changes Henry VIII's title 'Lord of Ireland' to 'King of Ireland'.

1542

- Many important Irish and Anglo-Norman chieftains submit.
- Conn Bacach O'Neill created Earl of Tyrone.
- The first Jesuits arrive in Ireland.

1543

- The earldom of Thomond (O'Brien of Clare) and the earldom of Clanricard (Burke of Galway) are created under the surrender and regrant policy.

1544

- Following the death of the first Earl of Clanricard, a war breaks out amongst his heirs.

1546

- Thomas Butler (Black Tom), cousin of the future Queen Elizabeth I, becomes the tenth Earl of Ormond.

1547

- Henry VIII dies. The accession of Edward VI. The beginning of the 'Edwardian Reformation'.

1548

- Lord Deputy St Leger recalled on suspicion of treason.

1549

- The First Act of Uniformity imposes *The Book of Common Prayer*.

1550

- St Leger is reinstated as Lord Deputy.
- The plantation (establishing of settlements) of Leix and Offaly begins (ends 1557).

1551

- The Scots carry out a massacre on Tory Island (Donegal).
- *The Book of Common Prayer* is the first book to be printed in Ireland.
- English liturgy is introduced into Irish churches.

1552

- The Cathedral at Clonmacnoise is looted and desecrated by Protestant Reformers.

1553

- Mary Tudor succeeds to the English throne and begins restoring the Catholic religion in Ireland (the 'Marian Restoration').

1554
- The Fitzgeralds are reinstated to the Earldom of Kildare.
- Married clergy are banned and ordered to be removed from office.

1555
- A papal bull reconciles Ireland with Rome.

1556
- Shane O'Neill, son of Conn Bacach, Earl of Tyrone, is forced to submit by Lord Deputy Radcliffe.

1557
- Armagh is burnt by the English.
- Shane O'Neill attacks the O'Donnells of Donegal.
- Lord Deputy Sussex begins the plantation of Offaly.

1558
- Queen Elizabeth I succeeds to the English throne.
- Sir Henry Sidney is appointed Lord Justiciar of Ireland.
- Shane O'Neill murders Matthew, Baron Dungannon – his half-brother and rival to the Earldom of Tyrone.

1559
- Shane O'Neill seizes the chieftainship of the O'Neills on the death of his father, Con Bacach.
- Hugh O'Neill, the son of Baron Dungannon, is taken to England for his safety and raised as an English nobleman.

1560
- The Acts of Uniformity and Supremacy restore the Protestant faith in Ireland and they enforce the use of *The Book of Common Prayer*.

1561
- Shane O'Neill is declared a traitor.

1562
- Shane O'Neill goes to London, where his Irish bodyguards cause much comment at Court and he submits to Elizabeth I.

1563
- Shane O'Neill is defeated at Tullahogue by Sussex.
- Adam Loftus appointed Archbishop of Armagh.

1564
- Leix and Offaly Irish rebel against the plantation of their territories.
- Shane O'Neill campaigns against the O'Donnells and the MacDonnells of Antrim.

1565
- Thomas Earl of Ormond, defeats his rival Gerald, Earl of Desmond, at the Battle of Affane.
- Shane O'Neill crushes the Scots of Antrim at Glenshesk, near Ballycastle.

1566
- Richard Creagh, the Roman Catholic nominee for Archbishop of Armagh, escapes from the Tower of London.

- Shane O'Neill burns Armagh Cathedral and attacks the English garrison at Derry.

1567

- Gerald, Earl of Desmond, is arrested on suspicion of treason and sent to the Tower of London.
- The O'Donnells defeat Shane O'Neill at Farsetmore. He flees to the Scots of Antrim and is killed by them at Cushendun, Antrim.
- Archbishop Loftus is moved from Armagh to Dublin.

1568

- James Fitzmaurice Fitzgerald begins a rebellion to restore the Earl of Desmond.
- Thomas, Earl of Ormond, builds an Elizabethan mansion at Carrick on Suir, Co. Tipperary.
- Sir Peter Carew is granted the Barony of Idrone in Co. Carlow.

1569

- Sir Henry Fitton is appointed President of Connacht, which is shired by a royal commission.
- Sir Peter Carew plans to colonise the surrendered estates of the Earl of Desmond.

1570

- The Fitzgeralds attack and plunder the town of Kilmallock in Limerick.
- Elizabeth I excommunicated by Pope Pius V.

1571

- Sir John Perrot, reputedly the illegitimate son of Henry VIII, is appointed President of Munster.

- Elizabeth I authorises a scheme to colonise the Ards Peninsula in eastern Ulster.
- In Dublin, a Gaelic language book is printed for the first time in Ireland.
- Catholic Bishop, Miler Magrath, changes faith and is appointed Protestant Archbishop of Cashel.

1572

- Sir John Perrot campaigns against the Munster rebels and captures Castlemaine.

1573

- The first Desmond rebellion ends.
- James Fitzmaurice Fitzgerald surrenders to Perrot.
- Gerald, Earl of Desmond, returns to Ireland. He is arrested but escapes to his castle at Tralee.
- The Earl of Essex lands at Carrickfergus with plans to colonise Ulster.

1574

- The Earl of Essex treacherously kills several hundred Irishmen at a banquet he holds in Belfast.

1575

- James Fitzmaurice travels to Europe seeking help for a Catholic rebellion.
- Essex is ordered to abandon his attempts to establish settlements in Ulster.

- Sir James Norrys massacres the MacDonnell inhabitants of Rathlin Island.

1576

- Nicholas Maltby is appointed Governor of Connacht.
- Protestant refugees from the Low Countries arrive in Dublin.
- Grace O'Malley, the notorius 'pirate queen' of Mayo, visits the court of Elizabeth I.

1577

- The papacy pledges its support to James Fitzmaurice Fitzgerald.
- *Holinshead's Chronicles* are published, containing information on Ireland by Richard Stanihurst.

1578

- A papal force leaves Italy en route to Ireland.

1579

- A contingent of papal soldiers lands at Smerwick, Kerry, under the leadership of James Fitzmaurice Fitzgerald.
- Rebellion breaks out in Munster after the Fitzgeralds kill two English envoys in Tralee, Kerry.
- James Fitzmaurice Fitzgerald is killed in a skirmish at Barrington's Bridge near Limerick.
- The Earl of Desmond assumes leadership of the rebels.
- Sir Nicholas Maltby defeats the Fitzgeralds at Monasternenagh.
- The Earl of Desmond sacks Youghal, Cork.

1580

- The Earl of Ormond institutes a scorched earth policy in Munster.
- Some 600 papal troops land at Smerwick and establish themselves at Dun-an-oir (September).
- James Eustace, Viscount Baltinglass and the O'Byrnes revolt in Leinster.
- Lord Deputy Grey is defeated in Glenmalure, Wicklow, by the O'Byrnes.
- The papal force at Smerwick surrenders and is massacred by English forces led by Grey and Sir Walter Raleigh.

1581

- English forces gain the upper hand in Munster.
- Nicholas Sanders, the papal legate, dies in Co. Limerick.
- John Derricke publishes *The Image of Irelande*, an illustrated account (in verse) of a military campaign in Ireland.

1582

- The brother of the Earl of Desmond killed by English forces.
- The scorched earth policy in Munster causes a famine that claims 30,000 lives in six months. There are reports of cannibalism.

1583

- The Desmond rebellion ends.
- Gerald, the fourteenth Earl of Desmond, is murdered by the O'Moriartys near Tralee after his followers steal some cattle.

1584
- Dermot O'Hurley, Archbishop of Cashel, is hanged in Dublin.

1585
- The Composition of Connacht: the majority of Irish chieftains in the region agree to submit to English administration and practices.
- The death of Richard Creagh, Roman Catholic Archbishop of Armagh, a prisoner in the Tower of London for 18 years.
- Rathfarnham Castle, Co. Dublin, is built by Archbishop Loftus.

1586
- Scottish mercenaries, hired by the Burkes, are massacred by Sir Richard Bingham, Lord President of Connacht, at Ardnaree, Mayo.

1587
- The Munster plantation begins and undertakers include Sir Walter Raleigh and the poet Edmund Spenser.
- Hugh O'Neill is granted the title of Earl of Tyrone.

1588
- At least 23 ships of the fleeing Spanish Armada are wrecked off the western coasts of Ireland. (September).
- The galleon *Girona* founders off Dunluce Castle, Co. Antrim.
- Sir Walter Raleigh is made Mayor of Youghal, Co. Cork.

1589
- The Burkes of Mayo and the O'Rourkes rebel because of mistreatment by Richard Bingham.

c1590
- Sir Walter Raleigh plants the first potatoes grown in Ireland (reputedly at Killua Castle, Co. Westmeath).
- Edmund Spenser publishes Part 1 of *The Faerie Queen*.

1591
- Red Hugh O'Donnell, heir to the Earl of Tyrconnell, escapes from Dublin Castle and finds refuge in the Wicklow Mountains with the O'Byrnes.

1592
- Red Hugh O'Donnell succeeds to the chieftainship of the O'Donnells. The Irish College at Salamanca, Spain, is founded.

1593
- Hugh O'Neill is inaugurated as 'The O'Neill'. Red Hugh O'Donnell leads a rebellion of O'Donnells and Maguires in Ulster.
- The Irish College at Lisbon, Portugal, is founded.

1594
- Bingham's army routed by Hugh Maguire at the 'Ford of the Biscuits'.
- Trinity College, Dublin, opens.
- The Irish College at Douai, Belgium, is founded.

1595

- Hugh O'Neill openly joins the Ulster rebellion.
- Sir Henry Bagenal's army defeated at Clontibret, Monaghan.
- Hugh O'Neill and O'Donnell petition King Phillip II of Spain for aid.

1596

- The Ulster leaders meet Alonso Cobos, Spanish envoy.
- Hugh O'Neill calls on Munster lords to join his revolt.

1597

- Fiach MacHugh O'Byrne ambushed and killed in Co. Wicklow.
- Hugh O'Donnell repels an English army at Ballyshannon, Donegal.
- Sir John Chichester, Governor of Carrickfergus, is killed by the MacDonnells of Antrim.

1598

- The Battle of the Yellow Ford – the combined forces of O'Neill, O'Donnell and Maguire overwhelm an English army led by Sir Henry Bagenal outside of Armagh.
- Rebellion breaks out throughout Ireland.

1599

- Robert Dudley, Earl of Essex, is sent to restore order in Ireland. English forces defeated at the Pass of the Plumes and Deputy's Pass. The Earl of Essex agrees a truce with Tyrone and returns to England.

- Sir Thomas Norrys builds a fortified mansion at Mallow, Co. Cork.

1600

- Mountjoy is appointed Lord Deputy by the English government and given a large army to subdue the rebels. He is assisted by Sir George Carew, President of Munster.
- Henry Dowcra lands in Lough Foyle and fortifies Derry. Mountjoy fights Hugh O'Neill at the Moyry Pass, enters Ulster and builds a fort at Mount Norris, Armagh.
- Rebel forces in Munster and Wicklow are defeated and then dispersed.
- James, fifteenth Earl of Desmond, is repudiated by his subjects when he attends a Protestant Church service in Kilmallock.

1601

- A Spanish army of some 2,500 under Don Juan de Aguila lands at Kinsale, Co. Cork (September). Lord Mountjoy lays siege to Kinsale.
- O'Neill and O'Donnell bring their armies from Ulster to aid the Spanish. Dunboy Castle on Bere Island, Co. Cork, is occupied by a Spanish garrison.
- At the Battle of Kinsale, Lord Mountjoy's smaller but well-deployed army routes the armies of Ulster (under O'Neill and O'Donnell) a few miles outside of the town (24 December).

- Hugh O'Neill retires to Ulster, while Hugh O'Donnell takes ship for Spain.

1602
- De Aguila surrenders to Mountjoy at Kinsale.
- Dunboy Castle is stormed and its defenders are put to the sword.
- Hugh O'Donnell dies in Spain.
- Lord Mountjoy invades Tyrone and destroys the stone inauguration seat of the O'Neills at Tullahogue.
- Rory O'Donnell, brother and successor of Red Hugh, surrenders to Mountjoy.
- Donal Cam O'Sullivan Beare begins his epic march from Glengarrif, in Cork to Ulster accompanied by about a thousand followers (December).

1603
- O'Sullivan Beare arrives in Leitrim with 36 men (January).
- The death of Elizabeth I. She is succeeded by King James I.
- Hugh O'Neill submits to Lord Mountjoy at Mellifont, Co. Louth.
- The end of the Ulster Rebellion, sometimes called the Nine Years War.
- Hugh O'Neill and Rory O'Donnell are pardoned and allowed to retain their titles and estates.

1604
- The death of Katherine Fitzgerald, 'the old Countess of Desmond'. She was reputedly 140 years old.

- A Friday market is opened in Belfast.

1605
- Gavelkind and the other practices of Gaelic feudalism are banned.
- The government declares all Irish people are subject to the Crown alone.
- Hugh Montgomery and James Hamilton are granted confiscated lands in Ulster.
- Attendance at Protestant services is made compulsory.
- Jesuits and other Roman Catholic priests are proscribed.
- The Catholic gentry of the traditionally pro-English counties around Dublin object to the new religious edicts.

1606
- The Brehon law code is formally abolished.
- The Franciscans found St Anthony's College at Louvain in Belgium.

1607
- The flight of the earls – Hugh O'Neill, Rory O'Donnell and other Ulster lords flee Ireland for Spain. Large areas of the six Ulster counties are confiscated.

1608
- A government survey of confiscated Ulster lands is initiated.
- Sir Cahir O'Doherty of Inishowen rebels; he is killed and his estates forfeited.

1609

- Some 500,000 acres in Ulster are made available for settlement.

1610

- The City of London undertakes to plant colonies in the area around Derry. Hugh Montgomery and James Hamilton plant the Ards and Clandeboye.
- Barnabe Rich publishes *A New Description of Ireland*.

1611

- By now there are almost 5,000 English settlers planted in Munster.
- John Speed's publishes a picture map of Dublin.

1612

- The first borough of the Ulster plantation is founded at Dungannon.
- Cornelius O'Devany, Bishop of Down, is executed for treason.

1613

- James I calls an Irish parliament in Dublin. Londonderry and Belfast are chartered.
- The first national convocation of the Irish Church is held in Dublin.

1614

- There are 3,000 Irish soldiers and 300 priests living in the territories of the King of Spain.
- Building work begins on the Crawfordsburn Inn, Co. Down, reputedly the oldest hotel in Ireland.

- The death of 'Black Tom' Butler, the tenth Earl of Ormond and the main Irish supporter of Elizabeth I.

1615

- The Dublin parliament of James I is dissolved.
- The Church of Ireland adopts the Confession of Faith.
- The tomb of Sir Francis Chichester and his wife is erected in St Nicholas's Church, Carrickfergus.

1616

- Hugh O'Neill, Earl of Tyrone, dies in Rome.

1617

- The fortified mansion of Portumna, Co. Galway, is completed.
- Fynes Moryson publishes *The Itinerary*, which includes an account of his Irish travels.

1618

- Donal Cam O'Sullivan Beare murdered in Spain by English agents.
- The walls of Derry completed.

1619

- Commissioners are appointed for the plantation of Longford.

1620

- Richard Boyle receives the title of Earl of Cork.
- Luke Gernon publishes *The Discoverie of Ireland*.

1621
- Further plantations in the Irish midlands are authorised.
- Custom House and a new wharf built in Dublin.

1622
- The English population of the Ulster plantations now numbers about 29,500.

1623
- The pamphlet *Advertisements for Ireland* comments that Ulster planters prefer Irish tenants as they are willing to pay higher rents.

c1624
- A Jacobean mansion is added to Donegal Castle by Sir Basil Brooke.

1625
- The accession of Charles I. James Ussher is appointed Archbishop of Armagh.

1626
- King Charles I offers his subjects 26 Graces (concessions) in return for subsidies to finance his army. Protestant bishops condemn the administration's tolerance of Catholicism.
- The Munster fisheries are worth 29,000 pounds, mainly due to an abundance of pilchards.
- The Franciscan, Michael O'Clery, returns to Ireland from Louvain, with the mission to collect old Irish manuscripts.

1627
- The offer of the Graces causes a confrontation between the Dublin administration and Irish Protestants.

1628
- Charles I grants 51 Graces for subsidies.
- Ulster planters are permitted to place Irish tenants on part of their lands.
- Michael O'Clery compiles *The Martyrology of Donegal*.

1629
- Attempts to close Catholic churches and ban public services cause riots in Dublin.
- The Provost of Trinity College bans all undergraduate plays.

1631
- Algerian pirates sack the town of Baltimore and kidnap its inhabitants.

1632
- Irish Catholics pay 20,000 pounds in subsidies to Charles I.
- The pilgrimage site of St Patrick's Purgatory on Lough Derg is destroyed by the local Protestant bishop.
- Stafford's *Pacata Hibernia*, an account of the Sir George Carew's campaigns in Munster, is published.

1633
- Thomas Wentworth, soon to be the Earl of Strafford, is appointed Lord Deputy.

- Edmund Spenser's *View of the Present State of Ireland* is published posthumously.
- The Protestant cathedral at Londonderry is completed.

1634
- The dispute between the archbishoprics of Armagh and Dublin over primacy is decided in favour of Armagh.

c1634
- Geoffrey Keating completes his *History of Ireland*, the first cohesive account written in the Irish language.

1635
- The Crown confirms its title to land in Roscommon, Sligo and Mayo.
- Thomas Wentworth provides open spaces on Stephen's Green and College Green so Dubliners can have a place to walk.
- Licensing laws are introduced to regulate Dublin's taverns.
- Michael O'Cleary, assisted by three other historians, compiles *The Annals of the Four Masters* – a chronology of Irish history from Gaelic sources.

1636
- The Crown confirms its title to land in Galway.
- Edward Bryce, a leading Ulster Protestant, is sentenced to perpetual silence after a dispute with Church of Ireland bishops.

1637
- Ireland's first professional theatre, the New Theatre, opens in Dublin.

1638
- Wentworth arrests Lord Chancellor Loftus.

1639
- The 'black oath' of conformity is imposed on Ulster Protestants by Wentworth.

1640
- War begins in Scotland. Wentworth raises an Irish army to support Charles I. He is accused of high treason by the 'Long Parliament' in England.

1641
- Thomas Wentworth is executed by the English Parliament.
- Patrick Darcey argues for the independent authority of the Irish parliament.
- Rebellion breaks out amongst the native Irish population of Ulster. Protestants are massacred at Portadown, Blackwatertown and other plantation settlements. The rebellion spreads. Old English landowners throughout Ireland take up arms in the Catholic cause. James, Earl of Ormond, assumes control of the royalist forces in Ireland.
- Catholics still own 59 per cent of Irish land at this date.

1642
- Fighting and massacres of Protestants continue.

- Sir Felim O'Neill fails to capture Drogheda after a three-month siege.
- The 'Confederation of Kilkenny' is formed by Catholic leaders. Owen Roe O'Neill arrives in Ireland and is appointed leader of the Irish army in Ulster.
- An army of Scottish Protestants under Robert Munro lands at Carrickfergus.
- Father Luke Wadding is appointed papal representative to the Confederation of Kilkenny.
- The first Irish Presbytery is opened in Carrickfergus by Scottish soldiers – comprises four elders and five ministers.

1643

- Ormond, on behalf of the royalists in Ireland, signs a one-year truce with the Confederation of Kilkenny. Charles I appoints Ormond, Lord Lieutenant.
- In Ulster, Owen Roe O'Neill defeats the Scottish army at Charlemont, Co. Armagh, but afterwards he is forced to retreat into Connaught.
- Derryhivenny Castle, Co. Galway, is erected by the O'Maddens (thought to be the last tower house built in Ireland).

1644

- The Solemn League and Covenant is taken by Munro's army. The Covenant becomes general amongst Ulster Protestants.

1645

- Papal envoy Rinnucini is sent from Rome to the Confederation of Kilkenny.

1646

- The Confederation of Kilkenny and Ormond formally make peace – Rinuccini condemns the agreement.
- Munro is defeated by Owen Roe O'Neill at the Battle of Benburb.

1647

- An English parliamentary army of 2,000 men is sent to Ireland. Ormond surrenders Dublin to the parliamentary force and leaves Ireland. The confederation army in Leinster is defeated at Dungan's Hill, Co. Meath. Lord Inchiquin, leading the parliament forces in Munster, sacks Cashel and defeats a confederation army at Knockanuss.

1648

- Lord Inchiquin switches allegiance to the royalists and signs a truce with the Confederation.
- Rinuccini alienates Catholic leaders by his refusal to make peace with the royalists and flees to Galway.
- The Confederation of Kilkenny holds its final meeting.

1649

- Charles I is executed in London. Royalists capture Drogheda and Dundalk.

- The royalists are defeated by the parliamentary army outside Dublin at the Battle of Rathmines.
- Oliver Cromwell arrives in Dublin. Drogheda is stormed and its inhabitants massacred on Cromwell's orders.
- Owen Roe O'Neill, the leader of the Ulster Catholic forces, dies.

1650

- Cromwell captures Kilkenny and Clonmel, then returns to England leaving General Ireton in command.
- Confederation forces in Ulster are routed at Scarriffhollis. Athlone, Carlow and Waterford surrender to parliamentary forces.
- Ormond, Inchiquin and other leading royalists leave for France.

1651

- Limerick surrenders to parliamentary forces.
- The Navigation Act restricts Irish maritime trade to English ships only.

1652

- Supporters of the confederation in Leinster surrender under the 'Articles of Kilkenny'.
- Galway, the last major royalist stronghold in Ireland, surrenders.
- The Act for the Settling of Ireland defines punishments for the population – including forfeiture of estates and transplantation to Clare and Connacht.

1653

- Inisboffin Island, the last royalist garrison in the British Isles, surrenders.
- Thousands of destitute and vagrant Irish are rounded up and shipped to the West Indies.
- Parliament declares the Irish Rebellion at an end.

1654

- The Down Survey lists and allocates forfeited lands.
- Transplantations of the Irish to Connaught begin; the estates they leave behind are given to adventurers or to Cromwell's soldiers in lieu of wages.
- The celebration of Christmas is forbidden.

1655

- The transplantation and expulsion of Catholics gathers pace – Dublin and Galway are cleared.
- Easter celebrations are forbidden.

1656

- Archbishop James Ussher (born 1581) of Armagh dies. The Archbishop was a noted Biblical scholar who had fixed the date for God's creation of the world at 4004 BC. His book collection is later used to start the Trinity College Library in Dublin.

1657

- The Settlement Act comes into being 'for the assuming, confirming and settling of lands in Ireland'.

Further harsh legislation is enacted against suspected Catholics.
- Erasmus Smith founds five elementary and five grammar schools.

1658
- Oliver Cromwell dies in England.

1659
- Army officers seize Dublin Castle in attempt to restore the authority of the English Pparliament.

1660
- Charles II is restored to the throne in England and proclaimed king in Ireland on 14 May.
- A new Navigation Act restores Irish maritime rights.

1661
- The Irish parliament, closed by Cromwell, is restored.
- James Butler is created Duke of Ormond and appointed Lord Lieutenant.
- The Church of Ireland is re-established.

1662
- The Settlement Act provides for restitution of unfairly confiscated properties, including those of some Catholics.
- The English parliament forbids the export of Irish wool.
- Foreign Protestants are encouraged to settle in Ireland.

1663
- Colonel Blood's planned rising of Cromwellian planters is foiled.
- The English parliament's Cattle Act restricts Irish cattle exports and trade with the colonies.

1664
- Around this date over 74 per cent of Irish exports are to England.

1665
- Smithfield Market, Dublin, is founded for the sale of feed and livestock.

1666
- The Act of Uniformity restricts religious, teaching and official positions to members of the Church of Ireland.

1667
- England and Scotland ban imports of Irish livestock.
- The College of Physicians is founded.

1668
- Around 12,000 Irish people have now been transported to the West Indies.
- The barn-style Middle Church at Upper Ballinderry, Co. Antrim, is consecrated.

1669
- George Fox, founder of the Quaker faith, visits Ireland.

c1670
- Jews from the Canary Islands flee the Inquisition and settle in Dublin.

1671
- The second Navigation Act restricts direct imports from the colonies to Ireland.

1672
- The *regium donum* grants to Presbyterian ministers are initiated.

1673
- The Test Act demands that all office holders take Church of Ireland sacraments.
- The first chart of Dublin Bay is drawn by Sir Bernard de Gomme.

1674
- The death of the Earl of Inchiquin.

c1675
- Hoare's Bank, the first in Ireland, opens in Cork.

1676
- Around this time, unfortified houses with Dutch gables like Eyrecourt, Co. Galway, and Beaulieu, Co. Louth, are built.

1677
- The Duke of Ormond is sworn in for a second term as Lord Lieutenant. Charles Fort is built to protect Kinsale Harbour (architect, Sir William Robinson).

1678
- Archbishop Talbot of Dublin arrested after Titus Oates accuses him of involvement in a 'Popish Plot'.

1679
- Oliver Plunkett, Archbishop of Armagh, is arrested on suspicion of involvement in the 'Popish Plot'.

1680
- Work begins on the Royal Hospital, Kilmainham, Dublin's first classical building.
- Three members of the audience are killed when the galleries of the Smock Alley Theatre collapse during a performance of Ben Johnson's *Bartholomew Fair*.

1681
- Oliver Plunkett is convicted of treason on false evidence and executed.

1682
- The 'Long Bridge', linking Belfast to the Down side of the River Lagan, is built at a cost of 12,000 pounds.
- Richard Southwell builds the Almshouses at Kinsale, Co. Cork.

1684
- The Dublin Philosophical Society is founded by William Molyneux.
- The first public dissection of a human corpse in Ireland takes place.

1685

- James II, widely considered to be sympathetic to Catholics, succeeds to the throne of England and Ireland.
- The first complete *Old Testament* in Irish is published in London (the translation was initiated in 1629 by William Bedel).
- William Petty's *Map of Ireland* is published.

1686

- Richard Talbot is made Earl of Tyrconnell and appointed Lieutenant General of the army.
- The government directs the Exchequer to pay Catholic bishops and archbishops.
- Jonathan Swift graduates from Trinity College.

1687

- Tyrconnell is sworn in as Lord Deputy.
- Public lighting is introduced in Dublin.

1688

- Apprentice Boys close the gates of Derry against Royal troops.
- William of Orange lands in England. James II flees to France.
- The percentage of land owned by Catholics is now only 22 per cent.

1689

- William of Orange and his wife Mary ascend the English throne.
- James II arrives in Ireland seeking help to reclaim his throne. James's

army fails to capture Londonderry after a siege of 15 weeks.
- Marshal Schomberg lands near Carrickfergus with a large Williamite army.

1690

- French troops arrive to support James II.
- William of Orange lands in Ireland at Carrickfergus.
- The army of James II is defeated at the Battle of the Boyne (July 1). James departs from Ireland three days later.
- Patrick Sarsfield attacks the Williamite siege train in a daring cavalry raid near Limerick (Sarsfield's Ride). William advances on Limerick but fails to take the city – he returns to England in September.
- The Duke of Marlborough captures Cork and the forts protecting Kinsale.

1691

- A French army under the Marquis de St Ruth sails into Limerick. At the Battle of Aughrim, General Ginkel's Williamite army defeats the French and Irish forces led by St Ruth, who is killed (July 12).
- Limerick is surrounded and besieged by the Williamites (25 August–24 September).
- The Treaty of Limerick is signed, allowing the defeated supporters of James II to leave Ireland and promising religious tolerance for Catholics. Sarsfield and other Irish

officers depart for France, becoming known in later years as the 'Wild Geese'.

1692

* Over 1,000,000 acres of land belonging to Irish supporters of James II are confiscated.
* The Irish parliament, now completely Protestant, meets for a short session.

1693

* Patrick Sarsfield dies after being wounded at the Battle of Landen.

1694

* William becomes the sole monarch of England and Ireland after his wife Mary dies.

1695

* The beginning of the era of the Anglo-Irish Ascendancy. The Irish parliament meets and passes acts which contravene the promise of tolerance in the Treaty of Limerick.
* Penal laws are passed forbidding Catholics their rights to bear arms and to educate their children or open schools.

1696

* Duties on Irish linen entering England are removed in order to encourage the industry.

1697

* Further penal laws ban burials in Catholic graveyards and exile all Catholic clergy.

* Two new parishes formed on north side of the River Liffey to cater for Dublin's expanding population.

1698

* Catholic clergy are expelled en masse.
* William Molyneux's tract *Case of Ireland being Bound by Acts of Parliament in England Stated* is condemned in Westminster.

1699

* Duties and restrictions are imposed on Irish wool exports to England.
* Molly Malone, the subject of the famous Dublin street song, is reputed to have died in this year.

1700

* The population of Ireland is now about 2,000,000.
* In the aftermath of the Williamite wars, the government holds over 600,000 acres of confiscated Irish land.

1701

* Work begins on Marsh's Library, Dublin.

1702

* The death of William of Orange. His successor, Queen Anne, is a strict Anglican.
* The Huguenot settlement at Portarlington, founded in 1667, is now a thriving market town.

1703
- The town walls of Cork are demolished to allow for the city's expansion.
- The first Irish newspaper begins publication (*Pue's Imperial Occurrences*).

1704
- Yet more penal laws are imposed – Catholic ownership and tenancy of land is restricted and dissenters and Catholics are excluded from public office.
- The Bible is printed in Ireland for the first time by James Blow (Belfast).
- Jonathan Swift publishes *The Tale of a Tub*.

1705
- British colonies in America are opened to direct trade in linen with Ireland.

1706
- Following the plantations and confiscations of the previous century only 18 per cent of Irish land now remains in Catholic ownership.

1707
- George Farquhar writes *The Beaux' Strategem* , which is considered to be the last great Restoration comedy.

1708
- Cork repeals by-laws which are hindering the activities of the city's Catholic merchants.

1709
- A palatine settlement is established in Rathkeale (Limerick).
- Sir Richard Steele publishes the first edition of *The Tatler* in London (ends 1711).

1710
- Smithwick's, Ireland's oldest surviving brewery, opens in Kilkenny.
- The last recorded wolf in Ireland is shot.
- The philosopher, George Berkeley, publishes *A Treatise Concerning Human Knowledge*.
- Jonathan Swift begins writing his *Journal to Stella*, an account of his life in London.

1711
- The commencement of an era of recurrent warfare between tenants and landlords which lasts nearly two centuries.
- In Connacht, the expropriation of land for pasture leads to the activities of the Houghers, who maim and slaughter thousands of sheep and cattle.
- The Linen Board is established to help promote the linen industry.
- The Medical School at Trinity College opens.

1712
- Building work begins on the Trinity College Library (architect, Thomas Burgh).

1713
- Jonathan Swift becomes Dean of St Patrick's Cathedral.

1714
- The accession of George I, the first Hanoverian king.

1715
- George I promises better treatment for dissenting Protestants.

c1716
- A series of bad harvests causes great distress in Irish rural areas.

1717
- The population of Ireland approaches 3,000,000.

1718
- Ulster Scots emigrate in large numbers to the American colonies.
- The Charitable Infirmary, Ireland's oldest hospital, is opened at Cork Street, Dublin (later moved to Jervis Street).

1719
- The Toleration Act exempts dissenting Protestants from the penalties imposed on Roman Catholics.
- *The Dublin Evening Chronicle* is published for the first time.

1720
- The Declaratory Act (Sixth of George I) lays down the supremacy of the English parliament over the Irish parliament.

1721
- Ireland is excluded from East India trade, except through British ports.

1722
- William Wood purchases the exclusive right to mint Irish coinage for 14 years from the Duchess of Kendal, mistress of George I.
- Work starts on Castletown House, Celbridge, Co. Kildare.

1723
- Parliament condemns Wood's patent.

1724
- The dispute about 'Wood's farthings' provokes Jonathan Swift to write *The Drapier's Letters*.
- Melodies by the Irish harpist, Turlough Carolan, are published for the first time.

1726
- The Presbytery of Antrim is established by non-subscribing Presbyterians.
- The Quaker School at Ballitore, Co. Kildare, opens. The orator, Edmund Burke, will become its most famous pupil.
- Jonathan Swift publishes *Gulliver's Travels*.
- The death of Egan O'Rahilly (born 1670), Munster poet and author of 'Gile na Gile' (Brightness of Brightness) and many other Gaelic lyric poems.

1727
- Thelkeld publishes *A Treatise on Irish Plants*.
- The death of Samuel-Louis Crommellin, the Huguenot

refugee who pioneered the Ulster linen industry.

1728
- A new Act removes the franchise from Catholics. Catholics are forbidden to practise as solicitors.
- The death of Stella (Esther Johnson), friend of Jonathan Swift and subject of his poem 'On Stella's Birthday'.

1729
- A new wave of Ulster Scots emigrates to the American colonies.
- The foundation stone is laid for the Parliament Building in College Green, Dublin (architect, Edward Lovett Pearce) – now the Bank of Ireland.
- Jonathan Swift publishes *A Modest Proposal*, satirising the treatment of Dublin's poor.

1730
- The potato is Ireland's staple diet for about three months of the year.
- Building starts on Bellamont Forest, Cavan, one of the earliest Palladian houses in Ireland (architect, E.L. Pearce).

1731
- The Irish parliament meets in the new College Green building for the first time.
- Thomas Molyneux founds the Dublin Society for Promoting Husbandry, Manufacturing and other Useful Arts.

- Work starts on Powerscourt House, Co. Wicklow (architect, Richard Cassels).

1733
- The government prohibits Irish trade with the West Indies.
- The Charter Schools movement is established to promote Church of Ireland education.
- Dr Steeven's Hospital opens in Dublin.

1734
- The philosopher, George Berkeley, is appointed to the bishopric of Cloyne.

1735
- George Berkeley publishes the first volume of *Queerist* (the third and final volume is published in 1737).

1736
- A linen cambric factory is opened in Dundalk by the Huguenot A. de Joncourt.
- Ireland's first daily paper, *The Dublin Daily Advertiser,* is published for the first time.

1737
- The first issue of Ireland's oldest surviving newspaper is published (*The Belfast Newletter*).

1738
- The death of Turlough Carolan (born 1670), Irish harpist.

1739
- The Francini brothers create the stucco ceilings at Carton House, Kildare.

1740
- There is a severe famine after a particularly harsh winter kills off livestock and destroys crops.
- The Irish actress, Peg Woffington, performs in Covent Garden, London, to great acclaim.

c1740
- The introduction of the first steam engines.

1741
- The famine worsens after a second bad winter.
- Newry is joined to Lough Neagh by Ireland's first canal.

1742
- Handel's 'Messiah' is performed for the first time at the New Music Hall, Fishamble Street, Dublin (13 April). The massed choirs of St Patrick's and Christchurch Cathedrals participate, with takings being donated to local charities.
- Work begins on Russborough House, Wicklow (architect, Richard Cassels).

c1743
- The Dublin Society founds its famous drawing schools and takes over an existing school run by the artist, Robert West.

1744
- Lord Lieutenant Chesterfield states 'the poor people of Ireland are used worse than negroes.'

1745
- Some 4,000 Irishmen fight for the French army against British and Dutch forces at the Battle of Fontenoy.
- Dr Bartholomew Mosse – 'man-midwife' – opens Ireland's first maternity hospital in George's Lane, Dublin.
- Work begins on Leinster House (architect, Richard Cassels), which becomes the home of the Irish parliament after 1924.
- The death of Jonathan Swift (born 1667), clergyman, satirist and commentator.

1746
- Irish parliament bans marriage between Catholics and Protestants.

1747
- John Wesley, the founder of Methodism, visits Ireland. He preaches at St Mary's Church, Dublin.

1748
- France harbours a large number of clergy fleeing the penal laws – there are 39 Irish priests in the Gironde region alone.

1749
- Work begins on St Patrick's Hospital for 'idiots and lunatics',

paid for by funds bequeathed by Jonathan Swift.

1750
- Some 300,000 cattle are slaughtered annually in Cork for the export trade. In the last 40 years, Cork has built an Exchange, a Customs House, a Corn Market and a new cathedral.

1751
- Work begins on the Rotunda Hospital, Dublin. Reputably Europe's oldest custom-built maternity hospital, it opens in 1757. The architect is Richard Cassels.
- The rebuilding of Essex Bridge, Dublin, on a cofferdam, is completed (architect, William Semple).

1752
- The Gregorian Calendar replaces the Julian Calendar.
- A regular coach service between Dublin and Belfast is opened.
- The building of the West Front of Trinity College, Dublin, begins.
- The first steeplechase is run between the church at Buttevant, Cork, and 'the spire of the St Leger Church' (Doneraile).

1753
- 'Money Crisis' – the Irish parliament clashes with the Dublin Castle administration when it wants to pay off the national debt with surplus revenue.

- A Delamain delphware factory is opened in Dublin (closes 1769).
- The death of George Berkeley (born 1685), philosopher and cleric.

1754
- The Brown Linen Hall is opened in Belfast.

1755
- The population of Belfast is about 7,500.

1756
- Work begins on the Grand Canal, linking Dublin to the River Barrow. By 1805, the canal will have been extended to join the Shannon waterway.
- St John's Square, Limerick is completed.

1757
- The Wide Street Commission is formed, which oversees the planning and laying out of Georgian Dublin.

1758
- Restrictions on the importing of Irish cattle and beef into England and Scotland are lifted. This encourages landlords to take over common land to increase their pasturage.

1759
- Arthur Guinness acquires a semi-derelict brewery at St James's Gate from Mark Rainsford on a 9,000-year lease at 45 pounds per annum.

- Work begins on the Provost's House, Trinity College, Dublin (architect, John Smyth).

1760

- The Catholic Committee is formed in Dublin.
- The French raid Belfast Lough and occupy Carrickfergus Castle for several days.
- The death of Peg Woffington (born 1718), the greatest Irish actress of her era.

1761

- Deep unrest amongst Irish peasantry leads to the emergence of the Whiteboy Agrarian Movement in Munster.
- Edmund Burke is appointed assistant to W.G. Hamilton, Chief Secretary of Ireland.

1762

- Merrion Square is laid out, marking the beginning of the modern city of Dublin.
- The first important Irish neoclassical house is built in Dublin. Today it is the Municipal Gallery of Art (architect, William Chambers) in Parnell Square.
- Oliver Goldsmith publishes *The Chinese Letters*.

1763

- The Whiteboy Agrarian Movement becomes active in Ulster.
- The first issue of *The Freeman's Journal* is published.

1764

- Work begins on the Rotunda Rooms at the north end of Sackville Street, Dublin.
- The Earl of Mornington (father of the Duke of Wellington) is appointed first Professor of Music at Trinity College, Dublin.

1765

- The English government purchases the Isle of Man (chief depot for Irish smugglers) from the Duke of Athol. Henceforth many illegal exports are shipped to Guernsey.
- Work begins on the Limerick Custom House (architect, Davis Duckart).

1766

- The Tumultuous Risings Act gives the government special powers to deal with the Whiteboys.
- Oliver Goldsmith publishes *The Vicar of Wakefield*.

1767

- The water-powered mill at Slane, Co. Meath, is completed at a cost of 20,000 pounds.
- Building work begins on Castletown Cox, Co. Kilkenny, one of the last Palladian houses built in Ireland (architect, Davis Ducart).

1768

- The term of the Irish parliament is limited to eight years (Octennial Bill).

1769
- Steelboy or Hearts of Steel movement becomes active in Ulster.
- The Cork Butter Market is established.
- Building is completed on the Marino Casino – a neoclassic villa near Dublin (architect, William Chambers).

1770
- There are agrarian riots in Ulster. Five farmers are killed when the army opens fire on Steelboy protestors in Belfast.
- The Assembly Rooms in Limerick are built.
- Oliver Goldsmith publishes *The Deserted Village*.

1771
- Benjamin Franklin visits Ireland.
- Peter Corcoran becomes the first Irish Bareknuckle Boxing Champion of England when he beats Bill Darts in a 'fixed' fight.

1772
- The Steelboys Act gives emergency powers to the authorities in Ulster.
- Catholics are permitted to lease bogland.

1773
- The 'Penny Post' is introduced in Dublin.
- British soldiers murder Art O'Leary near Millstreet for his horse. His wife writes the Gaelic poem 'The Lament for Art O'Leary'.

- Mayoralty House, Cork, later Mercy Hospital, is completed (architect, Davis Ducart).
- Oliver Goldsmith's *She Stoops to Conquer* is staged for the first time.

1774
- The Enabling Act permits Catholics to swear allegiance to the king.
- The White Linen Hall is opened in Donegall Square, Belfast.
- Oliver Goldsmith (born 1728) dies.

1775
- Henry Flood resigns as leader of the opposition Patriot Party in the Irish parliament after he accepts government office. Henry Grattan becomes the new leader of the Patriots.
- Two Whiteboys are executed following agrarian disturbances in Co. Wexford.
- The American War of Independence begins.
- Richard Brinsley Sheridan's *The Rivals* is staged for the first time.
- Nathaniel Hone paints 'The Conjuror'.

1776
- The Ranelagh Gardens open, rapidly becoming the centre of Dublin's social life.

1777
- The Presentation Sisters is founded in Cork by Nano Nagle.
- Richard Brinsley Sheridan's *School for Scandal* staged for the first time.

1778

- The threat of foreign invasion encourages Protestants to form Volunteer Companies in Belfast and Dublin. By the end of the year 40,000 Volunteers are enlisted.
- The American privateer, John Paul Jones, raids Belfast Lough.
- Gardiner's Catholic Relief Act restores the right to take long-term leases and inherit land.

1779

- Irish Volunteers celebrate William of Orange's birthday by parading in College Green with placards demanding free trade.
- In New York, the first St Patrick's Day Parade takes place.

1780

- The potato is now the staple diet for most of the rural population of Ireland.
- Ireland is allowed free trade with the colonies.
- Grattan proposes legislative independence for Ireland (rejected).
- Sacramental tests for dissenting Protestants are repealed.
- Arthur Young publishes *A Tour in Ireland*.

c 1780

- Brian Merriman writes the Irish poem 'Cúirt an Mheán Oíche' ('The Midnight Court').

1781

- Volunteers meet in Armagh and demand the reform of the Irish administration and independence for the Irish parliament.
- Work begins in Dublin on the new Customs House (architect, James Gandon; sculptures of riverine heads and the Arms of Ireland, Edward Smyth).

1782

- The Ulster Volunteers Convention in Dungannon calls for legislative independence and the repeal of all penal laws.
- The British parliament repeals the Sixth of George I Declaratory Act, conceding the independence of the Irish parliament. Poyning's Law is amended in favour of the Irish parliament (Yelverton's Act) and independence of the Irish judiciary is established (Forbe's Act).
- Gardiner's second and third Catholic Relief Acts restore property rights and permit Catholic schools.
- In Dublin, the Kildare Street Club is founded.

1783

- The Renunciation Act is passed by the new Whig government in Westminster, recognising the right of the Irish parliament to legislate independently. The Volunteer movement presents a Bill for parliamentary reform but it is rejected.
- The Penrose family open a glass factory in Waterford.
- The Bank of Ireland – the country's first joint stock bank – is established in Dublin.

1784

- The Belfast Volunteers invite Catholics to join their ranks and help fund the erection of St Mary's Chapel.
- The Irish government makes provision for a postal service.
- The 'Most Illustrious Order of St Patrick' is inaugurated in St Patrick's Cathedral.
- The deaths of Nathaniel Hone the elder (born 1718), artist, and George Barret (born 1732), landscape artist.

1785

- The population of Ireland has doubled since 1700 and now stands at about 4,000,000.
- Grattan's attempt to win free trade between Ireland and England fails when he rejects Prime Minister Pitt's amendments to his proposals.
- Ulster Catholics found a new agrarian secret society called the Defenders – it spreads across Ireland over the next few years.
- The Irish Academy is founded (becomes the Royal Irish Academy in 1786).
- Slane Castle, Meath, is gothicised (architect, Thomas Wyatt).
- The death of Davis Ducart, Sardinian architect. He was the last great exponent of the Palladian style in Ireland.

1786

- Work begins on Four Courts, Dublin (architect, James Gandon).

1787

- Continued agrarian unrest leads to the introduction of the British Riot Act (the so-called 'Whiteboys Act').

1788

- The madness of George III causes a constitutional crisis in England.

1789

- The Irish parliament votes for the Prince of Wales as Regent of Ireland.
- John Wesley visits Ireland for the twentieth and final time.
- The Whig Club is formed by Henry Grattan and other Patriots.
- Armagh Observatory is founded.
- Patrick's Bridge is opened in Cork. It joins the newly built Patrick Street to the northern slopes of the city.

1790

- Edmund Burke publishes *Reflections on the Revolution in France*.
- The death of Robert West, greatest of the 18th-century Irish stucco artists.

1791

- Samuel McTier and Robert Simms found the Society of United Irishmen in Belfast (14 October). The Society of United Irishmen of Dublin is established, with Napper Tandy as its first Secretary (9 November).
- Irish Catholics petition the king for relief from oppression.

- William Ritchie builds Belfast's first important shipyard. The population of the town is now over 18,000.
- Daly's Club, Dublin, is renovated into a sumptuous gambling house.
- Wolfe Tone publishes *Argument on Behalf of the Catholics of Ireland*.

1792

- The Belfast Volunteers Convention votes for immediate Catholic emancipation.
- Langrishe's Catholic Relief Act allows the practise of law and removes the legal ban on intermarriage.
- A Catholic convention in Dublin (the 'Back Lane parliament') decides to send a delegation to the English king.
- Wolfe Tone is appointed secretary of the Catholic Committee.
- A harp festival is held in Belfast. It inspires Edward Bunting to begin collecting the Irish airs later published in *Ancient Irish Music* (Volumes 1, 2 and 3 in 1802, 1809 and 1840 respectively).
- The first of Malton's prints of Dublin are published (series ends 1799).

1793

- Wolfe Tone and a delegation of Catholics meet King George III. Napper Tandy flees Ireland when he is accused of being a Defender.
- The Militia Act provides for local militias to be raised throughout Ireland.

- Government forces kill over 80 agrarian protestors at Taghmon, Co. Wexford.
- Hobart's Catholic Relief Act restores the vote and removes most remaining bars to Catholics, although higher state offices remain closed to them.
- St Patrick's College, the first Catholic institution for higher studies, is founded in Carlow.
- Castlecoole House, Fermanagh, is completed (architect, James Wyatt).

1794

- Dublin United Irishmen are suppressed. Wolfe Tone meets with French agents in Dublin.
- Catholics are enabled by law to attend Trinity College, Dublin.

1795

- The United Irishmen turn themselves into a secret society dedicated to the military overthrow of English power. Wolfe Tone leaves for America.
- Formation of the Orange Order in Loughall, Co. Armagh, after Presbyterians rout Catholic Defenders in the riot known as the 'Battle of the Diamond'.
- Grattan fails to obtain a further Catholic Relief Bill.
- The seminary of the Royal College of St Patrick, Maynooth, opens.
- Carlisle Bridge, Dublin is completed (architect, James Gandon).
- Work begins on the King's Inns, Dublin (architect, James Gandon).

- The Royal Dublin Society establishes the National Botanic Gardens at Glasnevin, Dublin.
- Maria Edgeworth publishes *Letters for Literary Ladies*.

1796

- Wolfe Tone arrives in France to seek aid for a rising.
- Lord Edward Fitzgerald joins the United Irishmen.
- The government suspends the Insurrection Act and implements habeas corpus.
- The leaders of the Belfast United Irishmen are arrested.
- Landlords are encouraged to raise a corps of armed Protestant Yeomen.
- Admiral Hoche's French invasion fleet – accompanied by Wolfe Tone – fails to land due to storms.
- The Orange Order holds its first Twelfth of July March in Lurgan.

1797

- Authorities impose martial law and proclaim the United Irishmen.
- The Catholic areas of Ulster are suppressed by General Lake.
- United Irishman, William Orr, is executed in Carrickfergus.
- Henry Grattan retires from parliament.
- Edmund Burke (born 1729), orator and political philosopher, dies in England.

1798

- A rising of United Irishmen is planned for May 23. Leinster United Irishmen leaders are arrested in Dublin (March). Lord Edward Fitzgerald (born 1763) is arrested in Dublin and dies of wounds received (4 June). The rising in the counties around Dublin fails. There are minor engagements at Naas, Prosperous, Kilcullen and elsewhere.
- In Wexford, massacres of Catholics at Dunlavin and Carnew panic the population. Near Harrow, a small force of local Catholics led by Father John Murphy clashes with a militia patrol – sparking an insurrection. Rebel forces camp at Vinegar Hill (29 May) and capture Wexford (1 June). Insurgent detachments defeated at Bunclody and New Ross. The main army routes the British at Tubberneering and advances north towards Dublin. At the Battle of Arklow, the Wexford army is decisively defeated and retreats back to Vinegar Hill. General Lake's army storms Vinegar Hill and Wexford town is recaptured on the same day (31 June).
- The Ulster Rising, predominantly Presbyterian, is confined to Counties Down and Antrim. The United Irish of Antrim are routed on 7 June by government troops (their leader, Henry Joy McCracken, is executed in July). The 7000-strong Down United Irishmen army, which includes several thousand Catholics, is defeated at the Battle of Ballynahinch (13 June).

- French forces under General Humbert land at Killalla, Mayo (August). The government garrison is routed in the 'Races of Castlebar'. Humbert advances towards Dublin but finds little support and faces a a much larger British army. He surrenders at Ballinamuck, Longford (8 September). The capture of Killalla ends major resistance in Ireland (23 September).
- The French invasion fleet is defeated off the Donegal coast, losing seven of its ten ships (10 October). Wolfe Tone (born 1763) is captured in Lough Foyle. He cuts his throat on 12 November when told he will be hung rather than shot as a soldier, and dies a week later.
- The Irish parliament is suspended in the aftermath of the Rebellion. Robert Stewart (Viscount Castlereagh) is appointed Chief Secretary.
- The Newtown Quaker school, Waterford, is founded.

1799

- Prime Minister Pitt proposes the Parliamentary Union of Ireland and Great Britain. Castlereagh launches a campaign of bribery and persuasion to secure the Union in the Irish parliament.
- Arthur Guinness turns the entire production of the St James's Gate brewery over to porter (a dark sweet ale brewed from black malt).

1800

- The last session of the Irish parliament opens. After Castlereagh packs it with pro-Union members, the Act of Union is carried on June 7.
- Henry Grattan returns from retirement to oppose the Union.
- Maria Edgeworth publishes *Castle Rackrent* anonymously. Thomas Moore publishes his translation of *The Odes of Anacreon*.
- Hugh Douglas Hamilton exhibits the painting 'Cupid and Psyche'.

1801

- The Union of Great Britain and Ireland, with a single parliament in London, is now a reality.
- The Copyright Act stops Irish publishers pirating books.
- Death of Michael Stapleton, stuccodore. His plasterworks include Slane Castle, Westport House and Belvedere House.

1802

- Robert Emmet returns from France to plan a new insurrection. Edmund Ignatius Rice opens his first school in Waterford.

1803

- Robert Emmet marches towards Dublin Castle with about 100 unruly followers; Lord Kilwarden (the Lord Chief Justice) and his nephew are murdered by the mob. The army disperses the crowd and Emmet flees (23 July). Emmet is arrested (25 August), tried for treason and executed in Dublin (20 September). Thomas Russell, chief co-conspirator of this 1803 Rising, is arrested in Ulster and executed in Downpatrick (21 October). Michael Dwyer, fighting a guerilla war in Wicklow Mountains since the 1798 Rising, surrenders and is transported to Australia.

1804

- Cork Street Fever Hospital, Dublin, is founded.
- James Barry paints his 'Self Portrait'.

1805

- The death of Brian Merriman (born c1747), Gaelic poet.

1806

- Lady Morgan (Sydney Owenson) publishes *The Wild Irish Girl*.

1807

- Thresher land agitation in Longford. Five Threshers are hanged for murdering an informer.
- The death of Dennis Hempson, last of the traditional Irish harpists.

1808

- The 'Veto controversy' arises over the Catholic hierarchy's right to appoint bishops to vacant sees.
- Edmund Ignatius Rice founds the Irish Christian Brothers, adapting the order's rules from those of the Presentation Sisters.

- Work begins on Nelson's Pillar in Dublin (height from base to top of statue, 144 feet (44 metres).
- Thomas Moore publishes the first volume of *Irish Melodies*, with music by Sir John Stevenson (tenth and final volume published in 1843).

1809

- The Catholic Committee re-established as the Catholic Board.

1810

- Legislation is drafted to curb rural secret societies (the Unlawful Oaths Act).

1811

- The Kish Lighthouse is erected in Dublin Bay.
- Kildare Place Society founded to promote non-denominational free schools.

1812

- The English poet, Percy Bysshe Shelley, arrives in Dublin to foment a revolution but he abandons his plans after two months and leaves Ireland.
- Martello towers are erected to guard harbours and strategic coastlines against the French.

1813

- Grattan's Relief Bill fails in the British House of Commons by four votes.
- The first Twelfth of July sectarian riots take place in Belfast.

- The largest meteorite recorded in Ireland, weighing 65 lbs (29 kg), lands in Co. Limerick.

1814
- Chief Secretary Robert Peel establishes an Irish police force (popularly known as the 'Peelers').
- Carlow Castle is blown up by a Dr Middleton to make room for a lunatic asylum.
- Work begins on the General Post Office (GPO) building in Sackville Street, Dublin.
- Belfast Academy is founded (it becomes Royal Belfast Academy in 1831).

1815
- The Battle of Waterloo takes place. The end of the Napoleonic Wars brings about economic recession in agriculture and urban industry.
- Daniel O'Connell kills John d'Esterre in a duel near Dublin.
- Charles Bianconi launchs his first mail-car passenger route, from Clonmel to Cahir, Tipperary.
- Mountjoy Square, Dublin, is completed.
- Irish prize-fighter, Dan Donnelly, wins a famous victory over the Champion of England on the Curragh, Kildare.

1816
- Famine and a typhus epidemic follow the failure of the potato crop.
- Halfpenny Bridge is built in Dublin.

- The death of Richard Brinsley Sheridan (born 1751), dramatist.

1817
- The typhus epidemic kills at least 50,000 people.
- The foundations of a new pier are laid at Kingstown, Co. Dublin. Kingstown becomes the main passenger terminal for Dublin.
- Maria Edgeworth publishes *Ormond*.

1818
- The Ulster Presbyterian Synod splits after the election of the Rev Henry Montgomery.
- The first steamboat crossing of the Irish Sea is made by the *Rob Roy*.
- William Carleton arrives in Dublin and soon embarks on a literary career.

1819
- Sullivan and Scanlan are hanged for the 'Colleen Bawn' murder of Ellen Hanly in Limerick – their crime inspires several famous literary works.

1820
- Ribbonmen disturbances in rural Connacht.
- Completion of the Wellington Obelisk in the Phoenix Park, Dublin.
- The Crow Street Theatre, Dublin, is closed down.
- Henry Grattan (born 1756) dies in London.

1821

- King George IV visits Ireland – the first visit by a British monarch since the flight of James II.
- Seventeen people are burnt to death in Tipperary by Rockite rural terrorists.
- The potato crop fails.
- The Bank of Ireland's monopoly on banking is abolished, except within Dublin.
- Dublin house prices are estimated to have fallen by 30 per cent since 1800.

1822

- Widespread famine and fever epidemics in rural areas.
- Robert Stewart (Lord Castlereagh), the main instigator of the Act of Union, commits suicide.
- Arthur Guinness II begins to brew Extra Strength Porter – the precursor of modern Guinness.

1823

- Daniel O'Connell forms the Catholic Association to agitate for emancipation.
- The harp is removed from Irish coinage.

1824

- A UK Act allows free trade in manufactured articles between Ireland and England.
- The Catholic Association introduces a subscription of one penny a month (the 'Catholic Rent').
- Henry Cooke becomes Moderator of the Synod of Ulster.

- William Rowan Hamilton develops the 'Theory of System of Rays' predicting conical refraction.
- Charles Robert Maturin publishes *Melmoth the Wanderer*.
- Bare-knuckle boxer Jack Langan loses two epic contests with the English champion, Tom Spring – at Worcester Racecourse (77 rounds) and Birdham Bridge (76 rounds).

1825

- The UK House of Lords rejects a Bill granting Catholic emancipation.
- The Pro-Cathedral (Catholic) in Marlborough Street, Dublin, is consecrated.

1826

- Catholic Association candidate, Richard Powers, defeats Lord Beresford in the Waterford election.
- The collapse of the weaving industry causes mass unemployment in the cities and riots in Dublin.

1827

- Sir Jonah Barrington publishes the first volume of *Personal Sketches of His Own Times* (third and final volume in 1832). Lady Morgan publishes *The O'Briens and the O'Flahertys*.

1828

- The Catholic Association holds a series of parish meetings simultaneously throughout Ireland.

- Brunswick Clubs are founded by Loyalist aristocrats in response to the Emancipation movement.
- Daniel O'Connell wins the Clare by-election but cannot enter parliament because of the 'Oath of Supremacy'.
- Dublin's first Catholic cemetery is opened at Golden Bridge.
- Francis Danby paints 'The Opening of the Seventh Seal' (now in the National Gallery of Ireland).

1829

- Catholic emancipation is granted by a Relief Act which allows Catholics to enter parliament, and to hold civil and military offices.
- The property qualification is raised from two pounds to ten pounds in an attempt to exclude Catholic voters.
- O'Connell is informed his election is invalid because the Act is not retrospective – he is re-elected unopposed to Clare.
- John O'Donovan appointed to the Ordinance Survey of Ireland. His notes and letters are to become a major historical source.
- Gerald Griffin publishes *The Collegians* (inspired by the 'Colleen Bawn' murder case).

1830

- Daniel O'Connell takes his seat in the House of Commons.
- Dublin Zoo, the third oldest zoo in the world, is opened by the Dublin Zoological Society.

- The Black Church, Dublin, is completed (architect, John Semple).
- William Carleton publishes *Traits and Stories of the Irish Peasantry* (second series published in1833).

1831

- The so-called 'tithe war' begins in Co. Kilkenny and spreads throughout Leinster, culminating in the death of 17 policemen in a riot at Carrishock, Kilkenny.
- The National Education Board is founded.
- Nine acres at Glasnevin, Dublin, are purchased for a Catholic cemetery.
- Samuel Lover publishes *Legends and Stories of Ireland*.

1832

- The Irish Reform Act increases Irish seats in the House of Commons from 100 to 105 and widens the franchise to include more Catholics.
- The government suspends tithes in the face of rural agitation.
- The cholera epidemic causes many deaths.
- The Tarbert Lighthouse, guarding the Shannon approaches to Limerick, is completed.

1833

- The number of Church of Ireland dioceses is reduced from 22 to 12 dioceses.
- The *Dublin University Magazine* is founded. It is noted for publishing poems by James Clarence Mangan and Samuel Ferguson.

1834

- Daniel O'Connell's motion on the Repeal of the Union is debated in the UK House of Commons.
- The most violent 'faction fight' of the century, at Ballyveigue, Co. Kerry, claims two dozen lives.
- Henry Cooke addresses a mass rally of Presbyterians at Hillsborough. He forges an alliance with the Church of Ireland against Catholics.
- The last sighting of a great auk in Ireland, at Waterford Harbour.
- Ireland's first railway, between Dublin and Kingstown (Dun Laoghaire), opens.
- Jockey Pat Connolly wins the first of two Epsom Derby victories on Plenipotentiary (wins on Coronation in 1841).

1835

- The Lichfield House Agreement allies O'Connell's Irish Party with the Whigs and Radicals.
- Thomas Drummond is appointed as Under Secretary of Ireland.
- The report of a royal commission on poverty reveals that labourers live and work in appalling conditions.
- The Association of Non-subscribing Presbyterians is formed.
- Wellesley Bridge – now Sarsfield Bridge – is opened in Limerick (architect, Alexander Nimmo).
- *Picturesque Sketches etc.* is published, including reviews by the artists George Petrie, Andrew Nicholl and Henry O'Neill.

1836

- The Royal Irish Constabulary and the Dublin Metropolitan Police are established to replace local constabularies.
- The Orange Order dissolves itself.
- The Synod of Ulster makes subscription to the Westminster Confession of Faith obligatory.
- The Ulster Bank is founded.
- Francis Mahony publishes *The Reliques of Father Prout*.

1837

- Queen Victoria ascends to the throne.
- Lord Kingsborough, eccentric and scholar, dies after being imprisoned for debts incurred in printing his ten-volume *Antiquities of Mexico*, which purport to prove that ancient Hebrews colonised Central America.
- The Irish composer, John Field, dies in Moscow.

1838

- The English Poor Law is extended to Ireland. It establishes the notorious workhouse system.
- Tithes are abolished and replaced by a less onerous fixed rent.
- Father Theobald Matthew begins his temperance crusade in Cork.
- Work starts on St Patrick's Roman Catholic Cathedral in Armagh (architect, Thomas Duff and after 1853, J.J. McCarthy).

1866
- Some 800 Fenians invade Canada from the United States – they occupy Fort Erie and fight a skirmish at Lime Ridgeway before withdrawing over the border.
- Archbishop Cullen of Dublin is made a cardinal.
- The death of George Petrie (born 1789), artist and antiquarian.
- The first Irish Derby is staged at the Curragh.

1867
- The Fenian rising in Ireland planned for March is betrayed and fails miserably. Thomas Kelly, leader of the Fenians, is arrested with his aide in Manchester. Fenians kill a policeman in an attempt to rescue Thomas Kelly (18 September). The 'Manchester Martyrs' – Allen, Larkin and O'Brien – are executed on 23 November. A Fenian bomb kills 14 in London (the Clerkenwell Explosion). In New York, Jerome J. Collins founds Clan na Gael.
- Work commences on St Fin Barre's Protestant Cathedral, Cork.
- William Lecky publishes *History of European Morals from Augustus to Charlemagne*.
- The death of William Parsons Earl of Rosse (born 1800), astronomer.

1868
- The Fenian bomber, Michael Barrett, is hanged in the last public execution in the British Isles.

- The Irish Parliamentary Reform Act halves the borough qualification and gives lodgers the franchise.
- The Irish National Teachers Association of Ireland is formed, with Vere Foster as its first president.
- In Canada, the Minister of Agriculture, Thomas D'Arcy Magee, a poet and former Young Ireland Patriot, is assassinated after condemning Fenian attacks.
- The first horse-jumping competition at the Dublin Horse Show is held over two fences.
- The death of Henry Cooke (born 1788), Presbyterian cleric.

1869
- The Amnesty Association is formed after reports that Fenian prisoners are being persecuted in prison.
- O'Donovan Rossa wins the Tipperary by-election in absentia (disqualified as a felon).
- Isaac Butt forms a new Tenant League.
- Charles Stewart Parnell is sent down from Cambridge University for rowdy behaviour.
- The Irish Church Act dis-establishes the Church of Ireland.
- The death of William Carleton (born 1794), writer.

1870
- Isaac Butt founds the Home Rule Association to campaign for a subordinate Irish parliament.

- Michael Davitt, leader of the IRB in England, is imprisoned.
- Gladstone's first Land Act fails to improve the position of tenants.
- *The Belfast Telegraph* is published for the first time.
- P.W. Joyce publishes the final volume of *The Origin and History of Irish Place Names.*
- The deaths of Daniel Maclise (born1806), artist, and Michael William Balfe, composer.

1871

- The census reveals that Ireland now has a population of 5,400,000.
- O'Donovan Rossa and 32 other Fenian prisoners involved in the Fenian raid on Canada are freed from prison.
- The Gaiety Theatre opens in Dublin.
- The Albert Memorial, London, is completed (the statue of Prince Albert and the 'Asia' sculptural group by John Henry Foley, the 'Europe' sculptural group by Patrick MacDowell).

1872

- Legislation provides for the secret ballot in parliamentary elections.
- There are sectarian riots in Belfast.
- The Catholic Union is formed.
- Trams begin running in Belfast and Dublin.
- The penny-farthing bicycle first appears in Ireland.

- Charles Lever publishes *Lord Kilgobbin*. Samuel Ferguson publishes *Congal*.

1873

- Isaac Butt founds the Home Rule League and the Confederation of Great Britain in Manchester. Butt also founds the Home Rule League in Dublin.
- The Irish Universities Act is defeated by Irish Members of Parliament, under pressure from the Catholic hierarchy, who object to its provision for non-denominational education. Trinity College abolishes its bar on Catholics enrolling.
- Dromore Castle, Limerick, is completed.
- Charles J. Kickham publishes *Knocknagow.*

1874

- Fifty-five supporters of Home Rule win UK parliamentary seats in the general election. Isaac Butt's motion proposing home rule for Ireland is defeated in the House of Commons.
- William Pirrie is taken into partnership by the Harland and Wolff shipyard.
- Dion Boucicault stages *The Shagraun*.
- J.P. Mahaffy publishes *Social Life in Greece from Homer to Menander*, noted for its frank treatment of homosexuality.
- The Irish Football Union is formed (Dublin).

1875

- Charles Stewart Parnell is elected to parliament in the Meath by-election.
- John Mitchel is elected to parliament for Tipperary but is denied his seat because he is a convicted felon. Mitchel is re-elected for Tipperary but he dies before he can be unseated again.
- The O'Connell centenary year is marked with celebrations.
- Catholic bishops ban Catholics attending Trinity College and repeat their opposition to the Queen's Universities.
- *The Dublin Evening Chronicle* closes after 156 years.
- England beats Ireland in the inaugural Rugby International between the countries.

1876

- The IRB splits with the Home Rule Party and demands that Fenian MPs withdraw from the House of Commons.
- In America, Captain Miles Keogh and 31 Irish-born soldiers in the US Seventh Cavalry die at the Battle of the Little Big Horn (Custer massacre).

1877

- A small group of Home Rule MPs led by Parnell obstruct the proceedings of the House of Commons.
- Parnell takes over the leadership of the Home Rule Confederation from Isaac Butt.

- Michael Davitt, a leading Fenian, is released from prison.
- The Society for the Preservation of the Irish Language is founded (Dublin).
- Percy French writes 'Abdallah Bulbul Ameer', his first famous song, for an amateur concert in Trinity College, Dublin.

1878

- Michael Davitt proposes the 'New Departure' – linking land reform to the Nationalist movement – in an article in *The New York Herald*.
- The Earl of Leitrim and two companions are murdered in Donegal by land agitators.
- A board is established for secondary schools (Intermediate Education Act).
- The Birr to Portumna railway line closes after only ten years – the shortest-lived Irish railway.
- Bram Stoker enters a long-standing business partnership with Sir Henry Irvine, renowned English actor.
- The death of William Stokes, medical scientist – the discoverer of Stokes-Adam's syndrome and Cheyne-Stokes respiration.

1879

- Michael Davitt founds the Mayo Land League. At a meeting in Irishtown, the League initiates the 'Land War' to secure the 'three Fs' (fair rent, fixity of tenure, free sale). Davitt forms the Irish National Land League with the support of C.S. Parnell.

- An apparition of the Virgin Mary appears at Knock, Co. Mayo.
- Exceptionally heavy rains contribute to near famine conditions in many western areas.
- Dan Lowry's Music Hall (today the Olympia Theatre) opens in Dublin.
- The Irish Rugby Union is founded.

1880
- Parnell tours America and addresses the US House of Representatives. Parnell is elected head of the Irish Parliamentary Party.
- The Land League begins 'boycotting' its opponents (a practice named after Charles Boycott, Lord Erne's agent in Mayo).
- In Dublin, the rebuilt Carlisle Bridge is renamed O'Connell Street Bridge.
- Lord Ardilaun presents St Stephen's Green to the city of Dublin.
- Tommy Beasley rides Empress, the first of three Aintree Grand National winners, to victory in the 1880 National (Woodbrook, 1881 and Frigate, 1889).

1881
- The census shows a population of under 5,200,000 – a decline of 3,000,000 since 1841.
- Parnell is acquitted of criminal conspiracy charges.
- Gladstone's Second Land Act grants the 'three Fs'. Parnell rejects the Land Act over arrears issue and

is imprisoned in Kilmainham Jail. The Land League is suppressed after issuing the 'No Rent Manifesto'.
- Dublin tram companies amalgamate into the Dublin United Tramway Company.
- The Dublin Horse Show is held at the Ballsbridge grounds for the first time.
- The Royal Belfast Golf Club is established, the first in Ireland.

1882
- In the 'Treaty of Kilmainham', Gladstone agrees to further reforms in return for Parnell ending the Land War.
- Chief Secretary Frederick Cavendish and Undersecretary Burke are murdered in Phoenix Park, Dublin, by a secret band called 'the Invincibles'.
- The Irish National League is established to replace the suppressed Land League.
- A family of five are murdered in Co. Galway (the Maamtrasna murders).
- The Tuke Committee is formed to give financial aid to emigrants – it helps thousands to leave for America.
- Oscar Wilde embarks on a lecture tour of the United States.
- The death of Charles J. Kickham (born 1828).

1883
- Five Invincibles are hanged for the Phoenix Park murders.

1884

- The Irish National League of America is founded.
- The first electric tram in Ireland runs from Portrush to the Giant's Causeway.
- The Wilton Lawn Tennis Club is established.

1884

- The Irish electorate increases by 350 per cent when Gladstone extends the vote to all householders.
- The IRB commence a 'Dynamite Campaign'. Four Fenians are sentenced to life imprisonment and three blow themselves up setting charges under London Bridge.
- The National Maternity Hospital, Holles Street, is opened.
- The first public libraries in Dublin (Capel Street and Thomas Street) are opened.
- The Gaelic Athletic Association (GAA) is founded in Thurles, Tipperary. Archbishop Croke of Cashel becomes its patron.
- Jack 'Nonpareil' Dempsey wins the first-ever middleweight world title boxing match at Great Kills, New York.

1885

- Parnell makes his 'No man has the right to fix the boundaries to the march of a Nation' speech in Cork.
- The Irish Party wins 85 seats in elections for the UK parliament, giving them the balance of power.
- Gladstone publicly gives his support to Home Rule (December).
- The Irish Loyal and Patriotic Union is founded to defeat Home Rule.
- The Orange Order calls on its lodges to demonstrate.
- Fenians bomb the House of Commons, Tower of London and Westminster Hall.
- The 'Ashbourne' Act makes funds available to grant full loans for tenants wishing to buy their land.
- Construction of the West Clare railway begins (opens 1887).
- Work begins on the National Library and Science and Art Museum, Dublin.
- The Irish Amateur Athletic Association is founded.

1886

- Gladstone's Liberals are restored to power, after Irish MPs vote out Lord Salisbury's Conservative administration. Gladstone introduces the First Home Rule Bill in the House of Commons – it is defeated by 30 votes on its second reading and parliament dissolves.
- The Conservatives win the subsequent general election, fought mainly on the Home Rule issue.
- The Irish Unionist Party is founded to oppose Home Rule with the support of Joseph Chamberlain.
- Lord Randolph Churchill makes the 'Ulster will fight; Ulster will be right' speech at the Ulster Hall, Belfast.

- There is widespread sectarian rioting in Ulster – 31 people are killed in Belfast during July and August. Evictions are carried out for arrears of rent by the Marquis of Clanricard in Co. Galway. There are serious disturbances at Woodford and Portumna.
- The Irish National Land League implements the 'Plan of Campaign' to fight landlords.
- George Moore publishes *A Drama in Muslin*.
- The death of Samuel Ferguson (born 1810), poet.

1887

- *The London Times* publishes a letter condoning the Phoenix Park murders, allegedly written by Parnell. It accuses Parnell of complicity in the Land War violence.
- Twenty-eight families are evicted in Bodyke, Co. Clare. Agitation for reform by Plan of Campaign supporters culminates in the 'Mitchelstown Massacre' in Cork, when the RIC shoot dead three demonstrators.
- Archbishop Croke denounces the GAA as a Fenian organisation after an IRB candidate wins its presidency.
- Lady Wilde publishes *Ancient Legends of Ireland*. Samuel Ferguson publishes *Oghm Inscriptions in Ireland, Wales and Scotland* posthumously.
- The first All Ireland finals are staged by the GAA. In hurling,

Thurles of Tipperary beat Meelick of Galway (1 April at Birr). In football, Commercials of Limerick beat Young Irelands of Dundalk (29 April at Clonskeagh).

1888

- A special commission begins to investigate accusations made by *The London Times* against Parnell. Parnell disassociates himself from the Land movement.
- The Institute of Chartered Accountants of Ireland is founded.
- The Catholic hierarchy condemn the Plan of Campaign.
- Sir John Lavery commissioned to paint Queen Victoria, establishing him as a society painter.
- Oscar Wilde publishes *The Happy Prince*. P.W. Joyce publishes *Irish Music and Songs*. William Butler Yeats publishes *Folk and Fairy Tales of the Irish Peasantry*.
- Ireland's first park racecourse is opened at Leopardstown, Co. Dublin.
- There are no All Ireland champions this year.

1889

- Richard Pigott is exposed at the special commission as the author of the 'Parnell' letters; he shoots himself in Madrid a month later. Parnell is vindicated and receives a standing ovation in the House of Commons. Captain W.H. O'Shea cites Parnell as co-respondent when he files for divorce from Kitty O'Shea.

- Eighty people die in one of Ireland's worst ever train crashes at Armagh.
- Horace Plunkett establishes the first co-operative creamery in Ireland at Drumcolliher in Limerick.
- The Pioneer League is founded by Father James Cullen.
- William Butler Yeats publishes *Wanderings of Oisin and Other Poems* and *Crossways*.
- The All Ireland champions are Dublin (hurling) and Tipperary (football).
- The death of the poet, William Allingham (born1824). The long poem 'Laurence Bloomfield in Ireland' is possibly his best known work.

1890
- Captain O'Shea divorces his wife (Parnell offers no defence as the guilty party) and wins custody of their children (17 November).
- Parnell is re-elected as leader of Irish Parliamentary Party (25 November).
- Gladstone states that Home Rule is impossible if Parnell remains as leader of the Irish Party.
- Five leading Irish MPs oppose Parnell. The Irish Party meets in Committee Room 15 to debate his leadership. Some 44 MPs walk out of the meeting and withdraw from the Party, leaving Parnell with only 28 followers (6 December).
- A study finds that the most common Irish surnames are Murphy, Kelly, O'Sullivan and Walshe.
- The Royal Society of Antiquaries of Ireland is founded.
- Douglas Hyde publishes *Beside the Fire*.
- The All Ireland champions are Cork (hurling) and Cork (football).
- The death of the actor and playwright, Dion Boucicault (born 1820).

1891
- The census shows a population 4,705,000.
- The Balfour Act makes more funds available for land purchase and sets up the Congested Districts Board.
- Anti-Parnellites form the Irish National Federation and win seats at Sligo North and Carlow.
- Parnell marries Kitty O'Shea in Steyning, Sussex (June).
- The death of Charles Stewart Parnell (born1846) in Brighton on 6 October – 200,000 people attend his funeral in Dublin.
- Michael Davitt, standing as an anti-Parnell candidate, is defeated by John Redmond in the Waterford City by-election.
- James Stephens, founder of the IRB, returns home after 25 years in exile.
- The *Irish Daily Independent* newspaper (from 1905, *Irish Independent*) is founded.
- Oscar Wilde publishes *The Picture of Dorian Gray*.

- The All Ireland champions are Kerry (hurling) and Dublin (football).

1892

- The Belfast Labour Party (the first socialist political party in Ireland) is established in Belfast.
- Free primary schooling and compulsory education up to the age of 14 is introduced through the Irish Education Act.
- Professor John Joly, of Trinity College, Dublin, invents the first practical colour photographic process.
- The Irish National Literary Society is founded.
- Oscar Wilde stages *Lady Windemere's Fan*.
- The first Irish Golf Championship is held.
- The All Ireland champions are Cork (hurling) and Dublin (football).

1893

- Gladstone's Second Home Rule Bill is defeated in the House of Lords.
- Opposition to Home Rule by Northern Protestants manifests in mass demonstrations in Belfast (4 April).
- Douglas Hyde and Eoin MacNéill found the Gaelic League.
- Consecration of St Mel's Cathedral, Longford, which took 53 years to build.
- Douglas Hyde publishes *Love Songs of Connacht*. William Butler

Yeats publishes *The Rose*. Oscar Wilde stages *A Woman of No Importance*.
- The All Ireland champions are Cork (hurling) and Wexford (football).

1894

- Gladstone retires from politics.
- The first meeting of the Irish Trade Union Congress.
- The Irish Agricultural Organisation Society (later the Irish Co-operative Organisation Society) is established under Horace Plunkett to encourage rural co-operative schemes.
- In the Bridget Cleary murder case in Tipperary, Bridget is killed by her husband because he believes she is a fairy changeling.
- Somerville and Ross publish *The Real Charlotte*. George Moore publishes *Esther Waters*.
- The All Ireland champions are Cork (hurling) and Dublin (football).

1895

- Michael Davitt enters the House of Commons as the Member of Parliament for South Mayo. He was refused entry on two previous occasions because of a felony rule.
- Oscar Wilde collapses under cross-examination by Edward Carson in his libel case against Lord Queensberry; later in the year he is imprisoned for two years on homosexuality charges.

- Oscar Wilde stages *An Ideal Husband* and *The Importance of Being Earnest*.
- The All Ireland champions are Tipperary (hurling) and Tipperary (football).

- Bram Stoker publishes *Dracula*. Amanda McKittrick Ros publishes *Irene Iddesleigh*.
- The All Ireland champions are Limerick (hurling) and Dublin (football).

1896

- James Connolly founds the Irish Republican Socialist Party.
- John Dillon assumes the leadership of the anti-Parnellite wing of the Home Rule Party.
- An extension to Balfour's Land Act makes 1,500 bankrupt estates available for sale to tenants.
- Ireland's first motor vehicle laws are introduced.
- The first electric tram runs in Dublin.
- The Limavady hoard of prehistoric gold objects is discovered by Tom Nicholl whilst ploughing.
- Ireland's first cinema shows are held at Dan Lowry's Music Hall, Dublin.
- John Pius Boland wins gold medals for tennis (singles and doubles) at the first modern Olympic Games in Athens.
- The All Ireland champions are Tipperary (hurling) and Limerick (football).
- The death of Lady Wilde (Speranza), writer and mother of Oscar Wilde.

1897

- The Irish Motor Car and Cycle Company begins operating.

1898

- The Local Government (Ireland) Act establishes popularly elected local authorities and gives qualified women a vote for the first time.
- James Connolly launches the weekly *Workers' Republic*.
- The Mary Immaculate College, Limerick, is founded to train Catholic women Catholic national school teachers.
- Dr John Colohan of Blackrock, Co. Dublin, imports the first petrol driven motor car (a Benz) into Ireland.
- The Gaelic League holds its first *féis* at Macroom, Cork.
- Oscar Wilde publishes *The Ballad of Reading Gaol*.
- The All Ireland champions are Tipperary (hurling) and Dublin (football).

1899

- The Boer War starts in South Africa. Major John McBride forms an Irish Brigade to aid the Boers. Michael Davitt withdraws from the House of Commons in protest at the Boer War.
- The first issue of Arthur Griffith's journal, *United Irishman*.
- W.B. Yeats and Edward Martin form the Irish Literary Theatre.

Their first production is Yeats's *The Countess Cathleen*.

- The Rathmines and Rathgar Music Society founded.
- Somerville and Ross publish *Experiences of an Irish RM*. William Butler Yeats publishes *The Wind Amongst the Reeds*.
- Tom Kiely establishes a world record in the hammer event and becomes the first man to throw the hammer more than 160 feet (49 metres).
- The All Ireland champions are Tipperary (hurling) and Dublin (football).

1900

- The Parnellite and anti-Parnellite factions of the Home Rule Party reunite under the leadership of John Redmond.
- Arthur Griffith founds Cumann na nGaedheal.
- The Irish Guards regiment of the British army is established.
- The earliest surviving film is made in Ireland (of Queen Victoria's visit to Dublin).
- The All Ireland champions are Tipperary (hurling) and Tipperary (football).
- Oscar Wilde (born1854) dies in Paris.

1901

- The census shows the population is 4,459,000.
- The Irish Literary Theatre stages the first professional performance

of a play in the Irish language (*The Twisting of the Rope* by Douglas Hyde).

- The All Ireland champions are London (hurling)and Dublin (football).
- The death of Vere Foster (born 1819), educationalist.

1902

- The UK Liberal Party abandons its support for Home Rule.
- The Dunraven Land Conference is held between tenants and landlords.
- W.B. Yeats stages *Cathleen ní Houlihan*. George Russell stages *Deirdre*. Lady Gregory publishes *Cuchulainn of Muirthemne*.
- The All Ireland champions are Cork (hurling) and Dublin (football).

1903

- Wyndham's Land Act helps tenants to buy out leases.
- St Patrick's Day is made an official holiday.
- The Independent Orange Order is founded in Belfast.
- The Irish Literary Theatre becomes the Irish National Theatre.
- The An Túr Gloine (the Glass Tower) stained glass studio is set up in Dublin.
- The first Gordon Bennet Race for Automobiles is held over a course in Laois, Offaly and Kildare.
- The All Ireland champions are Cork (hurling) and Kerry (football).
- The death of Ellen Blackburn, suffragette.

1904

- The Irish Reform Association is formed by Lord Dunraven to campaign for devolution.
- Rioters drive out Limerick's Jewish population (the Limerick Pogrom).
- Robert and Jack Chambers begin to manufacture Chambers automobiles in Belfast. They produce 16 different models over the next 21 years.
- Work begins on the Government Buildings, Dublin (architects, Webb and Deanne).
- The Abbey Theatre opens in Dublin with plays by W.B. Yeats and Lady Gregory.
- Bloomsday (June 10) – James Joyce meets Nora Barnacle in Dublin and later sets his novel *Ulysses* on this day.
- W.B. Yeats refuses to stage Shaw's *John Bull's Other Island* at the Abbey Theatre. J.M. Synge stages *Riders to the Sea*.
- Lady Gregory publishes *Gods and Fighting Men*.
- The All Ireland champions are Kilkenny (hurling) and Kerry (football).

1905

- Arthur Griffith proposes the Sinn Féin (We Ourselves) policy.
- The first of the Dungannon Clubs is formed in Belfast by Nationalists.
- The Ulster Unionist Council is founded. It helps forge links between Unionists and the Orange Order.

- The Independent Orange Order issue the Magheramore Manifesto.
- Electric trams begin running in Belfast.
- George Bernard Shaw stages *Major Barbara* and *Man and Superman*.
- George Moore publishes *The Lake*.
- *De Profundis* by Oscar Wilde is published posthumously.
- The All Ireland champions are Kilkenny (hurling) and Kildare (football).

1906

- A cross-channel boat service begins from Rosslare Harbour, near Wexford.
- The Belfast City Hall is completed (architect, Alfred Blumwell Thomas).
- The first issue of *Sinn Féin*.
- John McCormack makes his stage debut in Savona, Italy.
- The All Ireland champions are Tipperary (hurling) and Dublin (football).
- The death of Michael Davitt (born 1846).

1907

- Cumann na nGaedheal and the Dungannon Clubs become the Sinn Féin League (21 April). The National Council merges with the Sinn Féin League (5 September) and, in September 1908, it adopts the name Sinn Féin.
- The Evicted Tenants Act reinstates tenants and gives statutory purchase rights to the Land Commission on their behalf.

- James Larkin organises the Belfast Docks Strike, which lasts from May to September.
- Pope Pius X issues the Ne Temere Decree. It states that mixed marriages are only valid if the wedding service is held in Catholic churches and children from the union must be raised in the Catholic faith.
- Marconi begins his transatlantic wireless service between Clifden and Canada.
- There are riots in Dublin (Abbey Riots) after John Synge's *Playboy of the Western World* is first staged.
- Padraic Colum publishes *Wild Earth*. J.M. Synge publishes *The Aran Islands*.
- The All Ireland champions are Kilkenny (hurling) and Dublin (football).

1908
- The Irish Universities Act restructures the Royal University into the National University of Ireland (with colleges in Dublin, Galway and Cork) and Queen's University, Belfast.
- Patrick Pearse opens St Enda's School for Boys, Rathmines.
- The government sets up a fund to help local authorities house poorer classes. The old age pension is introduced.
- The Dublin Municipal Gallery is opened through the efforts of Hugh Lane.
- The All Ireland champions are Tipperary (hurling) and Dublin (football).

1909
- Fianna Éireann is formed under the leadership of Countess Marcievicz.
- James Larkin forms the Irish Transport and General Workers Union (ITGWU).
- Birrell's Land Act gives the congested Districts Board the right to compulsorily purchase land for the rationalisation of holdings.
- The first flight by an Irish plane is made by Harry Ferguson at Hillsborough.
- The Volta Cinema, Ireland's first cinema, opens in Dublin under the management of James Joyce.
- George Bernard Shaw's *The Shewing up of Blanco Posnet* is staged in Dublin after it is banned in London.
- Joseph Campbell publishes *The Mountainy Singer*.
- The All Ireland champions are Kilkenny (hurling)and Kerry (football).
- The death of John Millington Synge (born 1871).

1910
- Sir Edward Carson is elected leader of the Unionist Party.
- First issue of *Irish Freedom*, the IRB monthly newspaper.
- Irish is made compulsory for entry to the National University of Ireland.
- The White Star Liner *Olympic* is launched at the Harland and Wolff shipyard, Belfast.

- Sidney Olcott begins making films in Ireland with the US Kalem Company – the first film is *The Lad from Ould Ireland*.
- James Connolly publishes *Labour in Irish History*.
- The All Ireland champions are Wexford (hurling) and Louth (football).

1911

- The census of Ireland shows the population as 4,400,000 – almost halved since 1841.
- The Dublin Employers' Federation is established to oppose organised labour.
- The Irish Women Workers Union is formed. Qualified women win the right to membership of local councils and boroughs.
- The *Titanic*, sister ship of the *Olympic*, is launched at the Harland and Wolff shipyard.
- James Larkin publishes *The Irish Worker*, the newspaper of the ITGWU.
- The Parnell Monument in Sackville Street, Dublin, is inaugurated (sculptor, Augustus Saint Gaudens). The Cuchulainn Statue, now in the GPO building, is designed by Oliver Sheppard.
- The All Ireland champions are Kilkenny (hurling) and Cork (football).

1912

- Asquith introduces the Third Home Rule Bill. A Unionist amendment tries to keep Ulster in

the United Kingdom but it is defeated. On 'Ulster Day', almost 500,000 Ulster men and women sign the Solemn League and Covenant in protest against Home Rule.
- The Irish Labour Party is founded at the Irish Trade Union Congress in Clonmel, Tiperary.
- Father Browne, an Irish priest, takes photographs aboard the *Titanic* at sea. The *Titanic* hits an iceberg and sinks on her maiden voyage – some 1,490 people are drowned and 711 saved (14 and 15 April).
- D.W. Corbett makes the first aeroplane crossing of the Irish Sea.
- James Stephens publishes *The Crock of Gold*.
- The All Ireland champions are Kilkenny (hurling) and Cork (football).
- The death of Bram Stoker (born 1847).

1913

- The Third Home Rule Bill is carried in the House of Commons but defeated in the House of Lords twice (January and July).
- The Ulster Volunteer Force (UVF) is formed in Belfast.
- The Unionist council sets up a 'provisional government' under the leadership of Edward Carson.
- The League for the Support of Ulster is established in Britain.
- The Dublin 'lock-out' takes place from 26 August to early February 1914. William Martin Murphy

fires 40 members of the ITGWU (18 August). James Larkin responds with a general strike. There is then an Employers Federation lock-out of employees (26 August), followed by rioting in Dublin. James Connolly and James Larkin are imprisoned for short terms (August–September). The locked-out workers and their families suffer great hardship. The British trade union movement sends food ships to Dublin (27 September, 4 October).

- A citizen army is raised from Dublin workers. The Irish Volunteers are founded.
- Francis O'Neill, a Chicago policeman, publishes *Irish Minstrels and Musicians*. Joseph Campbell publishes *Irishry*.
- The All Ireland champions are Kilkenny (hurling) and Kerry (football).

1914

- The Curragh Mutiny – 57 officers of the British army declare they will refuse to implement Home Rule. The authorities take no disciplinary action.
- The UVF land a large shipment of arms from the vessel *Clydevalley* at Larne and Bangor.
- The provisional government of Ulster meets for the first time.
- The Home Rule Bill passes the House of Commons for the third time but is stalled in the House of Lords over the Ulster question (8 July).

- Robert Erskine Childers brings arms into Howth on the *Asgard*. British troops kill 4 and wound 27 on Bachelor's Walk.
- Britain declares war on Germany (4 August). The Home Rule Bill is suspended until hostilities cease.
- The Woodenbridge speech – John Redmond calls on the Irish Volunteers to serve with the British Armed Forces (20 September). The Volunteers split into the moderate National Volunteers and the militant Irish Volunteers.
- The report into the housing of the Dublin working classes reveals that almost 90,000 people are living in sub-standard accommodation. 'Darkest Dublin' – a collection of photographs of the slums of Dublin – is published.
- James Joyce publishes *Dubliners*.
- The All Ireland champions are Kilkenny (hurling) and Kerry (football).

1915

- The Military Council of the IRB is set up. Its leaders include Patrick Pearse, Eamon Ceannt and Joseph Plunkett, later joined by Thomas J. Clarke and Seán MacDiarmada.
- Militant Nationalists take control of the Gaelic League – Douglas Hyde is replaced as President by Eoin MacNéill.
- The *Lusitania* is sunk by a German submarine off the Cork coast. Sir Hugh Lane is among the 1,198 dead.

- The Dublin Fusiliers and Munster Fusiliers suffer heavy casualties in the Gallipoli landings, losing 600 and 550 men respectively (April).
- Francis Ledwidge publishes *Songs of the Earth*.
- The deaths of Viola Martin or 'Ross' (born 1862), writer, and Jeremiah O'Donovan Rossa (born1831). Patrick Pearse gives O'Donovan Rossa's funeral oration in Dublin (1 August).
- The All Ireland champions are Laois (hurling) and Wexford (football).

1916

- James Connolly joins the Military Council of the IRB – a rising is planned for 23 April, Easter Sunday.
- The *Aud*, with 20,000 rifles and munitions sails from Germany (9 April). A submarine follows with Roger Casement (12 April). The *Aud* is arrested in Tralee Bay by a British naval patrol (20 April), then scuttled by her crew in Cork Harbour (21 April). Roger Casement lands with two companions at Banna Strand, Fenit, near Tralee. He is arrested by British forces within a few hours (21 April).
- Eoin MacNéill places a newspaper advertisement cancelling Volunteer 'manouevres' on Easter Sunday. The IRB Military Council reverse the order (23 April).
- The Easter Rising begins; the GPO is occupied by Volunteers and Patrick Pearse reads the Proclamation of the Irish Republic from its steps. Boland's Mills, the College of Surgeons and other Dublin buildings are seized by the rebels (24 April). General Lowe declares martial law and moves British reinforcements into the centre of Dublin. The citizen army garrison in the College of Surgeons is overwhelmed (26 April). British troops secure the Liffey quays and isolate the GPO. A navy gunboat bombards the city centre. The Sherwood Foresters are ambushed at the Mount Street Bridge by Volunteers – they suffer over 230 casualties (26 April). Francis Sheehy-Skeffington (born 1878) and two others are murdered by Captain J.C. Bowen-Colthurst. An IRB force under Thomas Ashe attacks the RIC at Ashbourne Meath (27 April). Patrick Pearse surrenders to General Lowe at the GPO (29 April). The Easter Rising casualties (dead and wounded) include 184 insurgents, 530 British Forces and 2,300 civilians. Captured insurgents, including Eamon de Valera, Michael Collins and Countess Marcievicz, are sent to be interned in England.
- The following insurgent leaders are executed at Kilmainham Jail in Dublin: on 3 May, Patrick Pearse (born 1879), Thomas Clarke (born 1857), Thomas MacDonagh (born 1878); on 4 May, Edward Daly, Michael O'Hanrahan, William Pearse, Thomas Plunkett (born 1887, he marries Francis Gifford a

few hours before his execution);
on 5 May, John MacBride (born
1865); on 8 May, Eamon Ceannt
(born 1881), Con Colbert, Seán
Heuston and Michael Mallin; on
12 May, James Connolly (born
1868) and Seán MacDiarmada
(born 1884).
- Thomas Kent is executed in Cork
on 9 May.
- Roger Casement is tried in
England and sentenced to death
(29 June). The 'Black Journal'
(possibly forged by British intelligence) is circulated to discourage a
reprieve. Casement (born 1864) is
hanged at Pentonville Prison on 3
August.
- Lloyd George seeks to negotiate a
Home Rule agreement which
excludes six Ulster counties. This
is rejected by John Redmond (of
the Irish Parliamentary Party). The
first of the Easter Rising internees
in England are freed and return
home (December).
- At the Battle of the Somme in
France (1–11 July), the 36th
(Ulster) Division suffer over 5,000
casualties.
- The Twelfth of July Orange Marches
are cancelled and replaced with a
five-minute silence.
- The 16th (Irish) Division suffers
4,500 casualties at Ginchy in the
later stages of the Somme offensive
(September).
- Lennox Robinson stages *The
Whiteheaded Boy*.
- James Joyce publishes *Portrait of
the Artist as a Young Man*. James

Stephens publishes *Insurrection in
Dublin*.
- The All Ireland champions are
Tipperary (hurling) and Wexford
(football).

1917
- The remaining Easter Rising
internees are released from prison
(June).
- Eamon de Valera wins the Clare East
by-election (July 10). Other Sinn
Féin candidates win by-elections in
Roscommon North (February),
Longford South (May) and Kilkenny
City (August). Lloyd George con-
venes the Irish Convention but Sinn
Féin refuse to participate (25 July–1
August 1918). The Sinn Féin Ard
Féis is held at the Mansion House,
Dublin; Eamon de Valera is elected
President (25 October). The Irish
Volunteers elect de Valera as their
leader (26 October).
- At the Battle of Messines Ridge,
Flanders, the 16th (Irish) Division
fights alongside the 36th (Ulster)
Division.
- The All Ireland champions are
Dublin (hurling) and Wexford
(football).
- Thomas Ashe (born 1885) dies as
the result of a hunger strike in
Mountjoy Jail and Francis
Ledwidge (born 1887) is killed in
the second Battle of Ypres.

1918
- Voting rights are extended to all
men over 21 and qualified women
over 30.

1919

- The Military Service Act introduces conscription but it is abandoned when opposed by the Church, the Home Rule Party and Sinn Féin. Eamon de Valera and leading Nationalists are interned over the non-existent 'German Plot' (May).
- Five hundred are drowned when the *Kingstown*, a Holyhead mailboat, sinks.
- World War I ends (11 November) – some 350,000 Irishmen served with the British army , of whom at least 35,000 were killed.
- There is a general election in the UK. The Home Rule Party wins only 6 seats. Sinn Féin candidates, who state they will boycott parliament, win 73 seats. Unionist candidates win 26 seats. Countess Marcievicz, of Sinn Féin, is the first woman to win a seat in the House of Commons (December).
- Brinsley MacNamara publishes *Valley of the Squinting Windows*.
- The All Ireland champions are Limerick (hurling) and Wexford (football).
- The death of John Redmond (born 1856).

1919

- Sinn Féin convenes the first Dáil Éireann (Irish parliament), which issues a Declaration of Independence and elects Cathal Brugha as Acting President (21/22 January).
- The War of Independence begins at Soloheadbeag, Co. Tipperary, when two RIC men are killed by Volunteers (21 January). Eamon de Valera escapes from Lincoln Jail (February). The Dáil Éireann elects Eamon de Valera as President (1 April). Sinn Féin is suppressed, first in Tipperary then in other disturbed areas.
- There are widespread ambushes, arms raids and assassinations. British soldiers loot shops and homes in Fermoy and Cork City. The 'Limerick Soviet' seizes control of the city after local unions call a general strike (April).
- Alcock and Brown land in Clifden, Galway, after completing the first non-stop transatlantic flight.
- W.B. Yeats publishes *The Wild Swans at Coole*.
- The All Ireland champions are Cork (hurling) and Kildare (football).

1920

- 'Black and Tan' police units (composed of former British army soldiers recruited in England) arrive in Ireland to reinforce the RIC.
- Tomás MacCurtain, Mayor of Cork, is assassinated in his home by the RIC.
- The Irish Republican Army (IRA) is established and attacks police barracks throughout Ireland. Crown forces attack civilian property in Limerick, Mallow, Trim, Cork and other centres.
- The Black and Tans sack the small town of Balbriggan, near Dublin (20 September).
- Terence MacSwiney, Mayor of

Cork, dies while on a hunger strike in Brixton Prison (25 October).

- Kevin Barry, aged 18, becomes the youngest IRA man executed in the war (1 November).
- The Michael Collins' 'Squad' kill 14 British intelligence officers at locations throughout Dublin (night of 20 November). The Black and Tans open fire at Croke Park on the following day, killing 14 spectators and a player ('Bloody Sunday'). The UK parliament passes the so-called 'partition act' (the Act for the Better Government of Ireland).
- There is sectarian rioting in Derry (19 killed) and Belfast (13 killed). Hundreds of Catholic families living in Protestant areas flee during July and August.
- The Royal Ulster Constabulary and Ulster Special Constabulary are established.
- Irish soldiers of the Connaught Rangers mutiny in India – one man is executed and others receive long prison sentences.
- The All Ireland champions are Dublin (hurling) and Tipperary (football).
- The death of Percy French (born 1854), the composer of the popular song, 'The Mountains of Mourne'.

1921

- Sir James Craig replaces Edward Carson as leader of the Unionist Party.
- The first elections are held for the new Northern Ireland parliament.

- The Northern Ireland parliament is formally opened by George V (22 June). The Southern parliament is boycotted by Sinn Féin and adjourns (28 June).
- Custom House, Dublin, is burnt down by the IRA. A truce between Sinn Féin and the British government comes into operation (11 July). Anti-Catholic riots in Belfast in response to the truce claim 16 lives (July). Sinn Féin convenes the second Dáil Éireann (16 August) and sends a delegation led by Michael Collins and Arthur Griffith to London (9 October).
- At the Anglo–Irish Conference, Lloyd George insists that the six Ulster counties remain outside of an independent Ireland. He threatens to resume hostilities within three days (11 October–6 December). The Anglo-Irish Treaty is signed by the Irish delegation, excluding the six Ulster counties (6 December). De Valera rejects the Treaty (8 December).
- Proportional representation replaces the majority vote in local government elections.
- The All Ireland champions are Limerick (hurling) and Dublin (football).

1922

- The Dáil Éireann ratifies the Anglo–Irish Treaty by 64–57 votes (7 January). De Valera resigns as the President of Sinn Féin and leads the anti-Treaty faction out of the Dáil (9/10 January).

- Arthur Griffith is elected President of Dáil Éireann. Michael Collins is appointed Chairman of the provisional government. Dublin Castle is handed over to Michael Collins and British rule in Ireland ends (16 January). The 'League of the Republic' is formed by Eamon de Valera. Anti-Treaty IRA members form their own army council under Liam Lynch. The Four Courts, Dublin, are occupied by the anti-Treaty IRA (14 April).The first Irish Free State general election is held – the pro-Treaty candidates win a clear majority (16 June). The IRA Convention splits on the issue of the Treaty (18 June).
- The Irish Civil War begins. The Free State forces shell the Four Courts (28 June).
- The Free State government captures the Four Courts (30 June) and gains control of Dublin. The Free State army captures Waterford and Limerick (July), Cork city (10 August) and Fermoy (11 October). The Dáil Éirean gives military courts the right to sentence prisoners to death (October). Seventy-seven anti-Treaty Republicans are executed during the course of the war.
- During sectarian riots in Ulster in June and July over 450 people are killed in Belfast alone. Thousands of Catholics flee Ulster. The IRA assassinate Sir Henry Wilson (born 1864) in London.
- Michael Collins (born 1890) is killed in an ambush at Béal na mBláth, Co. Cork (22 August).
- The Dáil elects William Thomas Cosgrave as head of its provisional government (9 September).
- The All Ireland champions are Kilkenny (hurling) and Dublin (football).
- The UK Parliament Act establishes the Irish Free State (6 December).
- Arthur Griffith (born 1871) and Robert Erskine Childers (born 1870) are executed by the Free State.

1923
- De Valera orders anti-Treaty forces to cease fighting (27 April). The Civil War ends (24 May).
- W.T. Cosgrave establishes the Cumann na nGaedheal Party.
- In the Free State general election, W.T. Cosgrave retains power (Eamon de Valera and 43 other Sinn Féin members of the new Dáil abstain). The Irish Free State joins the League of Nations.
- The Garda Síochána are formed.
- The Free State abolishes workhouses.
- The Land Commission takes over the duties of the Congested Districts Board.
- An Irish film censor is appointed. The Appeals Board includes W.B. Yeats.
- The United Council of Christian Churches and Communions is formed, representing Methodists, Presbyterians and the Church of Ireland.

- W.B. Yeats wins the Nobel Prize for Literature.
- Seán O'Casey stages *Shadow of a Gunman*. George Bernard Shaw stages *St Joan*.
- Daniel Corkery publishes *The Hidden Ireland*.
- James Joyce publishes *Ulysses*.
- The All Ireland champions are Galway (hurling) and Dublin (football).
- The death of Edward Martyn (born 1859), co-founder of the Abbey Theatre.

1924

- The Boundary Commission meets in London.
- In the 'army mutiny', two government ministers resign after officers object to a reduction of the army by 25,000 soldiers; General Eoin O'Duffy is appointed the new Commander-in-Chief.
- The Free State Air Corps is founded.
- The Intermediate and Leaving Certificate Examinations are established.
- The first regular air service between Ireland and Britain is inaugurated (from Belfast to Liverpool).
- The filmcensor bans 104 films.
- The All Ireland champions are Dublin (hurling) and Kerry (football).

1925

- Boundary Commission findings are leaked by *The Morning Post*.

The two governments agree to retain the existing Ulster/Free State border.

- In the Northern Ireland General Election, the Unionists gain almost total control of the Northern Ireland Parliament.
- The IRA breaks with Eamon de Valera and forms an independent Army Council.
- Legislation allowing divorce is effectively barred in the Free State.
- Annual examinations for entrance into the Irish Civil Service are introduced.
- Construction work on the Shannon Hydro-electric Scheme begins.
- Production starts on the Thomond car – believed to be the first car manufactured in the Free State.
- The film *Irish Destiny* is released.
- Seán O'Casey stages *Juno and the Paycock*.
- Liam O'Flaherty publishes *The Informer*.
- The All Ireland champions are Tipperary (hurling) and Galway (football).

1926

- The Irish Free State census: 2,972,000. The Northern Ireland census: 1,257,000.
- Eamon de Valera breaks with Sinn Féin and founds the Fianna Fáil Party (16 May).
- The 2RN radio station is established in Dublin.
- The staging of Seán O'Casey's *The*

- The Northern Ireland parliament moves to a new building at Stormont, which is officially opened by Edward, Prince of Wales.
- Unemployed Catholic and Protestant workers riot in Belfast.
- The Eucharistic Congress is held in Dublin. It also commemorates 1,500 years of Irish Christianity.
- Maurice Walshe publishes *Blackcock's Feather*.
- The All Ireland champions are Kilkenny (hurling) and Kerry (football).

1933

- Fianna Fáil retain power in the Irish Free State general election.
- The Army Comrade's Association elects Eoin O'Duffy as President. It changes its name to the National Guard and members receive the nickname 'Blueshirts'. The National Guard is proclaimed as an illegal organisation (August). The National Guard merges with Cumann na nGaedheal and the National Centre Party to form the United Ireland Party (later Fine Gael) under the leadership of O'Duffy (2 September). The Communist Party of Ireland is re-founded.
- The All Ireland champions are Kilkenny (hurling) and Cavan (football).

1934

- Eoin O'Duffy resigns from the Fine Gael Party.

- Pensions are given to the anti-Treaty Civil War veterans.
- The Free State and UK governments sign a Coal-Cattle Agreement.
- Changes in the primary school syllabus place greater emphasis on the Irish language and nationalist attitudes.
- Irish is declared a compulsory subject for the Leaving Certificate.
- Robert Flaherty's documentary film *Man of Aran* is premiered.
- The All Ireland champions are Limerick (hurling) and Galway (football).

1935

- W.T. Cosgrave is elected chairman of Fine Gael.
- There is rioting in Belfast (May).
- The importation and sale of contraceptives is banned.
- The All Ireland champions are Kilkenny (hurling) and Cavan (football).
- The death of George William Russell (born 1867), the writer and artist known as AE.

1936

- The Irish Free State census: 2,969,000.
- The Free State government severs most of the remaining links with Britain in preparation for the introduction of a new constitution. The Senate of the Irish Free State is abolished.
- The IRA is declared an illegal organisation. The annual

commemoration at Wolfe Tone's grave in Bodenstown is banned. Fine Gael expels the Blueshirts. Henry Boyle Somerville, retired British admiral, is assassinated by the IRA.

- The Spanish Civil War begins. General Eoin O'Duffy leads 450 Blueshirts to join Franco's forces.
- Frank Ryan and other Republican sympathisers make their way separately to Spain, where they form the 150-strong James Connolly Column of the International Brigade.
- Irish Sea Airways – later Aer Lingus, the national airline – opens its first route, from Baldonnell Airport to Bristol using a DH 84.
- *The Dawn* is made in Killarney – the first Irish feature film with sound.
- Oliver St John Gogarty publishes *As I Was Going Down Sackville Street*. Seán O'Faolain publishes *Bird Alone*.
- The All Ireland champions are Limerick (hurling) and Mayo (football).

1937
- Northern Ireland census: 1,280,000.
- Eamon de Valera's new constitution of Eire is published. It allows for an elected presidency and a two-house parliament comprising a Legislature (the Dáil) and a vocationally based Senate.

- A referendum accepts the new constitution. Fianna Fáil comfortably win the general election which is held at the same time as the referendum. The constitution comes into effect on 29 December.
- Irish Volunteers in Spain fight on both sides in the month-long Battle of Jarama.
- Foynes, on the Shannon estuary, is inaugurated as a flying-boat stop on the transatlantic route.
- The All Ireland champions are Tipperary (hurling) and Kerry (football).

1938
- Douglas Hyde becomes the first President of Ireland under the new constitution.
- There is a Free State general election after the government unexpectedly falls on the issue of civil service arbitration. Fianna Fáil are returned with an increased majority.
- The 'trade war' ends when the UK and Irish governments negotiate agreements on land loans, treaty ports and economic issues. Ireland regains possession of the British naval bases in Cork Harbour, Berehaven and Lough Swilly.
- Michael Donnellan founds the Clan na Talmhan Political Party.
- Trolley-buses replace trams in Belfast.
- Patrick Kavanagh publishes *The Green Fool*. Samuel Beckett publishes *Murphy*.

- The All Ireland champions are Dublin (hurling) and Galway (football).

1939

- The IRA begin a bombing campaign in England (January). The Coventry bomb kills five people (August).
- The Irish government outlaws the IRA. The Offences Against the State Act establishes the Special Criminal Court for political offenders.
- World War II begins (1 September). The Dáil passes a Bill declaring Ireland's neutrality on September 3, which sees the start of the Emergency (the World War II years in Ireland).
- The UK government decides not to extend conscription to Northern Ireland after Catholic bishops state their opposition.
- The Irish Red Cross is founded.
- James Joyce publishes *Finnegan's Wake*. Flann O'Brien publishes *At Swim Two Birds*.
- The All Ireland champions are Kilkenny (hurling) and Kerry (football).
- The death of William Butler Yeats (born 1865).

1940

- John M. Andrews is appointed Northern Ireland Prime Minister.
- The Irish government introduces conscription.
- Three people are killed in an accidental German bombing at Campile, Co. Wexford.

- German agent, Herman Goetz, is arrested and interned.
- John Charles McQuaid becomes Catholic Archbishop of Dublin.
- The All Ireland champions are Limerick (hurling)and Kerry (football).
- The deaths of James Craig (born 1871) and Roderick O'Connor (born 1860), artist.

1941

- Germans bombers target Belfast, killing almost 900 people (April/May). In the worst attack, 1,500 houses are destroyed and fire engines from Republican Ireland cross the border to help (15/16 April).
- A German bomber mistakenly drops four bombs on Dublin – the largest lands on the North Strand and kills over 30 people (30/31 May).
- The terminal building at Dublin Airport is completed (architect, Desmond Fitzgerald).
- Kate O'Brien publishes *The Land of Spices*.
- The All Ireland champions are Cork (hurling)and Kerry (football).
- The deaths of James Joyce (born 1882), Michael Healy (born 1873) and John Lavery (born 1856), artist.

1942

- United States troops arrive in Northern Ireland. De Valera protests at their presence.

- The Federated Union of Employers is founded in Dublin.
- The Limerick Corporation begins demolishing parts of the Limerick 'Lanes'.
- The Irish Blood Transfusion Service is founded.
- The statue 'The Virgin of the Twilight', now in Fitzgerald Park in Cork, is sculpted by Seamus Murphy.
- Patrick Kavanagh publishes *The Great Hunger*. Eric Cross publishes *The Tailor and Ansty*.
- The All Ireland champions are Cork (hurling) and Dublin (football).

1943

- In the general election in Eire, Fianna Fáil is re-elected but does not have a clear majority.
- Sir Basil Brooke is elected Prime Minister of Northern Ireland.
- The Central Bank opens in Dublin.
- A sea-plane en route to Foynes crashes on Mount Brandon, Co. Kerry, killing nine people.
- The Northern Ireland Arts Council is set up.
- The All Ireland champions are Cork (hurling) and Roscommon (football).

1944

- Fianna Fáil achieves a clear majority of 14 seats in the general election in Eire.
- The National Labour Party is formed by breakaway Labour Party members.

- In the 'American note' incident, the Irish government refuses Allied demands to expel German and Japanese diplomats.
- The Children's Allowance is introduced for families with three or more children.
- Joyce Cary publishes *The Horse's Mouth*.
- The All Ireland champions are Cork (hurling) and Roscommon (football).
- The deaths of Joseph Campbell (born 1879), poet, and Eoin O'Duffy (born 1892).

1945

- Seán T. O'Kelly is elected President of Eire.
- The end of World War II. It is estimated that almost 200,000 Irish-born people served in the Allied Armed Forces.
- Winston Churchill attacks Irish neutrality in World War II. De Valera replies defending his position (May).
- Córas Iompair Éireann (CIE), the national transport service, begins operating.
- The first transatlantic passenger flight arrives in Shannon Airport. Aer Lingus transport 5,000 passengers during the year.
- Kate O'Brien publishes *That Lady*.
- The National Stud is established in Co. Kildare.
- The All Ireland champions are Tipperary (hurling) and Cork (football).

- The deaths of Count John McCormack (born 1884), Irish tenor, and Eoin MacNéill (born 1867).

1946

- Eire census: 2,955,000.
- The Russians veto Ireland's application to join the United Nations.
- Seán MacBride founds the Clann na Poblachta Party.
- The Irish government inaugurates the Departments of Health and Social Welfare.
- The Bord na Mona (Peat Board) is established to exploit Ireland's peat resources.
- The ESB begins the Rural Electrification Scheme.
- Pan-American Airlines, BOAC and TWA begin regular flights into Shannon Airport.
- The All Ireland champions are Cork (hurling)and Kerry (football).

1947

- The Republic of Ireland Health Act improves medical services and moots the controversial Mother and Child Scheme.
- Shannon Airport is declared a duty free area.
- Eamon Andrews begins his broadcasting career with Radio Éireann.
- The All Ireland champions are Kilkenny (hurling) and Cavan (football).
- The death of James Larkin (born 1876).

1948

- As a result of the general election in Eire, Fine Gael and the Labour Party form an administration under John A. Costello (the first coalition government in Ireland). Costello announces Ireland will become a republic (September). The Republic of Ireland Act is passed (21 December).
- An Taisce (the heritage and planning body) is established.
- *The Heat of the Day* by Elizabeth Bowen is published.
- The All Ireland champions are Waterford (hurling) and Cavan (football).

1949

- Eire officially becomes a republic and leaves the commonwealth.
- The Ireland Act is passed in Britain, giving Irish citizens special status and confirming Northern Ireland will remain part of UK.
- The Irish government declines to compromise its neutrality by joining NATO.
- The last Dublin to Dalkey tram runs.
- The All Ireland champions are Meath (hurling) and Tipperary (football).
- The deaths of Douglas Hyde (born 1860) and Edith Somerville (born 1858), writer.

1950

- Noel Browne proposes the Mother and Child Scheme. Catholic bishops voice their disquiet in a letter to the Taoiseach.

- The Irish and Northern Irish governments co-operate to establish the Erne Drainage and Electrification Scheme.
- The Irish Development Authority (IDA) is founded to promote industrial growth.
- The first turf-run power station opens in Portarlington.
- In the Tilson Case, the Irish Supreme Court upholds the Catholic position on mixed marriage by ruling that parents have equal rights in deciding their child's religion, and prenuptial agreements have legal force.
- The All Ireland champions are Tipperary (hurling) and Mayo (football).
- The deaths of James Stephens (born 1882), writer, and George Bernard Shaw (born 1856), who leaves a large sum to the National Gallery of Ireland.

1951
- Census figures show that the Republic of Ireland population stands at 2,961,000.
- Roman Catholic bishops condemn the Mother and Child Scheme. It is abandoned and Noel Browne resigns.
- After the general election in the Republic of Ireland, Fianna Fáil forms a new government under De Valera.
- Córas Tráchtála (the Irish Export Board) is established.
- The Republic of Ireland Arts Council is set up.

- The Abbey Theatre, Dublin, is destroyed by fire.
- The Rev Ian Paisley forms the Free Presbyterian Church.
- Professor E. Walton of Trinity College, Dublin, shares the Nobel Prize for Physics.
- The All Ireland champions are Tipperary (hurling) and Mayo (football).

1952
- Seán T. O'Kelly begins his second term as President.
- Legal adoption is introduced in the Republic of Ireland – the laws include clauses that prevent couples adopting children of a different religion and forbid couples in mixed marriages to adopt at all.
- The Bord Fáilte is established to encourage tourism in the Republic of Ireland.
- The Irish Management Institution is founded in Dublin.
- John Ford films *The Quiet Man* in Mayo.
- The All Ireland champions are Cork (hurling) and Cavan (football).

1953
- Liam Kelly founds Fianna Uladh.
- The *Princess Victoria* ferry disaster claims 128 lives on the Stranraer–Larne route (January).
- Radio Éireann inaugurates the annual Thomas Davis lectures on Irish history and culture.
- Gael-Linn is established to help revive spoken Irish.

- The Irish government bans news-reel films of the coronation of Queen Elizabeth II.
- The Chester Beatty Library opens in Ballsbridge, Dublin, comprising a collection of oriental and early manuscripts.
- The Busárus Building, Dublin, is completed (architect, Michael Scott).
- Samuel Beckett stages *Waiting for Godot*.
- The All Ireland champions are Cork (hurling) and Kerry (football).
- The death of Maud Gonne MacBride (born 1865).

1954
- In the general election in the Republic of Ireland, the Fine Gael and Labour coalition led by John T. Cosgrave ousts De Valera and Fianna Fáil.
- The flying of the Irish tricolour is effectively banned by the Northern Ireland Parliament.
- Liam Lynch founds Saor Uladh in Co. Tyrone.
- Michael Manning becomes the last man to be hanged in the Republic of Ireland.
- The first appearance of myxamatosis – over the next decade, it almost wipes out Ireland's rabbit population.
- The National Stud buys the horse, Tulyar, for 200,000 pounds – a world record at the time.
- Brendan Behan stages *The Quare Fellow*.

- Christy Brown publishes *My Left Foot*.
- The All Ireland champions are Cork (hurling) and Meath (football).

1955
- Ireland joins the United Nations.
- Fire destroys Cork Opera House.
- The first motorcars arrive on the Aran Islands.
- Brian Moore publishes *The Lonely Passion of Judith Hearne*.
- Christy O'Connor makes the first of ten successive appearances in the Ryder Cup golf competition (last appearance 1973).
- The All Ireland champions are Wexford (hurling) and Kerry (football).
  The death of Evie Hone (born 1894), artist.

1956
- Republic of Ireland census: 2,818,000.
- The Republic of Ireland gives persons born in Northern Ireland after 1922 citizenship rights.
- The IRA begins a new campaign of attacks in Northern Ireland.
- The first of the annual Cork Film Festivals is held.
- Ronnie Delaney wins a gold medal in the 1,500 metres at the Melbourne Olympics.
- The All Ireland champions are Wexford (hurling) and Galway (football).

1957
- De Valera and Fianna Fáil are returned to power in the general election in the Republic of Ireland.
- Gaeltarra Éireann is founded to encourage the commercial and industrial growth of designated Gaeltacht (Irish-speaking) areas.
- At the first Dublin Theatre Festival, the staging of Tennessee Williams' *The Rose Tattoo* causes controversy.
- The All Ireland champions are Kilkenny (hurling) and Louth (football).
- The deaths of Oliver St John Gogarty (born 1878), writer, and Jack B. Yeats (born 1871), artist.

1958
- The first Irish army soldiers serve in a United Nations peace-keeping mission as observers in the Lebanon.
- The Industrial Development Act encourages foreign investment in the Republic of Ireland. Restrictions on outside ownership of industrial concerns are lifted.
- Aer Lingus begins passenger services to the United States (April).
- The Ardmore Film Studio opens near Bray, Co. Wicklow.
- The All Ireland champions are Tipperary (hurling) and Dublin (football).
- The deaths of Paul Henry (born 1876), artist, and Lennox Robinson (born 1886), dramatist.

1959
- Eamon de Valera is elected the third President of the Republic of Ireland. Seán Lemass, Minister of Industry and Commerce, is appointed Taoiseach.
- The CIU and ITUC union confederations reunify into the Irish Congress of Trade Unions.
- The British and Irish governments reach a compromise on the disputed pictures in the Hugh Lane collection.
- Seán Ríada composes the score for the film *Mise Éire*.
- John B. Keane stages *Sive*.
- The All Ireland champions are Waterford (hurling) and Kerry (football).

1960
- F.H. Boland assumes the Presidency of the General Assembly of the United Nations.
- The 33rd Battalion of the Irish army joins the United Nations Peacekeeping Force in the Congo during the Congo Civil War.
- In an ambush at Niemba, Baluba tribesmen attack an Irish patrol, killing nine Irish soldiers – only two survive (8 November).
- PanAm begin the first scheduled jetliner passenger service between the USA and Ireland.
- Aer Lingus introduces the St Patrick, its first Boeing 707 jet, into service.
- The All Ireland champions are Wexford (hurling) and Down (football).

1961

- The Irish Republic census: 2,818,000. Northern Ireland census: 1,426,000.
- After the general election in the Republic of Ireland, Seán Lemass forms a minority Fianna Fáil government with the support of independent members.
- Ireland joins UNESCO.
- The Bord Bainne is set up to encourage milk production and marketing.
- A state-owned television service is inaugurated by Radio Telefís Éireann (May).
- The last of the Guinness Liffey steamers is taken out of service.
- The West Clare railway – the subject of Percy French's song 'Are Ye Right there Michael?' – closes down.
- The All Ireland champions are Tipperary (hurling) and Down (football).

1962

- The IRA abandons its six-year long campaign of attacks in Northern Ireland.
- Work begins on Liberty Hall, Dublin's first skyscraper (architect, Desmond R. O'Kelly).
- The first of Gay Byrne's weekly 'Late Late Shows' is broadcast by RTE Television (6 July).
- The All Ireland champions are Tipperary (hurling) and Kerry (football).

1963

- US President, John F. Kennedy, visits Ireland (June).
- Terence O'Neill succeeds Lord Brookborough as Northern Ireland's Prime Minister and leader of the Unionist Party.
- William Conway is appointed Catholic Archbishop of Armagh.
- 11 June is the wettest day on record to date – 7.25 inches (186 mm) of rain fall at Mount Merrion, Dublin.
- Kilkenny Design Studios is set up.
- Paddy Moloney forms the Chieftains – a traditional music group.
- Shay Elliot becomes the first Irishman to wear the leader's yellow jersey in the Tour de France.
- The All Ireland champions are Kilkenny (hurling) and Dublin (football).

1964

- The second Programme for Economic Expansion is published in the Republic of Ireland.
- An Irish Army detachment is sent to the UN Peacekeeping Force in Cyprus.
- The Campaign for Social Justice is established in Northern Ireland.
- The new American Embassy in Dublin is completed (architect, J. M. Johansen).
- The Ulster Folk Museum opens at Cultra, Co.Down.
- Brian Friel stages *Philadelphia Here I Come*.

- The All Ireland champions are Tipperary (hurling) and Galway (football).

  The deaths of Maurice Walsh (born 1879), Brendan Behan (born 1923) and Seán O'Casey (born 1880).

1965

- In the Republic of Ireland general election, Fianna Fáil form the government with independent support.
- Northern Ireland Prime Minister, Terence O'Neill, meets Irish Taoiseach, Seán Lemass, in Dublin.
- The human remains of Roger Casement are returned from England for burial at Glasnevin.
- The Clann na Poblachta Republican Party dissolves itself.
- England and Ireland sign the Free-Trade Area Agreement.
- The Nationalist Party in Northern Ireland enter Stormont as the official opposition.
- The Northern Ireland government decides to build the new town of Craigavon.
- Aer Lingus fly 1,100,000 passengers this year, 200 times as many as flew in 1945.
- John B. Keane stages *The Field*.
- The All Ireland champions are Tipperary (hurling) and Galway (football).
- The death of WT Cosgrave (born 1880).

1966

- Jack Lynch succeeds Seán Lemass as Taoiseach.

- Eamon de Valera is re-elected President.
- Nelson's Pillar on O'Connell Street is blown up by Republicans – pranksters steal Nelson's head.
- The Ulster Volunteer Force (UVF) is founded in Northern Ireland.
- Several banking groups merge to form the Allied Irish Bank.
- The new Abbey Theatre is opened in Dublin.
- Seamus Heaney publishes *Death of a Naturalist*.
- In horse racing, Vincent O'Brien is the top flat trainer in Britain, and Arkle wins his third consecutive Cheltenham Gold Cup.
- The All Ireland champions are Cork (hurling) and Galway (football).
- The deaths of Frank O'Connor (born 1903) and Flann O'Brien (real name Brian Nolan, born 1911).

1967

- The Northern Irish Civil Rights Association founded.
- An Aer Lingus passenger plane crashes a few miles north of Dublin Airport with three deaths.
- Censorship is lifted on all books which have been banned for 12 years or more.
- The New Library at Trinity College, Dublin opens.
- The first ROSC exhibition of contemporary art is held at the RDS, Dublin.
- The Dubliners ballad group achieve international success after recording *Seven Drunken Nights*.

- The All Ireland champions are Kilkenny (hurling) and Meath (football).
- The death of Patrick Kavanagh, poet (born 1904).

1968

- Austin Curry occupies a council house in Caledon, Tyrone, to protest against the unequal allocation of local government housing.
- The first major civil rights march takes place from Coalisland to Dungannon (24 August).
- The People's Democracy is founded by student demonstrators at Queen's University, Belfast.
- There is rioting in Derry (October).
- The Northern Irish government announces concessions to Catholics.
- Terence O'Neill's moderate 'Ulster at the crossroads' TV speech offends many Unionists and William Craig, Stormont Minister for Home Affairs, is dismissed.
- The Tuskar Rock plane crash – 61 people are killed when the Aer Lingus plane *St Phelim* crashes into the Irish Sea.
- The new University of Ulster opens in Coleraine.
- Ireland's first planetarium opens at the Armagh Observatory.
- Van Morrison releases *Astral Weeks*.
- The All Ireland champions are Wexford (hurling) and Down (football).
- The deaths of W.J. Leech (born

1881), artist, and William O'Brien (born 1881), trade unionist.

1969

- Fianna Fáil retain power in the general election in the Republic of Ireland.
- The Belfast to Derry civil rights march is ambushed at Burntollet Bridge (January 4).
- There are riots in Derry (April, July). The first death occurs in the disturbances at Dungiven (14 July). British troops move into Derry after sectarian attacks on the Bogside (14/15 August). Last elections are held for the Northern Ireland parliament. Terence O'Neill resigns as Unionist leader and is replaced by Major James Chichester-Clarke.
- Protestant mobs and the B Specials attack Catholic areas in Belfast – British forces intervene to protect Catholic communities (15 August). The Belfast 'peace line' is established by the British army. The Hunt Report recommends the abolition of the B Specials and the disarming of the RUC. The Ulster Defence Force (UDF) is founded by militant Loyalists. The UK government issues the Downing Street Declaration.
- Bernadette Devlin of the Unity Party, becomes the youngest MP to sit in the British House of Commons.
- The Republic of Ireland introduces special tax concessions for creative artists and writers.
- The Irish farthing and halfpenny

coins cease to be legal tender.

- The Wood Quay excavation of Viking Dublin begins.
- Samuel Beckett wins the Nobel Prize for Literature.
- The Clancy Brothers and the Tommy Makem ballad group disband.
- John B. Keane stages *Big Maggie*.
- James Plunkett publishes *Strumpet City*.
- The All Ireland champions are Kilkenny (hurling) and Kerry (football).

1970

- Ministers Charles Haughey and Neil Blaney are dismissed from Jack Lynch's Irish government for an alleged arms smuggling conspiracy (neither minister is convicted in a later trial).
- US President, Richard Nixon, visits Ireland.
- Gerry Fitt forms the Social Democratic Labour Party in Northern Ireland.
- The Republican movement splits into the Provisional IRA and the Official IRA.
- The Ulster Defence Regiment replaces the B Specials.
- Moderate Protestant and Catholics form the Alliance Party.
- The Catholic hierarchy removes its ban on Catholics attending Trinity College, Dublin.
- Irish banks go on strike for six months – many small businesses go broke as a result.
- 'All Kinds of Everything', sung by

Dana, wins the Eurovision Song Contest for Ireland.

- Van Morrison releases *Moondance*.
- Christy O'Connor is selected as Texaco Golf Sportstar of the Year (one of five times) and Supreme Sports Star. Nijinsky, trained by Vincent O'Brien, become the first horse to win the English Classic 'grand slam' since 1935.
- The All Ireland champions are Cork (hurling) and Kerry (football).

1971

- The first British soldier is killed in the current troubles (February 6).
- Internment is introduced in Northern Ireland (9 August). By the end of year, 1,500 people have been placed in custody.
- Brian Faulkner becomes Prime Minister of Northern Ireland.
- The Rev Ian Paisley forms the Democratic Unionist Party (DUP).
- The Republic of Ireland adopts decimal coinage.
- The 'Children of Lír' group (sculptor, Oísin Kelly) is unveiled in the Garden of Remembrance, Dublin.
- Donal Lunney, Christie Moore, Liam O'Flynn and Andy Irvine form the Irish folk group, Planxty.
- Mary Lavin publishes *Collected Stories*.
- The All Ireland champions are Tipperary (hurling) and Offaly (football).
- The death of Seán Lemass (born 1899).

1972

- Republic of Ireland voters opt to join the European Economic Community (EEC).
- The voting age in the Republic is lowered from 21 to 18.
- The Special Criminal Court (three judges, no jury) is initiated in Dublin to try political offences.
- 'Bloody Sunday' in Derry – 13 demonstrators are killed by soldiers of the Parachute Regiment (30 January).
- The British Embassy in Dublin is burnt down during riots (2 February).
- The Northern Ireland parliament is suspended in favour of direct rule by the British parliament. William Whitelaw becomes first Secretary of State for Northern Ireland.
- The 'Bloody Friday' bombings take place in Belfast – 19 people are killed and 130 injured (21 July). By the end of 1972, the 'troubles' have claimed 678 lives since 1969.
- A referendum removes the special status of the Catholic Church from the constitution of Ireland.
- The Irish government introduces value added tax (VAT).
- The Irish Farmers Association is founded.
- The NIHE, Limerick (now the University of Limerick), is officially opened.
- Radio na Gaeltachta begins broadcasting.
- Phil Lynott and Thin Lizzy have a UK hit with 'Whiskey in the Jar'.

- Seamus Heaney publishes *Wintering Out*.
- The All Ireland champions are Kilkenny (hurling) and Offaly (football).
- The death of Padraic Colum (born 1881), writer.

1973

- The Republic of Ireland joins the EEC. Northern Ireland joins the EEC with the United Kingdom.
- As a result of the Republic of Ireland's general election, a Fine Gael and Labour coalition is formed under Liam Cosgrave.
- Erskine Hamilton Childers becomes President of Ireland.
- The *Claudia* arms shipment is intercepted by the Irish Navy.
- Elections are held for the new Northern Ireland power-sharing assembly. The Ulster United Unionist Council (UUUC) is founded by the Orange Order, DUP and other Loyalist groups.
- At the Sunningdale Conference, Northern Irish political parties, the UK and the Republic of Ireland agree to establish a 'Council of Ireland'.
- The Irish Civil Service removes its bar on female employees marrying.
- The Supreme Court rules that the ban on importing contraceptives is unconstitutional.
- The compulsory pass in Irish is removed from the Intermediate and Leaving Certificate Examinations.

- Hugh Leonard stages *Da*.
- The All Ireland champions are Limerick (hurling) and Cork (football).

1974

- Cearbhall O'Dalaigh becomes the fifth President of Ireland (unopposed).
- Loyalist terrorists explode three bombs in the centre of Dublin (24 killed) and a fourth in Monaghan town (6 killed).
- Ireland's biggest robbery to date takes place near Tralee, Co. Kerry – 75,000 pounds are stolen from a Post Office van.
- The UUUC win 11 out of 12 Northern Irish seats in the British general election.
- A Loyalist general strike closes electrical services and blockades Belfast (May).
- The Northern Ireland power-sharing assembly is abandoned and the British government resumes direct rule.
- An IRA attempt to tunnel out of the Maze Prison is foiled.
- The Irish National Liberation Army is formed from militant dissidents in the Official IRA.
- In the UK, the Guilford bombing leaves 5 dead and the Birmingham pub bombings, 21 dead.
- The new Central Bank building in Dublin is ordered to be lowered by 13 feet (4 metres) after planners find it has exceeded its permitted height.
- An oil spillage from the tanker *Universal 1* threatens the West Cork coast.
- Powerscourt House, Co. Wicklow, is burnt down.
- Seán MacBride wins the Nobel Peace Prize.
- The All Ireland champions are Kilkenny (hurling) and Dublin (football).
- The deaths of Kate O'Brien (born 1894), and Seamus Murphy (born 1907), sculptor.

1975

- The IRA agree to a cease-fire in February, but this ends in November.
- Elections are held for the Northern Ireland Constitutional Convention. The proposed assembly fails when the UUUC reject power sharing.
- In the Miami Showband massacre, three band members and two UVF men are killed.
- Internment in Northern Ireland ends (5 December).
- The Herrema kidnapping and the Monasterevan siege take place (September–October).
- Five people are killed in the Clogh Bridge train disaster in Co. Wexford.
- The Blessed Oliver Plunkett, executed in 1681, is canonised.
- The Druid Theatre, in Galway, opens.
- The All Ireland champions are Kilkenny (hurling) and Kerry (football).
- The death of Eamon de Valera (born 1882).

1976

- President O' Dalaigh resigns on a point of constitutional principle – he is replaced by Dr Patrick Hillery.
- A report states that the Irish inflation rate is the highest in the EEC.
- 150,000 pounds are stolen in the Sallins mail train robbery.
- Christopher Ewart-Biggs, the British Ambassador, and his secretary are killed by a landmine near his Rathfarnham residence.
- In the Kingsmill massacre, Co. Armagh, ten Protestants are murdered in retaliation for the murder of five Catholics on the previous day.
- The Peace People movement is inaugurated in Belfast after three children die in a terrorist incident.
- The 'blanket protest' is initiated by H Block Republican prisoners against the removal of their 'special category' political status.
- A new Adoption Act permits couples in the Irish Republic to adopt children of a different religion.
- Máiréad Corrigan and Betty Wilson, founders of the Peace People, win the Nobel Peace Prize.
- Seamus Heaney publishes *North*.
- The All Ireland champions are Cork (hurling) and Dublin (football).

1977

- Fianna Fáil are re-elected with a clear majority in the general election in the Republic of Ireland. Jack Lynch forms the government. Dr Garret Fitzgerald succeeds Liam Cosgrave as leader of Fine Gael.
- The Workers' Party is founded after a split in Sinn Féin.
- 1,400 jobs are lost in Limerick when the Ferenka factory closes down after a long-running industrial dispute.
- The Treasures of Ireland Exhibition opens in the US.
- Alex Higgins wins the World Professional Snooker championship.
- The All Ireland champions are Cork (hurling) and Dublin (football).
- The death of Seán Keating (born 1889), artist.

1978

- An Irish army battalion is sent to join the UN Peacekeeping Force in southern Lebanon.
- Jack Lynch addresses the UN General Assembly.
- David Cook of the Alliance Party is elected as Belfast's first non-Unionist Mayor.
- In the La Mon hotel bombing in Co. Down, 16 people are killed.
- The Matt Talbot Memorial Bridge opens in Dublin (the first new bridge to cross the Liffey since 1880).
- The Dublin Institute of Technology (DIT) is founded.

- RTE 2, Ireland's second TV station, begins broadcasting.
- Bob Quinn screens *Poitín* (an Irish language film).
- Thin Lizzy release *Live and Dangerous*.
- The All Ireland champions are Cork (hurling) and Kerry (football).
- The death of Mícheál MacLiammóir (born 1899).

1979
- The Republic census: 3,365,000 (an increase of 13 per cent).
- Jack Lynch retires from politics. He is replaced as leader of Fianna Fáil and Taoiseach by Charles Haughey (December).
- European parliament elections are held for the first time (15 seats in the Republic of Ireland). Sucessful candidates in Northern Ireland (3 seats) include John Hume and the Rev Ian Paisley.
- The French oil tanker *Betelgeuse* explodes at Whiddy Island Oil Refinery in Bantry Bay, killing 50 people.
- The death of Lord Mountbatten and three others in the Mullaghmore boat bombing. On the same day, 18 British soldiers are killed in a bomb and gun attack at Warrenpoint, Co. Down (27 August).
- The Irish Republic joins the European Monetary System which means the end of parity between sterling and the punt.
- The Irish postal workers' strike lasts four months.
- Pope John Paul II visits Ireland:

1,000,000 people attend an outside mass at Phoenix Park. In Drogheda, the Pope appeals for peace in Northern Ireland.
- Tomás O' Fiaich, Archbishop of Armagh, is appointed Cardinal.
- The Irish Film Board is established.
- Seamus Heaney publishes *Fieldwork*.
- The All Ireland champions are Kilkenny (hurling) and Kerry (football).

1980
- Charles Haughey and British Prime Minister, Margaret Thatcher, establish the Anglo-Irish Committee at a summit meeting at Dublin Castle.
- Nearly 700,000 Irish PAYE workers join in a day of protest at the unfair tax system.
- A hunger strike is initiated by Republican prisoners in Northern Ireland. Cardinal O' Fiaich intervenes to avert deaths.
- The Derrynafflan Chalice is discovered on a national monument site in Tipperary.
- The Sense of Ireland Exhibition is held in London.
- Brian Friel stages *Translations*.
- The All Ireland champions are Galway (hurling) and Kerry (football).

1981
- The Republic of Ireland census: 3,443,405.
- After the general election in the

Republic of Ireland, the Fine Gael and Labour coalition form the government under the leadership of Garret Fitzgerald. Margaret Thatcher and Garret Fitzgerald set up the Inter-governmental Council.

- In the Stardust Ballroom disaster, 48 young people are killed in a fire at a Valentine's Night dance in Artane, Dublin.
- The IRA Hunger Strike at the Maze Prison lasts from 1 March to 3 October. Deaths begin after 66 days. The following strikers die: Bobby Sands, the elected MP for South Fermanagh whilst on strike (5 May); Francis Hughes (12 May); Patsy O'Hara (21 May); Raymond McCreesh (21 May); Joseph McDonnell (8 June); Martin Hurson (13 July); Kevin Lynch (1 August); Kieran Doherty, elected TD for Cavan-Monaghan whilst on strike (3 August); Thomas McElwee (8 August); Michael Devine (20 August).
- The National Concert Hall opens in Dublin.
- Pat O'Connor makes the TV drama *Ballroom of Romance*.
- The All Ireland champions are Offaly (hurling) and Kerry (football).
- The death of Christy Brown, writer.

1982
- As a result of the February general election in the Republic of Ireland, Charles Haughey forms a new

Fianna Fáil government but in the general election in November, Garret Fitzgerald's Fine Gael and Labour coalition are returned to power. Michael O'Leary resigns the leadership of the Labour Party and joins Fine Gael – he is replaced by Dick Spring.

- Ireland refuses to participate in EEC trade sanctions on Argentina during the Falklands War.
- Three IRA men are ambushed and killed by the RUC near Lurgan, Armagh, and this incident is later alleged to be part of a 'shoot-to-kill' policy.
- Droppin' Well pub bombing – INLA kill 11 off-duty soldiers and 6 civilians.
- Corporal punishment is banned in Republic of Ireland schools.
- Ireland win the Rugby Union Triple Crown championship.
- Alex Higgins wins the World Professional Snooker Tournament.
- The All Ireland champions are Kilkenny (hurling) and Offaly (football)

1983
- The 'Bugging Scandal' – it is revealed that the previous Fianna Fáil administration placed wire taps on journalists Bruce Arnold and Geraldine Kennedy.
- Inaugural meeting of the New Ireland Forum at Dublin Castle.
- The Irish Republic appoints its first Ombudsman.
- A policeman and a soldier are

killed during the rescue of kidnap victim Don Tidey, following the most intensive manhunt in the history of the Irish Republic.

- The race horse, Shergar, is kidnapped from the Ballymany Stud, Newbridge, Kildare – he is never found.
- The 'Supergrass' trials begin in Northern Ireland – 14 UVF members are convicted in the Joseph Bennet trial, and 22 IRA members in the Christopher Black trial.
- Nine prisoners escape in a mass break-out from the Maze Prison – a warder is killed.
- Two CIE trains crash near the town of Kildare and 8 persons are killed.
- The punt is devalued by 5 per cent.
- The Naas By-pass, the Irish Republic's first motorway, is opened.
- A referendum is held on whether to place an anti-abortion amendment in the Irish constitution – it is carried by 841,000 votes to 416,000.
- The concept of illegitimacy is abolished in the Irish legal code.
- Eamon Coughlan wins the 5,000 metres race at the Helsinki World Championships.
- The All Ireland champions are Kilkenny (hurling) and Dublin (football).

1984

- US President, Ronald Reagan, visits Ireland.

- The New Ireland Forum publishes a report suggesting three possible solutions for breaking the Northern Ireland impasse (May).
- Dominick McGlinchey, accused of murdering three worshippers in Darkley Pentecostal Hall in 1983, is extradited from the Republic to Northern Ireland.
- John Stalker begins an enquiry into the RUC killings of suspected Republican terrorists in Northern Ireland.
- The IRA bomb the Conservative Party Conference at the Grand Hotel, Brighton (October).
- Margaret Thatcher rejects the proposals of the New Ireland Forum in her 'Out! Out! Out!' speech (19 November).
- The Republic's Department of Post and Telegraph is divided into An Post (postal services) and Telecom Éireann (telecommunications).
- The Irish Shipping Company is liquidated. This heralds the end of the Irish merchant marine.
- The East Link toll bridge is opened in Dublin. The famous Liffey Ferry ceases its operations.
- Natural gas from the Kinsale field begins to be pumped into Dublin.
- The restoration of Kilmainham Hospital, Dublin, the finest seventeenth century building in Ireland, is completed.
- Neil Jordan screens *Company of Wolves*.
- U2 release *The Unforgettable Fire*.

- John Tracey wins a silver medal in the marathon at the Los Angeles Olympic Games.
- The All Ireland champions are Cork (hurling) and Kerry (football).
- The death of Liam O'Flaherty (born 1894).

1985

- The Anglo-Irish Agreement is signed between the UK and the Republic of Ireland at Hillsborough (15 November).
- Breakaway Fianna Fáil TDs and their supporters form the Progressive Democrat Party under the leadership of Desmond O'Malley.
- An Air India Boeing 747 crashes into the sea 80 miles off the Irish coast after a bomb explodes on board – all 329 people on board are killed.
- The Insurance Corporation of Ireland is in crisis – the Irish government intervenes with financial guarantees to protect the Allied Irish Bank.
- Knock Regional Airport, Mayo, receives its first commercial flight (official opening 1986).
- The phenomena of 'moving statues' arises – a shrine to the Virgin Mary at Ballinspittle, Co Cork, attracts thousands of pilgrims.
- Dublin musician, Bob Geldof, organises the Live Aid Concert to raise funds for victims of the Ethiopian Famine.

- Ireland defeat England in Dublin to win the Rugby Triple Crown.
- Barry McGuigan defeats Eusebio Pedroza to become the WBA featherweight champion of the world.
- The All Ireland champions are Offaly (hurling) and Kerry (football).

1986

- Republic of Ireland census: 3,541,000.
- John Stalker is removed from his enquiry into the RUC killings – there are allegations of a 'cover-up' by the British Intelligence Services.
- The Belfast Appeals Court overturns the convictions in the Christopher Black 'Supergrass' trial.
- The national transport company, CIE, is restructured into separate Bus, Rail and Dublin Bus services.
- A Goya and a Vermeer are amongst ten paintings stolen from the Beit Collection at Russborough House in a robbery masterminded by the Dublin criminal the 'General'.
- The ore carrier *Kowloon Bridge* runs ashore on one of the most beautiful stretches of the Dingle Peninsula, Kerry.
- Hurricane Charlie, the worst summer storm in living memory, causes unprecedented damage.
- A referendum in the Republic of Ireland rejects a constitutional amendment to permit divorce.
- The Pro-life movement takes court action under the Constitutional

Amendment to prevent family planning clinics advising on abortion facilities abroad.

- Pine martens, thought to be extinct in Ireland, are discovered in the Killarney National Park.
- The All Ireland champions are Cork (hurling) and Kerry (football).
- The death of Phil Lynott, rock musician.

1987

- A general election is held in the Republic of Ireland when the Labour Party withdraws from the coalition. A new Fianna Fáil government is formed under Charles Haughey. Garret Fitzgerald resigns from leadership of Fine Gael and he is succeeded by Alan Dukes.
- An Irish Republic referendum approves the Single European Act.
- The British army kills eight IRA members and a civilian in an ambush at Loughgall, Co. Armagh.
- Enniskillen bombing – 11 people are killed whilst attending a Remembrance Day service at the War Memorial. The *Eksund*, smuggling 150 tons of arms from Libya to Ireland for the IRA, is arrested by French authorities. A nationwide search for other arms dumps follows.
- Ireland's national debt spirals towards 260 billion pounds – Fianna Fáil implement cutbacks in government expenditure.
- The Poulnabrone portal tomb is excavated in Co. Clare.

- U2 release *The Joshua Tree*.
- Stephen Roche becomes the first Irish cyclist to win the Tour de France. He also wins the World championship at Villich, Austria, this year.
- Marcus O'Sullivan wins the first of three 1,500 metres at the World Indoor championships (others 1989, 1993).
- The All Ireland champions are Galway (hurling) and Meath (football).
- The death of Eamon Andrews (born 1922), boxer and broadcaster.

1988

- John Hume, leader of the SDLP, holds a meeting with Gerry Adams of Sinn Féin. He is criticised by other Northern Ireland parties.
- A Loyalist gunman kills three mourners at an IRA funeral in Milltown Cemetery, Belfast. Two days later, two British soldiers are dragged from their car and murdered by the IRA.
- The Irish government brings in a harsh budget to deal with the worsening economic crisis. A tax amnesty in the Republic of Ireland raises 500 million pounds.
- Aer Ríanta, the state-owned airport maintenance company, negotiates a contract to service the Russian Aeroflot fleet at Shannon Airport and to open duty free shops in Moscow and Leningrad Airports.
- The Grange Development wins compensation of two million

pounds from Dublin County Council when they are refused planning permission on land they own.

- Dublin celebrates its millennium; the Anna Livia sculpture is unveiled in O'Connell Street and soon gets the nickname 'the Floozie in the Jacuzzi'.
- The Republic of Ireland football team reach the European Cup Finals in Germany. They beat England 1–0 but do not progress beyond the first stage.
- The All Ireland champions are Galway (hurling) and Meath (football).
- The death of Seán MacBride (born 1904).

1989

- Charles Haughey forms a coalition Fianna Fáil and Progressive Democrat government.
- Mikhail Gorbachev, leader of the Soviet Union, makes a short visit to Ireland when his plane is refuelling at Shannon Airport.
- Johnston, Mooney and O'Brien, Dublin's oldest and best-known bakery, closes down.
- Century Radio, Ireland's first independent national radio station to operate legally, begins broadcasting.
- Jim Sheridan releases *My Left Foot*.
- Marcus O'Sullivan establishes a new world record in the indoor 1,500 metres.
- The All Ireland champions are Tipperary (hurling) and Cork (football).

- The death of Samuel Beckett (born 1906).

1990

- Mary Robinson is elected the Republic of Ireland's first female President.
- John Bruton replaces Alan Dukes as leader of Fine Gael.
- Brian Keenan, held hostage in Beirut for several years, is released and returns to Ireland.
- The Republic of Ireland football team reach the World Cup Finals for the first time – they lose 1–0 to Italy in the quarter-finals.
- Alan Parker releases *The Commitments*.
- Brian Friel stages *Dancing at Lughnasa*.
- The deaths of Cardinal Tomás O'Fiaich and Terence O'Neill (born 1904).

1991

- Republic of Ireland census: 3,526,000.
- An investigation is launched into alleged fraud and malpractice in the beef industry.
- The Irish government allows US airforce planes to refuel at Shannon Airport during the Gulf War.
- The 'Birmingham Six', wrongly accused of involvement in the 1974 pub bombings, are released from prison in England. The convictions of the 'Maguire Seven' are quashed.
- UVF gunmen murder three people

at a mobile shop in Craigavon, Co. Armagh.
- The legal age for purchasing condoms is reduced to 17; their sale is permitted in pubs and discos.
- Sonia O'Sullivan establishes a new world record in the 5,000 metres.
- The All Ireland champions are Tipperary (hurling) and Down (football).

1992
- Charles Haughey resigns and is replaced as Taoiseach by Albert Reynolds (February).
- The Irish public overwhelmingly approve the Maastricht Treaty in a referendum.
- The Democratic Left Party is formed after the Workers' Party split (Febuary).
- The UDA are banned in Northern Ireland.
- Nelson Mandela visits Ireland.
- The X Case: the Supreme Court allows a 14 year-old-girl to travel to England for an abortion. Further referendums on the abortion issue are held (3 simultaneously).
- Eamon Casey, Bishop of Galway, resigns after it is revealed that he is the father of a teenage son.
- Barcelona Olympic Games – Michael Carruth wins a gold boxing medal (welterweight) and Wayne McCullough wins a silver boxing medal (bantamweight).
- The All Ireland champions are Kilkenny (hurling) and Donegal (football).

1993
- Fianna Fáil and Labour form a coalition government under Albert Reynolds.
- Mary Harney succeeds Desmond O'Malley as leader of the PD Party.
- The Shankill Road bombing kills 10 people in Belfast. Within a week, Loyalist gunmen kill 6 Catholics in retaliation when they open fire in the Rising Sun public house.
- The Downing Street Declaration is signed by Albert Reynolds and John Major.
- The Irish punt is devalued after it is targeted by currency speculators.
- The budget deficiency in the Irish Republic has been reduced to 250 million pounds.
- Homosexuality is decriminalised in the Republic of Ireland.
- Jim Sheridan releases *In the Name of the Father.*
- Roddy Doyle publishes *Paddy Clarke Ha Ha Ha.* It wins the Booker Prize in London.
- The All Ireland champions are Kilkenny (hurling) and Derry (football).

1994
- A new Fine Gael and Labour Party coalition government is formed under John Bruton. Bertie Ahern replaces Albert Reynolds as leader of Fianna Fáil. The broadcasting ban on Sinn Féin is lifted by the Irish and UK governments.
- The IRA cease-fire is inaugurated

(30 August). Loyalist cease-fire is inaugurated (October 13).

- The Forum for Peace and Reconciliation meets in Dublin.
- The Emergency Powers Act in the Republic is revoked.
- The Irish government releases 9 IRA prisoners.
- Frank Delaney publishes *The Sins of the Mothers*.
- Catherine McKiernan wins the last of four consecutive victories in the annual World Cross Country Grand Prix Series. Sonia O'Sullivan establishes a new world record for the 2,000 metres.
- Ireland reach the last 16 of the Football World Cup Finals in the USA before they are defeated by Holland.
- The All Ireland champions are Offaly (hurling) and Down (football).

1995
- The Framework Document for Northern Ireland is launched by John Bruton and John Major.
- US President Clinton visits Northern Ireland and Dublin to help support the peace process.
- A referendum in the Republic of Ireland legalises divorce by the narrowest of margins – a majority of only 9,100 out of 1,630,000 votes cast.
- The Irish Republic legalises the provision of information and advice on abortion.
- Daytime British army patrols end in Belfast.

- The Irish Supreme Court allows the family of a woman who has been in a coma for 20 years to withdraw her life support system.
- Steve Collins beats Chris Eubank to win the WBO Super Middleweight title.
- The All Ireland champions are Clare (hurling) and Dublin (football).

1996
- Republic of Ireland census: 3,621,000.
- *The Sunday Independent* crime journalist, Veronica Guerin, is murdered by a drugs gang she has been investigating.
- The IRA cease-fire ends with the Canary Wharf bombings in London.
- Elections to the Northern Ireland Forum are held. Stormont multi-party talks begin (June).
- Orange Marchers confront local Catholics at Drumcree, Co. Down (July).
- Telifis na Gaeilge (the Irish language TV service) is launched.
- Ireland wins the Eurovision Song Contest for the 4th time in 5 years.
- Seamus Heaney wins the Nobel Prize for Literature.
- Frank McCourt publishes *Angela's Ashes*.
- Michelle Smith wins 3 gold swimming medals at the Los Angeles Olympic Games.
- The All Ireland champions are Wexford (hurling) and Meath (football).

1997

- Mary McAleese is elected as Ireland's second female president. As a result of the Republic of Ireland general election, Bertie Ahern forms a Fianna Fáil and Progressive Democrat coalition government.
- The McCracken Tribunal investigates payments to politicians.
- Father Brendan Smith is sent to prison for 12 years for sexual offences in the Republic of Ireland.
- Constables John Grahame and David Andrew Johnston become the 300th and 301st RUC men to be murdered in the current troubles.
- Sinn Féin candidates win 2 seats in the UK House of Commons.
- The IRA announces a new cease fire.
- The effects of the BSE scare are estimated to have cost the economy of the Republic of Ireland up to 1 billion pounds.
- The All Ireland champions are Clare (hurling) and Kerry (football).

1998

- The Good Friday Agreement is signed by all parties in Northern Ireland.
- The first all-Ireland ballot since 1918 approves the Good Friday Agreement (94.39 per cent in the Republic and 71.12 per cent in the North).
- A new enquiry into 'Bloody Sunday' is announced by the UK government.

- A car bomb planted by a dissident IRA group at Omagh, Co. Tyrone, kills 29 people.
- SDLP leader John Hume and Ulster Unionist leader David Trimble jointly receive the Nobel Peace Prize.
- The booming economy of the Republic of Ireland becomes known as the 'Celtic Tiger'.
- The Irish government implement measures to deal with huge increases in house prices.
- The Freedom of Information Act is passed in the Republic of Ireland.
- A monument to Ireland's World War I dead is opened in Belgium.
- Pat O'Connor screens *Dancing at Lughnasa*.
- The first stages of the Tour de France are held in Ireland.
- The Irish under-16 and under-18 football teams win the European Championships.
- The All Ireland champions are Offaly (hurling) and Galway (football).

1999

- Confrontations in Portadown follow the official banning of the Orange Order parade at Drumcree.
- The Irish economy's growth rate of 7 per cent is the highest in Europe.
- Jack Lynch, former Taoiseach, dies.
- It is announced that the RUC is to be awarded the George Cross.
- Power is devolved to the elected Northern Ireland Assembly (2 December).

- The British-Irish Agreement creates a North–South Ministerial Council and other cross-border institutions.
- The All Ireland champions are Cork (hurling) and Meath (football).

2000

- The deadlock over the decommissioning of terrorist weapons brings about the suspension of the Northern Ireland Assembly and the reimposition of direct rule (February).
- Inflation in the Irish Republic runs at 5.5 per cent.
- Lawyers in Northern Ireland are no longer obliged to swear an oath of allegiance to the Queen.
- The Northern Ireland Assembly resumes its functions (June).
- Poor Irish results in the Sydney Olympic Games provoke a reassessment of the country's athletics training programme.
- The Irish government commissions the Flood Report on ethics in public life.
- The All Ireland champions are Kilkenny (hurling) and Kerry (football)

2001

- Northern Ireland census: 1,685,267
- The Irish government is defeated in the Treaty of Nice referendum: 53.8 per cent vote against, on a 35 per cent turnout (June).

- Foot and mouth disease epidemic begins in Louth (March).
- John Hume resigns as SDLP leader.
- The IRA announces the start of arms decommissioning (October).
- David Trimble re-elected as the First Minister of Northern Ireland.
- Twelve weeks of demonstrations outside the Holy Cross Primary School, Belfast, end in December.
- Ireland is estimated to have 1,000,000 Internet users.
- The Royal Ulster Constabulary is renamed as the Police Service of Northern Ireland (November).
- The All Ireland champions are Tipperary (hurling) and Galway (football).

2002

- The punt is replaced as the Irish currency unit by the euro.
- General election results in the Republic: Fianna Fáil gains 81 out of 166 seats; Fine Gael drops from 54 to 31 seats; Sinn Féin gets 6.5 per cent of the votes (May).
- Bertie Ahern forms a new coalition government.
- Enda Kenny is elected leader of Fine Gael (June).
- Colm Murphy is convicted in Dublin of the Omagh bombing in 1998 (January).
- The IRA announces a second round of arms decommissioning (April).
- Alex Maskey becomes first Sinn Féin Lord Mayor of Belfast.
- Sinn Féin's offices at Stormont are raided by the police (4 October). Unionists demand Sinn Féin's

expulsion from the Stormont Assembly. Despite a series of crisis meetings, the Northern Irish Assembly is suspended (14 October).

- The Irish government's new referendum on the Treaty of Nice results in a 60 per cent 'Yes' vote.
- The All Ireland champions are Kilkenny (hurling) and Armagh (football).

2003

- Demonstrators protest against use of Shannon Airport by US military aircraft in the Iraq war.
- A US employee of Allied Irish Banks receives a jail sentence for one of the largest frauds in US history (US$691 million).
- Five Real IRA members are given long jail sentences in London for conspiracy to cause explosions in 2001 (April).
- Michael McKevitt, leader of the Real IRA, is sentenced to 20 years' jail in Dublin's Special Criminal Court, for directing terrorism.
- Peace Process talks collapse when David Trimble rejects the IRA's decommissioning acts as insufficient (October).
- In elections to the suspended Northern Ireland Assembly, the DUP has 25.71 per cent of the vote, Sinn Féin has 23.52 per cent, the UUP has 22.68 per cent, and the SDLP 16.99 per cent.
- The All Ireland champions are Kilkenny (hurling) and Tyrone (football).

2004

- Smoking is banned in all public places in the Irish Republic, except for prison cells, psychiatric hospitals and designated hotel rooms.
- The Cory Report in Northern Ireland recommends public enquiries into 4 murder cases where there may have been collusion with the security forces (April).
- The International Monitoring Commission finds 'disturbingly high' levels of paramilitary activity on both sides of the sectarian divide in Northern Ireland.
- Mary Harney is appointed Deputy to the Taoiseach in a cabinet reshuffle: two other women are in the cabinet (September).
- Sinn Féin accuses the UK government of planting a bugging device in its Belfast office (September).
- Mary McAleese is re-elected as President of the Irish Republic for a further seven years (October).
- In a raid on the Northern Bank, Belfast, £26,000,000 in cash is stolen. The authorities accuse the IRA of being involved in the robbery (December).
- Irish Finance Minister, Brian Cowen, presents a 'social inclusion' budget with big increases in public spending and an anticipated increase in GDP of 5.1 per cent.
- The All Ireland champions are Cork (hurling) and Kerry (football).

- Death of Joe Cahill, republican activist.

2005

- Ireland's GDP per head is recorded at 31 per cent above the 25-state European Union average.
- The IRA formally announces the end of its armed campaign (July).
- Belfast's bus service is renamed 'Metro'.
- Ryanair announce a $4 billion order of new aircraft from Boeing.
- David Trimble resigns as UUP leader following his defeat by the DUP in the British general election.
- A proposal to commemorate the fate of the *Titanic* by towing an iceberg to Belfast Lough is announced (February).
- Cork is European City of Culture this year
- The Irish Republic alters all road signs and regulations to kilometres.
- The All-Ireland champions are Cork (hurling) and Tyrone (football).
- Deaths of Gerry Fitt, politician; George Best, footballer; Dave Allen, comedian.

2006

- Census in the Republic shows highest population since 1861: 4,234,925, of whom 1,6000,000 live in Greater Dublin.
- Members of the Northern Ireland Assembly recalled (May) and given until 24 November to agree on a power-sharing executive.
- November deadline passes without agreement; direct rule continues, but the St Andrews Agreement offers a way forward.
- Ireland currently uses 50 per cent more oil per head than the European Union average for transport purposes.
- Armed Gardai remove 30 Afghan asylum seekers from St Patrick's Cathdral in Dublin.
- Laima Muktupauda publishes *The Mushroom Covenant,* describing the lives of Latvian mushroom pickers in Ireland.
- Belfast City Airport is renamed George Best Belfast City Airport.
- The hottest temperature so far in the century is recorded at Elphin, Co. Roscommon: 32.30C (88.70F).
- A medieval psalm book from the 8th–10th century is found in a bog in central Ireland.
- All-Ireland champions are Kerry (football) and Kilkenny (hurling).
- The last competitive rugby international takes place at Lansdowne Park before the development of the site.
- Ireland win rugby union's Triple Crown.
- Deaths of Charles Haughey, former Taoiseach; John McGahern, writer; Mella Carroll, first woman High Court judge in the Irish Republic.

2007

- Sinn Féin accepts the legitimacy of the Police Service of Northern Ireland, opening the way to a renewed Assembly and Executive.

- Northern Ireland's police ombudsman, Nuala O'Loan, confirms that officers in the former RUC colluded with UVF terrorists in shootings and other crimes over a ten-year period.
- General election in Irish Republic: Bertie Ahern wins a third term and sets up a new Fianna Fáil government with Green and PD support.
- Assembly election in Northern Ireland: DUP emerges as the biggest party. After getting approval from a DUP party conference, Ian Paisley agrees to become first minister in a power-sharing executive with Sinn Féin, with Martin McGuinness as Deputy First Minister. Paisley travels to Dublin for handshake and meeting with Ahern. Direct rule from London ends on 8 May and the new Executive assumes office.
- During road-building close to Tara, an important prehistoric site is unearthed.
- All-Ireland champions are Kerry (football) and Kilkenny (hurling).
- Deaths of Benedict Kiely, writer; Tommy Makem, folk-singer.

2008

- A massive slump in values in the Dublin stockmarket heralds a year in which the Irish economy falls into severe recession.
- Bertie Ahern resigns as Taoiseach following accusations of financial irregularities.
- Brian Cowen is elected leader of Fianna Fáil and Taoiseach (May).

- Ian Paisley resigns as First Minister of Northern Ireland; Peter Robinson is elected as leader of the DUP and becomes First Minister.
- Jamboree 2008 celebrates 100 years of Irish scouting.
- A national referendum rejects the Treaty of Lisbon by a majority of 53.4 per cent to 46.6 per cent, stalling the plans for a revised constitution for the European Union.
- The Seanad Éireann (Irish Senate) sits all night to pass the bill authorising state support for stricken banks.
- A state of economic recession is officially announced (September).
- Protests from students and pensioners follow budget proposals to increase university registration fees and scrap entitlement of all 70+ citizens to free medical treatment.
- The Irish government commits 10 billion euros to support six Irish banks threatened with financial collapse. A 'hidden loans' scandal and other irregularities are revealed, prompting the resignations of several senior bankers.
- 'Operation Seabight' seizes cocaine with an estimated value of 750 million euros from a yacht off the Cork coast.
- All Irish pork products are recalled following discovery of toxic levels of dioxins in animal feeds since 1 September.
- Ireland win 1 silver and 2 bronze medals at the Beijing Olympics, all in boxing.

- The All-Ireland champions are Kilkenny (hurling) and Tyrone (football).
- Pádraig Harrington wins the US PGA golf championship.
- Deaths of Paddy Canny, fiddle player; Patrick Hillery, former president; John O'Donohue, poet and philosopher; Nuala O'Faoláin, writer; Nollaig O'Gadhra, language activist and founder-member of Telefís na Gaeilge.

2009

- Economic crisis: Patrick Neary, head of the Financial Services Regulatory Authority, takes early retirement. 1900 jobs go at the Dell computer factory, Limerick, as unemployment rises to 9.2 per cent. Students engage in mass protests against reintroduction of university fees. Other groups protest in public against financial cutbacks. Anglo-Irish Bank is taken into state ownership.
- Child abuse scandal: the report of commission inquiring into child abuse at Roman Catholic church institutions reveals decades of 'terrorisation'. Murphy Report into the archdiocese of Dublin prompts the resignations of several bishops and assistant bishops.
- A second referendum on the Treaty of Lisbon yields a 67 per cent 'Yes' vote.
- Supreme Court rules that human embryos are not recognised or protected as unborn under the Constitution.

- Ireland's biggest bank robbery is staged at the Bank of Ireland in Dublin.
- Two British soldiers shot dead at Massereene Barracks, Co. Antrim: Real IRA claims responsibility.
- Deaths: Liam Clancy, singer; Cathal Daly, former Archbishop of Armagh; Justin Keating, politician; Hugh Leonard, writer; Vincent O'Brien, racehorse trainer.
- All-Ireland champions are Tipperary (hurling) and Kerry (football).
- Bernard Dunne is super bantamweight world champion (March–September).
- Ireland are Six Nations rugby champions.

2010

- Economic crisis: Ireland requests, and Eurozone countries agree, a financial rescue package of €75 billion. Protests against the austerity policy continue. AIB forced to cancel €40 million of staff bonuses. Irish Nationwide Building Society gets a €5.4 billion government bailout. Unemployment reaches 14 per cent.
- Cork–Dublin motorway is completed. Limerick–Galway railway reopens. Limerick Tunnel under the Shannon opens.
- Britain's Savile enquiry into the 'Bloody Sunday' shootings (1972) prompts an apology from the British prime minister.
- Peter Robinson, first minister of Northern Ireland, steps aside from

office for three weeks in the 'Irisgate' scandal about his wife's financial affairs; she resigns as MP and as a Member of the Legislative Assembly of Northern Ireland and withdraws from politics. Justice and policing are devolved to the Northern Ireland Assembly as of 12 April. Ian Paisley is made a life peer, as Lord Bannside.

• UNESCO names Dublin a 'City of Literature'.

• Dáil passes the Civil Partnership Act.

• Deaths: Paul Clancy, musician; Moira Hoey, actress; Tomás Mac Giolla, politician; Gerry Ryan, broadcaster.

• All-Ireland champions are Tipperary (hurling) and Cork (football).

2011

• Politics: Brian Cowen resigns as leader of Fianna Fáil after botched cabinet reshuffle; Micheál Martin elected. Green Party withdraws from coalition. General election results in victory for Fine Gael/Labour alliance. Fianna Fáil support collapses and Fine Gael win 76 seats. Enda Kenny is elected Taoiseach. Gerry Adams is elected as the member for Louth, and as leader of Sinn Féin, in the Irish parliament (Oireachtas). Two constitutional referendums held: power to reduce judicial salaries is approved; full investigative powers to Irish parliament committees is rejected. Michael D. Higgins (Labour) is elected president.

• Northern Ireland elections result in the continuance of the power-sharing DUP/Sinn Féin government, with Peter Robinson as first minister and Martin McGuinness as deputy.

• Economic crisis: new government maintains austerity programme. Protests and demonstrations continue. 'Occupy' movement stages occupation of Dame Street, Dublin. Prolonged sit-in at the Vita Cortex plant, Cork. Irish Bank Resolution Corporation (IBRC) formed by forced merger of AIB and Irish Nationwide Building Society. Irish bank bonds are reduced to junk status.

• Child abuse scandal: Cloyne Report uncovers further cases in the diocese of Cloyne.

• Queen Elizabeth is first British monarch to visit Ireland since independence. President Barack Obama also visits Ireland.

• Irish embassy to the Vatican is closed down in a cost-cutting drive.

• Deaths: Seán Cronin, republican activist; Lord Dunsany (Edward Plunkett), artist; Garret Fitzgerald, former Taoiseach; Joss Lynam, mountaineer; T.P. McKenna, actor.

• All-Ireland champions are Kilkenny (hurling) and Dublin (football).

2012

• Economic crisis: as Ireland falls further into recession, its Budget brings sweeping increases in prices and VAT (23 per cent), and a controversial €100 annual household tax. Carbon tax on fuel adds 1.5c a litre to prices. AIB cuts 2,500 jobs. A referendum is held to approve the European Fiscal Compact (guaranteeing national budgets to be in balance or surplus).

- Children's rights referendum passed by 58 per cent but not signed into law pending a legal challenge.
- A Bill proposing to legalise abortion in the event of danger to the mother's life is defeated in the Dáil.
- Mahon Tribunal finds Bertie Ahern, as Taoiseach, had accepted monies from property developers and financiers. He resigns from Fianna Fáil.
- In Belfast, Queen Elizabeth exchanges symbolic handshake with Martin McGuinness. Province-wide Loyalist protests and riots follow Belfast City Council's decision to fly the Union flag only on 18 designated days a year.
- Dublin is named European City of Science 2012.
- Aung San Suu Kyi receives freedom of Dublin (awarded in 2000).
- Rural dwellers protest about septic tank charges and inspections. Less than half of households have paid the €100 tax.
- RTE (national television and radio broadcaster of Ireland) fined €2,000,000 by the Irish Broadcasting Authority for the defamation of Father Kevin Reynolds, falsely accused of rape.
- The death of Savita Halappanavar at University Hospital, Galway, after she was refused an abortion, sparks widespread protests.
- A meteorite falls into the Irish Sea off Co. Louth. A tornado 700 metres high is seen near Buncrana.
- President Higgins' new volume of poetry is described by Professor Kevin Kiely as 'crimes against literature'.
- Deaths: Maeve Binchy, novelist; Mary Kate Byrne, Ireland's oldest person, aged 108; Máirín Egan, campaigner for autistic children; Barney McKenna, folk singer.
- All-Ireland champions are Kilkenny (hurling) and Mayo (football).
- London Olympics: 66 Irish competitors achieve best result since 1956 with one gold (Katie Taylor for boxing), one silver and three bronze medals. In the Paralympics, 49 participate, winning 13 gold, 11 silver and 18 bronze medals. The Paralympic team also win the 'People of the Year Award'.

2013

- Total population is estimated at 4,953,000. The birth rate has fallen 5 per cent since 2010. One third of babies are born outside of marriage. Net loss of population through emigration is 35,000.
- Economic crisis: the Irish Bank Resolution Corporation (IBRC) is liquidated overnight. Kenny

claims this will reduce Ireland's borrowing requirement by €20 billion. A new €1.4 billion economic stimulus campaign, using PPP (private-public partnership) schemes for schools, roads and police stations, is announced. Unemployment stands at 12.5 per cent.

- The government embarks on a worldwide 'promote Ireland' campaign. The US *Forbes* magazine describes Ireland as 'best place in the world for business'.
- The G8 group of nations holds a summit meeting in Co. Fermanagh.
- Bomb and letter bomb attempts by dissident republicans continue throughout the year in Northern Ireland.
- The Northern Ireland government introduces a plastic bag tax (applied in the Republic since 2002).
- Two referendums: the abolition of the Seanadd is rejected by 51.7 per cent of voters; new Court of Appeal is approved.
- High Court dismisses a challenge to the implementation of enhanced children's rights following the 2012 referendum.
- An official report finds 'state collusion' with Catholic Church organisations in placing girls and women in Magdalene laundries. Taoiseach apologises and promises a fund to help surviving inmates.
- Health Service Executive inquiry finds multiple failures in the hospital care of Savita Halappanavar.

- Food Safety Authority confirms presence of horse DNA in 'beef-burgers' on sale in supermarkets. Some 10 million are withdrawn.
- A national post-code system is announced, to be operative by 2015.
- Canadian astronaut Chris Hadfield tweets 'Tá Eire fíorálainn' from space.
- Pat Storey is elected Bishop of Meath & Kildare (Church of Ireland): first woman bishop in Ireland and Great Britain.
- Deaths: Joseph Cassidy, former Archbishop of Tuam; Seamus Heaney, poet; Milo O'Shea, actor; Peter O'Toole, actor; Dolours Price, republican activist; Christopher Robson, co-founder of Irish Lesbian and Gay Network.
- All-Ireland champions are Cork (hurling) and Mayo (football).
- Giovanni Trapattoni resigns as Ireland football manager following failure in World Cup qualifying matches. Martin O'Neill appointed manager, with Roy Keane as assistant.

2014

- Economic crisis: Ireland is first of the bailed-out countries to shake off 'Troika' controls, but austerity policy is maintained. Budget announces cuts in health tax relief and maternity benefits. Most welfare recipients have seen a 6.75 per cent drop in income since 2008.
- Price of farmland averages €9400

per acre, a fall of 5.6 per cent from 2012.

- Ireland's 'tax-haven' policies are criticised in the USA and elsewhere. Apple are said to have moved A$8.9 billion of income from Australia to Ireland between 2002 and 2013. Yahoo! announces transfer of its European HQ from Switzerland to Ireland to take advantage of the 'Double Irish Dutch Sandwich' tax arrangement.
- Peter Robinson threatens to resign as first minister of Northern Ireland over the disclosure that 180 'on the run' persons received official assurances about non-prosecution as part of the peace agreement of 2007.
- Evidence of unauthorised recording of telephone calls to and from Garda stations since the 1980s forces the resignation of Garda Commissioner Martin Callinan and an official apology from Justice Minister Alan Shatter to the Garda 'whistleblowers' who exposed the practice.
- Ireland are Six Nations rugby champions.
- Northern Ireland hosts the opening stages of the Giro d'Italia cycle race.

Index

Downing Street
Declaration 348
ethos of 47
factory building in 50
Framework Document
for 360
general strike by
Loyalists 351
housing, inequality in
allocations 348
internment 349, 351
Ireland Act (1949)
342
Irish tricolour, banning
of 344
leadership, new genera-
tion of 53–4
living standards in 50
Nationalist Party, official
opposition 347
parliament of 333, 335,
350
peace process 56–7
Police Service of 14, 362,
364
post-war decades in
49–50
proportional representa-
tion, abolition of 336
reaffirmation of partition
46
Secretary of State,
appointment of 52, 350
sectarian violence 51,
333, 334
Stormont, opening of
338
'supergrass' trials 355,
356
'troubles' (1971) 349
US troops in 340
'Welfare State' in 50
Northern Ireland Arts
Council 341

Northern Ireland
Constitutional
Convention 351
Northern Ireland Forum
elections 360
Northern Ireland Power-
sharing Assembly 350,
351
Northern Irish Civil
Rights Association 347
Northern Star, The 198
North–South Ministerial
Council 362
Northumbria 251
Norway, Viking fighting
fleet from 254

Ó Gráda, Cormac 40
Oates, Titus 290
Obama, Barack 367
O'Brian, Donal More 102
O'Brian, William 348
O'Brien, Connor, King of
Desmond 260
O'Brien, Donald Mór 263
O'Brien, Flann (Brian
Nolan) 347
O'Brien, Kate 340, 341,
351
O'Brien, Muirchertach
90, 106, 259
O'Brien, Turlough (1st of
'kings with opposition')
90, 258, 261
O'Brien, Vincent 347, 349
O'Brien, William Smith
227–8, 235, 312
O'Brien Kings of
Thomond 110, 116
O'Brien of Inchiquin
146–8, 152, 287, 288,
290
*O'Briens and the O'Flahertys,
The* (Owenson, S.) 307

O'Briens of Clare 274
O'Brien, Vincent 366
O'Byrne, Fiach MacHugh
134, 282
O'Byrne, John, Lord of
Wicklow 269, 270
O'Byrnes of Wicklow
131, 280, 281
O'Cahan, Donal 136–7,
139
O'Callaghan, Pat 336
O'Casey, Sean 247, 335,
336
O'Clery, Michael 61,
285, 286
O'Clery, Peregrine 62
O'Connell, Daniel ('the
Liberator') 203, 211,
212–15, 213, 214, 215,
216, 217, 218, 219–20,
227, 306, 308, 309,
310, 311, 312
O'Connell, General 36
O'Connell Monument 315
O'Connor, Aedh, King of
Connacht 105
O'Connor, Cathal 102
O'Connor, Christie 344,
349
O'Connor, Felim 106,
267
O'Connor, Frank 337,
347
O'Connor, James Arthur
310
O'Connor, Pat 354, 361
O'Connor, Roderick 340
O'Connor, Rory 37, 94,
95, 96, 98, 99, 102, 124,
261, 262, 263
O'Connor, Turlough 94,
260, 261
O'Connors of Connacht
115, 257